AFTER EFFECTS 4
In Depth

R. Shamms Mortier

CORIOLIS

The Coriolis Group, LLC
14455 N. Hayden Road, Suite 220
Scottsdale, Arizona 85260

480/483-0192
FAX 480/483-0193
http://www.coriolis.com

Library of Congress Cataloging-In-Publication Data
Mortier, R. Shamms.
    After Effects 4 in depth/by R. Shamms Mortier
        p. cm
    Includes index.
    ISBN 1-57610-310-2
      1. Cinematography--Special effects--Data processing.
2. Adobe After Effects. I. Title
TR858.M63 1999
778.5'345'02855369--dc21   99-17881
                         CIP

Printed in the United States of America
10 9 8 7 6 5 4 3 2 1

Publisher
Keith Weiskamp

Acquisitions Editor
Mariann Hansen Barsolo

Marketing Specialist
Gary Hull

Project Editor
Don Eamon

Technical Reviewer
Brian Little

Production Coordinator
Meg E. Turecek
Jon Gabriel

Cover Design
Jody Winkler
additional art provided by Brandon Riza

Layout Design
April Nielsen

CD-ROM Developer
Robert Clarfield

Other Titles For The Creative Professional

This book is dedicated to David Huber,
who knows the joy and pandemonium of visits with the muse.
—R. Shamms Mortier

ABOUT THE AUTHOR

Shamms Mortier has written over 800 articles and reviews on a wide range of computer graphics and animation applications; he has also written a dozen books. His column in *TV Technology*, "A Mix of Art and Engineering," is published biweekly. He is also a partner in two well-browsed subscription-based Web magazines: *Mastering 3D Graphics* and *3D Creature Workshop*. His first novel, *A Convergence of Worlds*, will be published in 2000.

ACKNOWLEDGMENTS

This book was a painstaking and challenging undertaking, and was only made possible with the help and effort of a number of individuals.

To all of the hard-working and dedicated folks at Coriolis, especially Mariann Barsolo, Don Eamon, Stephanie Wall, Jon Gabriel, Meg Turecek, Robert Clarfield, and Jody Winkler.

To my agent, David Fugate, and to his able executive assistant, Maureen Maloney, at Waterside Productions.

To Stephen Kilisky at Adobe and Michelle Jesse, for their courteous and exacting support.

To all the developers who supported this book, having created a wealth of magical plug-in effects for After Effects.

To the author's family, especially Diane, who provided tea and comfort during the long hours as the Vermont seasons danced by the studio window.

AT A GLANCE

CONTENTS

CONTENTS

TABLE OF

PART IV   EXTERNAL EFFECTS

Chapter 42
ISFX Image Tools 515

PART VI SPECIAL PROJECTS

INTRODUCTION

Welcome to the best and biggest book on Adobe After Effects. Besides providing you with an overview of the new features and attributes of After Effects version 4, this book is also a compendium of all of the latest volumes of external plug-in filters available at the time of this printing for After Effects. Of course, you will need to purchase these extras to be able to do the projects that involve their use, as detailed in the book.

How To Use This Book

Your use of the book and the accompanying CD-ROM depends on your experience with After Effects.

If you are an experienced professional and use After Effects in your work regularly, I suggest that you skim Chapters 1 through 4 to get some details on the new features available in After Effects 4. If your work involves integrating audio with your After Effects animations, read Chapter 5 carefully; After Effects 4 has some neat new audio capabilities (especially in the After Effects Production Bundle version). Your main use probably will focus on all the chapters that deal with the external plug-in volumes in your library or on ones that you are deciding to purchase. This book is a veritable encyclopedia of external plug-ins for After Effects, detailing what they do and how they do it. In no case does the text on external plug-ins suffice to replace that plug-ins documentation, but just to overview it and suggest places where it might be of use in your projects.

If you are a moderate-to-experienced videographics or multimedia professional but are new to After Effects, read the After Effects documentation (and do all the suggested exercises) from cover to cover before diving into this book. When you use this book, read it from cover to cover, paying special attention to all the options available to you in After Effects for crafting unbelievable animated effects in post-production. Decide which external effects volumes interest you, and purchase the one that fit your needs. Most After Effects users, like Photoshop users, are obsessed with plug-ins, and they usually acquire as many as possible for future creative use.

If you are a beginning digital artist and are interested in discovering how to apply animated effects to your 2D and/or 3D graphics and animations, then you must begin by purchasing After Effects and working through all of its documentation. You might want to invest in the standard version first and upgrade to the Production Bundle version as your needs and budget permit. Look at all of the chapters in this book that detail what external plug-ins offer, and begin to purchase those that contain the effects that interest you the most.

The Effects Icons

One of the unique features in this book is the use of specific icons to denote Effects Categories. You can thumb through the book, and see these icons used throughout, placed in the margins next to an Effect name. These are icons important because there are hundreds of effects available for After Effects, both internally and as external plug-ins. These icons separate each effect description into one or several of twenty-one effect types. This allows you to quickly identify an effect by its icon, and to compare different plug-ins from different developers with effects that do similar things. because it's a visual process, it is faster than listing these categories by name.

If you don't mind marking up your copy of the book, you can use a yellow marker to go over the icons of the effects that you find especially useful in your work, or you can even make small notes beside them. You also might want to make copies of the page in this Introduction that shows all of the "Effects" icons. If you find that some of the detailed descriptions of an effect listed in the book deserve more than its listed icon, in your estimation, you can cut out the icon and tape it alongside the one listed. This book is meant to be a production guide, so however you can find ways to make it serve your purposes, the better.

The Twenty-One Icons

Here are the icons used in the book, along with a short description of what their presence indicates:

Alpha Effects

 This Icon indicates the corresponding effect listing is best used to create or modify an Alpha channel or Alpha layer. Alpha channel effects are included in volumes from a number of developers.

Blurs And Sharpens

 Blur and Sharpen are standard image effects that do exactly what you would expect. There are Blur and Sharpen effects in volumes from many AE plug-in developers.

Channel Effects

 These effects are meant to address specific channels of a selected layer. They can apply modifications or swap one channel with another, and are common to a number of plug-in volumes.

Distortions

 When we think of effects, this category is the one that comes to mind most. It includes any filter that distorts the contents of the footage, animated or not. Pinch, Punch, Spherize, and many other effects are included in this category.

Environmental And Organic Effects

 Typically, these effects include any filters whose use results in natural phenomena. This includes fire, water, wind, earth, stars, or other effects noticed in the natural world.

Image Control Effects

 This category ranges from colorizing an image or footage to correcting brightness and contrast. This is one of the largest and most comprehensive standard effects categories.

Keying Effects

 Whenever you have a stack of layers and need to make part of a layer transparent so that the layers beneath show through, you have to get involved with applying a Key. many plug-in packages, as well as AE internal effects, are Key related.

Lights

 This is one category that has a specific chapter devoted to it: Chapter 25. Most of the filters that deal with lights and lighting are included in this chapter and are referenced by this icon.

Matte Tools

 Mattes are often used to mask out unwanted data when one layer is moving against another. Several external plug-in volumes offer excellent Matte filters.

Media Looks

 There are dozens of filters from many developers that allow you to transform your footage into pen and ink, oil paint, watercolor, and many other media looks. This icon can identify them.

Motion Effects

 Motion effects include After Effects Motion Math and other Keyframe Assistants.

Particle Systems

 After Effects and external plug-in developers have created a wealth of Particle System filters. These filters are used to create explosions, snow, rain, random spheres, and a number of other unique effects.

Perspective Effects

 Perspective Effects can include both 2D and 3D types. Commonly, Perspective Effects are used to fly a logo onto the screen from the background, but a number of alternate Perspective filters from different developers allow you to do much more than this.

Shadow Effects

 Shadow effects can be classified as any filter that allows you to create 2D or 3D shadows on other layers.

Stylize

 Stylizing effects do things such as transform footage into mosaics, brush strokes, or other Photoshop-like effects. Stylizing is closely associated with Media Looks (see preceding page).

Synthesize

 This icon indicates the After Effects 3.1 category, which is used to indicate Ramping effects. Ramps are also included in filters from other developers.

Text Effects

 A major use for After Effects is the development of titling and credits for films and multimedia, so it is necessary to have a separate category to target Text effect options.

Time Effects

 The Time Effects category includes Time Displacement and other similar effects. Most of these are found in After Effects as internal filters.

Transitions

 When you use a wipe to go from one layer to another, you are using a Transition. There are Transition filters in a number of external plug-in volumes, as well as internal to After Effects. The most notable Transition collection is Pixelan Software's Video Spicerack collection, detailed in Chapter 35 of this book.

Video Effects

 When you use Video footage, it has attributes that must often be adjusted, corrected, or both. These effects do just that.

Web

 Whether you are saving out your creations as GIF animations or doing something else that makes them Web-ready, the effects that show this icon point you in the right direction.

Contents Of The Book

This book is separated into several parts, each of which contains specific information to enhance your After Effects' knowledge.

Part I

This includes Chapters 1 though 5. These chapters are devoted to both the version 4 upgrade information and deepening your basic After Effects pursuits.

Part II

This includes Chapters 6 through 12, and centers upon all the internal filters and effects in After Effects 4. Each chapter targets specific effects categories.

Part III

This includes Chapters 13 through 15, which concentrate on the special attributes in the extended Production Bundle for AE4. The only distinction here is that the Production Bundle Audio Effects are folded into Chapter 4 because this chapter is all about audio effects.

Part IV

This is the largest section of the book, and it includes Chapters 16 through 43. Each chapter is devoted to the effects volumes from specific developers, The only exception is Chapter 25, which covers Light effects from a number of developers.

Part V

This includes Chapters 41 through 43. Each chapter covers useful tools from specific developers.

Part VI

This is Chapter 44, which contains three original projects you can explore using After Effects and various filters.

Appendixes

Here, you will find a number of references not covered in the main sections of the book.

Contents Of The Book's CD-ROM

This book's CD-ROM contains a wealth of value-added content. This includes:

- A complete trial version of Adobe After Effects 4.
- A complete trial version of Commotion (see Chapter 39).
- Demo versions of RayFlect's Four Seasons and PhotoTracer, two super filters for Photoshop (Mac and Windows).

- Over 200 animations, representing specific effects detailed, by chapter, in the text. Use these animations to get an idea of what a specific effect does. These are all QuickTime animations, so you need to have QuickTime installed. If you don't have it, get the details for downloading at **www.apple.com**. Windows users have to activate the QuickTime viewer once QuickTime is installed to load and view the animations. Mac users can simply double-click on the animation file.

- Content for the three original After Effects projects (see Chapter 44) is contained in the Projects folder on the CD-ROM. this content is original and copyright-free, so you may use it in any project you like.

We hope you enjoy this book, and that it helps you to maximize your use of Adobe After Effects 4.

PART I

OVERVIEW

IMPORTANT?

Version 4 of After Effects offers significant additions and enhancements over previous versions; nearly every area of the application has received some attention and upgrading. Even with all of these changes, After Effects 4 can still import your AE 3 and 3.1 project files. This chapter provides an overview of the enhanced features.

WHAT'S NEW AND

A Standard Adobe Interface

During the recent upgrades of Photoshop and Illustrator, Adobe made a dedicated effort to design the interfaces of both of these applications to have the same look and feel. This similarity helps artists and animators who often own and use both applications, offering them an easier and quicker way to apply their creative efforts. After Effects 4 has been integrated into this family of products, so that new After Effects users who have experience with either or both Photoshop and Illustrator will have a more comfortable and familiar After Effects environment in which to create.

The design of the new After Effects interface is crisp and clean, and it allow easier and more-intuitive access to tools (see Figure 1.1).

One thing you'll notice immediately, if you have used previous versions, is that every palette's content is tabbed. Instead of wandering through a maze of separate palettes that reference individual layers or alternate compositions, you can get there instantly by clicking on a tab. These tabs are one of the best production speed-up features of the new version.

The Palettes

Experienced users will have to take a few minutes to get used to the new interface, and the rearranged and redesigned tools and palettes. All of the palettes show some degree of redesign, and each of the palettes represents different balances between preview quality and speed.

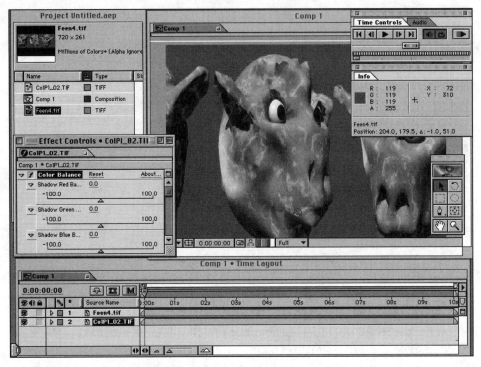

Figure 1.1
The new After Effects interface represents a major upgrade from previous versions.

Time Controls Palette

One of the best enhanced production items Adobe added to AE 4 is RAM Preview, which is accessed from the Time Controls palette. You have four options to preview animations: RAM, standard, manual, and wireframe. The RAM, standard, and manual previews are accessed using the Time Controls palette (see Figure 1.2).

Several Preview options are available from the Time Control's palette. RAM Preview plays a preview of the frames (including audio) at either the frame rate of your composition or as fast as your system configuration allows. The number of frames that are previewed depends

Figure 1.2
The new Time Controls palette. The controls represent (from left to right): First Frame, Frame Reverse, Play, Frame Advance, Last Frame, Audio, Loop, RAM Preview. At the bottom is the Time indicator, Jog control, and Shuttle control.

on the amount of available contiguous RAM that is allocated to the application. RAM Preview previews the span of time you specify as the work area.

Standard Preview provides a preview of all frames in your composition. Every frame is displayed as quickly as possible using the current settings of the layer switches, composition switches, and composition resolution. This preview generally plays slower than RAM Preview.

You access Manual Preview by the Shuttle control, the Jog control, and the Time indicator, which allow you to manually navigate through a composition, layer, or footage file. This mode is less precise with long compositions.

> *Note: Wireframe Preview (accessed by selecting Composition|Preview|Wireframe Preview) displays a preview of the frames for all layers in your active workspace. Each layer is represented by a rectangle, or by the outline of the mask or Alpha channel.*

Audio Controls Palette

The new Audio controls palette displays volume levels during playback and allows you to adjust the left and right levels of a selected layer. The Audio palette is conveniently linked to the Time Controls palette by a tab, which emphasizes the commitment of AE 4 to audio integration (see Figure 1.3).

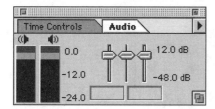

Figure 1.3
The new Audio controls palette is associated with the Time Controls palette by a tab.

> *Note: See Chapter 4 for detailed audio information.*

The Align Palette

The Align palette lets you align selected layers along any axis you select. Just multiple-select the targeted layers in the Time Layout window. You can also align layers along the horizontal axis, using the top, center, and bottom selection handles of the selected layers. You can distribute layers evenly along either the horizontal or vertical axis by using the proper alignment options (see Figure 1.4).

The Info Palette

The Info palette provides details about the area under the mouse pointer as you drag across a footage frame in the Composition, Layer, or Footage window. The palette displays values for the pixel color (RGB), Alpha channel (A), and X and Y coordinates of the current position

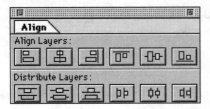

Figure 1.4
The Align palette.

When you modify a layer property, the bottom area of this palette displays precise values that relate to the layer instead of the pointer. As you drag a layer, the lower area of the Info palette displays the X and Y coordinates as related to the layer's anchor point (see Figure 1.5).

Effects Palette

The biggest change with the Effects palette is that this it is now tabbed, so you won't end up with stacks of confusing effects controls to toggle between. Just click on the tab for the targeted layer (see Figure 1.6).

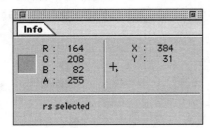

Figure 1.5
The Info palette.

Figure 1.6
Click on a tab to access the effects for that layer.

The Tool Palette

The Tool palette has been redesigned to appear similar to that in Photoshop. The left column shows the Selection, Marquee, Pen (Pen, Add Control Point, Delete Control Point, and Convert Control Point), and Move tools. The right column displays the Rotation, Oval, Pan Behind, and Zoom tools. See Figure 1.7.

Figure 1.7
The Tool palette.

> *Note: By using the Pan Mask tool, you can adjust the area that displays through a mask by panning (moving) the layer behind the mask in the Composition window. When you move a mask, the position values of the mask layer remain constant, and the mask moves in relation to other objects in the Composition window.*

> *Note: See Chapter 3 for a detailed look at the Time Layout window.*

Arranging Palettes

Use the following directions to arrange palettes:

- Click the palette's tab to make a palette appear at the front of its group.

- Drag the palette's title bar to move an entire palette group or the toolbox.

- Drag the tab for a palette to rearrange or separate a palette group.

- Drag a palette's tab to another group to move a tabbed palette.

- Choose Show|Palette Name in the Window menu to show or hide a palette (except the Align palette). Choose Window|Plug-In Palettes|Align & Distribute to show or hide the Align palette. Choose Show Tools in the Window menu to show or hide the toolbox.

- Choose File|Preferences|General to show or hide tabs in windows. Then select Tabbed Windows, and click on OK.

- Click the appropriate box in the upper right corner or double-click on a tab (or on the area alongside) to collapse a palette group to tabs only. Click on a button or double-click on the tab area to restore the group.

- If you have resized the Audio palette, double-clicking the tab area cycles through the new size, the default size, and the collapsed state.

Integration

After Effects 4 is now tightly integrated with the other trio of Adobe creative applications: Photoshop, Illustrator, and Premier.

Photoshop

When you export a Photoshop file for use in After Effects, the adjustment layer(s) and layer effects are preserved as well. Many Photoshop effects have also been added to AE 4 (as detailed in Chapters 6 to 10).

Illustrator

All Illustrator layers are preserved when an AI file is imported into After Effects 4. Illustrator paths can be copied and pasted, and the new rulers and guides will be familiar to Illustrator users.

Premier

All Premier 5.x projects can be imported as After Effects compositions. All edited clips appear as separate layers, and are properly arranged in the Time Layout window. Premier Audio plug-ins work when importing Premier content into After Effects as well.

Precision

Professional users will appreciate the precision capabilities of After Effects 4. You can now add up to 128 individual masks to any layer, increasing the effects potential of your project. Mask operations (add, subtract, intersect, and so on) can now be combined, and strokes and fills can be addressed as well. You can also copy and paste masks between Photoshop and Illustrator. The addition of adjustment layers allows you to globally address all of the layers beneath them in one step.

New Effects Galore

After Effects users crave effects, and AE 4 adds a wealth of internal filters, bringing the total to nearly 120. The bold items in the following list indicate Production Bundle filters:

> **Note: Chapters 4 and 6 through 15 detail the use of Production Bundle filters.**

- *Adjust Effects*—Brightness and Contrast, Channel Mixer, Color Balance, Curves, Hue/Saturation, Levels, Posterize, Threshold.
- *Audio Effects*—Backwards, Bass and Treble, Delay, **Flange and Chorus**, **High-Low Pass**, **Modulator**, **Parametric EQ**, **Reverb**, Stereo Mixer, **Tone**.
- *Blur and Sharpen Effects*—Channel Blur, Compound Blur, Fast Blur, Gaussian Blur, Motion Blur, Radial Blur, Sharpen, Unsharp Mask.

- *Channel Effects*—**Alpha Levels**, Arithmetic, Blend, Compound Arithmetic, Invert, MinMax, Remove Color Matting, Set Channels, Set Matte, Shift Channels.

- *Distortion Effects*—**Bézier Warp**, **Bulge**, **Corner Pin**, **Displacement Map**, **Mesh Warp**, Mirror, Offset, Polar Coordinates, PS+ Pinch, PS+ Ripple, PS+ Spherize, PS+ Twirl, PS+ Wave, PS+ ZigZag, **Reshape**, **Ripple**, Smear, Spherize, **Twirl**, **WaveWarp**.

- *Other*—Cineon Converter.

- *Image Control*—Change Color, Color Balance (HLS), Equalize, Gamma/Pedestal/Gain, Median, PS Arbitrary Map, Tint.

- *Keying*—Color Difference Key, Color Key, **Color Range**, **Difference Matte**, **Extract**, **Linear Color Key**, Luma Key, **Spill Suppressor**.

- *Matte Tools*—Matte Choker, **Simple Choker.**

- *Perspective*—Basic 3D, Bevel Alpha, Bevel Edges, Drop Shadow, Transform.

- *Render Effects*—Audio Spectrum, Audio Waveform, Beam, Ellipse, Fill, **Lightning**, PS+ Lens Flare, Ramp, Stroke.

- *Simulation*—**Particle Playground.**

- *Stylize Effects*—Brush Strokes, Color Emboss, Emboss, Find Edges, **Glow**, Leave Color, Mosaic, Motion Tile, Noise, PS+ Extrude, PS+ Tiles, **Scatter**, Strobe Light, Texturize, Write-on.

- *Text Effects*—Basic Text, Numbers, Path Text.

- *Time Effects*—Echo, Posterize Time, **Time Displacement.**

- *Transition Effects*—Block Dissolve, Gradient Wipe, Iris Wipe, Linear Wipe, Radial Wipe, Venetian Blinds.

- *Video Effects*—Broadcast Colors, Reduce Interlace Flicker, Timecode.

Extensibility

The proof of After Effects' extensibility lies in the abundance of third-party development. So many new effects volumes have been added by external developers (as we detail in Chapters 16 to 41) that hardly any effects area is not included. AE 4 also includes full support for QuickTime 3 (for both Macintosh and Windows). AE 4 also offers faster interactivity by caching frames while you work, so it doesn't have to render or retrieve them. After Effects 4, as we will demonstrate with the detailed information presented in this book, opens new worlds of interactive creativity.

COMPOSITION

If you are an experienced After Effects user, you probably have your own secret and tested methods for preparing new AE compositions. You may find a method or two in this chapter, however, that might make a new and valuable addition to your toolkit.

Whether your previous experience with After Effects is extensive or not, you will want to at least skim this chapter to see how the author's approaches might differ from yours. There's a good chance that you'll still learn something.

The AE Storyboard

If you have been involved in animation for any length of time, whether traditional or computer based, you are no doubt familiar with the necessity of creating a *storyboard* for any but the simplest productions. For those of you who may not be familiar with the storyboarding, a storyboard is simply a roadmap or plan of what is to take place (and when) in the animation. If you need to research the topic of storyboarding further, you can check out the available resources at your library. Many art and animation books on the market include a section on storyboarding.

To understand storyboarding is to understand the difference between *keyframes* and *tweens*. Keyframes, as any AE user knows, represent those times in an animation when some determined event or parameter changes. Tweens (from the term "in-betweens") represent all the intervening frames between keyframes. In computer animation, the computer determines the content of the tween, while the animator concentrates on the keyframe. This is also the way you create animations in After Effects.

Normally, a storyboard is a series of boxes that are drawn to represent various exact times in the animated sequence. Inside a box is a drawing of the content of that keyframe. Below the box are several lines of data, including the exact time of the keyframe in hours/minutes/seconds/frames (written as HH:MM:SS:FF). For example, if a keyframe is 12 seconds and 15 frames into the animation, this would be written as 00:00:12:15. Another line of data might mention what part of a musical soundtrack is referenced at that time, as well as any specific sound effects (such as a bang or plop, and so on). Any part of a narrator's track would also be written out under that keyframe. This, in a nutshell, is standard storyboarding.

PREPARING AN AFTER EFFECTS

However, for an AE storyboard, you should also indicate every effects keyframe that is implemented at that moment. This should include the name of the effect (internal or external plug-in), the exact settings involved, and all other associated data (such as keyframed geometries). This is exactly where this book becomes invaluable. By knowing in some global way the effect you want, you can look through the listings and find the icons that reference that effect category. From there, it's simply a matter of selecting your favorite among the effects that will do exactly what you want.

You can create your own AE storyboard form by drawing the box and the headings for the data lines in a drawing application (like FreeHand or Illustrator), printing it out, and making as many photocopies as you need to storyboard the production.

Starting A New AE Composition

The very first thing that you do after starting After Effects is to go to the Composition menu and select New Composition. When you do that, the Composition Settings dialog box pops up so you can configure the parameters of the composition (see Figure 2.1).

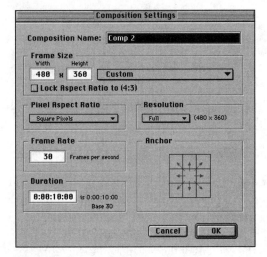

Figure 2.1
The Composition Settings dialog box.

The Composition Settings

You can input whatever data you need to customize your composition workspace in this dialog box. The following list describes the parameters of the composition workspace:

- *Composition Name*—Name your composition with a unique descriptive title so you can recognize it when it is stored on disk. If you have to quickly retrieve a composition for a client, there's nothing more embarrassing than having to search through drives and directories to find it.

- *Frame Size*—Will your work be written to NTSC, PAL, HDTV, Cineon, or film? Do you need to select a custom frame size because of special needs? Determine what you need, and input the corresponding frame size here. If your project will be output to more than one format, try to select a work format that will suffice for everything, perhaps with a little resizing later.

- *Pixel Aspect Ratio*—Square pixels are the default, but AE 4 addresses many other options. Choose a pixel aspect ratio that meets the demands of your output media.

- *Resolution*—Here's where you can optimize the space on your screen. If you have to work at a size that takes up the whole screen, leaving no room for palettes or windows (and you are confined to one monitor), then you can work at half, third, quarter, or a custom resolution to have a more manageable work area.

> **Note: Whatever resolution you set will represent the size of your footage at 100 percent in the Composition window.**

- *Frame Rate*—Frame rate is determined by your output needs. Different media requires different frame rates—from 24 frames per second (fps) for film, to 15 fps for most multimedia, to 30 fps for traditional broadcast output.

- *Anchor*—Placement of the anchor is very important when it comes to rotation and other applied effects. The default is the center of the composition. It's best to leave the anchor at its default, unless your storyboard calls for movements of the layers that are best served by altering the anchor placement.

- *Duration*—Duration is set in hours/minutes/seconds/frames. The Base Unit number represents the fps setting you have selected. A base unit of 30 means that there are 30 frames in one second of play.

After you configure your composition settings and select OK, your Composition window appears on screen. These same settings remain as the default if you quit and restart the application later.

Layers

The next step in the process is to import all of the layer footage content you will need in the composition. This content can be a mix of images, movies, music tracks, audio effects, and Photoshop, Illustrator, and Premier files. If you have more than one layer to import, select Import Footage Files from the File menu. That way, you can select multiple files without having to bring up the path dialog box each time. Just select Done when you have finished importing content.

Layer Properties

Layers that contain video or still images have both Mask (like Mask Shape) and Transform properties (such as layer position or rotation). A layer can also be the recipient of time remapping, and dozens of video effects and audio effects. You can animate a layer's properties graphically in the Composition or Layer window, or by entering numbers into a dialog box in the Time Layout window or in the Effects Controls window. To bring up the Layer window, simply double-click on the layer or on its name in any window it is listed in. You have to create masks in a Layer window, and not directly on the composition in the stack.

Adjustment Layers

Adjustment layers are new to AE 4. Because applying an effect to a layer affects only that layer and no others, you'll use an adjustment layer if you need an effect to exist independently of any layer. Unlike a normal layer, an adjustment layer does not display any source footage; it exists only to apply an effect. Effects applied to an adjustment layer will affect all layers below it in the composition's stacking order. An adjustment layer behaves exactly like a normal layer as far as using keyframes to adjust any adjustment layer's properties over time. Some global attributes, like brightening or adjusting the contrast of the entire stack, are best handled with an adjustment layer. You create an adjustment layer by selecting New Adjustment Layer from the Layer menu.

Aligning Layers

The Align palette can be used to line up or evenly space any number of multiselected layers. You can align or distribute layers along the vertical or horizontal axes of selected objects. When you align and distribute selected layers, keep the following points in mind:

- If you apply right-edge alignment, all selected layers align to the right edge of the selected object that is the farthest to the right.

- Selecting the distribution option evenly spaces selected layers between the two most extreme layers.

- Distributing layers by their centers will create equal space between the centers, but different-sized layers will extend by different amounts into the space between layers.

- Locked layers are not moved by any alignment or distribution options.

The Align and Distribute palette is accessed by selecting Plug-in Palettes|Align & Distribute from the Window menu.

Moving Layers Front Or Back In The Stack

Moving layers within the stack is easy. Simply highlight the target layer or layers and select the proper movement command from the Layer menu.

Layer Preview Quality

The Layer preview has three levels of quality: Best, Draft, and Wireframe. Higher-quality settings show more detail at higher resolution, but also tend to slow redraw and rendering speeds. "Best" displays and renders a layer using subpixel positioning, anti-aliasing, and complete calculation of any applied plug-in effects. "Draft" displays a layer so that you can see it, but only at rough quality. With draft quality, layers are displayed and rendered without anti-aliasing and subpixel positioning, and some effects are not precisely calculated. "Wireframe" represents a layer as a box with an X across it. Layers in wireframe are displayed and rendered faster than in other settings. Whereas the Wireframe mode is available only from the Quality list in the Layer menu, the Best and Draft settings are available by clicking on the Quality Switch (the slash) in the Time Layout window. If the slash leans to the right, quality is set to Best. If it leans to the left, Quality is set to Draft (see Figure 2.2).

Figure 2.2
The Quality Switch in the Time Layout window determines the preview quality of the selected layer. Top is Draft, and Bottom is Best.

Layer Stacking Order

When you add a new layer to a composition, it appears at the top of the layer stack by default. (This top layer is also the front-most layer in the Composition window.) Subsequent added layers also appear at the top of the stack. Changing the stacking order of an adjustment layer changes which layers it affects, because it affects all layers beneath it in the stack. The Time Layout window displays the layer stacking order. The top layer is listed at the top of the layer outline, the second layer second from the top, and so on. You can change the layering order in the Composition window or in the Time Layout window by simply dragging that layer to a new position (see Figure 2.3).

▷ ■	1	🖹 Feen4.tif
▷ ■	2	🖹 ColP1_02.TIF

Figure 2.3
Simply drag a layer to a new position in the stack in the Time Layout window.

Solid Color Layers

Select New Solid from the Layer menu, and a dialog box allows you to select the color of the new solid layer. Layers of solid color suffice for creating masks and many other purposes (see Figure 2.4).

Layer Transitions

You can cause one layer to transition to another in the stack in a number of ways and without resorting to any special-effects filters. The transitions include cuts, opacity transitions, size transitions, and position transitions. Transitions occur from the top visible layer to the next layer down in the stack.

Cuts

A *cut* is a sharp transition from one piece of footage to another, as in a slide show. But a cut in After Effects is different from a slide show because a cut can move from one animated

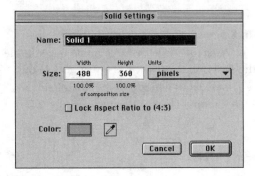

Figure 2.4
The Solid Settings dialog box appears when you select New Solid from the Layer menu. You can select its name, size, aspect ratio, and color.

piece of footage to another, as well as incorporate still imagery. Audio can also cut from one track to another in the same manner. To keyframe animate a cut, take these steps:

1. Decide on the footage that you want to include in your composition. Import it.

2. Check on the time of each piece of animated footage. You can do this by double-clicking on the layer name in the Time Layout window or on the layer itself (if it is at the top of the stack). Its Layer window will then appear, with its running length at the bottom. Write down the running length for each piece of animated footage in your stack (see Figure 2.5).

Figure 2.5
The movie's running length is shown at the bottom of its Layer window.

3. If you have imported still imagery for your composition, decide how long you want each image to remain on screen in the final piece. Note each of these times on your list as well.

4. Add the times to arrive at the new length for your composition.

5. Go to Composition Settings under the Composition menu, and change the length of the composition in the Duration box to match the new time you just calculated. Close the Composition Settings dialog box (see Figure 2.6).

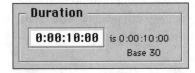

Figure 2.6
Change the listing in the Duration area of the Composition Settings dialog box to match your new calculations.

6. Now it's time to move your layers into position in the Time Layout window. Move each of the layer's length indicators horizontally, so that the end point of one lines up with the start point of the next one to appear. This is normally done so that layer 1 is followed by layer 2, and so on, but it does not have to be in this order. What is important is that each layer has its own time reserved for visibility that does not conflict with that needed by another layer. Preview and tweak as necessary (see Figure 2.7).

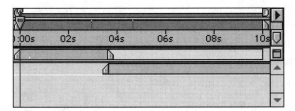

Figure 2.7
Move each layer in the Time Layout window so that its start point matches the end point of the previous layer's appearance.

Congratulations! You have just created a composition whose layers will be revealed by the cut method.

Opacity Transitions

Opacity can be set and altered in the Time Layout window alone. A layer is displayed at full opacity except for those areas that are excluded by a mask or Alpha channel as a default. You can adjust the degree of layer transparency by setting an Opacity value less than 100 percent. To change a layer's opacity for keyframe animation:

1. Select the layer you want to modify in the Time Layout window.

2. Press t (lower case) on your keyboard.

3. Click on the stopwatch to activate keyframe animation.

4. Click on the underlined Opacity value.

5. Enter a new value, and then click on OK.

The Opacity value can be keyframe animated in this manner. If Opacity is set to 100% at the start of an animation, and then altered to 0% at some later point, the next layer down will start to reveal itself.

Size Transitions

Using the same general methods as previously described for the opacity transition, you can cause your layers to shrink from view to reveal the next layer. However, you should observe some cautions:

• The idea is to start a layer at full size and to reduce the size to 0 to reveal the next layer, but this has to be keyframed carefully. The layer should be keyframed to start at 100%, and then to 99.9% about five frames before it is to disappear. Its last frame, of course, should be set to 0%. If you forget the 99.9% keyframe, the layer will start to reduce in size from the start of the animation. Unless you specifically call for this, it's not a good idea.

- The layers are not repositioned horizontally in the Time Layout window, unless their running time is shorter than where they need to appear in the temporal order. In this case, you can switch layers around in the stack to make sure they are where they should be when their visibility is called for.

- Realize that resizing will center on the layer's anchor point. To make the resizing center on a specific element of the layer, you have to move that layer's anchor point. To change the position of a layer's anchor point, take these steps:

  1. Double-click on the layer to bring up its Layer window.

  2. In the Layer window, click on the Layer options right-pointing arrow at the top right. This will present you with a list of options. Select Anchor Point Path.

  3. When you return to the Layer window, you will be able to reposition the anchor point for that layer.

  4. When you reposition a layer's anchor point, that new anchor point will line up with the composition's set anchor point, so you will have to manually reposition the layer in the stack once you close that layer's Layer window. Any resizing will now use the new anchor point as its center.

> Note: If you set the new anchor point outside the layer's frame space at one of the corners, you will be able to use a rotation transition to move the layer out of the composition. You can rotate the layer until it no longer appears in the composition, revealing the next layer in the stack.

Position Transitions

As you'll see, position transitions are probably the easiest of all. You can combine any or all of these transitions between any number of layers in the stack to create a more visually appealing composition.

Duplicating A Layer

You can duplicate any selected layer in the stack. After Effects copies all property keyframes, masks, and effects to the duplicate layer, which is added above the original layer and automatically selected. If you want to duplicate a layer without duplicating its keyframes, masks, or effects, add the original source footage file to the composition again. In a Composition or Time Layout window, select a layer and choose Edit|Duplicate or select Copy then Paste.

Flipping A Layer

The best way to flip a layer (horizontally or vertically) is to grab one of its control points in the Composition window and drag it past its anchor point. Hold down the Shift key while you're doing this to keep everything in proportion.

Showing And Hiding Layers

Use the Video switch (the eye icon at the left of the layer's name in the Composition window) to exclude or include layers from appearing. (The Video switch is on by default, so the layer displays in the Composition window.) When you want to speed up redraw or exclude a layer from appearing in both the preview and the rendered version, turn off the Video switch. (The icon will change to a closed eye.)

Locking A Layer

The Lock switch is located just to the right of the Audio switch, at the left of the layer's name in the Time Layout window. Activating this switch prevents the accidental selection of layers that you do not want to alter. When the Lock switch is on for a layer, you cannot select the layer in the Composition window or the Time Layout window. If you try to select or modify a locked layer, the layer flashes in the Time Layout window.

Renaming A Layer

The layer outline in the Time Layout window lists layers by the name of their source footage. You can rename any layer at any time to help you identify layer content and purpose in a composition. You can switch between displaying the original file name and the layer name you've chosen. After you rename a layer, all other layers in the composition will be displayed with brackets around their names. Renamed layers are displayed without brackets.

To rename a layer, take these steps:

1. In the Time Layout window's layer list, select the layer you want to rename.

2. Press the Enter (Windows) or Return (Mac) key on the keyboard. When the dialog box appears, type a new name.

3. Press Enter (Windows) or Return (Mac) again to apply the new name.

Reversing The Playback Of A Layer

It's easy to reverse the direction of a layer's playback. When you do this, all keyframes for all properties on the selected layer also reverse position relative to the layer (although the layer itself maintains its original In and Out points relative to the composition). This technique is used to play movies in reverse.

To reverse a layer's playback direction, take these steps:

1. In a Time Layout window, select the layer you want to reverse.

2. Press Ctrl+Alt+R (Windows) or Command+Option+R (Mac).

You can also enter a negative time-stretch value in the Time Stretch dialog box.

If you want to reverse the order of keyframes without reversing the layer's playback direction, select keyframes and choose Layer|Keyframe Assistant|Time-Reverse Keyframes. If you want to reverse a layer's playback direction without reversing the order of its keyframes, use time remapping to reverse the layer.

Rotate A Layer To Follow A Motion Path

You can make a layer rotate automatically as it moves along a motion path. For example, if you animate any layer content on a motion path, you can make the plane turn and change direction, following the motion path. This process is known as Auto-Orient Rotation.

> *Note: To take advantage of Auto-Orient Rotation, you first have to have created a motion path for the layer. This is done by keyframe animating its position over the length of the timeline.*

To use Auto-Orient Rotation, follow these steps:

1. In the Time Layout window, select the layer you want to modify.
2. Select Transform|Auto-Orient Rotation from the Layer menu.

> *Note: Read the After Effects documentation carefully to thoroughly familiarize yourself with layer terminology and techniques.*

> *Note: To apply eases to a selected layer's motion, use Easy Ease and other Keyframe Assistant processes. See Chapter 13 for more information.*

Masks

Masks are paths that you draw or import into a Layer window to create transparent areas for a layer. Everything outside of a closed mask area will be transparent in that layer. In the Time Layout window, you can set mask shapes and mask feather properties and change these properties over time.

You can create three types of closed masks: rectangular (or square, holding down the Shift key), oval (or circular, if you hold down Shift), and Bézier. Closed Bézier masks are created by using the Pen tool to draw a freeform Bézier path as a mask, creating any shape (see Figure 2.8).

Figure 2.8
Examples of a rectangular, oval, and Bézier mask on the same footage.

Figure 2.9
Text created by using the Rectangle and Bézier Pen in this layer's Layer window, resulting in text that uses the layer content as a texture.

A feature new to AE 4 is the ability to have up to 128 masks on any selected layer. This allows you to do things like create letter forms as a mask in the Layer window, which will create a text block whose texture will be the layer content (see Figure 2.9).

After you first create a mask, it can be resized or rotated, and you can change parts of it by grabbing and moving its control handles in the Layer window. The transparency information is stored in the layer's Alpha channel. When the Alpha channel of a layer doesn't meet your requirements, you can use any combination of Alpha channel effects to customize the mask. A mask, then, is a path or outline that modifies a layer's Alpha channel. Use a mask when you want to create areas of transparency in After Effects. A mask belongs to a specific layer, but each After Effects layer can contain multiple masks.

Stroking And Filling A Mask

A mask can be stroked to create a color border, and/or filled with color. To add a stroke to the mask, take these steps:

1. Select the layer containing the mask you want to stroke.

2. Choose Render|Stroke from the Effects menu.

3. In the Effect Controls window, choose the mask you want to stroke from the Path menu.

4. Specify the following options as necessary: brush size, brush hardness, opacity, and spacing frequency.

Select Render|Fill from the Effects menu to fill any mask on a targeted layer with color.

Precomposing

Precomposing is a method of nesting layers within an existing composition. When you want to change the order in which layer components are rendered, precomposing is a quick way to create intermediate levels of nesting in an existing hierarchy. Precomposing makes it easier to add an additional rendering stage before rendering the entire composition. When you precompose, your selected layers are moved into a new composition that takes the place of the selected layers. Precomposing also places the new composition in the Project window, available for use in any composition that follows.

> **Note: The Precompose command was called the Compify command in After Effects 1 and 2.02.**

When you precompose only one layer, you can transfer the keyframes and the mask, effects, and transform properties from the original layer to the new layer. You can also choose to keep the keyframes and properties with the original layer while it moves one rendering step further from the main composition. When you precompose more than one layer, the keyframes and properties stay with the original layers.

After Effects offers two options for working with layer properties and keyframes during precomposing:

• *Leave All Attributes In (the selected composition)*—With this option, the selected layer's properties and keyframes are left in the original composition. The frame size of the new composition is exactly the same as that of the selected layer. Use this option when you precompose layers only to simplify or reuse a composition, and not to change the rendering order of layer properties. After you precompose using the Leave All Attributes In option, the changes that you applied to the properties of the original layer are still applied to that layer in the original composition. This option is not available when you select more than one layer for precomposing.

• *Move all attributes into the new composition*—This option moves the properties and keyframes of one or more selected layers one level further from the main composition in the composition hierarchy. The frame size of the new composition is exactly the same as that of the original composition. Choose this option when you want to change the rendering order in the selected layers. For example, you use this option when you want to rotate a layer, but not its drop shadow. Select this option to organize selected layers into their own composition.

> **Note: It is especially useful to precompose multiple audio layers into their own premixed composition, once you have all of the mix information worked out. This creates a separate audio file that can be used as a track in another composition.**

Nesting

Nested compositions are organized into a hierarchy. Nesting combines two or more compositions into one from which the final movie is rendered. When you nest one composition inside another, it becomes a layer within that targeted composition. To nest one composition into another, simply import it and drag it into the stack.

Mattes

A *matte* is a layer (or any of its channels) that defines the transparent areas of that layer or another layer. You use a matte when you have a channel or layer that defines the desired area of transparency better than the Alpha channel, or in cases in which the footage does not include an Alpha channel.

After you have used any key to create transparency, you can further refine the matte to remove traces of key color and to create clean edges. The Production Bundle provides these matte tools: Simple Choker, Matte Choker, Alpha Levels, and Spill Suppressor (see Chapter 14).

Track And Traveling Mattes

When you want one layer to show through a hole in another layer, set up a track matte. You'll need two layers: one to act as a matte and the other to fill the hole in the matte. You can make the layer that will act as the track matte from a Ramp effect. You can also create it beforehand in Photoshop and save it out as a grayscale image. The matte becomes the transparency control layer for the next layer down, allowing the layer below that (the third layer) to show through. The third layer will show through where the matte is darkest, and become obliterated by the second layer's content where the new matte is lightest. (This is reversed if you reverse the transparency of the matte.)

When you animate the track matte layer, you create a traveling matte. This is the method used in films to place live actors in animated scenes. To create a track matte:

1. Import three pieces of footage. Two will serve as imagery, and one as the matte information. Make sure that the one to serve as matte data is a 256-level grayscale image. (Create it in a bitmap application, such as Adobe Photoshop.)

2. Make sure that the image to serve as the matte layer is on top of the stack. Go to the bottom of the Time Layout window, and click on the Switches/Modes lines at the bottom of the Switches column (see Figure 2.10).

3. Under the column TrkMat, you will see that no listing exists for the top layer. This is because the top layer will become the matte layer for the second layer down. Under the TrkMat column for the second layer, change None to Luma Matte. This makes the footage in layer 1 into a matte for layer 2, reading its brightness as transparency information. The result is that certain areas of layer 2 become transparent, revealing the content of layer 3.

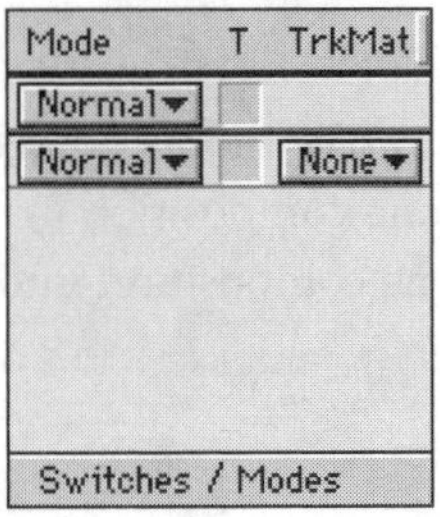

Mode | T | TrkMat
Normal▼
Normal▼ | | None▼

Switches / Modes

Figure 2.10
The Switches column is toggled to become the Modes column, with settings for developing a track matte.

4. If you want to explore the opposite effect, select Luma Inverted Matte instead of Luma Matte, and you will see that the areas that allow the content of layer 3 to show through have reversed (see Figures 2.11 and 2.12).

The examples shown in Figure 2.12 use normal mode. By altering the mode of the layer 2 footage, you alter the way that layers 2 and 3 combine (see Figure 2.13).

See Chapter 14 for details on the Matte Choker and Simple Choker filters.

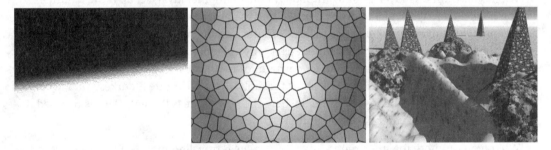

Figure 2.11
From left to right, layer content for layers 1, 2, and 3.

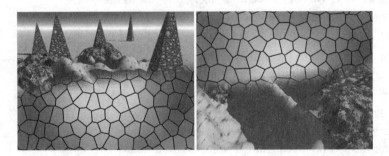

Figure 2.12
Same footage as Figure 2.11, but with a luma matte applied to the stack at the left, and an inverted luma matte applied to the stack at the right.

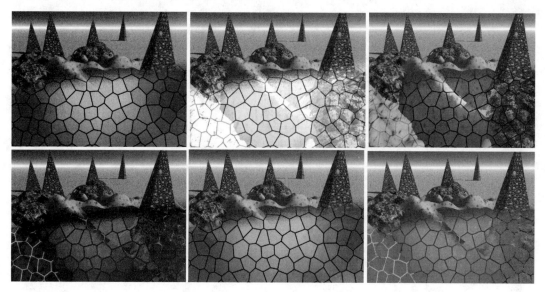

Figure 2.13
The different modes being used for the luma matte (top left to bottom right): normal, add, overlay, difference, luminosity, and exclusion.

RENDERING

After Effects is—more than anything else—an animation environment. With previous versions, we could have described it even more definitively as a 2D-animation environment, but that is no longer possible. With the release of AE 4, it's now earning a deserved reputation as a 3D-animation application.

With the addition of plug-ins such as HollywoodFX (Chapter 34), TILT (Chapter 38), and ZaxWerks Invigorator (Chapter 40), After Effects is accumulating credentials as a 3D-animation application as well. These effects filters, both internal and external, expand the list of options of *what* you can do with After Effects. Mastering the use of the Time Layout window and the incorporated timeline allows you to control *when* it is done. To create a good composition that is guaranteed to amaze, you have to understand and master both the *what* and the *when*.

The Time Layout Window

Understanding every facet and the importance of every option in the Time Layout window is a necessary first step toward crafting prize-winning animations in After Effects. In that regard, let's reinforce your understanding of the components of the Time Layout window (see Figure 3.1).

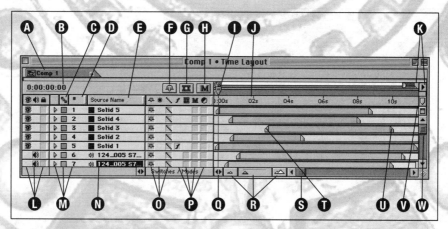

Figure 3.1
The Time Layout window, with call letters pointing out components to be detailed.

A Detailed Tour

For the following detailed text, refer to the alphabetical callouts shown in Figure 3.1.

Tab (A)

One of the new features added to After Effects 4 is the tabbed references to windows and palettes, which indicate the name of the environment you are currently working on. As you can see, this tab reads "Comp 1", and indicates that the time layout you are looking at here is for Comp 1. If we had more than one composition loaded, a tab would refer to each by name. This is another reason for using unique titles for all your compositions, thus allowing a more intuitive and faster access to them. For example, if you save a multitude of compositions saved as "Comp 1", and then import them into a AE project, each composition tab in the Time Layout window will read "Comp 1", and you won't know which is which when you need to configure or edit animations.

Current Time Display (B)

After Effects can display the current time as timecode, frames, or feet and frames. Selecting a time preference does not alter the frame rate of footage or a composite; it just changes how frames are numbered. Timecode counts frames per second and is the most common setting. Frames counts footage frames without reference to time and is used more to target certain frames for audio and other effects where counting the seconds is less important, or as a working mode prior to switching to timecode. Feet And Frames counts feet of 16mm or 35mm motion-picture film, and also counts fractions of feet in frames (35mm film has 16 frames per foot, and 16mm film has 40 frames per foot).

NTSC footage uses the 30-fps drop-frame timecode base. You can always change the starting frame number to match the time-counting method of another editing system you may be using. To change the time display:

1. Select Time from the File|Preferences menu (see Figure 3.2).

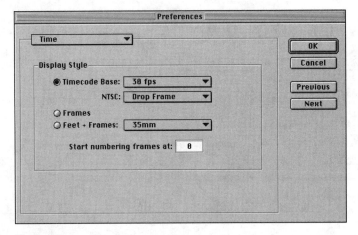

Figure 3.2
The Time Preferences dialog box.

2. Select a time preference: Timecode, Frames, or Feet and Frames

3. If you selected Timecode, then you can select from the following fps rates: 24, 25, 30, 48, 50, 60, and 100.

> *Note: To use drop-frame timecode for footage and compositions with a frame rate of 29.97 fps, click Timecode Base, then select 30 fps from the Timecode Base pop-up menu. To use non-drop-frame timecode for footage and compositions with a frame rate of 29.97 fps, click Timecode Base and select 30 fps from the Timecode Base pop-up menu and Non-Drop Frame from the NTSC menu.*

4. To use frames, click on Frames.

5. To use feet and frames, click on Feet + Frames. Select a film type from the Feet + Frames pop-up menu (16mm or 35mm).

6. Click on OK to assign your choice.

> *Note: If the composition is set to a frame rate of 29.97 fps, SMPTE 30 fps drop-frame timecode is assigned as the default. Drop-frame timecode makes adjustments for the slight difference between 29.97 fps frame rate and 30 fps frame rate. Non-drop-frame timecode is also available. When you use drop-frame timecode, the SMPTE-standard method of re-numbering the first two frame numbers of every minute, except at every tenth minute, is used.*

Label (C)

This is the Label column. The label's color indicates what type of footage layer is involved. To set the label color for a composition, video, audio, still, folder, and solid layer, select Label from the File|Preferences menu (see Figure 3.3).

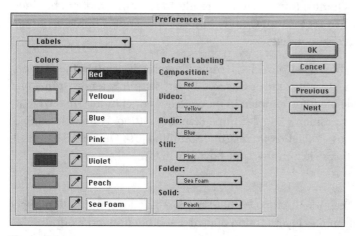

Figure 3.3

The Label Preferences dialog box allows you to customize your label colors.

Number (D)

This is the Number column. After Effects assigns a number to each layer in the stack.

Source Name/Layer Name (E)

Clicking on this title toggles you between the source name and the layer name. The source name always points to the name of the source file and cannot be altered. The layer name is by default taken from the source name, but it can be changed when you are in Layer Name mode. To rename a layer:

1. In the layer list of the Time Layout window, select the layer you want to rename.

2. Press Enter (Windows) or Return (Mac), and type a new name when the dialog box appears.

3. Press Enter (Windows) or Return (Mac) again to apply the new name.

Hide Shy Layers Switch (F)

Activating this global switch hides all of the layers in the layer list for which the Shy Switch is turned on. Note that this does not hide the content in the Composition window, but only the layer data in the Time Layout window stack. This makes it easier to perform keyframe animations on the layers that are not "shy," because you don't have to scroll to get to them.

Frame Blending Switch (G)

Frame Blending is set in the Render Settings dialog box, but using this switch on selected motion layers allows you to select specific layers for Frame Blending, by setting it to On For All Checked Layers. Frame blending slows previewing and rendering, so you might want to apply frame blending without displaying it. By selecting the Enable Frame Blending button at the top of the Time Layout window, you can control whether layers that use frame blending affect redraw and rendering. The Quality setting you choose also affects frame blending. When the layer is set to Best Quality, frame blending results in smoother motion, but may take longer to render than when set to Draft Quality. You can also enable frame blending for all compositions when you render a movie.

In the Render Settings dialog box (see Figure 3.4), Frame Blending determines the frame blending settings for all layers. Use the On For Checked Layers setting to render frame blending only for layers with frame blending enabled in the Switches panel in the Time Layout window, regardless of the composition's Enable Frame Blending setting. Frame Blending can be found in the Render Settings dialog box under Time Sampling. Use On For All Checked Layers if you are activating this switch in the Time Layout window.

Motion Blur Switch (H)

The faster an object moves, the more it blurs. Without motion blur, layer animation appears less real. Adding motion blur makes layer motion appear smoother and more natural. Motion blur cannot be added to motion that already exists within a animation or movie that was imported as a layer. Smoothing the content of a video layer is accomplished by Frame

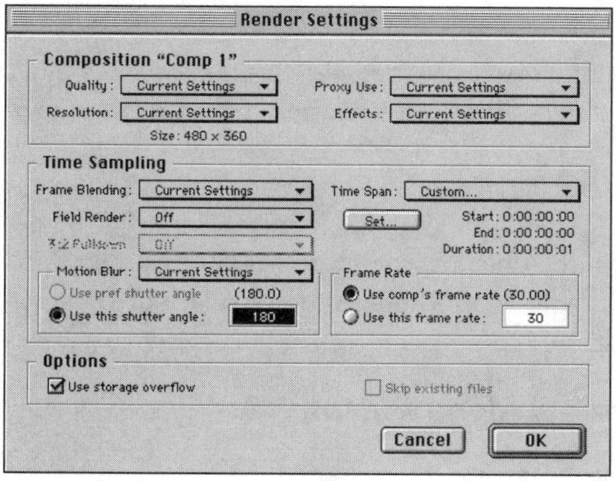

Figure 3.4
The Render Settings dialog box.

Blending. The Motion Blur switch creates a true motion blur based on a layer's movement and a shutter angle you specify.

The Enable Motion Blur button lets you control whether layers that use motion blur affect redraw and rendering. You can also enable motion blur for all compositions when you render a movie, using the Render Settings dialog box.

Shutter angle is set in the General Preferences dialog box. The shutter angle is measured in degrees and simulates the exposure produced by a rotating shutter. Setting the shutter angle has no effect unless you are applying motion blur. The shutter angle is computed using the footage "frame rate" to determine the necessary exposure. Entering a shutter angle of 1 degree applies almost no motion blur at all, while entering 360 degrees applies the maximum amount of blur. The shutter angle is set to 180 degrees as the default (see Figure 3.5).

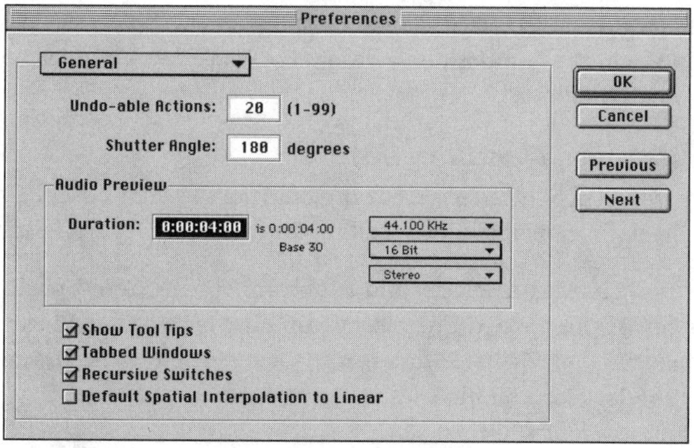

Figure 3.5
The shutter angle is set in the General Preferences dialog box, but only takes effect when you activate Motion Blur.

Current Time Marker (I)

Moving this marker advances the composition display to the point in time indicated by the marker. This is the most common way to select a frame for keyframing or to advance to a specific time in the composition.

Time Ruler (J)

These ruler marks tell you where you are in the timeline, so that moving the Current Time Marker can be done effectively. The ruler is notated in whatever time marks match the settings you have selected in Time preferences.

Compress Ruler Control And Window Menu Button (K)

Move the Compress Control to zoom in on the time marks so that you can position the Current Time Marker more effectively.

The Window Menu button displays the Time Layout window, which includes functions affecting layers and keyframes, as well as providing access to the Composition Settings dialog box. The listings are as follows:

- Composition Settings (which gives you instant access to the Composition Settings dialog box).
- Hide Shy Layers.
- Enable Frame Blending.
- Use Keyframe Icons/Use Keyframe Indices. Keyframe indices place a small number inside every keyframe Icon.

AV Panel (L)

The Audio/Video (A/V) Features panel in the Time Layout window lets you lock layers, control which layers display in the Composition window, and control which layers appear in a preview and a rendered version. You can also see at a glance if the layer is a visual or an audio file. Clicking on the audio or visual icon so it does not display makes that layer invisible (or silent, in the case of audio) in the Composition window. Locking a layer means that you cannot accidentally alter it while editing.

Openers, Color Keys, And Layer Numbers (M)

The most important item here is the Layer Openers. These are the Triangle icons pointing to the right. When you click on them, they open the layer editing attributes (see Figure 3.6).

Opening a layer for editing exposes its Masks, Effects, and Transform options. You can edit masks and effects only if they have been applied. Transforms can always be edited. Video transforms include Anchor Point, Position, Scale, Rotation, and Opacity. Activate keyframe animation by clicking in the timeclock icon on the left, moving to another frame, and changing the appropriate value (see Figure 3.7).

If you open an Audio layer, there is one more attribute—Audio. This attribute has separate parameters that cannot be keyframe animated, but just list various data. Notice that there

Figure 3.6
When a layer is opened for editing, its masks, effects, and transforms can be keyframe animated.

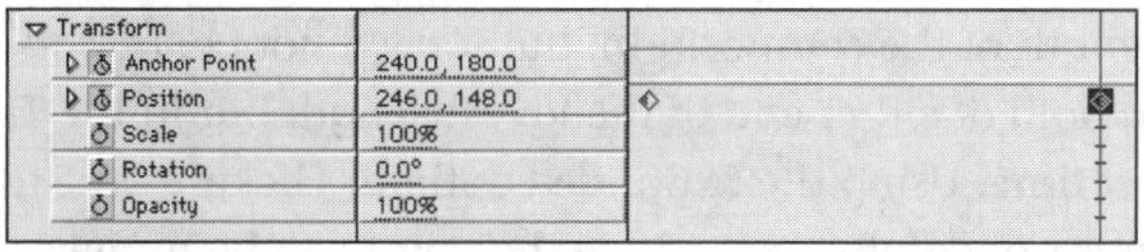

Figure 3.7
The timeclock icon is activated for Position, showing the keyframed icons on the Position attribute's timeline.

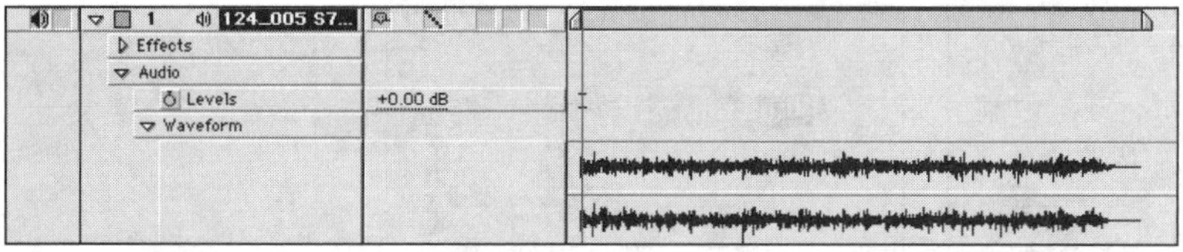

Figure 3.8
Opening an Audio layer exposes yet another attribute list that cannot be keyframe animated.

are no timeclock icons present for activating keyframing (see Figure 3.8). For more information about handling audio, see Chapter 4.

Source/Layer Name (N)

This is the source or layer name. You can alter the layer name.

Switches 1 (O)

These switches are for Shy, Collapse Transformations/Continuously Rasterize, and Quality.

> *Note: The Layer Switches (for both Switches 1 and Switches 2) panel shares space in the Time Layout window with the Transfer Modes panel, so it isn't visible if the Transfer Modes panel is visible. You can change instantly between the Layer Switches panel and the Transfer Modes panel by clicking on the Switches/Modes button in the Time Layout window. See Chapter 2 for Transfer Modes.*

Switches 2 (P)

These switches are for Effects, Frame Blending, Motion Blur, and Adjustment Layer.

Expansion Button For Expanded Display (Q)

Clicking on the Expansion button adds more content to the Time Layout window, as shown in Figure 3.9.

	In	Out	Duration	Stretch	0 :00s
	0:00:00:01	0:00:11:07	0:00:11:07	100.0%	

Figure 3.9
The Expanded Time Layout window components: In Point, Out Point, Duration Time, and Stretch.

The In and Out Point refer to the times that the layer appears in the composition, and when it disappears. Often, this is set to the length of the composition, but it need not be. In and Out Points can also be set by grabbing hold of either end of the layer's length bar in the Time Layout window and moving it to a new time. Using the Expanded options, clicking on either or both the In and Out Point time brings up a dialog box where the point can be numerically indicated (see Figure 3.10).

Figure 3.10
You can alter the In and/or Out Point of the layer by clicking on the time in the Expanded options in the Time Layout window.

Duration and Time Stretch really mean the same thing, the first numerically and the second by percentage. This is the total length of the layer in time. You can stretch the time by clicking on either number. They both bring up the same dialog box, where time can be stretched by time increments or by percentage. Note that stretching a movie longer makes it play a little slower (frames are added), and stretching it shorter makes it play quicker (frames are removed). Stretching an Audio layer distorts the playback (see Chapter 4 on Audio). See Figure 3.11.

Zooming (R)

These three icons allow you to zoom in or out of the timeline. From left to right, they are: Zoom Out, Interactive Zoom, and Zoom In. Zooming out allows you a better global view of the timeline, whereas zooming in allows you more detail and a closer view of each frame.

Figure 3.11
The Time Stretch dialog box.

Horizontal Timeline Slider (S)

Unless you are zoomed out all the way, you will see only a portion of the timeline at one time. Use this slider to move horizontally to see different portions of the timeline.

In Point (T)

This symbol on the left edge of a layer allows you to adjust its In Point by moving it to the right.

Out Point (U)

This symbol on the left edge of a layer allows you to adjust its Out Point by moving it to the left.

Comp Marker And Comp Family (V)

Drag a Comp marker to any point on the timeline important enough to mark for a return visit, perhaps because a vital transition is happening at that point. Clicking on the Comp Family icon opens the Composition window if it is closed. This is especially helpful when you have multiple Comps in a project, but the one you want has been closed. Just click on its tab in the Time Layout window, and then click on the Comp Family icon.

Vertical Slider (W)

If you have many layers in your composition, you may need to use this slider to get to the one you want to edit. You can avoid this necessity by making all the layers not needed for editing Shy.

Rendering

You can render both single graphics of any frame in the Composition window, or a full animation of your project. Whether you elect to render a single-frame graphic (Save Frame As File or Photoshop Layers from the Composition menu), or as a movie (Make Movie from the Composition menu), the same Render dialog box appears. You can even save a single frame as a QuickTime movie file, though why you might select this option would be a mystery. When rendering out either a single-frame graphic or a movie, the first dialog box that appears after you name the output file and select a save path is the Render Queue (see Figure 3.12).

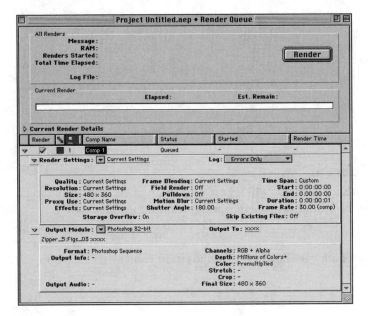

Figure 3.12
The Render Queue dialog box.

If you open both the Render Settings and Output Module lists, you will see a lot of information that lists all the details of your current composition. The Render Settings lists allows you to select Current, Best, Draft, or Custom. Select either Best or Custom for your final rendering. When you select Custom, or when you click on the selected Render Setting name, the Render Settings dialog box will pop up. This gives you the capacity to customize your render settings (see Figure 3.13).

The Render Settings Dialog Options

The following options are found in the Render Settings dialog box:

- *Quality*—This determines the quality setting for all layers. The options include Current Settings, Best, Draft, and Wireframe. Finished rendering should be done with the highest quality possible.

- *Resolution*—Your selection here determines the size and clarity of the rendered composition, relative to the original composition dimensions. You should set the Quality option to Draft when rendering at reduced resolution. Selecting Best quality in this case does not produce a clear image, it just takes longer to render.

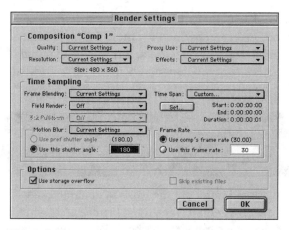

Figure 3.13
The Render Settings dialog box.

- *Proxy Use*—This setting whether proxies are used when rendering. A *proxy* is a lower-resolution or still version of existing footage used to replace the original to save processing time, used when you want to speed up previewing in the rendering of test movies. Use any file available as a proxy. The attributes and keyframes you apply to the proxy are transferred to the actual footage when you do a final render.

- *Effects*—Determines which effects are enabled for the rendered composition. You can choose to use current settings or to turn on or off all effects. If you select All On, all applied effects are used in a composition or a layer. If you select All Off, all effects for the composition are disabled.

- *Frame Blending*—Apply the frame blending settings for all layers. The options are Current Settings, On For Checked Layers, and Off For All Layers.

- *Field Render*—Select the field rendering technique used for the final rendered composition. Choose Off if you are rendering for film or for display on a computer screen.

About Field Rendering

Most broadcast video is *interlaced*, where each frame consists of two fields displayed in turn, so a 30 fps video is really 60 fps, considering that there are really two separate interlaced fields for each frame. Your computer, however, displays noninterlaced video, so that each frame is displayed completely from top to bottom. When you finish creating a movie for display on a television, After Effects can render it back to fields, which is needed for high quality for broadcast display. The two interlaced fields are known as Field 1 and Field 2, even and odd, or upper and lower. Movies in After Effects need to be field-rendered to produce the correct broadcast video signal for NTSC or PAL formats. Each separate field contains every other horizontal line in the frame. A TV displays one field and than the other, so you see a unified frame. Interlaced video describes a frame with two passes of alternating scan lines. In noninterlaced video, like that displayed on your computer and in a movie theater, scan lines are drawn in order from top to bottom in a single pass.

You have to separate fields as you import and field-render the composition to a finished movie file if you plan to use interlaced video in a composition or want to use an After Effects movie in an interlaced-video medium such as NTSC. If you want to incorporate digitized field-rendered footage in an After Effects project, you should separate the video fields when you import the footage.

> **Note: When you import interlaced video that was originally transferred from film, remove the 3:2 pulldown that was applied during the transfer from film to video as you separate fields to prevent distortion.**

After Effects accurately converts the two interlaced frames in the video to noninterlaced frames, while preserving image quality, which is essential when applying effects. Each field-separated frame has only half the data of the source frame, so it's best to view the results at best quality, allowing After Effects to interpolate between the scan lines. High-quality interlaced frames are created when the final rendering occurs, which is perfect for videotape.

- *3:2 Pulldown*—This sets the phase of 3:2 pulldown. Please refer to the After Effects documentation for a complete overview on this option.

- *Motion Blur*—This sets Motion Blur for the composition. The options are Current Settings, On For Checked layers, and Off For All Layers.

- *Shutter Angle*—The amount of motion blur is affected by this value. Telling After Effects to Use Pref Shutter Angle uses the shutter angle selected in General Preferences. If you want the preferences setting to be overwritten, set another value here.

- *Use Storage Overflow*—If checked, the rendering continues when the first assigned storage volume overflows. If not checked, rendering stops when the first assigned storage volume reaches capacity.

- *Time Span*—The options are: Work Area Only, Length Of Comp, or Custom. Your choice sets the length of the rendering. Custom (or clicking Set) brings up another dialog box, allowing you to enter Timecodes for Start, End, and Duration.

- *Frame Rate*—Determines the sampling frame rate used to render the composition. Select Use Comp's Frame Rate to use the frame rate specified in the Composition Settings dialog box, or select Use This Frame Rate to type in a different frame rate. The actual frame rate of the composition is unchanged.

- *Skip Existing Files*—When checked, you can re-render part of a sequence of files (do not use it if you've saved out a movie file, but only for single-frame sequences). This current sequence and existing sequence must share the same name. The starting frame number, frame rate, and time span must also be the same. Use this option to render single-frame sequences on multiple systems.

Rendering Photoshop Files

If you select to Save Frame As Photoshop Layers in the Composition menu, you can import the saved data to Photoshop, and all the layers will be intact. This reemphasizes the integration offered by AE 4 among all Adobe applications.

Output Module Settings

The Output Module listing in the Render Queue dialog box are only part of the story. To bring up the full Output Module options list, you have to click on the current option, bringing up the Output Module Settings dialog box (see Figure 3.14).

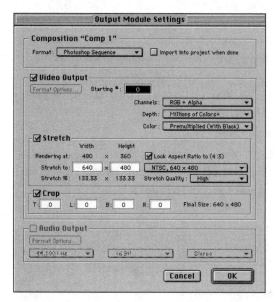

Figure 3.14
The Output Module Settings dialog box.

AE 4 contains an upgraded list of output module options for the specific video and audio output format that you require, as well as all the video compression options you need. The following options are listed:

- *Format*—Specify the format for the output file or sequence of files. The File formats include: TIFF Sequence, Targa Sequence, SGI Sequence, PNG Sequence, Pixar Sequence, PCX Sequence, JPEG Sequence, FLC/FLI, Filmstrip, Cineon (AE format) Sequence, BMP Sequence, Animated GIF, Amiga IFF Sequence, ElectricImage IMAGE, PICT Sequence, ElectricImage, Photoshop, QuickTime (Mac), Video for Windows (Windows), and file types available from plug-in file format modules.

- *Import Into Project When Done*—Checking this option imports the rendered movie into the current project. This option is used to import pre-rendered compositions back into a project.

- *Format Options*—Clicking here opens a dialog box with format-specific options waiting for your input (such as compression and other options).

- *Channels*—Your options are RGB, Alpha, and RGB+ Alpha. All files created with a color depth of Millions Of Colors+ have labeled Alpha channels, so that data describing the Alpha channel is stored in the file.

- *Depth*—Choose the color depth of the rendered movie, remembering that certain formats may limit depth and color settings. Your options are: Black And White, 4, 16, 256, Thousands, Millions, Millions+, 4 Grays, 16 Grays, and 256 Grays.

- *Color*—This option determines how colors are created with the Alpha channel. Choose from either Premultiplied (With Black) or Straight (Unmatted). Many imported file formats may already include an Alpha channel, including: Adobe Photoshop, ElectricImage IMAGE, TGA, TIFF, QuickTime (saved at a bit depth of Millions Of Colors+), and Adobe Illustrator. After Effects automatically converts empty areas to an alpha channel for Adobe Illustrator files.

- *Stretch*—This is the size of your rendered movie. Select Lock Aspect To if you want to retain the existing frame aspect ratio if you stretch the frame size. Choose Low Stretch Quality for tests, and High Stretch Quality for final rendering.

- *Crop*—You can trim or add pixels to the edges of a rendered movie. Select the number of pixels to be added or subtracted from the top, left, bottom, and right sides of the movie. Positive values will crop the movie, and negative values will add pixels.

- *Audio Output*—This setting sets the Sample Rate (from 5.564 to 96.000 kHz), Sample Depth (8 Bit or 16 Bit), and the Playback Format (either Mono or Stereo). The sample rate should correspond to the capability of the output format.

    Movies playback on most computers—22.050 kHz (8-bit sample depth)

    Compact Disc Audio—44.100 kHz (16-bit sample depth)

    Digital Audio Tape (DAT)—48 kHz (16-bit sample depth)

> **Note: For hardware that supports 16-bit playback, you may also select 16-bit sample depth.**

Alpha Channel Types

The two Alpha channel types are Unmatted and Premultiplied. The following list describes these two types:

- In an Unmatted (also called "Straight") Alpha channel, the transparency information is kept in the Alpha channel only, not in any of the visible color channels. With a straight Alpha channel, the effects of transparency are not visible until the image is displayed in an application that supports straight alpha.

- In a *premultiplied* Alpha channel, the transparency data is kept in the Alpha channel, and also in the visible RGB channels, which are modified (or multiplied) with a background color. A premultiplied Alpha channel is also known as *Matted Alpha* with a background color. The colors of semitransparent areas, such as feathered edges, are shifted toward the background color in proportion to their degree of transparency.

Output Preferences

One last item to consider when rendering your output is the Output dialog box in the Preferences menu. The following settings are important when you think that your movie or sequences might be too large to fit on the current targeted drive (see Figure 3.15).

- *Make Movie Contingencies*—This is where you set the Overflow Volume names, which can be any storage device mounted on your system. You specify multiple volumes to which rendered compositions can be directed in case one volume gets too full. You can select up to five drives.

- *Segment Sequences*—This input value sets the limit on how many sequence segments may be targeted to a drive before overflow occurs.

- *Segment Movie Files*—This input value sets the limit on many megabytes of a movie file may be targeted to a drive before overflow occurs.

- *Minimum Diskspace Before Overflowing*—You may not reach the set overflow limit for sequence segments or the megabytes for a saved movie before your disk runs out of space. Set the amount of memory that is to be the limit the drive has to reserve to trigger overflow here.

- *Audio Block Duration*—This value sets the duration of the Audio Block.

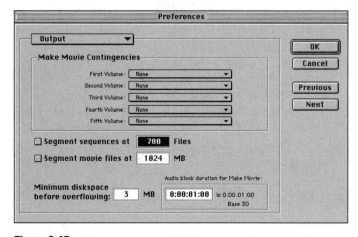

Figure 3.15
The Preferences Output dialog box.

AUDIO

ALL ABOUT

After Effects 4 has greatly expanded its capacities to integrate audio into a composition, and this chapter covers all of its audio capabilities.

This chapter covers the following areas: importing audio tracks, audio control window operations, internal audio effects (backwards, bass and treble, delay, stereo mixer), Production Bundle audio effects (flange and chorus, high-low pass, modulator, parametric EQ, reverb, tone), render audio effects (spectrum and waveform), playing audio, re-timing audio samples, and layering audio.

Importing Audio Tracks

You can import a variety of audio file formats directly into After Effects. (You may get a file conversion dialog box on some; just select a place to store the converted audio file.) Audio files appear as layers in the Time Layout window just like any other footage. You can adjust the audio preview settings, such as sample rate, in the General Preferences dialog box (see Figure 4.1). These settings change the quality of audio playback when you preview the composition, not when you render it.

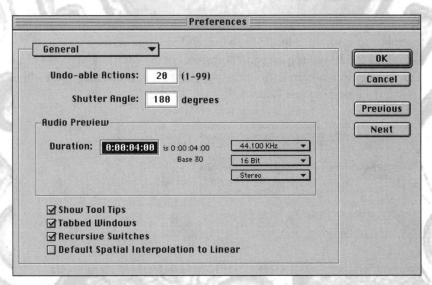

Figure 4.1
Set the audio preview settings in the General Preferences dialog box.

You can import and export QuickTime (Mac and Windows) and WAV (Windows only) audio files into After Effects 4. QuickTime supports AIFF, AU, WAV (Mac OS only), and Mac Sound (Mac OS only) files. Check the Adobe Web site for possible updates or additions to these formats.

When you render a movie to a file, you can set the Audio Output parameters. You can specify the sample rate (from 5.564 to 96.000 kHz), sample depth (8-bit or 16-bit), and play-back format (mono or stereo). Choose a sample rate that corresponds to the capability of the specific output format. A sampling rate of 22.050 kHz is a standard for movies on most computer systems; 44.100 kHz is standard for compact disc audio; and 48 kHz is standard for digital audio tape (DAT). Choose 8- or 16-bit sample depth, depending on the expected output format of the movie. Choose an 8-bit sample depth for playback on a computer, and a 16-bit sample depth for compact disc and digital audio playback (or for enhanced hardware that supports 16-bit playback). You may also have 16-bit sampling depth available to you on a high-end audio card installed in your system.

Previewing Audio

Follow these two steps to preview audio:

1. Go to the Composition or Time Layout window, and move the current time marker to the time where you want your preview to start. When you first preview an audio track, it's a good idea to start at the beginning of the track, so you can hear and see where components of the audio are on the timeline.

2. Select Composition|Preview|Audio (Here Forward), or press the period key (.) on the numeric keypad. The audio will play from that point. To stop the audio preview, click anywhere on screen.

You may want to preview the audio and video tracks of only part of the composition. To do this, set a specified work area. In the Time Ruler window, move the left and right work area markers to mark the beginning and end of the part of the composition you want to use as a work area. The work area markers indicate the part of the composition that will be displayed for previewing or rendering (see Figure 4.2).

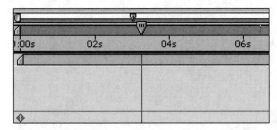

Figure 4.2
The work area markers set the parameters for the previewed audio or audio/video layers.

Audio Control Window Operations

If you click on the triangle in the upper right corner and choose Options in the Audio palette, the Audio Options dialog box appears, from which you can select either Decibels (to display audio levels in decibels) or Percentage (to display audio levels as a percentage, where 100 percent equals 0 dB).

From the Slider Minimum menu, select the minimum decibel level you want to display in the Audio palette, and then click on OK (see Figure 4.3).

While previewing audio, After Effects displays signals to indicate when the audio is "clipping," the distortion that occurs when the audio signal exceeds the maximum level of the audio processing equipment. After Effects also displays a volume unit (VU) meter in the Audio palette that actively displays audio levels during playback. To view the VU meter and levels controls in more detail, increase the height of the Audio palette. The VU meter can be seen at the bottom of the Audio palette displayed in Figure 4.3.

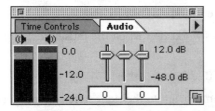

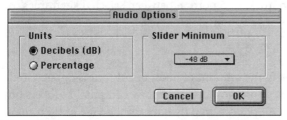

Figure 4.3
The Audio palette (top) and the Audio Options dialog box (bottom).

In the same window as the Audio palette is the Time Controls palette, with each control having its own tab. In the upper right corner of the Time Controls palette is an important audio tool, with three vertical slashes and a right-pointing triangle. Clicking on this triangle to preview all the audio content in the composition that isn't switched off in real time, and all switched on audio layers are mixed. The system reads them into RAM first, one of AE 4's best new features (see Figure 4.4).

Internal Audio Effects Filters

AE 4 offers a group of filters for customizing your audio content: Backwards, Bass/Treble, Delay, and Stereo Mixer. These filters can be found under the Audio listings in the Effects menu.

Figure 4.4
The RAM load icon at the upper right in the Time Controls palette reads all of the composition's audio content into RAM, and then gives you real-time playback. If you plan to preview just the audio, make all other layers invisible first.

Backwards

The Backwards effect reverses audio footage by playing it from the last frame or keyframe to the first frame or keyframe. The frames remain in their original order however, when viewed in the Time Layout window.

The following are some possible uses for the Backwards effects:

- Reverse a section of an effects track to create bizarre sounds for bizarre footage.

- Reverse a musical track to create unique music. This works best when the music track has a lot of percussion.

Only one control allows you to adjust the Backwards filter's parameters:

- *Swap Channels*—Swap Channels swaps the data from the left to the right stereo channel, or vice versa. Otherwise, the entire audio track, or a portion between selected keyframes, is reversed. This is the Backwards effect's only option.

Bass/Treble

Using the Bass/Treble filter, you can specify the amount of boost or cut that is applied to the low frequencies of the audio layer. This is important, because many computer speakers have terrible bass quality, so if you're creating AE projects to play back on the Web or on a computer CD-ROM, you have to consider boosting the bass.

This list discusses some possible uses for the Bass/Treble effect:

- Boost all audio bass if the project is for the Web or a CD-ROM playback.

- Use this filter to create unique audio sequences, by keyframing the bass and treble values to switch dominance during an animation.

The following controls allow you to adjust the parameters of the Bass/Treble filter:

- *Bass*—Alter the dominance of the bass channel in the mix, with settings from –100 to 100.

- *Treble*—Alter the dominance of the treble channel in the mix, with settings from –100 to 100.

Delay

The Delay effect repeats the sounds in the audio footage after a specified amount of time. This can be used to simulate a sound bouncing off a surface some distance away, like an echo. This effect can help simulate the acoustic environment of different rooms. Some possible uses for the Delay effect are:

- Boost the Wet value to accentuate the delay, making the audio mimic sound in a large gymnasium.

- Use a Feedback value that is very high when you want repeated echoes.

The following controls allow you to adjust the Delay filter's parameters:

- *Delay Time*—This control specifies in milliseconds the interval of time between the original sound and its echo. Drag the slider to the right to increase the time between the original sound and its echo. The values range from 0 to 30,000.

- *Delay Amount*—This control specifies the level of the first delayed audio. Drag the slider to the right to increase the amount of the original sound that is sent as echo. The values range from 0 to 1,000.

- *Feedback*—This specifies the amount of the echo that is fed back into the delay line to create subsequent echoes. Drag the slider to the right to increase the amount of echo signal that is fed back into the delay line. These values also range from 0 to 1,000.

- *Dry Out, Wet Out*—These values (from 0 to 400) specify the balance of the original (dry) sound to the delayed (wet) sound in the final output. Values of 50% represent the default.

Stereo Mixer

Using the Stereo Mixer effect, you can mix the left and right channels of an audio layer and pan the entire signal from one channel to the other.

The following are some possible uses for the Stereo Mixer effects:

- Pan the sound from one channel to another to create audio that travels in space.

- Shift the sound to one direction by panning it either left or right. This leaves the other channel free for another track altogether, thus creating real stereo.

The following controls allow you to adjust the parameters of the Stereo Mixer filter:

- *Left Level, Right Level*—These values (from 0 to 400) specify the level of the left or right audio channel of an audio layer.

- *Left Pan, Right Pan*—These values (from –100 to 100) shift the mixed stereo signal from one audio channel to the other.

- *Invert Phase*—This control inverts the phase of both channels of the stereo signal. Use this to prevent two sounds at the same frequency from canceling each other out.

Production Bundle Audio Filters

You get more audio filters if you purchase the AE 4 Production Bundle. These include Flange and Chorus, High-Low Pass, Modulator, Parametric EQ, Reverb, and Tone.

Flange And Chorus

This effect combines two separate audio effects, Flange and Chorus, into a single effect. Chorus is commonly used to add depth and character to audio footage that contains a single instrument or voice, giving it a slightly off-balance sound. The Chorus effect makes one voice sound like a chorus.

Flange applies a detuned copy of the sound (one that is played at a frequency slightly offset from the original). By experimenting with the voice separation time and the modulation depth, you can create a number of unique sounds. The default settings apply to the Flange effect alone.

The following are some possible uses for the Flange and Chorus effects:

- Use Flange controls to warp a standard sound into a space-age sound.
- Use Chorus to create multiple voice effects.

The following controls allow you to adjust the parameters of the Flange and Chorus filter:

- *Voice Separation Time (ms)*—This value (from 0 to 3,000) specifies the milliseconds that separates each voice (the delayed versions of the original sound). Low values are commonly used for flange, and higher values for chorus.
- *Voices*—This value (from 0 to 32) specifies the number of voices in the processed or "wet" audio.
- *Modulation Rate*—This value (from 0 to 1,000) specifies the rate in Hz for frequency modulation.
- *Modulation Depth*—This setting (expressed in percentages from 0 to 100 percent) specifies the total amount of frequency modulation.
- *Voice Phase Change*—This setting specifies the modulation phase difference between each subsequent voice. The setting can range from 0 to 360 degrees.
- *Invert Phase*—This control inverts the phase of the processed (wet) audio. Inverting the phase will accent more of the high frequencies. Not inverting the phase will accent more of the low frequencies.
- *Stereo Voices*—This control alternates each voice between two channels so that the first voice appears in the left channel, the second in the right channel, the third in the left, and so on. To hear stereo voices, you must preview the audio in stereo (by choosing File|Preferences|General, and then Stereo for the Audio Preview selection) or render the movie in stereo.
- *Dry Out/Wet Out*—This setting specifies (in a range from 0 to 400) the mix of unprocessed (dry) audio to processed (wet) audio in the final output. A value of 50 percent is the default.

High-Low Pass

The High-Low Pass effect sets a limit above or below which frequencies can pass. High Pass allows frequencies above the limit and blocks frequencies below. Conversely, Low Pass allows frequencies below the limit and blocks frequencies above the limit.

The following are some possible uses for the High-Low Pass effect:

- Change the focus from one sound to another over time. For instance, if the audio contains both music and voice, fade out the music while gradually bringing in the voice.

- Direct certain frequencies to specific sound reinforcement equipment.

The following controls allow you to adjust the parameters of the High-Low Pass filter:

- *Filter Options*—This control specifies whether to apply the High Pass or the Low Pass filter.

- *Cutoff Frequency For High Pass*—This value (from 1 to 20,000) specifies the frequency below which the footage is not audible. For Low Pass, this value specifies the frequency above which the footage is not audible.

- *Dry Out/Wet Out*—This control specifies the mix of unprocessed (dry) audio to processed (wet) audio in the final output. The setting can range from 0 to 400, although the default is 0% for Dry Out and 100% for Wet Out.

Modulator

The Modulator effect adds both vibrato and tremolo to audio by modulating (varying) the frequency and amplitude. Using the Modulator, you can even create a Doppler effect, as when the pitch of a train's whistle raises as the train approaches an observer, and lowers as it passes.

The following are some possible uses for the Modulator effect:

- Use a Triangle Modulation with a Modulation Rate of 20 and a Modulation Depth of 100% to create a muted, ethereal sound.

- Use a Sine Modulation with a Modulation Rate of 6, a Modulation Depth of 50%, and an Amplitude Modulation of 100 to create a sound like a series of dog barks.

The following controls allow you to adjust the parameters of the Modulator filter:

- *Modulation Type*—This specifies the type of waveform to use. Sine waves produce the purest sounds, and triangle waves produce sounds that are more distorted.

- *Modulation Rate*—This value specifies the rate in Hz at which the frequency modulates. This setting can range from 0 to 1,000.

- *Modulation Depth*—This setting (from 0 to 100) specifies the degree of frequency modulation.

- *Amplitude Modulation*—This value (from 0 to 100) specifies the amount of amplitude (volume) modulation.

Parametric EQ

The Parametric EQ (equalization) effect either emphasizes or attenuates specific frequency ranges. Parametric EQ is useful for enhancing music, for example, by boosting the lower frequencies to increase the bass. Using this effect, you can enhance up to three different bands of the audio footage. As you specify controls, a frequency-response graph indicates the combined

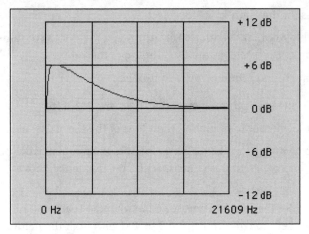

Figure 4.5
Parametric EQ's frequency-response graph.

equalization curve you have created. On the frequency-response graph, Band 1 is red (currently, the only one displayed in Figure 4.5), Band 2 is green, and Band 3 is blue.

Following are some possible uses for the Parametric EQ effects:

- Isolate and cut the frequency range of an offending background sound to attenuate it. You may need to experiment with several settings to isolate the appropriate frequency range.
- Accentuate a frequency in the audio layer.

The following controls allow you to adjust the parameters of the Parametric EQ filter:

- *Band Enabled*—Activates an equalization band and its controls.
- *Frequency*—This setting (from 1 to 21,609) specifies which frequency to modify. The frequency you select here will act as the peak of the effect (the center of the specified bandwidth).
- *Bandwidth*—This value (from 1 to 99) determines the range of frequencies to enhance above and below the frequency you chose to modify.
- *Boost/Cut*—This value (from –100 to 100) specifies the amount of boost or cut to be applied to the amplitude of the frequencies inside the specified bandwidth. (Positive values boost; negative values cut.)

Reverb

The Reverb effect allows you to simulate a spacious or acoustically "live" interior environment by simulating the random reflections of a sound off surfaces.

Some possible uses for the Reverb effects are:

- Creating the ambience of a large space, such as the Grand Canyon, by setting the following parameters: Reverb Time 15, Diffusion 70, Decay 70, Brightness 15, Dry Out 0, and Wet Out 100.

- Creating a muted background track by using the following parameters: Reverb Time 300, Diffusion 50, Decay 0, Brightness 100, Dry Out 100, and Wet Out 20.

The following controls allow you to adjust the Reverb filter's parameters:

- *Reverb Time (ms)*—This value specifies the average time in milliseconds between the original audio and the reverberated audio. The setting can range from 0 to 5,000.
- *Diffusion*—This control specifies how much the effect scatters the original audio. More diffusion can make the audio sound further from the microphone. The value can range from 0 to 100.
- *Decay*—This control specifies the amount of time it takes for the effect to subside (with settings from 0 to 100). A longer decay simulates a larger space.
- *Brightness*—This value (again from 0 to 100) specifies the amount of detail that is preserved from the original audio. More brightness can simulate a room with live, or highly reflective, acoustics.
- *Dry Out/Wet Out*—These settings (from 0 to 400) specify the mix of the unprocessed (dry) audio to the processed (wet) audio in the final output.

Tone

The Tone effect synthesizes simple tones to create effects such as low rumbles, telephone rings, laser blasts, and more. You can add up to five tones for each effect to create a chord, and you can apply the Tone effect to a layer that has no audio. At rendering time, make sure that you select an output format that supports audio (QuickTime or Video for Windows). Some possible uses for the Tone effects are:

- Creating a chord with tones, and using another audio filter to modify it further.
- Creating laser blasts in time with the visual effect.

The following controls allow you to adjust the Tone filter's parameters:

- *Waveform Options*—This choice specifies the type of waveform to use: sine, square, triangle, or saw. Sine waves produce the purest tones. Square waves produce the most distorted tones. Triangle waves are close to sine, and saw waves are close to square.
- *Frequency*—Specifies the frequency in Hz (from 0 to 30,000) of the first through the fifth tones. To disable a tone, set its frequency to 0.0.
- *Level*—This setting (from 0 to 100) changes the amplitude of all tones. If you hear clicking when you preview or play the audio, the level may be set too high.

Render Audio Effects

Under the Render list in the Effects menu, you will find two important audio accessory filters: Audio Spectrum and Audio Waveform. If you have an audio layer in your stack, you can use either of these filters to render the audio waveform or spectrum so it is visible. This is a valuable feature for many reasons:

- You can render the waveform or spectrum so that, as the sound plays, the waveform can be used as an interesting part of your composition.

- You can use the rendered waveform or spectrum as a guide to place a keyframed object, and then make the waveform invisible for the final rendering. The object will be seen to move in accordance with the frequency or amplitude of the audio.

- You can use the rendered waveform or spectrum as a deformation source to drive the effects of another visual layer. This allows the deformation to occur in sync with the audio.

- Apply an audio spectrum to imported vector text to see the spectrum outline the text. Use a Hue Interpolation value of 360 degrees or more to make the form multicolored.

Audio Spectrum

The Audio Spectrum effect displays the magnitude of frequencies in the range you define with the Start Frequency and End Frequency centroids. This effect then displays the audio spectrum in any number of ways, including along a Bézier path of a layer. You apply the effect to a layer that contains a solid color or an image, and then select where the audio is to be taken from (see Figure 4.6).

The following controls allow you to adjust the parameters of the Audio Spectrum effect:

- *Audio Layer*—This is the layer that contains the audio that you want to display as a spectrum.

- *Start Point/End Point*—Placing these centroids specifies the position at which the spectrum starts and ends (if Path is set to None). If Path is not set to None, the audio spectrum is displayed along the selected path of the layer.

- *Use Polar Path*—When this is selected, the path will start from a single point and be displayed as a radial graph.

- *Start Frequency/End Frequency*—Sets the first and last frequency in the range of frequencies being displayed. Values can range from 1 to 22,050 Hz.

- *Frequency Bands*—This value (from 1 to 4,096) specifies the number of frequencies displayed.

Figure 4.6
You can apply an audio spectrum to any path, as shown in these three examples.

- *Maximum Height*—This control sets the maximum height of a displayed frequency (from 1 to 32,000 pixels).

- *Audio Duration*—This control sets the duration of audio (from 0 to 30,000 milliseconds) that is used to calculate the spectrum.

- *Audio Offset*—This control specifies the time offset (from –30,000 to 30,000 milliseconds) used to retrieve the audio.

- *Blend Overlapping Colors*—If this option is checked, overlapping spectrums will be blended. This is useful when a path bends back on itself.

- *Hue Interpolation*—If Hue Interpolation is not set to 0, the frequencies displayed will rotate through the hue color space. Rotations of multiple turns will force multiple spectral banding. Values can range from 0 to 360 degrees times any number of rotations.

- *Dynamic Hue Phase*—If this is selected and if Hue Interpolation is not 0, the start color will be shifted to the maximum frequency in the range of displayed frequencies. This allows the hue to follow the fundamental frequency of the displayed spectrum as it changes, and is a great way to have the spectrum follow a musical sequence.

- *Color Symmetry*—If selected, the start and end colors will be the same when Hue Interpolation is not 0. This creates color continuity on closed paths.

- *Display Options*—The options are Digital, Analog Lines, and Analog Dots, with each creating a different spectral look.

- *Side Options*—Select whether to display the spectrum above the path (Side A), below the path (Side B), or both (Side A and B).

- *Duration Averaging*—When checked, the audio frequencies are averaged together to create less randomness in the form.

> **Note: Explore this effect for creating astounding components for music videos.**

Audio Waveform

The Audio Waveform effect displays the waveform amplitude of any selected audio layer. You can display the audio waveform in a number of different ways, including along a Bézier path created by an open or closed mask of a layer. You can also import an Illustrator file as the path. You apply the effect to a layer that contains a solid or an image, and that may contain audio, or select the audio from anywhere in the stack (see Figure 4.7).

The following controls allow you to adjust the parameters of the Audio Waveform effect:

- *Audio Layer*—Select the layer that contains the audio that you want to display as an amplitude waveform.

- *Start Point/End Point*—Use the centroids to the positions at which the waveform starts and ends, as long as Path is set to None. If Path is not set to None, the audio waveform is displayed along the selected path of the layer.

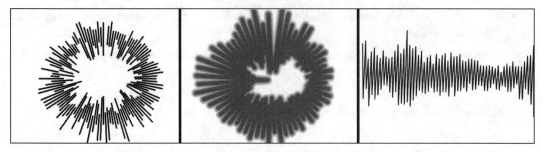

Figure 4.7
A selection of Audio Waveform renderings.

- *Displayed Samples*—This control sets the number of samples (from 1 to 44,100) to display when graphing the waveform.

- *Maximum Height*—This control specifies the maximum height (from 1 to 4,000 pixels) of a displayed frequency.

- *Audio Duration*—This control sets the duration of audio, from 0 to 30,000 milliseconds.

- *Audio Offset*—This control sets the time offset used to retrieve the audio. You can select from –30,000 to 30,000 milliseconds.

- *Waveform Options*—This control specifies how to display the audio waveform, as mono, left, or right. Mono combines the left and right channels of the audio layer. If the audio source is mono, the Waveform Options property has no effect.

- *Display Options*—This control specifies how to display the audio waveform (as digital, analog lines, or analog dots). Digital displays each sample as a single vertical line connecting the minimum and maximum source sample. Analog Lines displays each sample as a line connecting the previous and next sample, from either the minimum or maximum audio source sample. Analog Dots displays each sample as a dot representing either the minimum or maximum audio source sample.

Playing Audio

You can play an audio file in the following ways:

- When you load the file, it's likely that you will be presented with a player in the Load dialog box. Click on it to hear it play before you commit to loading it (see Figure 4.8).

- Double-clicking on a file in the Project List window will bring up an audio player (see Figure 4.9).

- After you add the audio layer to the stack, you can use the VCR controls in the Time Controls palette to play the audio file. Clicking on the speaker icon at the upper right of the palette loads the audio sample into RAM for real-time playback (see Figure 4.10).

Make sure that the smaller speaker icon and the looping icon are also selected, so you can hear the audio file and also have it loop (see Figure 4.11).

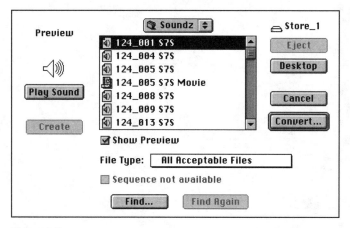

Figure 4.8
You may be presented with a player in the Load dialog box.

Figure 4.9
The Preview Audio player.

Figure 4.10
Click on the speaker icon at the upper right of the Time Controls palette to load the sample into RAM for real-time playback.

Figure 4.11
Make sure that these two icons in the Time Controls palette are also activated.

Retiming Audio Samples

Audio Files can be retimed as easily as other media files, by selecting Time Stretch from the Layer menu (with your audio layer selected). Doing this brings up the Time Stretch dialog box, where you can make the layer time either longer or shorter (see Figure 4.12).

Time can be stretched in one of three ways: Layer In-Point, Current Frame, and Layer Out-Point.

Figure 4.12
The Time Stretch dialog box.

- Layer In-Point holds the layer's current starting time, and time-stretches the layer by moving the Out point.

- Current Frame holds the layer at the position of the current time marker (also the frame displayed in the Composition window), and time-stretches the layer by moving the In and Out points.

- Layer Out-Point holds the layer's current ending time and time-stretches the layer by moving the In point.

What Happens When You Time-Stretch An Audio Layer?

To understand what happens to an audio layer that is time-stretched, it might be helpful to first think of a visual layer that undergoes the same operation. Let's say that, on a video layer, we show a woman at frame one walking toward her car. The last frame shows the woman in the car, starting to drive away. If we make the layer longer, it will take more time for her to get to the car. If we compress the time of the layer in half, she gets to the car twice as quickly as the sequence was filmed.

Now take that same understanding to an audio layer and run it through the same process. Suppose that you have a waltz melody that starts at keyframe one and runs for 10 seconds before ending at the last frame. Let's also suppose that the After Effects composition is also 10 seconds long. If you time-stretch the waltz to 20 seconds long, and the composition remains 10 seconds long, you will obviously have room for only half of the waltz in the composition. You can move the waltz layer back and forth, finding the best starting and ending points for half of the melody. But there's more.

By time-stretching the waltz, you also alter the pitch of the music. Because the melody is stretched out over a longer period, the music sequence will sound much lower and dragged out. What was once a sprightly waltz now becomes a dirge. If you want a dirge because of what is going on visually, then this is no problem. If you don't, however, then using a time stretch to multiply the time the melody takes to complete isn't the way to go.

If you time-stretch the waltz in the other direction (compressing the time), the melody quickens in tempo and the pitch gets higher. What was once a waltz is now a mazurka. It's not only faster but trumpets become flutes, and voices sound like the singers have breathed too much helium. If the total melody is now five seconds, and the AE composition is still 10 seconds long, the song takes only half of the composition to play. You can then move the song, sliding it back and forth on the layer's timeline so that its shortened duration begins and ends where you want.

Another technique is to truncate the audio layer. This is done by simply moving the end nodes, one or both, toward the center of the audio segment. This winds up cutting off either or both the start and/or end of the audio. Doing this carefully, and previewing the results as you do, allows you to have just one portion of the music for playback. Unlike time-stretching, truncating the audio layer doesn't alter the pitch or tempo of the sound.

Time stretching is especially important when you are creating sounds from audio segments that are unique. An audio sample of a cat, for example, can be augmented in this manner to sound like a lion or dinosaur if it is expanded, and like a bird if it's compressed. That way, a small library of sampled sounds can suffice for thousands of uses. This is all possible when you use the Stretch Time capacity of After Effects.

Layering Audio

Using simple copy-paste commands, you can duplicate any audio layer as many times as needed. When you have the amount you require, they can each be treated in different ways to create a chorus of different sounds. In this way, you could make the sound of a sparrow sound like a jungle full of exotic birds, or you could make one car sound like rush hour. The only trick is to preview your explorations often, moving things around and applying whatever effects are necessary until the result you want is achieved.

Try This!

Here's an experiment that accentuates the bass of a musical sequence. I have found that it works effectively if the sequence is funk oriented. (To paraphrase a quote by Louis Armstrong, "If you gotta ask what funk is, you'll never know.").

1. Open a new composition. Make it any size you like. Create a 10-second animation at 30 fps.

2. Import or create any image or video footage you like, with whatever effects look good.

3. Open a musical sequence, preferably one as long as your timeline. Look for a funky sequence (although you can explore this technique by using any musical style).

4. Place the musical sequence in the stack.

5. Now copy and paste the sequence again, so that there are two identical musical tracks in the stack.

6. Move the second sequence to the right four frames to create a delayed echo of the sequence.

7. With the second sequence still active, apply a Bass and Treble audio effect from the Effect menu. Set Bass to maximum, and switch Treble to 0. This doubles the bass frequencies for the music. Preview to make sure you like it, and record to disk.

Note: Any time you double a soundtrack, you make it pop out more, and the accents are amplified.

Audio Controlled Footage

You can use an audio track to control the contents of a video track. The best filters to use for this option are ones that deal with displacement. A readily available displacement filter is the Displacement Map filter found in the Distort listings in the Effects menu. To create a composition with an audio track controlling a video track:

1. Import an audio track.

2. Create a new color layer.

3. With the color layer selected, select Effect|Render|Audio Spectrum. You are going to create a visible audio waveform based on the audio file.

4. In the Effects Controls window, apply the following parameters to the Audio Spectrum effect: Select your audio layer for the Audio Layer; Hue Interpolation to 360 degrees; Maximum Height, 5,000; Thickness, 20; Softness, 100; and Analog Lines for Output Options. This creates a multicolored waveform.

5. Precompose these two layers, selecting to move all attributes into the new composition. Now you will have just one layer, containing both an animated waveform and the audio track that drives it.

6. Import an image for the top layer.

7. With the image selected, select the Displacement Map filter from the Effects/Distort list.

8. Set the following parameters: Select your recently generated precomposition as the Displacement Map; max Horizontal, 20; max Vertical, 100; and use Luminance channels for both horizontal and vertical displacements. Leave all other settings at their defaults. Preview the results, and render to disk if you are satisfied.

What's really happening here? In reality, the audio layer is controlling the waveform layer, and the waveform layer is controlling the displacement map. You can control your visual footage with an audio layer in other ways, but this is one of the best ways.

Note: Be aware that After Effects 4 can also import Adobe Premier projects that contain extensive Premier audio effects.

PREPARATION

In this chapter, you'll look at the two applications that most computer artists and After Effects users are already familiar with—Adobe Photoshop and MetaCreations Painter.

Because After Effects simply applies its effects on the available content of existing compositions, it is important that you know how to prepare a range of content elements for use in your After Effects projects. You thus need to learn how to get around in a number of other applications, from 2D to 3D, and maybe even audio applications as well. It would be impossible for any single book to include even a brief mention of all of the diverse applications that might be used to prepare content for After Effects Compositions. I can, however, mention an important few as examples and allow you to take it from there. So, we should start with the applications that are most important for creating After Effects content: 2D bitmap applications.

Of course, the most common tools are Photoshop and MetaCreations Painter. If you have already mastered both of these 2D bitmap applications—and feel that you know all you need to so that you can prepare After Effects content—please browse this chapter anyway. There may be a few ideas here that you can add to your skills collection. If these applications are completely new to you, then you will want to purchase them and first learn the basics by working through all the documentation and tutorials. That way, this chapter will increase your appreciation of the possibilities.

Adobe Photoshop

Why is Photoshop recommended as a primary content-creation environment for After Effects?

- Because it is the most popular 2D bitmap creation and editing application on the market. Other similar applications have tools that Photoshop lacks, but Photoshop remains the core application for preparing and editing bitmaps.

- Photoshop is the primary target for the development of bitmap-effects plug-ins. Some of Photoshop's effects will not work in any other bitmap application. Additionally, with the release of After Effects 4, many more of Photoshop's native effects have been integrated into After Effects, with animatable parameters. Learning how to apply these effects in either Photoshop or After Effects gives you a jump-start in applying them in the other application.

- Because Adobe is the developer of both Photoshop and After Effects, the two applications are very similar in terms of tool use, effects processing, and the general design of the icons and interface. This similarity makes one the natural complement of the other.

- If you are doing professional digital work, it is essential that you "speak" Photoshop, no matter what other bitmap applications you are using.

So, with all of these points in mind, look at some specific ways that you can use Photoshop to develop content that is intended for use in your After Effects compositions.

> *Note: Please remember that this is not a Photoshop book, so this chapter touches on only a few options. If you need a great Photoshop book, see* **Photoshop 5 In Depth,** *by David Xenakis and Sherry London, 1998, The Coriolis Group.*

Creating A Matte Effects Layer

There is more than one way to accomplish this task, but this is my favorite. The task is to create an Alpha layer for an image in Photoshop that ports to After Effects for Alpha use. The benefit is that you can use all of Photoshop's tools to create the exact Alpha required, and Photoshop has more and better tools than After Effects for this task. Here's what to do:

> *Note: Photoshop 5 was used to develop these tutorials.*

1. Select an image that has a background with more than just one color. This is important because you want to use the original image as the basic footage, while using only part of the image as the content for the Alpha channel, which you will have to outline in Photoshop. See Figure 5.1.

Figure 5.1
This is the original image you are using. It's a piece of wood I picked up because it resembles a deer head. The piece was propped up against some shutters, and the picture was taken with a digital camera.

Note: You can find this image in the CH_05 folder on the companion CD-ROM.

2. Using Photoshop's Selection or Pen tools, outline the foreground element that is to be used as Alpha channel data in After Effects. If you do not know how the Pen tools work, read the Photoshop documentation, or read the section on Selections and Paths in the Photoshop book mentioned previously.

3. When the figure is outlined and still selected, use the Copy and then the Paste command. The outlined element will be pasted to another layer in Photoshop (see Figure 5.2).

Figure 5.2
Here is the outlined figure, now on its own layer in Photoshop.

4. Save the layered image to disk as a Photoshop file (because the Photoshop format preserves the layer information).

5. Now go to the Photoshop Layer menu, and delete the background layer completely. (Throw it in the palette's trash can.) Now all you have is the outlined figure. Go to the Image menu, and select Grayscale. You are asked if you want to delete the color information. Click on OK. Now you have a 256-level (8-bit) grayscale image of just the foreground element. Save this as a TIFF file (see Figure 5.3).

6. Now you are ready to do some work in After Effects. Quit Photoshop, and open After Effects.

7. Let's first work with just the grayscale image you saved. Import it, and place it in a new composition (see Figure 5.4).

8. Load another image layer. Use any image you like, although clouds work well for this example. Place the new layer under the grayscale layer.

Figure 5.3
The grayscaled foreground is now a separate image.

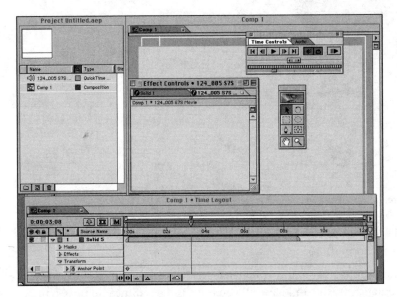

Figure 5.4
The grayscale image is placed in a new composition.

9. With the grayscale layer selected, go to the Keying list in the Effects menu, and select Color Key. This is a simple color-keying effect that will allow you to drop out a single color. Use the eyedropper to select the white background of the grayscale image. Immediately, it drops away, displaying the background image behind it. To sharpen the border of the foreground grayscale image, move the slider in the Edge Thin control to 1 (see Figure 5.5).

Figure 5.5
The Color Key effect is used to drop out the background of the grayscale image, displaying the background layer beneath.

10. Go to the Channel listing in the Effects menu, and select the Set Matte effect. You are going to set the grayscale data as the Matte data layer. Under Take Matte From, select the grayscale layer. Under Use For Matte, select Full, although you can also explore Luminance to drop out some of the grayscale data for a later experiment.

11. Now it's time to apply an image effect to the Matte layer. First, let's add some color to the grayscale image. Select the Tint effect from the Image Control list in the Effects menu. Set Black to Red, and White to Yellow. This should tint the grayscale brown (red plus yellow equals brown).

12. From this point, you can add any additional effects you like. For instance, you can add the Texturize effect from the Stylize list. This effect allows you to select any layer in the stack and apply it as a texture to the source layer, our grayscale image. The result of this effect can be seen in Figure 5.6.

13. You can layer any number of effects that you need. For example, if you add a Mirror Distort effect at this point, you will wind up with an image that resembles Figure 5.7.

Creating A Foreground Effects Layer

After you create separated layers in Photoshop and save them in Photoshop format, you can use After Effects to add effects to the layer elements. Let's see how this works with the separated Photoshop layers you have created:

1. In a new After Effects composition, import the Photoshop layered graphic mentioned at the start of the chapter. It will import as separate layers, so that the foreground image is separated out of the overall background. Place both the layers

Figure 5.6
A texturize effect is added, using the same image as the texture. This adds embossed dimensionality to the grayscale, just as a Bump Map would.

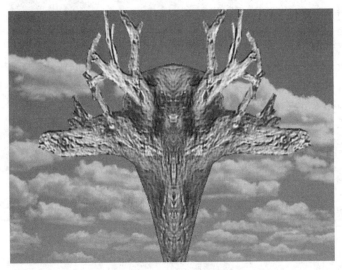

Figure 5.7
Using the Mirror Distortion effect, the image looks like an animal skull against a sky backdrop, much like a painting by Georgia O'Keeffe. Compare this image with the original Photoshop version you started with in Figure 5.1.

in the composition, so that the cutout foreground is on top. If you used the deer image on the companion CD-ROM, you will see an image similar to Figure 5.8.

2. Because each layer is a separate and complete image with RGBA channels, applying Channel Effects to the top layer will make it seem as if they are being applied to the background layer as well. This happens because the foreground image data was

Figure 5.8
The starting footage, using both Photoshop layers. Because the top layer was cut out of the background layer, it looks like a single image.

cut out of the background with the selection marquee and pasted as a duplicate to the next layer in the stack. Because this was accomplished entirely in Photoshop, you needn't go through the process of using any cutout processes in After Effects.

3. Go to the Blur And Sharpen list in the Effects menu, and select Channel Blur. This filter allows you to apply a blur to any or all of the RGBA channels in the Foreground layer. Set the RBA (red, blue, and Alpha channel) values to 127, and you will create an image resembling that shown in Figure 5.9.

Figure 5.9
Channel Blur is applied, resulting in a foreground that pops out of the background.

Popping Out The Foreground

After you have created a layered Photoshop graphic that has a selection from the overall image as one of its layers, you can use After Effects to sharpen the foreground elements so that they pop out of the background more effectively. Here's one way to do it:

1. In a new After Effects composition, import the Photoshop layered graphic mentioned at the start of the chapter. Again, it imports as separate layers, so that the foreground image is separated out of the overall background. Place both the layers in the composition so that the cutout foreground is on top. You will see an image similar to Figure 5.10, if you used the deer image from the companion CD-ROM.

Figure 5.10
The imported layered Photoshop file, with the unaltered foreground layer on top.

2. Apply the Sharpen filter from the Blur And Sharpen Effects list, at a value of 200, to the foreground layer. Notice how the grain in the foreground layer is emphasized (see Figure 5.11).

Creating A Photoshop Alpha Channel

Because so many After Effects filters can be applied to only the Alpha channel, you should understand how to create Alpha channels for images in Photoshop. The following steps show how to use the same layered Photoshop image that was created previously to do just this:

1. Open Photoshop, and load the layered Photoshop deer image from the companion CD-ROM. It will resemble Figure 5.12.

2. Using the Layers menu, make the background invisible (see Figure 5.13).

3. Use the Magic Wand tool and click on an empty area of the layer. Choose Select Similar from the Selection menu. All of the blank parts of the layer will be selected. Now select Inverse from the Selection menu, and only the image content will be selected.

Figure 5.11
The Sharpen filter is applied to the foreground layer.

Figure 5.12
The Photoshop layered graphic is loaded.

4. Go to the Channels tab, and click on the Make New Channel icon at the bottom (the icon next to the trash can). You have just created an Alpha channel for the image. Use the visibility "eye" icons to turn off the RGB channels. The selection marquee should be visible in the Alpha channel. Fill this area with solid white (see Figure 5.14).

5. Now return to the Layers tab, and throw away the Foreground layer. You don't need it anymore. You now have the image with a built-in Alpha channel. Save it to disk as a TIFF image for After Effects import.

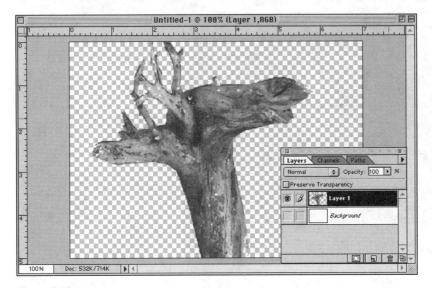

Figure 5.13
The background is made invisible.

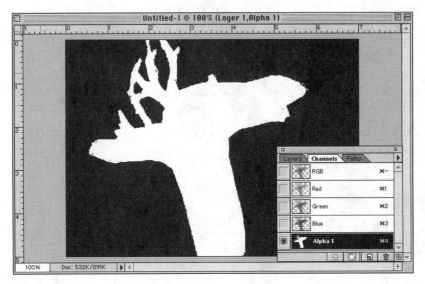

Figure 5.14
The Alpha selection is filled with solid white.

6. Open After Effects, and import the Alpha channel image. When the Interpret Footage dialog box appears, click on Treat As Straight (unmatted) and on Invert. The imported image will show the foreground as Alpha transparent. Any image or footage you place in the next layer down from this one will show through the foreground outline (see Figures 5.15 and 5.16).

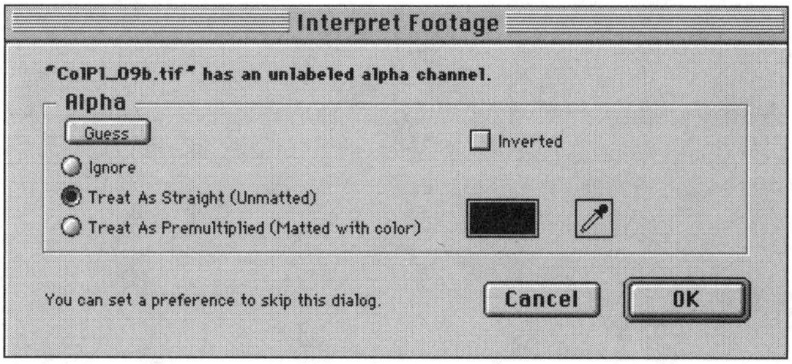

Figure 5.15
The Interpret Footage dialog box.

Figure 5.16
Any image or footage placed a layer below the source Alpha will be seen through the foreground silhouette.

Photoshop Plug-Ins

Most effects you apply to your After Effects footage will be done in (what else?) After Effects. Some filters, however, are custom designed for Photoshop and are not compatible with After Effects. Some of these also work with what are called "Photoshop-compatible" bitmap-editing applications, like Corel's PhotoPaint and MetaCreations Painter. Some of these filters, although not animatable, can produce just the background or texture you might be looking for when it comes to a specific After Effects project. Photoshop is the mother of all filter effects environments, so let's look at some examples from just three filter plug-in packages that you may find useful for generating images to import into After Effects. You will use the graphic displayed in Figure 5.17 as the target image to apply various Photoshop filters.

Figure 5.17
This image is an original 3D rendering that the author created in MetaCreations Ray Dream 5.

AlienSkin's Xenofex

Chapters 16 and 17 of this book cover the uses of AlienSkin's Eye Candy filters for After Effects. The Xenofex filters are made especially for Photoshop and compatible applications, and are different from those found in the Eye Candy collection. They include the following 16 filters: Baked Earth, Constellation, Crumple, Distress, Electrify, Flag, Lightning, Little Fluffy Clouds, Origami, Puzzle, Rounded Rectangle, Shatter, Shower Door, Stain, Stamper, and Television. See Figures 5.18 to 5.21.

Figure 5.18
Left top to right bottom: Baked Earth, Constellation, Crumple, and Distress.

Figure 5.19
Left top to right bottom: Electrify, Flag, Lightning, and Little Fluffy Clouds.

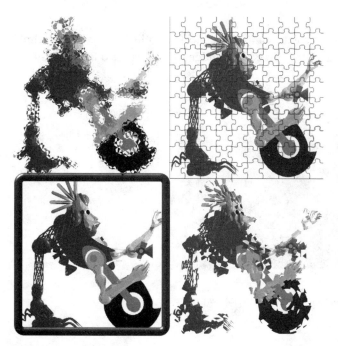

Figure 5.20
Left top to right bottom: Origami, Puzzle, Rounded Rectangle, and Shatter.

Figure 5.21
Left top to right bottom: Shower Door, Stain (Red Wine), Stamper, and Television.

XAOS Tools' Terrazzo

XAOS Tools' Terrazzo allows you to create some of the most versatile tiled backdrops that you could ever imagine for use in After Effects. The image we will use as a basis for these examples is shown in Figure 5.22. See Figure 5.23 for a display of some of the tiled looks that Terrazzo makes possible.

Figure 5.22
The source image used for the Terrazzo filter effects that follow.

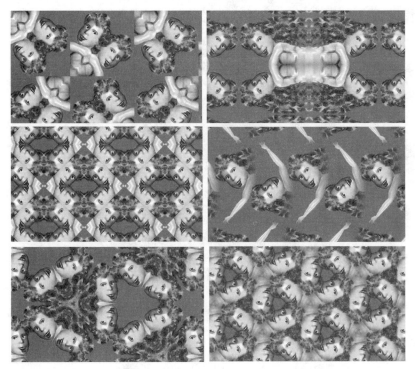

Figure 5.23
Six examples of various tiled effects made possible by the Terrazzo plug-in filter from XAOS Tools.

KPT 5

Kai's PowerTools from MetaCreations is a set of Photoshop-compatible filter plug-ins that no After Effects user will want to be without. These Photoshop 5 filters add the following items to the already extensive version 3 set (version 4 was skipped): Blurrr, Noize, Radial Warp, Smoothie, Frax4D, FraxFlame, FraxPlorer, FiberOptix, Orbit, and ShapeShifter. The image that was used as a source to create the displayed KPT 5 effects can be seen in Figure 5.24. You can see the effects in Figure 5.25.

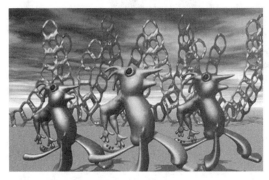

Figure 5.24
The original source image.

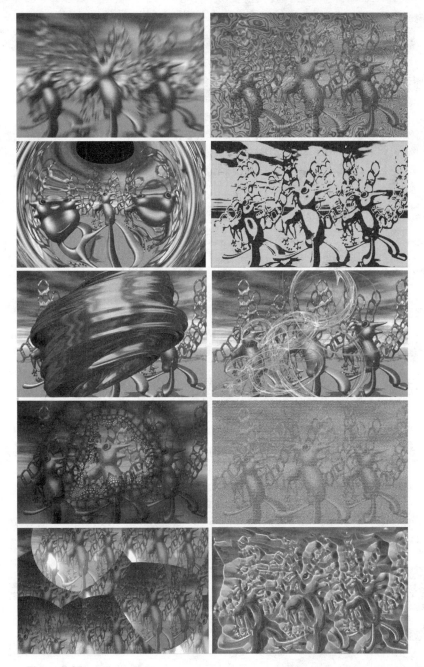

Figure 5.25
Upper left to bottom right: Blurrr (Spin), Noize (Soft RGB), Radial Warp, Smoothie, Frax4D, and FraxFlame (Swirl), FraxPlorer, FiberOptix, Orbit, and ShapeShifter.

MetaCreations' Painter

As far as digital painting goes, no other application on the market offers you as extensive an effects list or as many natural media options as does MetaCreations' Painter. Unless you are an experienced Painter user, however, your best bet is to study the documentation carefully, purchase and use a separate Painter book, and spend a good amount of time exploring Painter's way of doing things. Doing all of this, you can master Painter and create startling digital artwork. Painter has another attribute that makes it a perfect environment for editing After Effects output and preparing alternate images and animations for import. Unlike most other bitmap applications, Painter can read and write QuickTime and AVI movie files. When reading in movies, Painter separates them into single frames, so you can custom paint each frame in the stack, before saving the animation out again (see Figure 5.26).

Painter has hundreds of unique effects that can't be duplicated anywhere else. Here's just one.

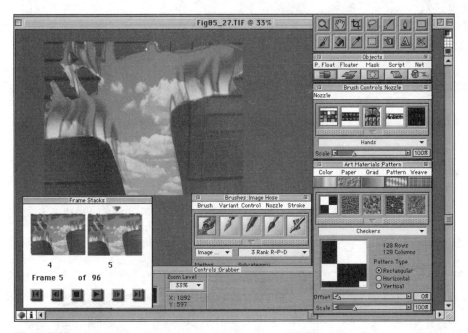

Figure 5.26
Painter allows you to import movie files for customized painting. Then, you can save them out again and import them into After Effects.

Glowing Tiles

Using Painter, here's a way to customize any animation saved out from After Effects or anywhere else. When saved, you can import it back into After Effects for more animated processing. It's called "Glowing Tiles" because it translates the animation into tiled areas that look like stonework and colorizes the frames according to the underlying hues. The following steps guide you through it:

1. Load an animation into Painter. As long as it's a QuickTime movie (Mac) or an AVI file (Windows), it will load fine. The only restriction will be the RAM in your system. (Longer movies require more RAM.) For experimentation, import a 30-frame animation (see Figure 5.27).

Figure 5.27
Import any animation you like into Painter. It will come in as a sequence of single frames. This frame is from an After Effects animation.

2. Make sure that the animation is on Frame 1. Go to the Custom Tile filter in the Esoterica listing in the Effects menu. A dialog box will appear (see Figure 5.28).

3. Input the following settings: Paper type, Blur Radius 1, Blur Passes 1, Thickness 1, Use Grout, and Threshhold of 125. Repeat this action for each frame, leaving the settings the same (see Figure 5.29).

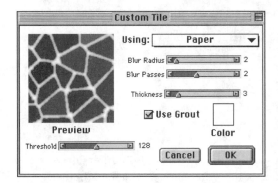

Figure 5.28
The Custom Tile dialog box.

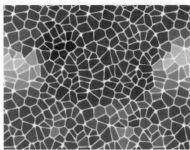

Figure 5.29
This is the result of the Custom Tile operation in Painter.

Creating An Original Animation In Painter

Here's a way to create an animation in Painter that you can import as footage into After Effects, and then apply more animated effects. We'll use my favorite Painter tool, the Image Hose. Here's what we do:

1. Open Painter, and select New from the File menu. A dialog box will pop up (see Figure 5.30).

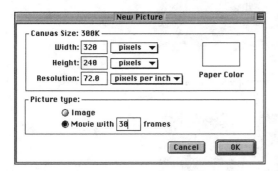

Figure 5.30
The New Picture parameters dialog box in Painter.

2. Use the following parameters: 320×240 pixels at 72 DPI, and 30 frames. When the New Frame Stack dialog box appears, make the animation 24-bit color with an 8-bit Alpha channel, and two layers of Onion Skin (see Figure 5.31).

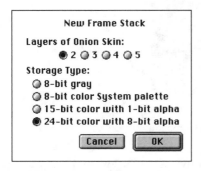

Figure 5.31
The New Frame Stack dialog box.

3. Select the Image Hose from the Brushes menu, and use the Grass Nozzle. Spray a row of grass on each of the 30 frames at the bottom (see Figure 5.32)

4. Save the animation. This animation will display a row of grass in wild motion because every frame is different. Now import the animation as a layer in After Effects. Place it over a layer that displays a cloud image or animation. Use a Color Key filter on the Grass layer, targeted to the background color so it drops out. The footage will now look like that in Figure 5.33.

Figure 5.32
Spray a row of grass with the Image Hose at the bottom of each frame, using the Grass Nozzle.

Figure 5.33
The composited footage with the Painter-animated grass in the foreground.

Render the animation, and save it to disk. As an alternative, if you just want a stable row of grass, you can just create a single image, using the same Image Hose Nozzle. Import it into After Effects as a layer, and drop out the background. The variations are limitless.

For examples, see the Grass and Grassy animations on the companion CD-ROM.

So Much More...

This chapter just gives you a taste of how to use Photoshop and Painter to create footage for After Effects projects. You can also learn to use any of dozens of 3D applications to prepare animated 3D scenes and then import the finished rendered animation into After Effects. You can use video footage, and even still images from a video camera, for After Effects compositions. The choices are limitless.

PART II

INTERNAL EFFECTS

BLURS AND SHARPENS

INTERNAL EFFECTS:

The internal effects covered in this chapter allow you to add different kinds of blurs to your footage, as well as remove fuzziness from images.

In this chapter, you will learn about the following filters, which ship with After Effects: Channel Blur, Compound Blur, Fast Blur, Gaussian Blur, Motion Blur, Radial Blur, Sharpen and Unsharp Mask; they are listed under Blur and Sharpen in the Effects menu.

Channel Blur

 Use a channel blur when you want to affect each RGB channel separately. This can create interesting color effects as well as image blurs (see Figure 6.1). The following are some possible uses for the Channel Blur effect:

- As a transition, create an animation that shows RGB channels blurring one at a time in succession. The result is footage that moves from a color to a blur effect.

- Use the Channel Blur effect to create flashes or explosions with an Alpha layer. Use an Alpha layer that displays a starburst, and keyframe animate the Alpha channel blur to move sporadically from a setting of 0 (which displays the Alpha channel footage) to a setting above 500 (which blurs out the Alpha channel footage). The result will be a flashing Alpha channel whose fades affect the full extent of the underlying footage.

Figure 6.1
Left: The unaffected image. Center: A blur of 15 set to the green channel. Right: A blur of 15 set to all RGB channels.

The following controls allow you to adjust the Channel Blur effect:

- *Blurriness*—Use the sliders to set the Blur values from 0 to 32,767 for each of the RGB or Alpha channels separately. Settings of 100 are usually sufficient to completely blur the image when you're working on all RGB channels simultaneously. Higher settings are more effective when working on one or two channels or when animating the blurs.

- *Edge Behavior*—This is normally checked as the default. If unchecked, pixels outside the image area will be transparent, which forces the pixels on the edge of the image area to be semi-transparent. This is not something you want in most cases, so leave this item checked.

Flash In The Pan

Take a look at the ChanBlur file on the companion CD-ROM. A channel blur is applied to the Alpha channel, causing a flash effect on the underlying footage. The channel blur uses keyframe settings of 0 (full Alpha visible) to 777 (Alpha footage invisible) to achieve the effect.

Compound Blur

 This is a rare blur effect. It gives you both a blur and an inversion (negative) of the targeted footage (see Figure 6.2). Some possible uses for the Compound Blur effect include:

- Use this effect if your footage has facial elements involved, since the inversion process looks very dreamlike on a face.

- Use this effect on a layer whose content is a cutout from the footage. The compound blur creates a very smooth movement toward transparency when applied.

The following controls allow you to adjust the Compound Blur effect:

- *Blur Layer*—Target any selected layer in your footage stack. You'll really appreciate the way this effect works when applied to a cutout layer.

- *Maximum Blur*—The settings for this control range from 0 to 4,000.

- *Stretch Map To Fit*—No matter how small the target layer is, you can check this option and have the compound blur applied to the entire image area.

Figure 6.2
Left: The original footage, displaying the overlaid footage on the right (a cutout of the background footage). Center: A compound blur of 30 is applied to the layer. Right: A compound blur of 60 is applied.

- *Invert Blur*—This option takes the uniqueness away from the effect by removing the inversion look. So, in most cases, leave this unchecked.

Blurry Flurry

The CompBlur animation on the companion CD-ROM centers on the Compound Blur effect. The effect is applied to a second layer, which is a partial cutout of the background. The values of the keyframes range from 0 to 100 at different places in the animation.

Fast Blur

 This is the simplest blur of all, with just one control for blurriness. Use this effect when all that's called for is a simple and fast blur (see Figure 6.3).

The following control allows you to adjust the Fast Blur effect:

- *Blurriness*—This is Fast Blur's only control. Its values range from 0 to 32,767, with values over approximately 300 tending to obliterate the targeted footage.

Figure 6.3
Left: Original footage. Center: A fast blur of 10. Right: A fast blur of 50.

Gaussian Blur

 The Gaussian Blur effect is a little slower than Fast Blur, but it does a better job of removing any noise from the footage. Use this effect when all that's called for is a simple, quick blur, but with a little more quality than the Fast Blur effect (see Figure 6.4).

Figure 6.4
Left: Original footage. Center: A Gaussian blur of 10. Right: A Gaussian blur of 50. Compare these images with those in Figure 6.3.

The following control allows you to adjust the parameters of the Gaussian Blur effect:

- *Blurriness*—Within settings ranging from 0 to 1,000, this slider controls the intensity of the blur.

Motion Blur

The Motion Blur effect adds a direction component to the Blur effect (see Figure 6.5). The following are some possible uses for the Motion Blur effect:

- To add speed lines to elements moving in one or more directions, use a motion blur in the selected footage.

- Use a high-value motion blur when something is speeding across the scene.

The following controls allow you to adjust the Motion Blur effect:

- *Direction*—This control sets the direction of the blur with a radial dial.

- *Blur Length*—The Blur Length settings can range from 0 to 1,000, although settings above 100 are very seldom needed.

> Note: Make your footage overlap the Composition window by about one-quarter inch in all directions. This effect causes a gray border to appear in either the horizontal or vertical footage frame, and overlapping will make the border invisible.

Faster Than A Speeding Bullet

Open the MotBlur file on the companion CD-ROM. In this animation, the footage shows the effects of an applied motion blur. The blur was rotated 360 degrees during the animation.

Figure 6.5
Left to right: Motion Blur settings of 0, 10, and 100.

Radial Blur

This is the best blur to select for moving footage, especially when the footage shows a smaller item (like a ball or a meteor) moving around in the frame (see Figure 6.6). The following are some possible uses for the Radial Blur effect:

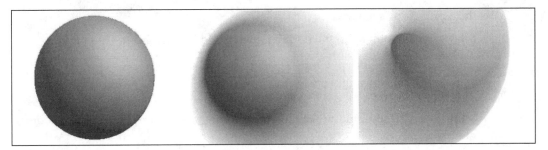

Figure 6.6
Left: Original footage. Center: Zoom radial blur applied. Right: Spin radial blur applied.

- Use a zoom radial blur to cause motion trails behind moving objects in the footage. Keyframe the blur center by following the object during the animation and keeping the center in front of the blur motion.

- Use a spin radial blur to evoke blurred rings that move with your footage.

The following controls allow you to adjust the parameters of the Radial Blur effect:

- *Amount*—The Amount control has two components: a visual display of the radial type and an associated intensity slider. The cursor that places the center of the blur is better avoided. Instead, just interactively move the center in the visual display. No numbers are associated with the intensity slider; it just moves left (for less intensity) and right (for more intensity). As the slider is moved, however, you do get visual feedback that displays the rays associated with the blur.

- *Center*—Avoid this placement cross in favor of the interactive placement of the center of the blur in the visual display.

- *Type*—You can choose from two radial blur types: Spin (concentric rings) and Zoom (raylike projections). Use the Zoom type when you want the footage element to show a blurred trail. Use the Spin type to generate blurred rings that follow the movement.

- *Antialiasing*—You may select between Low and High. Select High as the default, and use Low to preview the resulting radial blur.

Circling The Blur

Open RadBlur from the companion CD-ROM. This animation displays a zoom radial blur in action. The center of the blur moves in a 360-degree circle around the footage.

Zoom Blur Project

Do the following to create a Zooming Blur effect:

1. Add still or animated footage of your choice to the Composition window.

2. Activate the Radial Blur effect from the internal Blur and Sharpen options.

3. Set the parameters as follows:

- Set the Center point at an interesting target on the footage, Zoom type, High Antialiasing.

- Set the Amount slider all the way to the left so there is no effect applied to the first frame of your animation, and keyframe it.

- Set the Amount slider all the way to the right for the last frame of your animation, and keyframe it.

4. Render and save the animation to disk. For an example of what this produces, see the ZmBlr animation on the companion CD-ROM.

Sharpen

You can employ the Sharpen effect in two ways. First, you can use it to sharpen footage that is a little fuzzy. Use Sharpen at lower settings (below 100) to remove the fuzziness from footage. Use Sharpen at higher settings (especially above 1,000) to add a color-embossing effect to footage (see Figure 6.7).

The following control allows you to adjust the Sharpen effect's parameters:

- *Sharpen Amount*—This is the only control for the Sharpen effect, and the values range from 0 to 4,000. To remove fuzziness from footage, stay below 100, or you will begin to introduce color-embossing effects. If color-embossing effects are what you desire, set the Amount value to 1,000 and above.

Figure 6.7
Left: Original footage. Center: Sharpen Amount set to 100. Right: Sharpen Amount set to 4,000.

UnSharp Mask

This filter makes the image sharper and gives you exacting control over the threshhold points (see Figure 6.8).

The following are some possible uses for the UnSharp Mask effect:

- Explore various settings to bring out the details in an image, such as the grain in a slice of bread or the striations in weathered rock.

- Use multiple UnSharp Mask effects to create unique sculpted looks.

Figure 6.8
Left: Original footage. Center: Amount set to 500, Radius at 1. Right: Radius increased to 10.

The following controls allow you to adjust the UnSharp Mask filter's parameters:

- *Amount*—This control adjusts the strength of the sharpness, from 0 to 500. Values over 200 starts to create posterized looks.

- *Radius*—This control sets the area being affected, from .1 to 500. At smaller radius settings, you can *pop out* the details. Each image is different, so you need to explore the best radius each time you use this filter.

- *Threshhold*—This control's settings range from 0 to 255. The default setting is 0, which means that all areas of the image or footage will be affected. As you increase the Threshhold value, less of the image or footage is affected.

EFFECTS AND KEYING

*The following AE plug-ins are included in the
After Effects software and are listed under the
Effects menu in the Channel Effects group. They
include Alpha Levels, Arithmetic, Blend,
Compound Arithmetic, MiniMax, Set Channels,
Set Matte, and Shift Channels.*

Channel Effects/Alpha Levels

  The Alpha Levels filter is perfect to use after creating an Alpha layer
with BorisFX Linear Color key (see Figure 7.1). The following are
some possible uses for the Alpha Levels effect:

- Animate several layers in your footage stack, each with its own Alpha Levels filter, to get complex crossfades between layers.

- Animate the Input Black and Input White levels going in opposite directions to
  achieve footage that minimizes movement in the Alpha channel layer.

The following controls allow you to adjust the parameters of the Alpha Levels effect:

- *Input Black/White Level*—The values for the Input Black/White levels (0 to 255) are
  remapped to the Output Black/White levels, creating fades in the Alpha channel.

- *Gamma*—Gamma influences the apparent brightness of the footage (its settings
  range between 1 and 10).

Figure 7.1
Left: Original footage (church is the Alpha layer). Center: Input Black at 255 and Output Black at
175. Right: Input Black at 255 and Output Black at 125.

- *Output Black/White Level*—Resetting the Output Black/White levels is the final step in remapping the Alpha grayscale levels, which affects the transparency of different elements in the Alpha channel.

AlphaLev

The AlphaLev animation (found on the companion CD-ROM) demonstrates the Alpha Levels effect. The top (Alpha) layer is an image of a church, and the background is colored squares. The Alpha levels parameters that are keyframe animated are Input Black (0, 1 at midpoint, and 255 at the end), and Output White (0 to 255 at midpoint). Gamma is set to 4.

Channel Effects/Arithmetic

 This filter allows you to adjust the mix of RGB channel colors with different operators (see Figure 7.2). The following are some possible uses for the Arithmetic effect:

- Select the RGB values that you want, and apply an operator that creates a posterizing effect on the footage.

- Animate the channel values to get a palette that shifts colors.

The following controls allow you to adjust the parameters of the Arithmetic effect:

- *Operators*—Thirteen operators are available to you, and each mixes the RGB channels in different ways. These controls should be explored before you settle on one.

- *RGB Values*—These values (in a range of 0 to 255) determine the mix of the RGB channels. Setting them all to 0 results in the footage being displayed in its original color mix, unless the operator is Max, Block Above, Slice, or Multiply. Setting all channels to 255 creates different effects based on your choice of operator.

- *Clipping*—The default for this channel is on (checked), which limits the color range of the effects. Color anomalies can occur if this is unchecked.

Figure 7.2
The same values are used with different operators. The common values are red 117, green 149, and blue 191. The operators (left to right) are Difference, Add, and Slice.

By The Numbers

The Arithmetic file on the companion CD-ROM shows an example of the Arithmetic effect in action. The RGB channels are all animated and assigned to the Alpha overlays (the eyes of the subjects).

Channel Effects/Blend

The Blend effect works to combine two selected layers, according to your choice of mode (see Figure 7.3). The following are some possible uses for the Blend effect:

- Use a Crossfade as a transition from one footage layer to another.

- Use Tint Only to create subtle blends of layers based on their hues.

The following controls allow you to adjust the Blend effect's parameters:

- *Blend With Layer*—From any layer in the stack, select the layer you want to blend the footage with.

- *Mode*—There are five modes: Crossfade, Color Only, Tint Only, Darken Only, and Lighten Only. Crossfade blends in the alternate layer as a transparency, according to the Blend percentage. Color Only blends in the color and is harsher than Tint Only. Darken Only and Lighten Only use the Luma (brightness) values of the alternate image on the initial layer.

- *Blend With Original*—This control adjusts the Blend value from 0 to 100 percent. Nothing is shown but the alternate layer with a setting of 0, whereas a setting of 100 displays only the primal layer.

- *If Layer Sizes Differ*—You can either center the selected layer or resize it to fit.

Figure 7.3
Left: A Crossfade of 45%. Center: Darken Only at 0%. Right: Lighten Only at 0%.

Channel Effects/Compound Arithmetic

Compound Arithmetic is a more extensive version of the Blend effect and gives you more options for blending layers together (see Figure 7.4). Some possible uses for the Compound Arithmetic effect are shown in the following list:

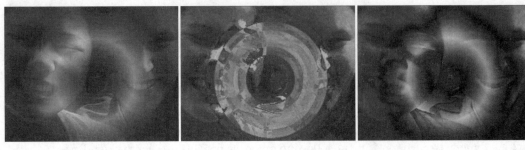

Figure 7.4
Left: The Copy operator at a 45% blend. Center: The XOR operator at a 30% blend. Right: The Difference operator at a 10% blend.

- Use this filter whenever you want more Blend options than the Blend filter can provide.

- Use the Hard Light operator at 0 percent to create a blend effect that allows the hue of the alternate footage (stable or moving) to colorize the initial footage.

The following controls allow you to adjust the parameters of the Compound Arithmetic effect:

- *Second Source*—With this control, you select the second source layer to blend with.

- *Operator*—You can choose among 15 operators. Explore all of them to decide on the look that's right for your footage.

- *Operate On Channel*—You can target the blended footage's RGB, RGBA, or Alpha channels. The default setting is RGB.

- *Overflow Behavior*—These options indicate how pixel values that exceed the allowed range are treated. The default setting is Clip. The other options are Wraparound and Scale. (Check the After Effects documentation for a more detailed discussion of these options.)

- *Stretch Second Source*—If the second source layer is a different size, check this box.

- *Blend With Original*—This control sets the layer mix from 0 to 100 percent. A setting of 0 maximizes the effect, and a setting of 100 percent displays only the original layer. Values within this range adjust the blending.

Channel Effects/Invert

 The difference between this inversion filter and a simple inversion effect is what can be inverted. This filter allows you a very wide range of options (see Figure 7.5). The following are some possible uses for the Invert effect:

- Use the RGB, YIQ, or Luminance channel options to create the standard footage inversion (negative image). RGB and YIQ produce a greenish cast at 0 percent.

- Use one of the RGB channels to generate more posterized footage.

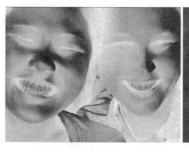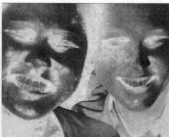

Figure 7.5
Left: RGB blend of 0%. Center: Red blend at 0%. Right: HLS blend of 0%.

The following controls allow you to adjust the Invert effect's parameters:

- *Channel*—The Invert effect provides a wide range of channel options. They include: RGB Composite or Separate RGB Channels, HLS Composite or Separate Hue-Saturation-Lightness Channels, YIQ, Luminance, In Phase Chrominance (hue), Quadrature Chrominance, and Alpha. Explore all of these options before deciding on one.

- *Blend With Original*—This control blends the effect with the original footage in percentages from 0 to 100. A setting of 0 maximizes the effect, whereas 100 displays just the original footage.

Channel Effects/MiniMax

 MiniMax creates a blocky mosaic pattern over the image. A maximum setting generates a whiter block, and a minimum setting a blacker block (see Figure 7.6). The following are some possible uses for the MiniMax effect:

- Keyframe animate a Maximum Horizontal and Vertical color channel, starting from 0 and ending at 200 for a blocky fade to white.

- Keyframe animate a Minimum Horizontal and Vertical color channel, starting from 0 and ending at 200 for a blocky fade to black.

Figure 7.6
Left: Original footage. Center: Horizontal and Vertical Maximum Radius of 3 on the color channel. Right: Horizontal and Vertical Minimum Radius of 3 on the color channel.

The following controls allow you to adjust the MiniMax effect's parameters:

- *Operation*—The options are Minimum, Maximum, Minimum Then Maximum, or Maximum Then Minimum. In general, Maximum sets the blocks or streaks to white, and Minimum to black.

- *Radius*—The settings for this control range from 0 (no effect) to 32,000. A setting of 3 is usually sufficient for small blocks, whereas 200 will obliterate most footage.

- *Channel*—Select RGB, RGB plus Alpha, any separate RGB channel, or just the Alpha channel.

- *Direction*—The default setting is Horizontal And Vertical, which creates blocks. As suspected, Horizontal creates horizontal streaks and Vertical creates vertical streaks.

Oil Painting

To create an oil-painted look for your footage, do the following:

1. Import your still or animated footage to the Composition window.

2. Select the MiniMax filter from the Channels list in the Effects menu.

3. Use the following parameters: Maximum Operation, Color Channel, and Horizontal And Vertical Direction.

4. Set the Radius between 2 and 6 to achieve the best oil-painted look. Higher settings obliterate the image content.

Render and save the picture or animation to disk.

Open Minimax from the companion CD-ROM. This animation moves from a maximum type of 200 to 0 at the center, and then from a minimum setting of 0 to 150 at the end. The layer is split in half, with the MiniMax effect assigned to each half separately.

Channel Effects/Set Channels

 This filter allows you to blend up to four layers, according to their channel settings (see Figure 7.7). The following are some possible uses for the Set Channels effect:

- For the simplest composited results in combining four layers, assign them in order to the red, green, blue, and Alpha channels.

- Use this effect to create extremely abstracted transparent composites from four separate layers. This works best when the footage is moving on and off screen, and is especially valuable when all of the layers are text blocks.

The following controls allow you to adjust the Set Channels effect:

- *Source*—Select separate source footage for four footage layers. These can be any layers in the stack. Layer 1 is the red channel, Layer 2 is the green channel, Layer 3 is the blue channel, and Layer 4 is the Alpha channel.

Figure 7.7
The images from left to right display some variants when combining the same three layers of footage.

- *Set RGBA To Source*—The options here allow you to select what determines the channel mapping. It can be Red, Green, Blue, Alpha, Luminance, Hue, Lightness, Saturation, Full, or Off. So many cross-connections are possible that the only way to settle on a combination is to keep exploring until you find something you like.

- *Stretch*—This checkbox stretches any offsized layers to fit.

> **Note: You'll have better luck configuring this effect at first if you stick with two layers instead of trying to mix four. Include three or four layers after you get the hang of it.**

Channel Effects/Set Matte

 This effect is used to select a traveling matte, a composite of layers that is joined together as one. Traveling mattes are commonly used to show moving footage either inside of other moving footage or against a moving backdrop. The matte is an intervening Alpha channel that treats the primary footage so that the secondary footage can show through (see Figure 7.8). The following list shows some possible uses for the Set Matte effect:

- Select a patterned matte layer, and use it to glue the matte to the primary layer so that the secondary layer can show through where the Alpha is transparent.

- Make the secondary layer invisible in the timeline to display only the composited matte and the primary layer, with the color of the matte dominant.

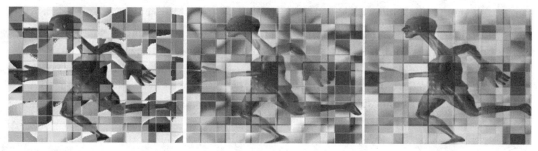

Figure 7.8
Left to right, alternate composite types for the Set Matte effect: Hue, Saturation, and Lightness.

Note: *After a traveling matte is set, the footage layers are glued together and can be moved, resized, or rotated as one composite. The normal stacking order would be the primary layer on top, the secondary layer beneath it, and the matte layer on the bottom. You can also explore placing the matte layer between the primary and secondary layers.*

The following controls allow you to adjust the parameters of the Set Matte effect:

- *Take Matte From*—This control allows you to select any layer in the stack as the matte.

- *Use For Matte*—This control sets the channel through which the matte works: Red, Green, Blue, Alpha, Luminance, Hue, Lightness, Saturation, Full (displays only secondary footage), or Off (displays only primary footage).

- *Invert Matte*—If this control is checked, you can invert (make a negative of) the matte effect.

- *Sizing*—If the layers are offsized, checking one or more of these alternatives will compensate Stretch Matte To Fit, Composite Matte With Original, and Premultiply Matte Layer. (Read the After Effects documentation on Premultiplied Alpha channels, a way of adding color components from the background to an Alpha layer.)

Look at the RotMat file on the companion CD-ROM. Using a Luminance Set Matte effect, the matte layer is rotated against the composited footage.

Channel Effects/Shift Channels

 This effect does something very basic, but with some interesting results. It allows you to select any channel as the source of information for the RGB and Alpha channels (see Figure 7.9). The following list shows some possible uses for the Shift Channels effect:

- Take the RGB channels from their original sources and take the Alpha channel data from the hue information. The result will be primary footage that is semi-transparent and shows through the background footage.

- To create a text block that shows through a moving background footage, simply select the text block's Alpha channel data to come from the Luminance or any RGB channel. A stenciled outline of the text will show the footage below it.

The following control allows you to adjust the Shift Channels effect:

- *Take Channel From*—You can take the Alpha, red, blue, or green channel data from a selection of channels: Alpha, Red, Green, Blue, Luminance, Hue, Lightness, Saturation, Full On, and Off. This control is especially valuable for creating Alpha channel effects because it allows you to develop instant Alpha channel transparencies even when there is no Alpha channel in the stack. Very complex traveling mattes can be created in seconds.

Figure 7.9
RGB channels in these examples were kept referenced to themselves, but the Alpha channel drew its data from other sources. From left to right, the Alpha channel was referenced to the Hue, Lightness, and Saturation channels.

Channel Effects/Remove Color Matting

This filter allows you to remove halos caused when an Alpha channel drops out parts of the footage to reveal a color or content layer below, and the contrast between the two colors at the dropout points is too wide. Simply select another matte color with the eyedropper or from the system palette, and try to remove the halo. Experimentation is necessary to get this perfect. The following are some possible uses for the Remove Color Matting effect:

- Use this filter to remove color halos that result when a facial portrait is composited against a complex backdrop.

- This filter works well when a Difference Matte is used first because it allows you to fine-tune the color range of the Difference Matte.

The following control allows you to adjust the Remove Color Matting filter:

- *Background Color*—This is the only control. Use either the eyedropper or the system palette to select the color removed.

Keying/Color Key

Color Key is a basic key. You use this filter to drop out areas of the top layer based on its RGB color (see Figure 7.10). The following are some possible uses for the Color Key filter:

- Use this filter with a small Tolerance level to create small transparent areas on the targeted layer.

- Use this filter with keyframe-animated Tolerance to create a wipe based on Tolerances that increase in size from 0 to 255.

The following control allows you to adjust the Color Key filter:

- *Key Color*—Select the color to be used as the Key Color.

- *Color Tolerance*—The lower the Tolerance, the smaller the dropout areas. This control's setting ranges from 0 to 255.

Figure 7.10
Left: Original footage. Center: Color Tolerance of 75 and Blur of 10. Right: Tolerance increased to 150.

- *Edge Thin*—Adjusts the edge boundary where the dropout areas meet the footage content. This control's setting ranges from –5 to 5.

- *Edge Feather*—Feather the edges (in a range from 0 to 100) to create smoother blurred transitions.

Keying/Luma Key

This filter is a basic Keying filter that allows you to control the transparency of the footage, based on its bright and dark areas (see Figure 7.11). The following are some possible uses for the Luma Key filter:

- Use this filter to key out bright areas on footage that contain mixed brights and darks.

- This filter works well when used to key out a backdrop that has an even luminescence different from the foreground.

The following controls allow you to adjust the Luma Key filter:

- *Key Type*—You can key out the brightness or darkness of the footage, or compare the footage with the underlying layer to key out similar or dissimilar areas.

- *Threshold*—This is the main control that adjusts (in a range from 0 to 255) for the extent of the dropout areas.

Figure 7.11
Left: Original footage. Center: Key Out Brightness, with a Threshold of 75. Right: Same Threshold value with key Out Darkness selected.

- *Tolerance*—The lower the Tolerance (in a range from 0 to 255), the smaller the dropout areas, though this control has far less effect on the footage than the corresponding control in the Color Key filter.

- *Edge Thin*—Adjusts the edge boundary where the dropout areas meet the footage content. This control's setting ranges from –5 to 5.

- *Edge Feather*—Feather the edges (in a range from 0 to 100) to create smoother blurred transitions.

EFFECTS

8

This chapter covers the AE filters that are featured in the Effects/Distort menu: Displacement Map, Mirror, Offset, Spherize, and Wave Warp. Many Photoshop filters are also discussed.

Displacement Map

The Displacement Map effect allows you to use the channel information from one layer to alter the contents of another layer. The primary layer becomes a tiled backdrop, while the secondary layer becomes a foreground that is mapped with the footage of the primary layer (see Figure 8.1).

The following are some possible uses for the Displacement Map effect:

- Keyframe animate the horizontal and vertical displacement from –333 to +333 with Luminance channel settings. The result is a moving primary footage in the background that is mapped onto the secondary footage. The look is a similarly animated, reflected crystalline glass on the secondary footage.

- For an appearance that is more speckled, use displacement values over +10,000 and under –10,000.

Figure 8.1
Left: The original layer image. Center: The displacement map layer image. Right: Displacement mapping activated for the two layers.

The following controls allow you to adjust the parameters of the Displacement Map effect:

- *Displacement Map*—The displacement map is your secondary image, although it will displace the present foreground layer as the dominant footage. Select it from any layer in the stack.

- *Use For Horizontal/Vertical*—You can choose among the following channel selections for each of the horizontal and vertical displacement parameters: Red, Green, Blue, Alpha, Luminance, Hue, Lightness, Saturation, Full, Half, and Off. Each selection creates a different look to the displacement mapping.

- *Max Horizontal/Vertical Displacement*—Set each of these displacement values independently. (Its settings range from –32,000 to +32,000.) Larger values make the background move very fast.

> **Note: Using values over +400 or under –400 will cause the background to flash wildly. Also be aware that movement from positive to negative displacement values in an animation causes the background to scroll down, while movement from negative to positive values causes it to scroll up.**

- *Displacement Map Options*—If the map isn't sized according to the rest of the footage, you may choose to center it, stretch it to fit, or tile it.

- *Edge Behavior*—This checkbox should remain marked. Unmarking it causes anomalies in the displacement map footage.

He's Been Displaced

There are three displacement animations on the companion CD-ROM. The first is DispMap. This is a displacement map animation with vertical and horizontal displacement values that run from –333 to +333 with Luminance channel settings.

DispMap2 is a displacement map animation with vertical and horizontal displacement values that run from +12,000 to –9,000 with Saturation channel settings.

DispMap3 is a displacement map animation with vertical and horizontal displacement values that run from +200 to –200 and back to +200 with Lightness channel settings.

Mirror

 Mirroring is a symmetry function, so that the selected footage is mirrored along a selected axis (see Figure 8.2). The following list shows some possible uses for the Mirror effect:

- Mirror a text block at 180 degrees, with the reflection center set to the bottom of the text, to create a reflection as if the text were sitting on a mirrored surface.

- Animate the reflection angle, creating a rotating, continuously referenced symmetry.

The following controls allow you to adjust the Mirror effect's parameters:

- *Reflection Center*—Place the crosshairs anywhere in the Composition window (or even outside it) to set the placement of the mirrored symmetrical halves.

Figure 8.2
Left: Reference footage. Center: Reflection angle of 90 degrees, with center on composition center. Right: Reflection angle of 180 degrees, with center on composition center.

- *Reflection Angle*—The reflection angle, set by this radial dial, determines the angle that the mirroring will reference.

Mirror, Mirror

Take a look at the Mirror file on the companion CD-ROM. Using the Mirror effect, with the center of rotation placed at the center of the composition, the reflection angle was animated one full turn (360 degrees).

Tile Slide

This exercise uses the Mirror effect to create footage that tiles and moves at the same time. Do the following:

1. Import either still or animated footage into the Composition window.
2. Select Effects|Distort|Mirror filter from the Distort list in the Effects menu.
3. Set Blend With Original to 0%.
4. Keyframe the Center to the upper lefthand corner of your footage for the first frame, and keyframe the Center to the lower righthand corner of your footage for the last frame.
5. Render the animation and save to disk.

You will see that the footage starts at the upper left as a quarter-screen tile, becomes a full centered frame in the middle of the animation, and moves to a quarter-screen position at the lower right at the end. See the TileSld animation on this book's CD-ROM.

Offset

 Offsetting footage creates tiled footage (see Figure 8.3). Some possible uses for the Offset effect include:

- Creating a tiled backdrop for foreground footage.
- Animating the placement of the Offset crosshair to get a moving, tiled backdrop. Reduce the size of your footage to get more tiles.

Figure 8.3
Left: Original footage. Center: Offset footage. Right: Offset footage blended with original at 40%.

The following controls allow you to adjust the Offset effect's parameters:

- *Shift To*—Placing this crosshair allows you to shift the footage center anywhere on or off the Composition window.

- *Blend With Original*—You can blend the offset footage back with the original footage.

PS Pinch

 This is a Photoshop filter, which uses the same interface as its Photoshop counterpart. Use it to pinch or bloat the footage (see Figure 8.4). Some possible uses for the PS Pinch effect include:

- Creating a throbbing animation by keyframe animating the PS Pinch parameter from low to high values.

- Using a series of PS Pinch effects to pinch the footage into more distorted areas.

The following controls allow you to adjust the PS Pinch effect's parameters:

- *Pinch Amount*—This control's settings range from –100 to 100. Zero does nothing. Negative values bloat the footage, and positive values pinch it inward.

- *Blend With Original*—Blends the effect with the original footage. (This control's settings range from 0 to 100 percent.)

Figure 8.4
Left: Original footage. Center: PS Pinch Value of –100. Right: PS Pinch value of 100.

PS Ripple

This is another Photoshop filter. PS Ripple uses the same interface as its Photoshop counterpart. Use it to add an animated ripple to the footage (see Figure 8.5). Some possible uses for the PS Ripple effect include:

> **Note: The PS Ripple filter doesn't create concentric rings; rather, it generates a series of parallel distortions.**

- Ripple the footage from –999 to 999, and then use a Color Key to remove parts of the effect, to create a distorted ripple wipe.

- Use multiple PS Ripple filters on a stack of semi-opaque layers to create 3D water effects.

The following controls allow you to adjust the PS Ripple effect's parameters:

- *Amount*—This control (with a settings range from –999 to 999) adjusts the strength of the rippled effect on the footage.

- *Blend With Original*—Blends the effect with the original footage. Its settings range from 0 to 100 percent.

Figure 8.5
Left: Original footage. Center: A value of 300. Right: A value of 999.

PS Spherize

This is yet another Photoshop filter, and it uses the same interface as its Photoshop counterpart. It has less variability than the standard AE Spherize filter (see Figure 8.6). Some possible uses for the PS Spherize effect include:

- Using the PS Spherize filter to warp a face into a rounder form.

- Using a negative PS Spherize effect over a negative Pinch to emphasize a reverse bloating of the footage.

The following controls allow you to adjust the PS Spherize effect's parameters:

- *Amount*—This control adjusts the strength (with settings that range from –100 to 100) of the PS Spherize effect on the footage. Negative values act to zoom the footage out, and positive values add a fisheye lens-like effect.

Figure 8.6
Left: Original footage. Center: A value of –100. Right: A value of 100.

- *Blend With Original*—Blends (with a setting range from 0 to 100 percent) the effect with the original footage.

PS Twirl

Here's another Photoshop filter, which uses the same interface as its Photoshop counterpart. Use it to reshape the footage around a twirled center (see Figure 8.7). Some possible uses for the PS Twirl effect include:

- Adding just a touch of PS Twirl to warp and distort mechanical objects so they look more cartoony.

- Keyframe animating PS Twirl to make it seem as if the footage is being pulled down a drain.

The following controls allow you to adjust the PS Twirl effect's parameters:

- *Twirl Angle*—Use the rotation control to set the degree of the PS Twirl. This control's settings range from 0 to 360 degrees times the number of rotations.

- *Blend With Original*—Blends (from 0 to 100 percent) the effect with the original footage.

Figure 8.7
Left: Original footage. Center: Rotation of 35 degrees. Right: Rotation of 90 degrees.

PS Wave

This is a Photoshop filter that also uses the same interface as its Photoshop counterpart. Use it to translate the footage via a waveform (see Figure 8.8). Some possible uses for the PS Wave effect include:

- Animating the PS Wave effect so that its values coincide with the amplitude values of the Audio track. The footage will look as if it is being distorted by the audio.

- Keyframe animating the Number Of Generators from 3 to 8, and applying it to footage that is to act as the background for an underwater scene.

The following controls allow you to adjust the PS Wave effect's parameters:

- *Wave Type*—Select from Sine, Triangle, or Square.

- *Undefined Areas*—Wraparound or Repeat Edge Pixels are the options. Explore each for your footage.

- *Number Of Generators*—This sets (in a range from 1 to 999) the quantity of waves. Use a small number (below 10) if you want to see the footage content.

- *Horizontal/Vertical Scale*—This sets (in a range from 0 to 100) the scale of the horizontal and vertical wave components independently. Set either to 0 and the other to 100 to emphasize parallel waves.

- *Min/Max Amplitude*—This controls the strength of the wave. Its settings range from 1 to 999.

- *Min/Max Wavelength*—The shorter the Wavelength, the more waves you will see on the footage. The settings range from 1 to 999.

- *Blend With Original*—Blends (in a range from 0 to 100 percent) the effect with the original footage.

Figure 8.8
The following three PS Wave types use the same parameters: Wave Generators setting of 1, Horizontal and Vertical Scale of 100, Min/Max Amplitude from 5 to 10, and Min/Max Wavelength of 1 to 100. Left: Sine Wave. Center: Triangle Wave. Right: Square Wave.

PS ZigZag

This is a Photoshop filter, and it employs the same interface as its Photoshop counterpart. A zigzag is another version of concentric ripple effect (see Figure 8.9). Some possible uses for the PS ZigZag effect include:

- Using the PS ZigZag effect under a PS Ripple effect, and setting the Ripple center away from the PS ZigZag center. This creates a wavy ripple.

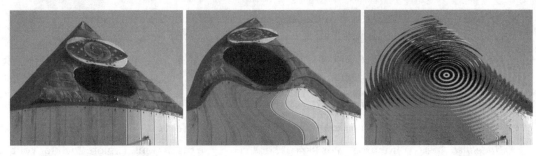

Figure 8.9
Left: Original footage. Center: Amount of 100 with just 1 Ridge. Right: Amount of 100 with 20 Ridges.

- Using the same technique described above, but keyframe animating the PS Ripple center to create multiple ripples with distortion patterns.

The following controls allow you to adjust the PS ZigZag effect's parameters:

- *Amount*—Similar to Sine waves, this controls the quantity of ZigZag waves. (Its settings range from –100 to 100.)

- *Ridges*—This control sets the number of ripples out from the center. (Its settings range from 1 to 20.)

- *Blend With Original*—Blends the effect (in a range from 0 to 100 percent) with the original footage.

Smear

Smearing the footage breaks it up into pixelated noise and then adds separation to the image content (see Figure 8.10). Some possible uses for the Smear effect include:

- Using this effect to animate a face going through all manner of contortions.

- Using different Mask Offsets to warp your footage.

Figure 8.10
Frames from a Smeared animation, showing how centroid placement can warp just the area in which you're interested.

The following controls allow you to adjust the Smear effect's parameters:

- *Masks*—You can set two separate layers to act as the Source Mask and Boundary Mask.

- *Mask Offset*—Use the centroid to place the offset distance.

- *Mask Rotation*—Use the Rotation control (in settings from 0 to 360 degrees) to spin the mask.

- *Mask Scale*—Use this control (in settings from 0.1 to 2) to size the mask area.

- *Percent*—Settings range from 0 to 100.

- *Elasticity*—Set the Elasticity of the mask from Stiff to Super Fluid. Explore the listed options to see what works best for specific footage.

- *Interpolation*—Select from among Discreet, Linear, and Smooth. Select the one that works best with your specific footage.

Spherize

The Spherize effect bulges out the footage in an amount determined by the Radius setting, from the placement of the Center crosshair (see Figure 8.11). The following are some possible uses for the Spherize effect:

- Animate the Radius value from 0 to 2,500 to get a fisheye zoom of the footage.

- Set the Radius value to 2,000 and move the crosshair in a keyframed animation. The result is a close-up panning of the footage.

The following controls allow you to adjust the Spherize effect's parameters:

- *Radius*—The Radius value (from 0 to 2,500) determines the amount of spherical bulge, interpreted as a fisheye zoom, for the footage.

- *Center Of Sphere*—Wherever you place the crosshairs will become the center of the spherical zoom.

Figure 8.11
Left: Original footage. Center: Radius of 300 with center on composition center. Right: Radius of 2,500 with center moved to upper left of footage.

AND PERSPECTIVE EFFECTS

9

This chapter covers effects that are included with After Effects. The three major categories of effects are Adjust, Image Control, and Perspective Effects. You can find the related filters under the Effects menu.

The following AE filters are included in your After Effects software and can be found under the Effects menu in the Adjust, Image Control, and Perspective directories. Adjust: Brightness/Contrast, Channel Mixer, Color Balance, Curves, Hue/Saturation, Levels, Posterize, and Threshold. Image Control: Brightness/Contrast, Change Color, Color Balance, Color Balance HLS, Equalize, Gamma/Pedestal/Gain, Levels, Median, and Tint. Perspective: Basic 3D, Bevel Alpha, Bevel Edges, and Drop Shadow.

Adjust: Brightness/Contrast

This is a basic brightness/contrast control (see Figure 9.1).

Use this filter when you need to alter the brightness and/or contrast of the footage.

The following controls allow you to adjust the parameters of the Brightness/Contrast effect:

- *Brightness*—Brightness is controlled by the slider. Its settings range from –100 to +100.

- *Contrast*—Contrast is similarly controlled by the slider. Its settings also range from –100 to +100.

Figure 9.1
Left: The original footage. Center: Brightness and Contrast settings increased to 25. Right: Brightness and Contrast settings lowered to –25.

Adjust: Channel Mixer

The Channel Mixer filter allows you to control every combination in the RGB Channel mix (see Figure 9.2).

The following are some possible uses for the Channel Mixer effect:

- Use this filter to color correct hue anomalies in your footage.
- Create emotional tones over your footage by adjusting the RGB channels.

The following controls allow you to adjust the Channel Mixer filter's parameters:

- *RGB Mix Sliders*—Use these sliders (in a range from –200 to 200) to control every possible combination of RGB channel mixes, from the selected channel to the degree that it mixes with other channels.

- *Monochrome*—Checking this box translates the footage to grayscale.

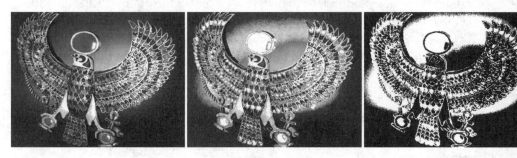

Figure 9.2
Left: Original footage. Center: Increasing the Red-Red value to 200. Right: Decreasing the Red-Red value to 75.

Adjust: Color Balance

This is a basic RGB color-balance filter, allowing you to alter the amount of red, blue, and green in the mix.

Use this filter when your footage is out of balance for the RGB mix, or when you want to create animated color-channel effects.

RGB Balance allows you to alter the mix of each RGB color channel within the Color Balance effect, with a range of settings from –100 to +100.

Adjust: Curves

Curves allow you to adjust the darks and lights of the footage separately (see Figure 9.3).

The following are some possible uses for the Curves filter:

- Adjust small areas of RGB anomalies by using the Curves filter.

Figure 9.3
Left: Curves interface. Center: Original footage. Right: Footage adjusted with Curves.

- Use Curves to create customized posterizations by adjusting the RGB curves in more radical ways.

To master the Curves filter, you must spend some time exploring and playing with the adjustment curve for each footage layer you need to address. Alternate image content responds differently each time you use the Curves filter. Because this filter is similar to using Curves in Photoshop, you can transfer what you learn about Curves to either application. Every adjustment you make brightens or darkens a range of RGB selections.

Adjust: Hue/Saturation

Adjusting Hue and Saturation allows you to make subtle or radical alterations in the look of your footage (see Figure 9.4).

The following are some possible uses for the Hue/Saturation effect:

- Adjust the Hue to tint the footage any way you like. Just select Colorize.
- Move the Saturation slider to 0 to instantly translate the footage to grayscale, or keyframe animate this effect to move to or from grayscale as you like.

The following controls allow you to adjust the Hue/Saturation filter's parameters:

- *Master Hue*—Use the Rotation control to shift the Hue spectrum to a new position. Look at the color bars in the dialog box to see the new spectrum you have chosen.

Figure 9.4
Left: Original footage. Center: Lightness of –30. Right: Lightness of 30.

- *Master Saturation*—Adjust the overall Saturation of the image (ranges from –100 to 100). A setting of 0 creates a grayscale image. Setting the value higher than 0 starts to introduce pixelated anomalies into the footage.

- *Master Lightness*—This control (with settings from –100 to 100) either darkens or brightens the footage.

- *Colorize*—To add tinted monochromatic color to the footage, select this checkbox. When Colorize is on, it has its own separate Hue, Saturation, and Brightness sliders.

Adjust: Levels

The Levels tool is the most accurate way to adjust the Input/Output of all footage channels. For this reason, it requires an advanced knowledge of color and transmission theory, and is not for the beginner. To begin to master this filter, read all the After Effects documentation carefully, and then read every Photoshop book on color that you can. Take a class or two in color theory, and visit the technicians at your local TV station. Otherwise, you can explore what these channel controls do, but don't take on any assignments that require their use and mastery until you have attained the required knowledge and experience.

Channel levels can be altered by using the sliders and also by interactively adjusting the histogram presented in the Levels Effects Interface (see Figure 9.5).

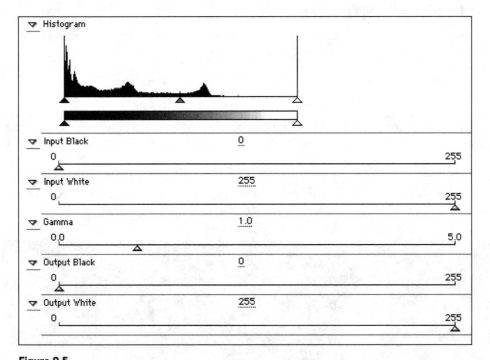

Figure 9.5
If you aren't a master of color and signal transmission theory, you can explore the global transformation of channel adjustment by manipulating the sliders under this interactive histogram for the indicated channels.

Adjust: Posterize

Posterizing reduces the number of colors in the available palette, so that some hues are transposed along the way to other available hues (see Figure 9.6).

The following are some possible uses for the Posterize effect:

- Use a Posterize value of 2 to create a dream sequence look.
- Keyframe animate the Posterize control to introduce subtle hue alterations in your sequences.

The following control allows you to adjust the Posterize filter's parameters:

- *Level*—This is the only control (with settings ranging from 2 to 255), and its sets the degree of Posterization. Lower settings produce more posterizing.

Figure 9.6
Left: Original footage. Center: Posterize value of 5. Right: Posterize value of 2.

Adjust: Threshhold

The Threshhold filter is best used to create an Alpha map from RGB footage (see Figure 9.7).

The following are some possible uses for the Threshhold filter:

- Use the Threshhold filter to create an Alpha map of composited effects.
- Use Threshhold to create dynamic black-and-white footage.

Figure 9.7
Left: Original footage. Center: A level of 50. Right: A Level of 80.

The following controls allow you to adjust the Threshhold filter's parameters:

- *Level*—This is the only control, with settings ranging from 0 to 255. Zero creates totally white footage, and 255 all black. In between, the footage content is revealed in discreet amounts.

Image Control: Change Color

This filter allows you to alter any selected color or color range in the footage, so that you can correct for bad color or create color effects (see Figure 9.8).

The following are some possible uses for the Change Color effect:

- Animate the Lightness Transform values from 0 to 100 to make a color sparkle. Randomize the keyframe placement.

- Animate the Hue Transform settings from –100 to +100 to wash the footage in an array of colors.

The following controls allow you to adjust the Change Color effect's parameters:

- *View*—You can select to view either the corrected layer or the color-correction mask that has been created. Switching to Color Correction Mask during the modification process is instructive.

- *HLS Transform*—Hue (in a range of settings from –1,800 to +1,800), Lightness (settings from –100 to +100), and Saturation (–100 to +100) may be altered separately. This allows you fine control over the altered footage palette.

- *Color To Change*—Use either the eyedropper to select a color or color range in the footage that you want to alter.

- *Matching Tolerance/Softness*—This control allows you to fine-tune the mask. For that reason, switch to the Color Correction Mask View when using these controls. Its settings range from 0 to 100.

Figure 9.8
Left: Original footage. Center: Results of a hue transform. Right: Viewing the color-correction mask.

- *Match Colors*—You can match the selected colors using RGB, Hue, or Chroma. RGB is the default.

- *Invert Color Correction Mask*—By checking this option, you can instantly invert the mask values, getting negative values for the colors. Animating this switch produces a strobe effect.

Image Control: Color Balance HLS

This basic HLS balance filter allows you to alter the hue, lightness, and saturation of the footage. Use this filter when your footage is out of balance for the RGB mix or to create animated color channel effects.

HLS Controls let you adjust the hue, lightness, and saturation of your footage. This can be done for correction purposes or to create animated changes in the footage.

Image Control: Equalize

Equalize is a basic and quick way to balance your channel ranges.

The following controls allow you to adjust the Equalize effect's parameters:

- *Equalize Style*—You may equalize the footage by using RGB, brightness, or in a Photoshop style.

- *Amount*—In a range from 0 to 100, the settings allow you to better equalize the balance in the footage.

Image Control: Gamma/Pedestal/Gain

Unlike other filters, this one requires knowledge and mastery of the more technical side of RGB channel balancing.

Use this filter when you want to perform extremely complex and detailed balancing of the RGB channels for your footage. This filter is especially useful if you're trying to match the footage to other footage for color anomalies.

The following controls allow you to adjust the parameters of the Gamma/Pedestal/Gain effect:

- *Black Stretch*—Black Stretch is used to remap the low pixel values of all channels. Its settings range from 1 to 4, and maximizing it lightens the dark areas of the footage.

- *RGB Gamma*—Gamma pushes up the brightness without washing out the color. Its settings can range from 1.5 to 32,000.

- *RGB Pedestal*—RGB Pedestal specifies the lowest attainable output for a channel. Its values can range from –32,000 to +32,000.

- *RGB Gain*—Gain specifies the largest attainable output for a channel. Its values also range from –32,000 to +32,000.

Image Control: Median

Median is a Blur Convolve filter, allowing you to assign an image blur to the footage in pixelated blocks (see Figure 9.9).

The following are some possible uses for the Median effect:

- Use this filter on an Alpha channel to spread out the Alpha effects, and also to blur the edges of the Alpha mask.

- Animate the radius setting from 0 to 50 or more to blur out the targeted footage.

The following controls allow you to adjust the Median effect's parameters:

- *Radius*—Radius sets the range of the effect. Its settings range from 0 to 1,009, but values over 100 tend to create one large color block.

- *Operate on Alpha Channel*—You may select to use this filter on the Alpha channel.

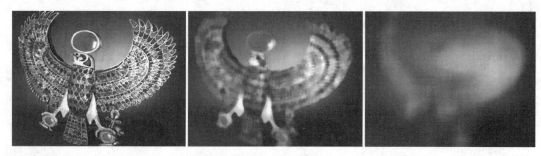

Figure 9.9
Left: Original footage. Center: A Radius setting of 5 is applied. Right: A Radius setting of 20 is applied.

Image Control: PS Arbitrary Map

The PS Arbitrary Map adds degrees of posterization to the footage (see Figure 9.10).

The following are some possible uses for the PS Arbitrary Map effect:

- Keyframe animate from 0 to 360 to create animated posterizations.

- Use this filter to create solid color areas that can be color keyed out of the footage.

Figure 9.10
Left: Original footage. Center: A Phase of 260. Right: A Phase of 225.

The following controls allow you to adjust the PS Arbitrary Map filter's parameters:

- *Phase*—Use the Rotation control to adjust the Phase of the mapping.
- *Apply Phase Map To All*—Activating this checkbox tends to darken the footage. Default is off.

Image Control: Tint

The Tint effect transforms your footage into a two-color palette at its highest Amount setting, or it can blend with the original footage colors (see Figure 9.11).

The following are some possible uses for the Tint effect:

- Map the black to a light color and the white to a dark color to get a negative-tinted footage.
- Animate the amount setting so that the footage fades in and out of the tint. Fading to a tinted footage from full color is an effect often used in documentaries because tinted footage looks older than color footage.

The following controls allow you to adjust the Tint effect's parameters:

- *Map Black/White To*—Tint allows you to map the blacks (dark hues) and whites (light hues) to any two colors you want.
- *Amount Of Tint*—The Amount slider sets the blend between the tint and the original footage palette. Its settings can be between 0 and 100.

Figure 9.11
Left: Original footage. Center: Black mapped to a light color and white to a dark color produces a tinted negative at an amount setting of 100. Right: The tint blended with the original palette at an amount of 60.

Perspective: Basic 3D

This is a basic 3D Planar effect. It offers little fine-tuning control. The professional user is advised to look at the BorisFX or MetaCreations planar effects for more fine-tuning for this effect (see Figure 9.12).

The following are some possible uses for the Basic 3D effect:

- Use this effect to fly a logo up from the background.
- Use this effect to add perspective to a text block.

Figure 9.12
Left: A Swivel setting of 0 and a Tilt of 45 at a distance of 30. Center: Swivel changed to 45. Right: Distance of –35 brings the footage a lot closer.

The following controls allow you to adjust the Basic 3D effect's parameters:

- *Swivel*—This radial dial adjusts the perspective of the footage on its vertical axis.

- *Tilt*—This radial dial adjusts the perspective angle of the footage related to the horizon.

- *Distance To Image*—Distance adjusts the closeness of the footage to the camera. Its settings range from –30,000 to +30,000; the lower the value, the *closer* the footage.

- *Specular Highlight*—When checked, a blurred highlight is added to the footage to increase depth perception.

- *Preview Wireframe*—This option toggles a wireframe preview on and off.

Basic 3D Flyup

To create an animation that shows a graphic flying up to the full screen from the background, do the following:

1. Select any image you want that fits the size of your Composition window and import it. Make this animation 12 seconds long, at 30 fps.

2. After you place the image in the Composition window, select Effects|Perspective| Basic 3D. Switch Highlight off.

3. You will set three keyframes during this 12-second animation for Swivel, Tilt, and Distance to Image. These keyframes will be at 0, 4, and 10 seconds.

4. At 0 seconds, set the values for Swivel, Tilt, and Distance to Image to 0 degrees, zero degrees, and 8,000 respectively.

5. At 4 seconds on the timeline, set the keyframe values for Swivel, Tilt, and Distance to Image to 1×, 1×, and 1,000, respectively.

6. At 10 seconds on the timeline, set the keyframe values for Swivel, Tilt, and Distance to Image to 2×, 2×, and 0, respectively.

Render the animation and save it to disk.

The Plane, The Plane

The Basic3D animation on the companion CD-ROM demonstrates how the Basic 3D effect allows this footage of a plane to fly into the distance.

Perspective: Bevel Alpha

 This filter places a beveled frame around your footage (see Figure 9.13).

The following are some possible uses for the Bevel Alpha effect:

- Add a frame to pop your footage out from a backdrop, and add a 3D look to its edges.

- Use a frame around a text block, and it will look like a plaque. If the text is cut out, the actual text will take on a 3D look.

The following controls allow you to adjust the parameters of the Bevel Alpha effect:

- *Edge Thickness*—Although the settings for this control range between 0 and 200, the most common settings are between 10 to 35 for an acceptable frame.

- *Light Angle*—This radial dial allows you to adjust the directional light source that adds dimension to your frame.

- *Light Color*—You may select any color for the light source, which will be reflected on those parts of your frame facing the light.

- *Light Intensity*—Brighten the Intensity value (0 to 1) if the footage is dark.

Figure 9.13
A frame is added to the footage with the Bevel Alpha effect.

Perspective: Bevel Edges

 This filter adds a frame around footage that doesn't have an Alpha channel, or footage where you would prefer to add the frame directly to the image (see Figure 9.14).

Use the Bevel Edges effect when you want to apply the frame directly to the footage.

The following controls allow you to adjust the Bevel Edges effect's parameters:

- *Edge Thickness*—The settings for this control range from 0 to 0.5, but the most common settings for an acceptable frame are between 0.1 and 0.25.

Figure 9.14
A frame is added to the footage with the Bevel Edges effect.

- *Light Angle*—This radial dial allows you to adjust the directional light source that adds dimension to your frame.

- *Light Color*—You may select any color for the light source, which will be reflected on those parts of your frame that face the light.

- *Light Intensity*—Brighten the Intensity value (0 to 1) if the footage is dark.

Perspective: Drop Shadow

  This effect adds a drop shadow behind the footage. To see a drop shadow, your selected footage has to be smaller than the background (see Figure 9.15).

The following are some possible uses for the Drop Shadow effect:

- Add a drop shadow to text so that it seems to be floating above the footage in the background.

- Use the Drop Shadow effect when several layers are moving across the backdrop to add dimension to the scene.

The following controls allow you to adjust the parameters of the Drop Shadow effect:

- *Shadow Color*—Select any color you like, depending on the background. Use a color that is complementary to the background color, or select black.

Figure 9.15
A drop shadow added to a footage layer.

- *Opacity*—Opacity determines the transparency of the shadow and what can be seen through it. Explore this control to find the best looking settings for your footage. Its settings range between 0 and 100, and the best beginning default is 50.

- *Direction*—Set the direction of the shadow with this radial dial.

- *Distance*—Distance sets the perceived height of the footage against its background. Its settings range between 0 and 4,000. The larger the value, the higher the footage seems to be placed.

- *Softness*—Softness (with a range from 0 to 50) blurs the edge of the shadow. As a rule, shadows become softer as the distance from the light source increases.

Casting A Shadow

Take a look at the DrpShad animation on the companion CD-ROM. As this footage flies away from and above the background, its shadow gets fuzzier and larger.

Perspective: Transform

This filter is takes the Basic 3D idea and expands on it, including more controls to fine-tune an animated 3D planar sequence (see Figure 9.16).

The following list shows some possible uses for the Transform effect:

- Keyframe animate exacting logo fly-ups with this filter.

- Use the Opacity control with keyframe animation settings from 0 to 100 to make your target layer appear out of the mist.

The following controls allow you to adjust the Transform filter's parameters:

- *Anchor Point and Position*—Normally, these two centroids are placed at the same position. They can be moved independently however, making positional animation easier.

- *Scale*—The Height and Width of the footage can be scaled separately. Its settings range from –30,000 to 30,000.

Figure 9.16
Left: Original footage. Center: Scaled at 50%, with a Skew of –30 on a Skew Axis of 35 degrees, and a Rotation of 45 degrees. Right: Same settings, with a Skew Axis of 90 degrees and a Rotation of –40.

- *Skew*—Skewing (with settings ranging from –70 to 70) causes the footage to rotate on the Z axis, and using the Skew Angle control (from 0 to 360 degrees) allows you to adjust the deformation caused by skewing.

- *Rotation*—This is also rotation (from 0 to 360 degrees) on the Z axis, taking whatever the Skew settings are into consideration.

- *Opacity*—You can control the Opacity (from 0 to 100 percent) of the targeted layer.

- *Shutter Angle*—Controls the angle of the Camera Shutter, or the viewing eye.

RENDER EFFECTS

10

This chapter concentrates on the filters in the Stylize directory of the Effects menu, which are included in your After Effects package. They include Brush Strokes, Color Emboss, Emboss, Find Edges, Leave Color, Mosaic, Noise, Scatter, Strobe Light, and Texturize.

Stylize: Brush Strokes

This effect adds a painterly look to your footage (see Figure 10.1).

The following are some possible uses for the Brush Strokes effect:

• Use this effect to add a random look to your footage.

• Use this effect on a background, so that foreground layers stand out.

These controls allow you to adjust the parameters of the Brush Strokes effect:

• *Brush Size*—The Brush Size settings determine the thickness of the brushed strokes. You can select a thickness from 0 to 5. The thicker the stroke, the more the image deteriorates.

> **Note: Be warned that this effect requires excessive rendering time and may not be worth the trouble for animated footage**

Figure 10.1
Left: Original footage. Center: A Brush Size of 4, Stroke Length of 20, Density of 2, and Paint Surface on the image. Right: A Brush Size of 5, Stroke Length of 40, Density of 2, and Paint Surface of paint on white.

- *Stroke Length/Density/Randomness*—Although the settings for stroke length range from 0 to 40, it is best left at 10 or lower to prevent overly long rendering times. Density is the visibility of the stroke on the footage. Its range is from 0 to 2. The Stroke Randomness settings (from 0 to 2) add a more painterly character to the footage at higher values.

- *Paint Surface*—Paint Surface options are Original Image, Transparent, White, and Black. Painting on the original image is the default for most cases. Using the other options tones down the visibility of the effect.

- *Blend With Original*—Leave this setting at 0 for the maximum effect.

Stylize: Color Emboss

This effect superimposes a cloned layer over the footage at an offset from the original. It's not a very pretty effect (see Figure 10.2).

Some uses for the Color Emboss effect include:

- Use it to add interest to an image layer.

- Animate the Contrast setting from 400 to 0, with Relief at 200. This produces an animation that starts with the colors separated into layers, and ends with the cohesive image.

The following controls allow you to adjust the Color Emboss effect:

- *Relief*—Relief sets the apparent depth of the effect. Although its settings can range from 0 to 1,000, it's best kept around 20.

- *Contrast*—Contrast sets the layered clone apart from the original. Its range of settings is from 0 to 32,767. At higher settings, it creates a complete separation of the apparent plates. It's best defaulted to about 50.

- *Blend With Original*—Leave this control set to 0 to maximize the effect.

Figure 10.2
Left: Original footage. Center: Relief settings of 10 and Contrast of 200. Right: Relief boosted to 200, resulting in a confusion of layers. High Contrast settings combined with high Relief settings create this result.

It's Boss

For an example of the Color Emboss effect, see the ColEmb animation on the companion CD-ROM. Relief is set to 30, and the Contrast setting moves from 1,200 to 0, revealing the unembossed footage.

Stylize: Emboss

 This is by far a better option than Color Emboss, and it can create carved-block effects (see Figure 10.3).

The following are some possible uses for the Emboss effect:

- Use the Emboss effect on moving footage, and you'll create an animated linoleum cut.
- Use Emboss on a text block to make it look carved into a surface. This is a great effect for titles.

The following controls allow you to adjust the Emboss effect's parameters:

- *Direction*—Use this radial dial to determine the direction of the shadows.
- *Relief*—Relief sets the apparent depth of the effect. Its settings range from 0 to 1,000, but are best kept around 20.
- *Contrast*—Contrast sets the layered clone apart from the original. Its range of settings is 0 to 32,767. At higher settings, it creates a complete separation of the apparent plates. It's best defaulted to about 50.
- *Blend With Original*—Leave this set to 0 to maximize the effect.

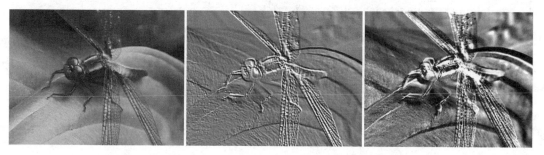

Figure 10.3
Left: Original footage. Center: Relief setting of 2 and Contrast of 200. Right: Relief boosted to 10.

Stylize: Find Edges

 This filter creates a stunning look that is reminiscent of a pencil or charcoal drawing (see Figure 10.4).

The following are some possible uses for the Find Edges effect:

- Use this effect to emulate pencil or ink drawings. Another option is to keyframe animate the Blend control from 100 to 0, which will cause the footage to go from photographic to graphic over time.
- Blend in the effect at 70 percent to add darken the outline of shapes that may be too light in the footage.

Figure 10.4
Left: The Find Edges effect with a Blend of 0. Center: Find Edges with Blend at 70%. Right: Find Edges with Blend at 0 and Invert checked on.

The following controls allow you to adjust the parameters of the Find Edges effect:

- *Invert*—This inverts the effect, producing negative imagery.

- *Blend With Original*—Leave this set to 0 to maximize the effect.

Stylize: Leave Color

 This has become a very popular commercial effect. It allows you to gray out everything but one selected color (see Figure 10.5).

The following are some possible uses for the Leave Color effect:

- This effect works best when your footage displays only a small amount of the color you want to leave, like someone holding a head of green lettuce with no other greens in the scene.

- Use this as an animated transition effect to pop out a text block that is in the color you want to leave. Everything else will suddenly gray out.

The following controls allow you to adjust the Leave Color effect:

- *Amount To Decolor*—This setting allows you to determine how grayscaled the rest of the footage will become. Its settings range from 0 to 100.

Figure 10.5
Left: The original footage. Right: Everything is grayed out but the orange in the trees.

- *Color To Leave*—Use the eyedropper to determine what color in the footage will be left untouched.

- *Tolerance*—Set the Tolerance value (in a range from 0 to 100) to determine how many associated hues will remain untouched.

- *Edge Softness*—Applying a softer edge makes the remaining color blend in better. Its settings range from 0 to 100, and you should explore the best value to use.

- *Match Colors*—You may select to base this operation on either the RGB or Hue value.

Stylize: Mosaic

 A mosaic is an array of blocks that hide the image content to some degree (see Figure 10.6).

The following are some possible uses for the Mosaic effect:

- Mosaic is a good effect to use when you want to animate an image being brought into, or moving away from, clarity. Just adjust the size of the blocks over time.

- Turn Sharp Colors on when you want to make the viewer suspect what the footage looks like. Turn it off to mute the view and make it more unrecognizable.

The following controls allow you to adjust the parameters of the Mosaic effect:

- *Horizontal Blocks/Vertical Blocks*—Settings for both of these controls have a range from 1 to 4,000. A setting of 1 creates a single color block, while 4,000 is far more than you need to show a clear image (unlocked). Usually, settings between 20 and 50 will show the mosaic at its best, but you have to explore the value to use dependent on the size of your footage.

- *Sharp Colors*—Use this option when you want to make each block stand out from the rest. When this option is off, the effect is muted and blurry.

Figure 10.6
Left: Horizontal and Vertical Blocks set to 75 with Sharp Colors on. Center: The same settings with Sharp Colors off. Right: Horizontal and Vertical Blocks set to 30 with Sharp Colors on.

Mo' Mosaic

Open the Mosaic file on the companion CD-ROM. The color blocks move from 0 to 300 and back to 0 in this example of the Mosaic effect.

Stylize: Motion Tile

This filter creates a tiled effect (see Figure 10.7).

The following are some possible uses for the Motion Tile effect:

- Keyframe animate the Width and Height from 100 to 0 to create an animation that moves from the original image to shrinking tiles to a gray screen.

- Use Mirror Edges to create kaleidoscopic animations.

These controls allow you to adjust the parameters of the Motion Tile effect:

- *Tile Center*—Use the centroid to place the center of the Tiling.

- *Tile Width and Height*—Set the Tile size, according to the width and height you require. (The settings range from 0 to 100.)

- *Output Width and Height*—This sets the Output Size (0 to 30,000).

- *Mirror Edges*—Check this option to create kaleidoscopic patterns.

- *Phase*—(0 to 360 degrees) Use this rotation control to set the amount of Phase Shift.

- *Horizontal Phase Shift*—Check this option to shift the image data horizontally, as set in the Phase dial.

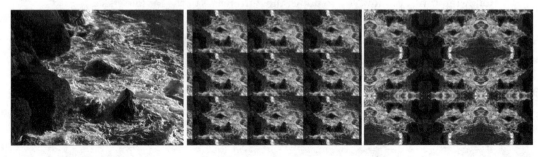

Figure 10.7
Left: Original footage. Center: Width and Height set to 31. Right: Same settings, with Mirror Edges checked on.

Stylize: Noise

Noise can make your footage look like a pointillist painting, or like a chaotic cloud of dots (see Figure 10.8).

The following are some possible uses for the Noise effect:

- Use noise with Clipping on to create an effect that simulates a stippled painting.

- Use noise with Clipping off to create an animation that moves from clarity to chaotic dots, or vice versa.

Figure 10.8
Left: Clipping on, with the Amount of Noise set to 30. Center: Clipping off, with the Amount of Noise set to 30. Right: Clipping on with the Amount of Noise set to 100.

The following controls allow you to adjust the Noise effect's parameters:

- *Amount Of Noise*—The Amount setting (in a range from 0 to 100) determines the quantity of noise in the image. With Clipping on, this can be maximized. When Clipping is off, a setting of 50 will probably be your best high value.

- *Noise Type*—Color Noise is the default setting. With this option unchecked, the dots are black.

- *Clipping*—Leave Clipping on in most cases. With it off, the footage deteriorates into chaotic dots.

Stylize: PS Extrude

 The PS Extrude filter creates 3D zooming tiles (see Figure 10.9).

The following are some possible uses for the PS Extrude effect:

- Keyframe animate the Depth Size (from 1 to 255) for an exploding 3D tiled zoom.

- Keyframe animate the Block Size (from 2 to 255) while the Depth is keyframe animated from 100 to 1. The result is an animation that resolves from chaos to coherency, using 3D tiles.

Figure 10.9
Left: Original footage. Center: Block Size of 42 and Depth of 40. Right: Block Size 20 and Depth of 200.

These controls allow you to adjust the parameters of the PS Extrude effect:

- *Block Size*—(parameters range from 2 to 255) A value of 255 creates a block as large as the original footage, while setting the value to 1 creates the tiniest block.

- *Depth*—The 3D depth of the tiles is controlled here, in a range from 1 to 255.

- *Blend With Original*—This controls the mix of the effect footage with the original source footage. The settings range from 0 to 100.

Stylize: PS Tiles

 This is a Photoshop filter that breaks the footage up into tiled columns and rows (see Figure 10.10).

The following are some possible uses for the PS Tiles effect:

- Use this filter to give footage the look of a mosaic construction.

- Keyframe animate the Number Of Tiles from 1 to 99 to break up the footage.

These controls allow you to adjust the parameters of the PS Tiles effect:

- *Foreground Color*—This is the color used for the spaces in between the tiles, selected with the eyedropper or the system palette.

- *Number Of Tiles*—The larger the number (in a range from 1 to 99), the larger the tiles.

- *Maximum Offset*—The Offset value (from 1 to 90) adds a scattered randomness to the tiles.

Figure 10.10
Left: Original footage. Center: Number Of Tiles = 10 and Maximum Offset = 10. Right: Number Of Tiles = 35 and Maximum Offset = 30.

Stylize: Strobe Light

 It's disco time! Use this animation effect to generate a flashing strobe that illuminates your footage (see Figure 10.11).

The following are some possible uses for the Strobe Light effect:

- Use a Xor Strobe operator to generate a posterized image each time the strobe goes off.

- Use a Subtract Strobe operator to create a dark strobe effect.

THE DANGERS OF STROBE USE

Use this effect sparingly because strobe lights can be annoying. The effect may also be dangerous for epileptics (it can cause seizures), so try to place a warning about the Strobe effect in your presentation.

The following controls allow you to adjust the parameters of the Strobe Light effect:

- *Strobe Color*—Select any color you like for your Strobe Light effect. The color only tints the image with some operators.

- *Blend With Original*—Select 0 to get the full effect, or values higher than 0 to mute the effect.

- *Strobe Duration and Period*—The Duration setting (in a range from 0 to 32,000) sets the amount of time the strobe remains activated. The Period setting determines the time lag between flashes. This setting also ranges from 0 to 32,000.

- *Random*—This setting introduces a random factor into the effect. Its range is from 0 to 100.

- *Strobe Type*—The two options are Operates On Color Only and Makes Layer Transparent. If the layer is transparent, the composition will display the underlying footage each time the strobe goes off. If you're operating on the color, then the footage will display whatever operator is applied.

- *Strobe Operator*—Explore the looks of these 13 operators to see which is best for your purposes.

Note: You have to move the Time slider to a place on the timeline where the strobe is active to see the results of the operator.

Figure 10.11
Left: A Difference Strobe operator. Center: A Darker Strobe operator. Right: An Xor Strobe operator.

A Strobe Of Genius

In the Strobe animation on the companion CD-ROM, Duration is set to 0.15 and Period to 0.45. The Xor operator was used.

Stylize: Texturize

This filter embosses another selected layer over the footage (see Figure 10.12).

The following are some possible uses for the Texturize effect:

- This effect works well when you want to emboss a logo on the footage.
- Use this effect to animate an embossed footage on an unmoving image.

> **Note: If you use the same layer for both the footage and the texture layer, the footage will look embossed on its own.**

The following controls allow you to adjust the Texturize effect:

- *Texture Layer*—Select any layer in the stack as your texture.
- *Light Direction*—Use the radial dial to set the lights and shadows.
- *Texture Contrast*—This control sets the apparent depth of the texture. Its settings can range between 0 and 2.
- *Texture Placement*—If the texture layer is a different size than the footage, you can tile it, center it, or stretch it to fit.

Figure 10.12
Left: The original footage. Center: The texture Layer. Right: The result of texturizing with a Contrast setting of 2.

Superimposing Texture

The Texturize effect can create interesting superimpositions of footage, as demonstrated in the Txtrizer animation on the companion CD-ROM.

Stylize: Write On

This filter allows you to "write" on a selected layer over the footage (see Figure 10.13).

The following are some possible uses for the Write On effect:

- Write a text line on the footage.
- Draw an arrow on the footage that points to an element of interest.

Figure 10.13
Left: Original footage. Center: Animated text written using the Write On effect. Right: An arrow drawn with the Write On filter.

These controls allow you to adjust the parameters of the Write On effect:

- *Brush Position*—Place the centroid where the brush stroke is to be at that particular frame.
- *Color*—Select the Color with the eyedropper or the system palette. Note that this can be keyframe animated to produce a brush stroke that blends multiple colors over time.
- *Brush Size*—Measured in pixels, with settings ranging from 0 to 50.
- *Brush Hardness*—Hardness values (from 0 to 100 percent) determine the fuzziness of the edge of the stroke. The lower the value, the softer the edge.
- *Brush Opacity*—You can create semi-transparent brushes (in a range from 0 to 100 percent) by selecting Opacity values below 100%.
- *Brush Stroke Length*—You will have to explore the best setting for your footage. Its values range from 0 to 3,000. Lower values create a line whose starting strokes start to disappear as the animation progresses, while higher values make strokes that decay less.
- *Brush Spacing*—Higher values create strokes that are segmented into smaller strokes (values range from 0.001 to 3,000). Explore what looks best for your footage.

Render: Beam

The Beam can suffice for a beam of light, or a solid stroke (see Figure 10.14).

The following are some possible uses for the Beam effect:

- Creating laser rays shooting from one object to another.
- Creating a spotlight by setting Softness to 50, with a Beam sized small at the start to large at the end.

These controls allow you to adjust the parameters of the Beam effect:

- *Starting and Ending Points*—Place the centroids anywhere you want to on the layer.
- *Length*—Adjust the length (from 0 to 100 percent) as needed for your project.
- *Time*—Keyframe animate this setting (from 0 to 100 percent) to create a Beam that is generated over time.

Figure 10.14
Left: Original footage. Center: A beam starts at an object small and ends at another place in the footage wider. Right: A Beam with an ending Width of 450 can be generated with no Softness, creating a more solid construct.

- *Starting and Ending Thickness*—These controls allow you to shape the size (from 0 to 4,000) and form of the Beam.

- *Softness*—This control has a setting from 0 to 100 percent. Use 100% Softness to blend the Beam into the background. Lower settings create harder-edged Beams.

- *Inside/Outside Colors*—Use the eyedropper or system palette to set the Beam's colors.

- *3D Perspective*—When checked, the Beam is created facing the supposed 3D camera pointing into the screen.

- *Composite On Original*—There is no percentage of blend here, but simply a yes-or-no option.

Render: Ellipse

This filter creates an Ellipse (see Figure 10.15).

The following are some possible uses for the Ellipse effect:

- Creating an oval that highlights an area you want to emphasize.

- Generating an exploding nova ring by keyframe animating the sizes from 0 to 500.

Figure 10.15
Left: Original footage. Center: An Ellipse with a Width and Height of 180 and a Thickness of 50 is overprinted on the footage layer. Right: A Size of 440 and a Thickness of 500 creates a glowing arc.

These controls allow you to adjust the parameters of the Ellipse effect:

- *Center*—Place the centroid anywhere you want to on the layer.
- *Width and Height*—These controls (with settings ranging from 0 to 2,000) alter the size and shape of the Ellipse.
- *Thickness*—Set the thickness of the Ellipse from 0 to 1,000. Values over 200 tend to fog out the content.
- *Softness*—This control's settings range from 0 to 100 percent. Use a Softness of 100% to blend the Ellipse into the background. Lower settings create harder edged Ellipses.
- *Inside/Outside Colors*—Use the eyedropper or system palette to set the Ellipse's colors.
- *Composite On Original*—Select this option to place the Ellipse over the footage content.

Render: Fill

 This effect is applied to a mask layer to create transparent feathered areas (see Figure 10.16).

The following are some possible uses for the Fill effect:

- Creating opacity maps for any mask layer.
- Using a keyframe-animated feathering to bring the footage content into or out of a fog.

These controls allow you to adjust the parameters of the Fill effect:

- *Fill Mask*—Select the Mask layer to address.
- *Color*—Select the Color of the Mask layer.
- *Horizontal and Vertical Feathering*—Feather the mask either or both Horizontally and Vertically, to create transparency. These two controls' settings range from 0 to 999.

Figure 10.16
Left: Original footage. Center: A solid mask is created and placed over the footage. Right: The Fill effect, with a Horizontal and Vertical Feathering of 555, is applied.

Render: Ramp

 A ramp is a graduated tone, or a blend between two colors. Ramps are of two general types—linear and radial—and can be used on any layer, including the Alpha layer (see Figure 11.17).

Some possible uses for the Ramp effect include:

- Create a radial color ramp between any selected colors. Animate the Scatter setting from 0 at the start to 512 at the end to generate an interesting explosion.

- Use a linear ramp that ranges from dark blue at the bottom to light blue at the top (or the reverse) for graduated sky backdrops.

The following controls allow you to adjust the parameters of the Ramp effect:

- *Start/End Ramp Placement*—Use the crosshairs to place the start and end of the ramp. Wider settings produce better gradated tones.

- *Start/End Ramp Color*—If you are targeting an Alpha layer, select black/white or white/ black as the colors. If you are creating a color layer, select any two colors.

- *Ramp Shape*—Select either Linear or Radial. Linear ramps produce nice effects like horizons and skies, while radial ramps produce graduated bursts.

- *Ramp Scatter*—With a range of 0 to 512, you can control the pixelization of a ramp. Higher settings disperse the pixels more.

- *Blend With Original*—You may select to display nothing but the ramp layer (0 percent), to hide the ramp layer completely (100 percent), or anything in between these two extremes.

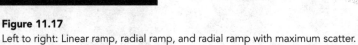

Figure 11.17
Left to right: Linear ramp, radial ramp, and radial ramp with maximum scatter.

Animated Radial Ramping Burst

To create a graduated radial layer, do the following:

1. With After Effects open, go to the Layers menu. Create a new solid color layer.

2. Open the Ramp filter in the Effects menu.

3. Select your start and end colors from the System Palette by clicking on the appropriate swatches in the Ramp dialog box. They can be any two colors you like.

4. Select Radial Ramp from the Ramp Shape list.

5. Use a Ramp Scatter setting of 222, which adds a pixelated look to the radial burst, and leave the Blend With Original value at zero.

6. Keyframe animate the End of Ramp centroid so that it is on top of the Start Of Ramp centroid for your first frame, and as far away from it as possible, but within the bounds of the Composition window, for your last frame.

Render the animation, and save to disk. You have created an exploding burst using the Ramp filter.

Render: Stroke

 This filter creates a border around either a selected path or a mask layer (see Figure 10.18).

The following are some possible uses for the Stroke effect:

- Add a border to a path that encloses an area of interest.
- Add a border around a mask layer to pop it out.

These controls allow you to adjust the parameters of the Stroke effect:

- *Path*—Select either an Illustrator path or a Mask layer for the border.
- *Color*—Select the color of the border with the eyedropper or from the system palette.
- *Brush Size*—(0 to 50) Select the size of the brush according to the look you need.
- *Brush Hardness*—The softer the brush (0 percent), the lower this value, up to 100 percent. Soft brushes blend into the footage.
- *Opacity*—The border can fade into the footage at lower values. (The settings range from 0 to 100 percent).

Figure 10.18
Left: Original footage. Center: A new Mask layer is placed over the original content. Right: The Stroke filter is used to generate a border around the masked area.

- *Spacing*—The higher this value (from 0 to 100), the more space between the circular strokes that make up the border.

- *Paint On*—Select from Original Layer or Transparent. Transparent causes the original content to remain invisible.

TEXT AND TIME

INTERNAL EFFECTS:

The following internal After Effects filters are covered in this chapter: Basic Text, Numbers, Path Text, Time Echo, and Posterize Time. All of these give you the power to play with text and time.

This chapter presents a close look at two areas of After Effects internal effects filters. You can use these effects to generate and manipulate text and number blocks, to use paths to animate text, and employ various filters to alter time itself—well, to manipulate the representation of time within footage.

Basic Text

This very useful filter allows you to generate text blocks (see Figure 11.1).

Some possible uses for the Basic Text effect are:

- Creating footage with subtitles for the hearing impaired.

- Create an animation that starts with the text size at maximum and ends with it at the right size for viewing. The text will seem to fly into the footage.

> **Note: When you first access this filter, a dialog box allows you to enter the text and select among the style options for its display. You can alter these settings anytime by selecting the Options command in the Effect dialog box.**

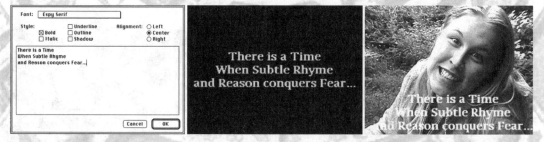

Figure 11.1
Left: The Basic Text dialog box. Center: Text with Ccompositing off. Right: Text with Compositing on.

The following controls allow you to adjust the parameters of the Basic Text effect:

- *Size*—The size can be set from 0 to 512. Select the size that best fits the footage or composition area.

- *Position*—Place the crosshairs to control the horizontal and vertical placement of the text.

- *Text Color*—Select any color for the displayed text.

- *Composite Over Original*—With this option unchecked, your text will be displayed on a black backdrop. When it is checked, the text will be displayed over the selected footage layer.

Numbers

 This is the filter to use if you need to display number blocks of any type, from dates to timecodes to basic number data (see Figure 11.2). You can do a number of useful things with numbers, including:

- Time your footage exactly. Select the Timecode type (normally, the Timecode 30 selection). Set the Timecode at 0 at the start frame. Move the Timeline Slider to the last frame and read the Timecode numbers.

- If you want to be reminded of the current time, here's a trick. Open a new composition window, reduce it, and place it on the side of the display area. Select the Time type, and set the offset to 0. The display now shows the exact time as indicated by your computer's clock. Size the display so that you notice it at a glance.

The following controls allow you to adjust the settings for the Number effect:

- *Type*—Select the type of number display you need. The options are: Number, Number With Leading Zeros, Timecode (30, 25, and 24), Time, Numerical Date, Short Date, Long Date, and Hexadecimal.

- *Random Values*—With this control, you can randomize the numerical data when set.

- *Value Offset*—Increment or decrement the numerical settings (from –30,000 to +30,000 units).

Figure 11.2
The following number styles are displayed on an overlay layer, from left to right: Timecode, Long Date, and Short Date.

- *Decimal Places*—Set the number of decimal places you want.

- *Size*—Determine the vertical size of the number set (0 to 512). Use a size that is best suited to your footage.

- *Position*—Place the crosshair to determine the center of the number block.

- *Text Color*—Select any color for the number block you need.

- *Composite On Original*—Check this option to display your numbers over the selected footage layer. With this option unchecked, your numbers will be displayed on a black background.

Path Text

Using this filter, you can add lines of text assigned to a path (see Figure 11.3). You can do a number of useful things with the Path Text filter, including:

- Creating wiggly animated text simply by keyframe animating the path by moving the control points.

- Placing a text line around a circular area.

The following controls allow you to adjust the settings for the Path Text effect:

- *Shape Type*—Select from Bézier, Circle, Loop, and Line. You can change the Type at any time and preview what it looks like. You should not keyframe animate this setting because the text will simply snap to the new Type when the keyframe is reached.

- *Information*—The data is updated as you create new parameters.

- *Path Control Points*—Place the centroids to determine the path shape, although it's easier to simply move them in the Composition window.

- *Path*—Select any path in the stack. This item is useful after you import a path from Illustrator or Photoshop.

- *Margins*—Keyframe animating the left and/or right margins (in a range from –30,000 to 30,000) allows you to fly the text across the screen horizontally.

Figure 11.3
Left: The Path Text dialog allows you to select the font and input the data. Center: The Bézier path option allows you to edit the curved path. Right: Text can also be placed on a line.

- *Alignment*—The options are Left, Right, Center, and Force. The Force option makes the text adhere to the entire path, just as justified text in a DTP application.

- *Tracking*—Sets the Tracking values, in a range from –8,000 to 8,000.

- *Kerning*—Allows you to set all the Kerning Pairs in thousandths of an em, so the text reads more clearly and appears more balanced. If you have no experience doing this, don't wait for a rush project to learn it. Explore kerning beforehand in a DTP application such as PageMaker.

- *Baseline Shift*—Allows you to shift the text baseline by discreet amounts (–8,000 to 8,000).

- *Character Rotation*—This is a great keyframe animation option. Rotate each of the characters on the text path by any amount (from 0 to 360 degrees) you desire.

- *Perpendicular To Path*—If this option is unchecked, all the characters in the text will be parallel to the first character.

- *Vertical Writing*—Check this option to force the characters in the text to be written vertically to the Path.

- *Horizontal Shear*—(–70 to 70) This control adds obliqueness to the characters, like that created in italics.

- *Size*—Change the global size (in settings that range from 0 to 1,024) of the text block.

- *Horizontal/Vertical Scale*—Use these controls to create condensed and expanded type styles. The settings for these controls range from 0 to 2,000.

- *Visible Characters*—At a value of zero (the settings range from –1,024 to 1,024), which allows the text to be invisible on every frame. At higher or lower settings, the text appears either left to right (positive values) or right to left (negative values) when keyframe animated. Exactly what values are to be used to create the text letter by letter depends on your specific project and must be explored each time.

- *Fade Time*—A setting of 0 (the settings range from 0 to 100) makes each letter of the text pop into view, while higher values allow the text characters to fade up slowly. The smoothest fades occur when this value is set to 100.

- *Mode*—The options are Normal and Difference. Normal is the default; Difference blends the text with the footage layer (if the Composite On Original option is checked).

- *Text Color*—Select any color for the text. Keyframe animate this setting to create text that changes color over time.

- *Composite On Original*—Check this option to show the text overlaid on the source footage.

- *Jitter*—Automatically add animated Jitter to the Baseline (in a range from –2,000 to 2,000), Kerning (–2,000 to 2,000), Rotation (0 to 360 degrees), and Scale (–500 to 500) factors.

Time Echo

Time Echo is a filter that helps you create multiple composites that can be spectacular and dreamlike (see Figure 11.4). Some ethereal effects you can make include:

- Creating *out of body* footage with this filter. Select footage that shows a person lying in a bed and slowly rising. Applying a time echo will superimpose the rising figure over the figure lying down.

- Using this effect on a text block to create a hallucinogenic title sequence.

The following controls allow you to adjust the Time Echo effect:

- *Echo Time*—This control specifies the time in seconds (–30,000 to +30,000) that echo samples are taken from.

- *Number of Echoes*—With this control, you can specify the number of frames (0 to 30,000) in the echo effect.

- *Starting Intensity*—This control sets the opacity (0 to 1) of the starting frame in the echo sequence.

- *Decay*—You can set the ratio of intensity value (0 to 100) for subsequent time echoes. The default is 1.

- *Echo Operator*—This control sets the type of composite being applied: Add, Maximum, Minimum, and Screen. Composite in Front or Back can be used on a footage Alpha channel.

Figure 11.4
Left to right: Starting footage, composited with Maximum type, and composited with Screen type.

Dream Time

The Timecho file on the companion CD-ROM displays a truly spectacular effect. Here, the Time Echo filter is used to create dreamlike footage. This animation displays a Maximum Time Echo type.

In Timecho2, a variation of the Time Echo effect was created by animating all the parameter settings and selecting the Screen type.

Posterize Time

 This filter creates a strobe effect on the selected animated footage. You can use the Posterize Time effect to:

- Achieve slow-motion and fast-motion effects.

- Create old-time movie effects by using a fast frame rate (60 and above).

> **Note: It doesn't make any sense to show images from Posterize Time footage, because this is an animation effect. It is best appreciated by viewing the Ptime 1 and 2 animations in the Animations folder of this book's CD-ROM.**

You can adjust the parameters of the Posterize Time effect with the Frame Rate control (in a range from 0 to 99), which sets the new frame rate to the selected footage in frames per second. Fast frame rates show more footage in the allotted time, while slow frame rates show less.

Ptime 1

For a sample of the Posterize Time effect applied at a setting of 10, see Ptime 1 on the companion CD-ROM. Then look at Ptime 2 for the same footage at a setting of 99.

> **Note: The footage used in these Posterize Time animations are from ArtBeats' REEL Explosions collection.**

ANIMATIONS, AND TEXT EFFECTS

TRANSITIONS, VIDEO OPTIONS, GIF

This chapter covers the following internal After Effects filters: Transitions (Block Dissolve, Gradient Wipe, Linear Wipe, Radial Wipe, and Venetian Blinds), Video Options (Broadcast Colors, Reduce Interlace Flicker, and Timecode), Text Effects, and GIF Export. Transitions are useful in segues from one sequence of footage to another. The video options are vital if you plan to use your output in a broadcast TV medium. The Text and GIF options add further usefulness to After Effects output designed for use on the Web.

Internal Transition Effects

Transitional wipes (Block Dissolve, Gradient Wipe, Linear Wipe, Radial Wipe, and Venetian Blinds) take you from one footage layer to the next in an animated sequence (see Figure 12.1). Some possible uses for the Transition effects include the following:

- Use the Radial transition with both Clockwise and Counterclockwise options on, and a maximum feathering, for one of the softest possible reveals between layers.

- Use the Venetian Blinds transition with a steady width of 40 and a vertical direction of 0 to place your footage "behind bars."

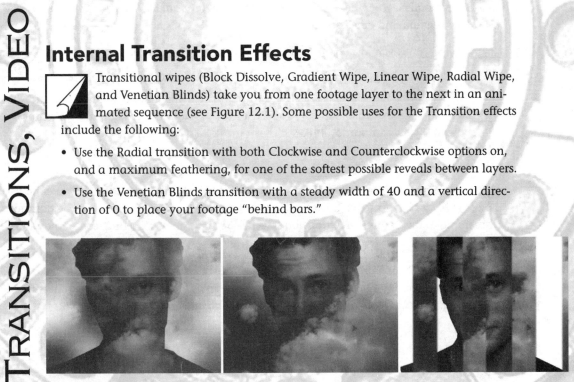

Figure 12.1
Example frames from the following transition, from left to right: Block Dissolve, Radial Wipe, Venetian Blinds.

All of the transitions have the same basic controls for creating a wipe that reveals either the layer below the selected layer, or a layer in the stack that you can select. The one parameter worth mentioning specifically is the Feather option. Add feathering when you want the effect to be subtler, revealing the target layer with a softer look.

Making The Transition

The files on this book's companion CD-ROM provide examples of the following:

- The Block Dissolve transition; Blkdslv.

- An example of an inverted Gradient Wipe transition; GradWipe.

- An example of a Radial Wipe transition that moves both clockwise and counterclockwise at the same time; RadWipe.

- An example of the Venetian Blind transition, with Width and Feather keyframed; VnBlind.

Broadcast Colors

You can adjust your video color display with this filter, which is especially useful for broadcast displays. Use this filter as needed to adjust the signal for a video display. Until digital video supplants NTSC broadcast standards, it is essential that video color displays be modified when needed to tone down colors that are too "hot" (saturated) or they will cause bleeding and other anomalies.

The following controls allow you to adjust the Broadcast Colors effect:

- *Broadcast Locale*—Select either NTSC or PAL. (The SECAM standard is not represented.)

- *How To Make Color Safe*—This list displays ways in which you can adjust the amplitude of the footage to make it color safe for broadcast transmission: Reduce Luminance (reduces brightness); Reduce Saturation (takes some of the color "edge" off the colors); Key Out Unsafe (makes unsafe colors transparent, so use with care); and Key Out Safe (good for a preview of what is left over).

- *Maximum Signal*—This control allows you to adjust the IRE level boundary for pixel adjustment (100 to 120). Any pixels that fall within a range above your setting will be adjusted according to the Color Safe option you selected. Settings above 110 may cause anomalies.

Reduce Interlace Flicker

Use this filter to reduce the flicker that is sometimes observed when the signal is interlaced, especially when the footage contains a lot of thin horizontal lines.

This effect has only one control. The Softness control (0 to 1,000) allows you to soften the edges of horizontal lines in the display, which makes the lines less likely to cause flickering when broadcast.

Warning! Do not use this filter to deinterlace a signal (separate its dual fields).

Use Reduce Interlace Flicker whenever your footage contains too many horizontal lines, and you observe them flickering in a video transmission. This is especially useful if your footage contains charts and graphs with a lot of horizontal content.

Timecode

When all you need is Timecode—and not other, more extensive numeric options—this is a good option in place of the Numbers filter.

The following controls allow you to adjust the Timecode effect:

- *Mode*—You can choose to display the current timecode, display the encoded timecode (if the footage already contains a timecode stripe), encode the current timecode (if the footage has already been timecoded), or encode and display the current timecode.

- *Display Format*—Select from either SMPTE (HH:MM:SS:FF), or Frame Numbers. Note that the SMPTE option is not as full-featured as that offered in the SMPTE options in the Numbers filter.

- *Time Units*—Set your frames-per-second rate here. (This will typically be 30, but it may vary depending on your footage.)

- *Starting Frame*—This control (–100,000 to +100,000) is usually set to 0 as the starting frame, but you can set it to a wide range of numbers to help you stitch things together in the edit room.

- *Text Position*—This crosshair sets the upper-left-corner position of the timecode display.

- *Text Size*—Change the timecode display size to whatever you need; settings between 20 and 30 are the most common.

- *Text Color*—Display the timecode in any color you want. It will always be displayed on a black rectangular background.

> **Note: If you save the Timecode information with the footage, do not use any distortion or compression on the footage. Doing so will destroy the Timecode data, which is stored on the blue channel in the bottom row of pixels.**

GIF Animation Saves

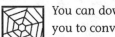

You can download this free internal export filter from the Adobe Web site. It allows you to convert your After Effects animations to GIF format for Web display.

To access this filter, make a movie. (Choose Make Movie in the Composition menu.) After the Render dialog box appears, select the Custom option from the Output Module list. Select GIF Animation when the Custom Rendering dialog box appears—and then Format Options—and you'll see the GIF Animation options dialog box (see Figure 12.2).

You can use this output type when you want to display your After Effects work on the Web.

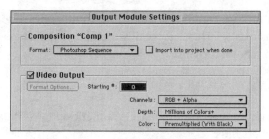 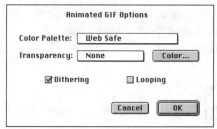

Figure 12.2
After accessing the Custom Rendering dialog box (on the left), select GIF Animation, then click on the Format Options button. The Animated GIF Options dialog box will appear (right).

Note: Your footage must have a 256-color palette for GIF animations to display on the Web.

Use the following controls to adjust the GIF Animations parameters:

- *Color Palette*—Always set this to the Web Safe option, so that both Mac and IBM-compatible PC users will view the same animation colors when the movie is posted to the Web.

- *Transparency*—If your movie has a single-color background, turn on Transparency and select the background color as a dropout color. This looks nicer on a Web display than a single-color background because it shows the Web page itself as the background. If you have a cartoon-like content, select Hard Edge; if the content is more photographic, select Soft Edge.

- *Dithering*—If your footage is photographic, select Dithering On, since that allows an emulation of a larger palette display. Dithering does have some problems, because its larger file size leads to slower display on the Web. Flickering may also result if the animation has a lot of movement. Explore different settings and view the results.

- *Looping*—It's a good idea to leave this option selected. Otherwise, your Web GIF animation will just play once.

Text On A Path

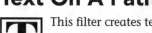 This filter creates text that can be curved on a path. It's free and can be downloaded from the Adobe Web site. (See Figure 12.3 for an example of this filter's effect.)

The following are some possible uses for the Text On A Path effect:

- Set the Jitter rate for both Size and Rotation to 300 at the start of an animation, and 0 at the end to create a text block that shudders like Jell-O at the start, and stabilizes at the end.

- Animate Horizontal and Vertical Size from 0 to the sizes you want, and watch as the text grows from invisible to your desired size.

Figure 12.3
Left to right: Text in a circle, text on a Bézier path with Perpendicular off, and text on a line with Rotation and Scale jittered.

You can adjust the Text On A Path filter with the following controls:

- *Shape Type*—You can select to have your text on a configurable Bézier path or a circle, loop, or line.

- *Margins*—Set the left and right margins (–30,000 to +30,000) to move the text away from the edges by that number of pixels. Use this control to center your text, and to keep it away from overprinting important parts of the footage.

- *Alignment*—You can set the alignment as Left, Right, Center, or Forced. Forced Alignment forces the text to obey the left and right margin settings.

- *Tracking*—This value (–8,000 to +8,000) specifies the distance in pixels between text characters after kerning is applied.

- *Kerning*—Some pairs of letters (such as an uppercase "T" followed by a lowercase "o") need to be kerned—moved closer or farther apart so the spacing looks right. This tool does just that.

- *Baseline Shift*—The text path is usually the imaginary line on which characters in your text sit. Shifting the baseline moves the text either above or below that imaginary line.

- *Character Rotation*—Setting this radial angle adjusts the angle of each character in the text. You can select to have the characters remain perpendicular to the path or not.

- *Horizontal Shear*—Adjusting this angle adds an italic look to the text.

- *Size*—The size of the text (0 to 1,024) is determined by the size of your composition, and can be adjusted. Large non-Postscript or non-TrueType font sizes show the aliasing (jaggedness) of the characters.

- *Horizontal and Vertical Scale*—These controls allow you to stretch the text block vertically and horizontally, so that the text fits the composition more naturally.

- *Visible Characters*—If you select 0, your text block will disappear. Adjusting the value higher allows just a portion of the right-hand text to become visible. Adjusting the value lower forces the characters to become visible from right to left.

- *Fade Time*—The Fade Time control (0 to 100) is tied to the Visible Characters control. Selecting no fade time makes a character become visible instantly. With various fade times set, the character fades into visibility.

- *Mode*—Two options exist for the Mode control—Normal and Difference. Sometimes, characters in a text block can overlap. With Normal Mode selected, the overlapping characters maintain their color setting. With Difference selected, the parts of a character that overlap are colored black.

- *Text Color*—With this control, you can select any color for your text block.

- *Composite On Original*—With this unchecked, your background is black. With it checked, the text is composited over your footage.

- *Tangents and Vertex*—You can alter the shape of your curved baselines using these four crosshairs. It takes a little practice to master their placement.

- *Jitters*—Jittering adds a randomness to the selected parameter. You can jitter the baseline, kerning, rotation, and scale. Apply a little jittering to alter the mechanical look of a text block when needed.

> *Note: Whenever you access the Option command in the Effects dialog box, you bring up the Message dialog box. This allows you to select another font or style, or to alter your text message.*

The Path To Text Success

The Text On A Path filter was used to create the Txtpath1 animation on the companion CD-ROM. Jitter Size and Rotation were set to 222 at the start and 0 at the end. Vertical Size ranged from 50 to 30.

In Txtpath2, the Horizontal and Vertical Sizes were keyframed from 0 to their final sizes. A little change of color and rotation jitter was added for interest.

PART III

PRODUCTION

BUNDLES

MOTION PACK

This is the first of three chapters that detail the contents of the After Effects production bundles. The production bundles consist of three effects volumes sold separately by Adobe: the Motion pack, the Keying and Matte Tools pack, and the Distortion pack. Each of the Production Bundles is loaded with a vast array of options that no professional After Effects user will want to be without.

The following production bundle After Effects filters are covered in this chapter and are listed as Keyframe Assistants under the Layer menu: Motion Math, Smoother, Wiggler, Easy Ease, and Motion Sketch.

Motion Math

 Motion Math uses its own prioritized programming language and mathematical algorithms to create scripts that automatically generate keyframed animations. Learning Motion Math can be slow, but—once you master it—you can save much time when creating very complex animations. Unless you are an experienced C programmer (the C language is similar to the Motion Math language), the best way to learn Motion Math is to load the sample scripts, run them, and then alter some of the variables to preview what happens. Selecting Motion Math from the Layer|Keyframe Assistants command brings up the initial Motion Math dialog box (see Figure 13.1).

To work with the Motion Math effect:

• Use the Gravity Motion Math script when you want a layer to fall to the bottom of the composition with a bounce at the end.

• Use the Spring script to tie layers together as one moves in relation to the other.

The Script Editor

This area is where the script is assembled. If a script is loaded, it's loaded into this area of the Motion Math interface. Sample scripts are located in the MMScript folder in the After Effects folder on Windows systems, or in the Sample Motion Math Scripts folder in the After Effects folder on the Macintosh (see Figure 13.2).

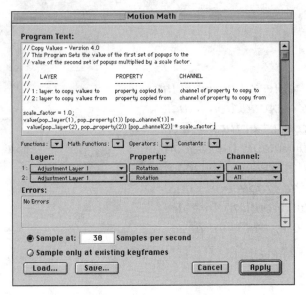

Figure 13.1
The Motion Math Keyframe Assistant dialog box.

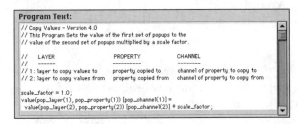

Figure 13.2
The Script Editing area in the Motion Math dialog box.

Language Element Pop-Up Menus

Using the functions and other elements in these pop-up menu selections, you can insert commands and variables in your scripts. See the Production Pack documentation, pages 68 to 72, for a detailed description of all of the elements contained in these pop-ups (see Figure 13.3).

Figure 13.3
The Language Element pop-up menus.

Substitution Pop-Up Menus

Select the layer(s) that you want to target, the properties (opacity, rotation, position, anchor point, size, and more) that you want to alter with the script, and the channels that are targeted for selection. These items will define what the script operates on. Motion Math also displays any errors it encounters when it runs a script on your targeted footage layers (see Figure 13.4).

Figure 13.4
Select the layer, property, and channel that will receive the scripted operators.

Sample, Load/Save, And Apply

The Sample input area allows you to tell the Motion Math script how many keyframes it should create. The default is 30, but you'll want to keep this to a maximum of 10 in most cases. Load/Save operations allow you to import any previously saved script (like the included examples), and to save out your own customized favorites. The Apply button is the last step, and you'll use it to apply the Motion Math script to your composition (see Figure 13.5).

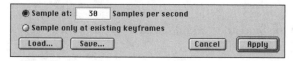

Figure 13.5
The Sample, Load/Save, and Apply controls in the Motion Math dialog box.

Realtime Interactive Editing Of The Motion Math Script

After a script is applied and you have previewed it, you may find that certain parameters need to be tweaked, in either a major or a minor way. At this point, either you may run Motion Math again to change elements of the script, or you can edit the animation in the composition window. Motion Math places a series of control points over your footage that can be moved interactively, resulting in a change in the animation. Use both the re-scripting and the interactive methods interchangeably, depending on your editing needs.

I Second That Motion

The MotMath1 file on the companion CD-ROM shows the Spring Motion Math script applied to position, while MotMath2 displays the Gravity Motion Math script applied to a layer.

Smoother

The Smoother is a keyframe assistant that removes excessive keyframes from an animation (see Figure 13.6).

If you used Motion Math to generate an animation and absentmindedly left the default sample rate set to 30, you will wind up with way too many keyframes in your animation. This isn't bad in itself, but it can lead to severe problems when you try to alter the position or another parameter of the keyframe. Instead of playing smoothly, the motion will jump at that point—which is where the Smoother keyframe assistant comes in handy. Just draw a marquee around all of the keyframes in the animation (except the first frame)

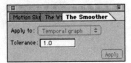

Figure 13.6
The Smoother dialog box.

until they are highlighted in the Time Layout window. Go to the Layer|Keyframe Assistants command to access the Smoother. In the dialog box that pops up, you will see a Tolerance input area. Set the Tolerance to any value you like, realizing that the higher the value, the more the curve of the action will be smoothed. Values set too high will severely redraw the keyframe curve. Select OK to apply Smoother, and a number of excessive keyframes on the motion curve will be removed.

Wiggler

The Wiggler does the opposite of the Smoother, adding randomly positioned keyframes to a selected motion curve (see Figure 13.7).

Figure 13.7
The Wiggler dialog box.

Using The Wiggler Keyframe Assistant

The Motion Math animation you produce may look too smooth and mechanical, so it may be time to call on the Wiggler. Just draw a marquee around any or all of the keyframes in the animation (except the first frame) until they are highlighted in the Time Layout window. Go to the Layer|Keyframe Assistants command to access the Wiggler. The Wiggler dialog box shows a number of options:

- *Apply To*—Select either Temporal Graph or Spatial Path, depending on the property that is addressed by the selected keyframes.

- *Dimension*—This allows you to apply the Wiggler to only one axis of the property (like size for the X value), independent of each other or in unison.

- *Frequency*—This control allows you to set the number of additional keyframes that will be added to the selected time range.

- *Magnitude*—This control sets the relative strength of the new effect produced by the Wiggler.

- *Noise Type*—Smooth Noise creates gradual changes, and Jagged Noise creates sudden changes between keyframes.

Wiggle And Jiggle

To create a randomized motion in your animation, do the following:

1. Place a graphic in the Composition window.

2. In the Timeline, go to the graphics Geometrics list. Activate the Position item, and move the graphic to different positions for a number of frames in your animation. You have created a motion path for the graphic to follow.

3. Using the mouse, encircle all of the keyframes on the timeline with a marquee. They will all indicate they are selected by changing to white in a black square.

4. Go to the Wiggler Keyframe Assistant in the Layer menu.

5. In the Wiggler dialog box, apply the following parameters: Apply To Spatial Path, All Dimensions Independently, Frequency 8, Magnitude 10, and Jagged.

Select OK, and notice that a large number of new keyframes have been inserted between each of your original keyframes. Preview the animation. If you need to change it, go back to the Wiggler Keyframe Assistant dialog box again. When satisfied with the movement, render the animation and save to disk.

Easy Ease

Eases are applied as soon as you access the command, with no dialog box for setting parameters.

You can use eases in all types of animation to make the global movement less mechanical and false. For instance, when a ball is dropped, it initially accelerates downward due to gravity. When a ball is tossed into the air, it rises, but eventually slows, stops, and then begins to accelerate downward. This acceleration and deceleration is what eases are all about.

To use Easy Ease, just draw a marquee around any or all of the keyframes in the animation (except the first frame) until they are highlighted in the Time Layout window. Go to the Easy Ease command, and this effect is automatically applied. Your keyframes are adjusted over time.

Motion Sketch

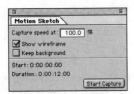

Draw your motion paths with Motion Sketch (see Figure 13.8. for the dialog box).

Motion Sketch is a lot easier to use than Motion Math when it comes to configuring a motion path, and it is especially geared toward visual users. You have to decide on four options in the Motion Sketch dialog box before you can sketch a path:

- *Show Wireframe*—I prefer to keep the wireframe of the selected layer invisible so I can concentrate more fully on the shape of the path. Of course, you may prefer having it visible.

- *Don't Erase Contents*—Checking this option leaves the image in the display. I dislike this in most cases because it creates confusion when drawing a path. However, in some cases—say, when you want to make sure that a certain part of the image is being targeted—you may want to check this option.

- *Preview Audio*—This option is useful because it shows you the amplitude of the audio track (if your footage has one). You can create paths that respond visually to the amplitude of the audio by checking this option.

- *Capture Motion At*—Whatever value you place in this input box, After Effects will adjust the recording speed of your drawing. A value of 1 is the default, making the recording of your drawing move at the same speed as the animation in frames per second. Selecting 2 would allow you to draw twice as fast as the current frame rate. I prefer a setting of 3 in most cases, so I can take a little more time getting the keyframes and motions where they are wanted.

Selecting the Start Capture option brings you back to the composition window. When you start to draw the path, the clock starts ticking, and the frame counter advances in the Time Layout window.

Figure 13.8
The Motion Sketch dialog box.

MotSktc1 And 2

These two Motion Sketch animations reveal two effects that this filter is capable of producing. Compare them, and notice how the movements vary. You can create an infinite number of motions for your graphic and animation layers by using this filter.

TOOLS PACK

14

This is the second of three chapters on the After Effects production bundles. Here, you'll explore effects that let you alter your footage content by changing color components and adjusting the Alpha layer.

The following After Effects production bundle filters are covered in this chapter: Color Difference Key, Color Key, Color Range, Difference Matte, Extract, Linear Color Key, Luma Key, Spill Suppressor, Alpha Levels, Matte Choker, and Simple Choker.

Color Difference Key

The Color Difference key creates an Alpha matte from two partial mattes. You can interactively alter either the partial matte or the Alpha matte (see Figure 14.1 and 14.2 for examples). Use this filter to create unique transparencies that are based on the creation and blending of three matte layers.

The following controls allow you to adjust the parameters of the Color Difference Key effect:

- *Eyedroppers and Channel Selectors*—As shown in Figure 14.1, the eyedroppers are used to darken and lighten areas of either the Partial A, Partial B, or Alpha matte channels of the image. (You select channels by clicking on the selectors beneath the preview.)

- *View*—Select any of the channels—or all four at the same time—for viewing in the Composition window.

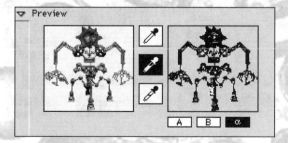

Figure 14.1
The three eyedroppers (combined with a fourth, which is out of view) allow you to darken and lighten either of the partial mattes or the Alpha matte itself to create a composited final image.

Figure 14.2
Left and center: Two different final composites based on variations in the matte sandwich. Right: All four views (both Partial mattes, the Alpha matte, and the Final composite) can be previewed at any time.

- *Key Color*—The Key Color control enables you to select a drop-out hue from the image in the Composition window.

- *Color Matching Accuracy*—Select either Fast or Accurate. So many variations are possible that the author suggests you leave this setting to Accurate.

- *Fine Tuning the Channels*—Adjust the Black, White, and Gamma setting for all three component channels for both In and Out options to fine-tune the transparencies until you achieve what you want.

Color Key

This isn't a production bundle filter, but it's included here because of similarity of use. This is the most basic key in After Effects, but also one of the most effective (see Figure 14.3). You can use the Color Key to do the following:

- Drop out a background color to reveal the layer behind the image.

- Drop out a color inside the image, play with the tolerance and feathering, and create a pattern inside the image.

Figure 14.3
Left: The cat's background is dropped out to reveal the flowers. Center: Feathering is increased to 88, so that the cat's edges fade into the flower layer. Right: The key color is selected from the cat's fur, and feathering is added. The result: The flower pattern is superimposed on the fur.

The following controls allow you to adjust the parameters of the Color Key effect:

- *Key Color*—Drop out any color in the image. By increasing the Tolerance setting, a range of colors is dropped out.

- *Color Tolerance*—If you set this control at 0, only the selected color drops out. Setting the control higher than 0 causes more colors to drop out the higher the value gets.

- *Edge Thin*—Explore the use of this control to remove any outlines from your image.

- *Edge Feather*—Feather the drop-out color to create transparent areas that blend more smoothly.

Color Range

Color Range allows you to create image transparencies by manipulating a range of color areas of the image (see Figure 14.4). You may also do the following:

- Animate the Fuzziness from 0 to 255 to create liquid transparent effects.

- Use different color ranges in an animation to create transparent movements between the foreground and background footage.

The following controls allow you to adjust the parameters of the Color Range effect:

- *Preview*—Use the eyedroppers to alter the transparent areas of the selected layer.

- *Fuzziness*—Fuzziness (0 to 255) can fade the entire layer or just a portion of it.

- *Color Space*—Select from LAB, YUV, or RGB. Each one reacts differently to the alterations in the color ranges.

- *Fine Tuning*—Use the Min/Max settings to fine-tune your transparent areas.

Interactive Color Range Keying

The best thing about using this filter is that it allows you to work interactively to create a complex dropout effect. To do so, take the following steps:

1. Import two content layers into the Composition window. The top layer will have part of its content made transparent so the lower layer will show through.

Figure 14.4
Left to right: A variety of image effects created with the Color Range filter.

2. Open the Color Range filter under the Keying/Effects menu.

3. All your work will be done by using the preview screen in the Color Range dialog box. Notice that three eyedropper icons appear in the dialog box. The first icon selects the initial color range, the second adds to it (with a plus sign), and the third subtracts from it (with a minus sign).

4. Click in the Preview image in the dialog box with the first eyedropper to indicate the initial color range that will be dropped out. Watch your Composition window for the results. Use the Fuzziness slider (0 to 200) to adjust the transparent area to increase or decrease. Moving the slider to the left decreases the selection; moving it right increases the range.

5. To add a different Color Range, use the eyedropper with the plus sign. To subtract a Color Range, use the eyedropper with the minus sign.

When your top layer shows just the right amount of transparency for the bottom layer to show through, render the image or animation, and save it to disk.

Fuzzy Range

By altering the fuzziness and the color ranges, the Color Range animation (ColRang on the companion CD-ROM) achieves a number of alternate transparency levels.

Difference Matte

  The Difference Matte control compares the Source and a Difference layer, and keys out pixels that are the same color and in the same position (see Figure 14.5). You can use it to do the following:

• Push the Softness setting above 60 to achieve some beautiful chrome-like effects.

• Vary the Tolerance setting to drop out different areas of the image.

The following controls allow you to adjust the effect's parameters:

• *View*—View the source, matte, or final output (default).

• *Difference Layer*—This layer is compared to your source layer for pixel color and position.

• *If Layer Sizes Differ*—Use this control if the layers are of different sizes. Options are Center or Stretch to Fit.

• *Matching Tolerance*—Adjusting the Tolerance setting (0 to 100%) creates different levels of transparency, and creates alternate fades (both in and out) when animated.

• *Matching Softness*—Softness values above 50 create chromatic, semitransparent areas.

• *Blur Before Difference*—Blur (0 to 1,000) can wash out a layer if set too high. Usually it works best at no higher than 10.

Figure 14.5
Altering the Tolerance values creates different transparency combinations between layers.

What's The Dif?

The Difference matte animation (DifMat on the companion CD-ROM) displays what happens when you vary both Tolerance and Softness from 0 to 100 over time.

Extract

Extract "keys out" a range of the image based on its luminance or brightness (see Figure 14.6). The following list shows some possible uses for the Extract effect:

• Use this filter when the footage contains different levels of brightness.

• Use this filter to set levels of transparency on a layer when the image has high contrasted elements.

The following controls allow you to adjust the effect's parameters:

• *Channel*—Luminance is the default, but you may also apply this filter to the red, blue, green, or Alpha channels.

• *Black Point/White Point*—Set the Black Point and White Point values to determine the degree of transparency for the channel.

• *Black and White Softness*—Softness smoothes the edges of the opaque parts of the image.

• *Invert*—Invert allows you to address the underlying layer.

Figure 14.6
Three layer composites altered with the Extract filter.

Linear Color Key

 The Linear Color Key is another keying option, which is particularly useful in creating composited imagery (see Figure 14.7). The following are some possible uses for the Linear Key effect:

- If you use this filter when the selected footage is on a color layer, the footage will exhibit highlights based on the background color.

- Use a Matching Tolerance value of 85 to 90, and a Softness of 100 to add a slight foreground-based texture to the background layer.

The following controls allow you to adjust the effect's parameters:

- *Preview*—Use the preview thumbnails and the eyedropper tools to add and subtract colors from the Linear Color progression.

- *View*—You can preview the Final Output (default), Source Only, or Matte Only layers. These options can help when you're using the eyedropper tools to alter transparencies.

- *Key Color*—Select a key color from the image in your Composition window.

- *Match Colors*—Adjust the Match Colors slider (0 to 100) to adjust the selected color range.

> **Note: Using the RGB selection allows for a wider range of tolerances. Hue and Chroma effects seem to be applied faster, obliterating the selected target footage.**

- *Matching Tolerance*—Adjust the Tolerance slider (0 to 100) to alter the transparencies by adding or eliminating associated Key Color ranges.

- *Matching Softness*—The Softness value (0 to 100) allows the transparent areas to blend without hard edges.

- *Key Operation*—Your can choose for your color selections to be Keyed Out or Kept, allowing you to switch back and forth until you find a suitable transparency for the layer.

Figure 14.7
An example of the Linear Color Key effect. Left: The background layer. Center: The foreground layer. Right: The finished composite, with a matching Tolerance of 30 and a Softness of 75.

Low Tolerance

The LinKey file on this book's companion CD-ROM displays the application of the Linear Color key filter. Tolerance moves from 0 to 30, and Softness from 0 to 100 over the length of the animation.

Luma Key

 This filter isn't part of the production bundle, but it's included here because of similarity of use. The Luma Key filter allows you to create transparent areas by targeting image brightness (see Figure 14.8 for an example). Following are some possible uses for the Luma Key effect:

- Create a glow around the foreground image (as long as it sits on a solid color) by using an Edge Thin value of –5 and a Feathering of 20 or more.

- To create a very balanced transparent overlay, use the following settings: Threshold of 240, Tolerance of 150, Edge Thin of 0, and an Edge Feathering of 100.

The following controls allow you to adjust the Luma Key effect's parameters:

- *Key Type*—You can key out brighter, darker, similar, or dissimilar elements. If your image has a light backdrop you want to key out, choose Lighter, and, if dark, choose Darker.

- *Threshold and Tolerance*—Adjust the Threshold and Tolerance levels until the transparency has the desired effect.

- *Edge Thin*—You can use a higher Edge Thinning value (–5 to +5) to create a border around your image. The lower the setting, the thinner the border.

- *Edge Feather*—Feather the edge to create a glow. Choose No Feather when you want a harder edge.

Figure 14.8
Left: Brighter keyed out (Tut is on a white backdrop) and Tolerance of 250. Center: Key Out Darker, Threshold of 90, and an Edge Thin of –1. Right: Key Out Brighter, Threshold of 240, Tolerance of 150, Edge Thin of 0, and an Edge Feathering of 100.

Spill Suppressor

This filter allows you to suppress the color selected by removing it from the observable palette. You can use this filter to adjust the palette of footage that displays hues you want to remove.

The following controls allow you to adjust the parameters of the Spill Suppressor effect:

- *Color to Suppress*—Select the color in the Composition window with the eyedropper.

- *Color Accuracy*—The options are Faster and Better. For any colors but red, green, and blue, use Better.

- *Suppression*—You can suppress the selected color on a range from 0 to 200.

Alpha Levels

This filter is best used to tweak the transparency effects of an existing Alpha channel (see Figure 14.9). Use this filter to adjust the transparency of the Alpha channel.

The following controls allow you to adjust the effect's parameters:

- *Insert Black and White Levels*—Explore the Input values until the image reaches your desired effect.

- *Gamma*—Adjust the Gamma value (0.1 to 10) to alter the transparency of the dropout color.

- *Output Black and White Levels*—Explore the Output values until the image achieves the desired effect.

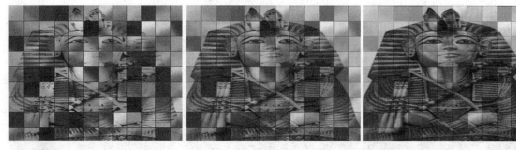

Figure 14.9
These three images all use the settings at their defaults, except for Output Black Level. That ranges, left to right, from 20, to 90, to 150.

Matte Choker

This filter allows you to adjust for holes and leftover pixels in a matte by applying two choking operations, so that the overall shape is preserved.

The following controls allow you to adjust the parameters of the Matte Choker effect:

- *Choke 1 Alterations*—Use the Geometric Softness, the Choke 1 values, and the Gray Level Softness values to spread the areas of the matte that have holes.

- *Choke 2 Alterations*—After the holes have been filled by using the Choke 1 alterations, adjust the Geometric Softness, Choke 2 values, and the Gray Level values until the outlines of the matte look as they should.

- *Iterations*—The Iteration value (1 to 100) applies the Choke operations that number of times. If the image displays complex and ragged mattes, you should set the Iterations higher.

Simple Choker

 Use this filter to make quick adjustments to the content of a matte (see Figure 14.10 for an example).

The following controls allow you to adjust the Choke Matte effect:

- *View*—View either Final Output or Matte. Select Matte when fine-tuning the choke.

- *Choke Matte*—Set the Choke value from –100 to +100. The more choke you apply, the more the transparent color spreads out.

Figure 14.10
Left to right: A matte layer with Choke Matte values of 0, 1, and 2.

Pack

Distortion

This is the third of three chapters covering the After Effects production bundles. I'll show you how to use these filters to twist and warp your footage in ways that will attract the viewer to your creations.

This chapter covers the following After Effects filters: Bulge, Corner Pin, Displacement Map, Glow, Lightning, Ripple, Scatter, Time Displacement, Twirl, and Wave Warp.

Bulge

 The Bulge effect distorts the footage by creating areas that are either zoomed in or on (see Figure 15.1 for an example). The following are some possible uses for the Bulge effect:

- Create a magnifying glass graphic that floats above your footage, and apply a positive bulge to the glass. As the magnifying glass moves over the underlying layer (or the layer moves under the glass), the area will appear magnified.

- Create interesting facial warps.

The following controls allow you to adjust the Bulge effect:

- *Radius*—The bulge is confined to an oval area. You can determine the Horizontal and Vertical Radius values for that area (0 to 8,000).

- *Bulge Center*—Placing the bulge center with the crosshairs sets the maximum Bulge effect at those coordinates.

- *Bulge Height*—The height of the bulge (-4 to +4) determines the extent of the warping. Negative values draw the image inward, while positive values push it outward.

- *Taper Radius*—Adjusting the Taper Radius (0 to 255) adds subtleties to the Bulge effect, allowing you to move a mouth as if it's speaking, or to blink an eye.

- *Antialiasing*—Use Low when you're configuring the effect, and High when you record it.

- *Pinning*—Checking this box pins down the edges of the footage so that the borders don't warp. It is best left on in most situations.

Figure 15.1
Left: Bulge with a Height of 4 applied to an eye. Center: Bulge of Height -2 applied between the eyes. Right: Bulge with Height of 2 and Horizontal Radius of 120.

Battle Of The Bulge

Open the Bulge1 animation on the companion CD-ROM. At high Horizontal and Vertical Radius values (in this case 400), and with the corners pinned down, the Bulge effect creates a squared-off area. The bulge applied in the Bulge2 animation shows the power and use of the Taper parameter, which is used to move the mouth.

Corner Pin

 All footage has four virtual corner pins: upper left and right, and lower left and right. Moving them distorts the plane of the image (see Figure 15.2). Following are some possible uses for the Corner Pin effect:

- Use this filter to create a perspective view of the footage.

- Reverse the upper and lower corner pins to flip the image vertically during an animation, or reverse the left/right corner pins to flip it horizontally.

The Corner Pin Placement control allows you to move any or all of the corner pins to distort the image plane.

Figure 15.2
Depending on where you place the corner pins, the image will be warped by their magnetic pull.

Displacement Map

The Displacement Map effect writes another image or selected footage over the target layer, displacing it by the amounts indicated (see Figure 15.3 for an example). Following are some possible uses for the Displacement Map effect:

- Animate the horizontal displacement with a separate layer selected as the displacement layer, and the foreground will be panned: left/right (positive horizontal), right/left (negative horizontal), down/up (positive vertical), or up/down (negative vertical).

- Use the Luminance option to place the selected displacement layer in front of the foreground layer.

The following controls allow you to adjust the Displacement Map effect:

- *Displacement Map*—Select a layer in the stack to use as the displacement map. Note that this layer will become the background for your foreground footage.

- *Use For Horizontal*—Select a channel to use as the horizontal displacement map mode. Luminance is the default, but explore all of the options before deciding on one.

- *Max Horizontal Displacement*—This value (–32,000 to +32,000) sets the horizontal location of the displaced layer. Negative values move left, and positive values move right. Values lower than –500 or higher than +500 can show distortion patterns.

- *Use For Vertical*—Select a channel to use as the vertical displacement map. Luminance is the default, but explore all of the options before deciding on one.

- *Max Vertical Displacement*—This value (–32,000 to +32,000) sets the vertical location of the displaced layer. Negative values move down, and positive up. Values lower than -500 or higher than +500 can show distortion patterns.

- *Displacement Options*—If the target layer and displacement map layer are different sizes, the layers can be centered, stretched, or tiled.

- *Edge Behavior*—The default is Wrap Around. Leave this checked for most situations.

Figure 15.3
Left: Foreground. Center: Background. Right: Composite using displacement mapping.

Power Of Displacement

DispMap1 on this book's companion CD-ROM offers a displacement map animation that demonstrates the power of this effect. Luminance was used for the horizontal, with a horizontal displacement that ranges from –44 to –999 and back to –444. The blue channel is used for the vertical, with no vertical displacement.

DispMap2 is one of the simplest yet most stunning animations on the CD-ROM. Displacement mapping was used on a layer with a lens flare, and a layer with a cloudy sky was selected as the displacement map. Horizontal displacement (from –100 to +100) was keyframed. The result is an animated lens flare that seems to be behind the clouds.

DispMap3 is a more radical version of displacement mapping, using lower and higher values for both horizontal and vertical displacements.

Glow

 Glows add illumination to the lightest elements in the targeted footage layer. (See Figure 15.4.) The following are some possible uses for the Glow effect:

- Add a glow to your text blocks to force them to "pop out" of the composition.
- Create a diffraction-patterned glow by selecting the Alpha channel, and Hard Light with A & B colors. Make the colors black (A) and yellow (B). Keyframe animate the Glow Radius from 75 to 150.

The following controls allow you to adjust the parameters of the Glow effect:

- *Glow Based On*—Select Alpha Channel or Color Channels. Use the Alpha Channel option to create diffraction patterns.
- *Threshold, Radius, Intensity*—Explore these settings to alter the quality and type of the glow.
- *Composite*—Composite the glow On Top or Behind the layer. Select Behind only if it's a floating layer.
- *Glow Operation*—Explore all of these operation types before settling on any one. They each create very different looks.

 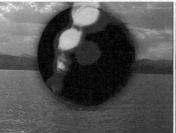 

Figure 15.4
Three different glow operations, left to right: Add, Overlay, and Hard Light.

- *Glow Colors*—Select from Original, A & B, or Arbitrary Map. Using the original colors creates standard glows. Using the A & B colors leads to interesting effects. Selecting Arbitrary Map allows you to get the colors from another image on file.

- *Color Looping*—This setting applies when you select A & B colors. Select either the Triangle or the Sawtooth options.

- *Color Loops*—Color loops (1 to 127) determines the thickness of the diffraction patterns. The higher the value, the thicker the patterned bands will be.

- *Color PhWSe*—The A & B pattern has a wave phase. Select it here.

- *A & B Midpoint*—The midpoint (0 to 100) determines what color will dominate (less than 50 for A and more than 50 for B), or if they will both be equal (50).

- *Color A & B*—Select colors for A and B with the eyedropper.

All Aglow

The Glow1 file on the companion CD-ROM shows a diffraction-pattern animation, created by animating the Color Loops parameter between 20 and 70. The glow was based on the Alpha channel. Other settings include Threshold and Radius of 100 with a Intensity of 45, a Difference Operation with A & B Colors, and a BAB Color Loop.

Lightning

 This is probably the most popular effect in the production bundle Distortion Pack, leading to all sorts of pyrotechnics (see Figure 15.5). The following list shows some possible uses for the Lightning effect:

- Use lightning to liven up your animated logos.

- Select the eye of a person as the start point, and the eye of another as the endpoint, and animate. Is it animosity or love?

The following controls allow you to adjust the parameters of the Lightning effect:

- *Start & End Points*—The lightning is always centered at the start point, and targets the end point.

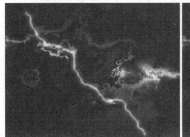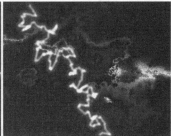

Figure 15.5
Left to right, frames from a Lightning animation.

- *Segments*—The segments value (3 to 25) determines the straightness of the bolt. A value of 3 defines a fairly straight bolt; a bolt with 25 segments will wander all over the place.

- *Amplitude*—Set the amplitude from 0 to 50.

- *Details*—The values for the detail level (0 to 8) sets either a low detail for fuzzy bolts, or high for sharper. Detail Amplitude (0 to 1) determines the strength of the detail throughout.

- *Branching*—It is the branching of lightning—the treelike structure—that gives lightning its recognizable character. You can set Branching (0 to 1), Rebranching (0 to 1), Branch Angle (0 to 60), Branch Segment Length (0 to 10), Branch Segments (0 to 40), and Branch Width (0 to 10). Explore all of these values to get the lightning characters you need.

- *Speed*—This is an animation setting: The higher the value (1 to 20) the more erratic and variable the strokes.

- *Stability*—Ranging from 0 to 10, this value sets the probability of the random variations in the strokes.

- *Fixed End Point*—Without this checked, the bolt will wander all over instead of to a selected target area.

- *Width*—Set the Width value (1 to 100) according to your needs, realizing that Width values of more than 40 tend to create streaks of light rather than lightning. Width Variation (0 to 1) alters the width from frame to frame.

- *Color*—You can select the internal and external colors of the bolt, but this is affected by whichever blending mode you choose.

- *Pull*—The Pull Force value (1 to 1,000) determines how much the Pull Direction setting controls the bolt. Pull Direction can be set from 0 to 90 degrees.

- *Random Seed*—A random number generator (0 to 100) shapes the overall bolt structure.

- *Blending Mode*—Setting the blending mode makes a lot of difference as far as colors are concerned. The Normal mode will apply the colors as you have selected them. The Add mode takes cognizance of the layer colors and blends the values instead of the hues. Screen is a variation of the Add option.

- *Simulation*—When Rerun At Each Frame is checked, the lightning will behave the same way at the same frame each time it is run; otherwise, it will never be the same twice. If you see what you like in the preview and want exactly that, check this option.

Lightning Target

Check out the Litning file on this book's companion CD-ROM for an example of the Lightning effect with an animated target point.

Ripple

This filter causes a rippled wave to warp the selected layer (see Figure 15.6). Following are some possible uses for the Ripple effect:

- Create rippled effects on a watery surface.

- Create ripples with a limited radius on an eye.

The following controls allow you to adjust the Ripple effect's parameters:

- *Radius*—Sets the overall Radius (0% to 100% of the layer) of the ripple.

- *Center of Ripple*—Place the crosshairs where you want the ripple centered.

- *Type of Conversion*—Asymmetric or Symmetric. Asymmetric ripples look more realistic and cause more distortion. Symmetric ripples cause less distortion, and travel out from the center point alone.

- *Wave Speed*—This is an animation setting with values from –15 to +15.

- *Wave Width*—Wave Width (2 to 100) determines the width from crest to crest.

- *Wave Height*—Height (0 to 400) determines the strength of the distortion involved.

- *Ripple Phase*—You can tap into the wave at any point in its phase by setting this radial dial.

Red Ripple

The Ripple file on the companion CD-ROM shows you what can happen to a group of tomatoes when you apply the Ripple filter.

Figure 15.6
Various Ripple effects.

Scatter

Scatter scrambles the pixels, adding an effect not unlike an explosion (see Figure 15.7 for an example). The following are some possible uses for the Scatter effect:

- Use an Amount value of 0 at the start of an animation and 127 at the end to simulate a grainy explosion.

Figure 15.7
Left to right: Original image, Scatter Amount of 127 with no Grain, Scatter Amount of 127 with Vertical Grain.

- Animate a Scatter effect with a constant Amount (whatever you want) with the Randomize setting on. The Scatter particles will move around on their own, similar to Brownian motion.

The following controls allow you to adjust the Scatter effect:

- *Scatter Amount*—Set the Amount from 0 to 127. Higher values add more noise to the selected layer.

- *Grain*—The default is None, which applies the scatter evenly. The Horizontal and Vertical options apply the scatter with a bias in those directions.

- *Scatter Random*—If this is checked, the scatter moves on each frame, rather like a chaotic particle system.

Time Displacement

Time Displacement is an animation effect that works on moving footage. The frame is recombined with a frame that is a set distance behind or in front of the current frame, based on the Luminance values (see Figure 15.8). Use the Time Displacement effect to create composited art from any selected animation.

The following controls allow you to adjust the parameters of the Time Displacement effect:

- *Time Displacement Layer*—Select the footage layer whose content will displace the targeted layer. You can use the same layer as well.

Figure 15.8
The original footage is on the left, followed by two Time Displacement-altered frames.

- *Max Displacement*—Set the maximum displacement time in seconds –3,600 to 3,600).

- *Time Resolution*—Set the number of times per second the pixels are replaced (usually the same number as the frame rate).

- *If Layer Sizes Differ*—Checking this option stretches layer sizes to fit (if they are not the same size).

Twirl

Twirl causes a twirling warp on the selected footage (see Figure 15.9). Following are some possible uses for the Twirl effect:

- Use the Twirl effect to segue from one piece of footage to another. Animate the footage you're coming from to move from an angle of 0 to 4X at a Radius of 100, and animate the footage you're going to from an angle of 4X to 0, at a Radius of 100. Then stitch the two together.

- Use Twirl to create a whirlpool on water footage.

The following controls allow you to adjust the Twirl effect's parameters:

- *Angle*—The Angle value spins the entire frame.

- *Twirl Radius*—The Twirl Radius sets the XY limits of the Twirl effect.

- *Twirl Center*—Place the crosshairs to define the twirl's center.

Figure 15.9
Left: Original footage. Center: Twirl Angle of 126 degrees and a Radius of 50. Right: Twirl Angle of 2X + 0 degrees and a Radius of 100.

Wave Warp

Wave Warp is a wave generator. The waves warp the footage they're targeted to (see Figure 15.10 for an example). The following are some possible uses for the Wave Warp effect:

- Use a Sine Wave Type to make a waving flag. Set the Speed at 1.

- Use a Circle Wave Type, and animate the Direction from 0 degrees to 1X 0 degrees. The effect is mesmerizing.

Figure 15.10
Three wave types. Left to right: Circle, Triangle, and Sine.

The following controls allow you to adjust the Wave Warp effect:

- *Wave Type*—You can select from a number of wave types, each with its own unique personality. The Sine Wave is the most common, and Noise the most chaotic.

- *Wave Height and Width*—Wave height and width can range between –32,000 and +32,000. Smaller sizes (below 35) create interference patterns.

- *Direction*—The direction of the wave is set and can be animated with this radial controller.

- *Wave Speed*—This is an animation control. Settings between 0 and 2 will usually suffice, but values from –100 to +100 are possible. Negative values for wave speeds move the waves left (and positive right).

- *Pinning*—To prevent the borders of the footage from being warped by the wave distortions, you can pin the footage down in several ways. The most stable is All Edges, but other selections can be used for various effects.

- *Phase*—You can tap into the wave phase at any point in its generation, shifting the wave effect to a new point in its cycle.

- *Antialiasing*—Low, Medium, and High are the options. Use Low when configuring the effect, and High for your final rendering.

Animated Slats

To transform your footage into a moving series of animated vertical slats, do the following.

1. Import a graphic or animation to the Composition window.

2. Open the Wave Warp filter from the Distort list in the Effects menu.

3. Use the following parameters: Wave Width 15, Direction 90, Speed 3, Pinning All Edges, and Phase 0. Use Low Antialiasing for previews, and High for the final render.

4. Keyframe animate the Wave height to 0 at the first frame, 100 for the middle frame of the animation, and 0 again for the last frame. This allows the animation to endlessly loop.

Render the animation and save to disk.

Wavy Gravy

The Wave Warp settings that created the WaveWarp animation on the companion CD-ROM are Circle Wave Type, Wave Height and Width of 100, Speed of 1, Center Pinning, and keyframed animation of the Direction from 0 degrees to 1X 0 degrees.

PART IV

EXTERNAL FILTERS

EYE CANDY I

In this chapter and also in Chapter 17, we'll take a look at AlienSkin Software's Eye Candy AE plug-ins, which give you the power to create effects such as flames, metallics, and basket weave patterns.

Although the Eye Candy collection is based on the Eye Candy plug-ins for Adobe Photoshop, it is an external set of plug-ins that has to be purchased separately. If you have experience with the Eye Candy plug-ins in Photoshop, applying these effects in AE will be easier. The plug-ins come on a CD-ROM and are available for both Power Mac and Pentium Windows 95-98 and NT (2000) platforms. A standard install script places the plug-ins in your AE plug-ins directory.

The complete Eye Candy AE plug-ins include Antimatter, Carve, Chrome, Cutout, Fire, Fur, Gaussian Blur, Glass, Glow, HSB Noise, Inner Bevel, Jiggle, Motion Trail, Outer Bevel, Perspective Shadow, Smoke, Squint, Star, Swirl, and Weave. In this chapter, we'll look at Antimatter, Chrome, Fire, Fur, Glass, HSB Noise, Jiggle, Smoke, and Weave. The balance of the Eye Candy effects are covered in Chapter 17. The effects have been separated into two groups so that they can be described according to similar usage, as indicated by the descriptive icons that accompany each effect.

Antimatter

The Antimatter effect allows you to adjust the luma (brightness) of a graphic or animation, without affecting either hue or contrast. Applied at 100%, this produces surrealistic solarized images or frames. Lesser percentages tend to blur the graphic content by varying degrees (see Figure 16.1).

Figure 16.1
From left to right, the images display the following Antimatter percentages: 0%, 35%, and 100%.

Antimatter contains one control slider that allows you to adjust the amount of the effect applied by percentages from 0 to 100.

You can use Antimatter over time to move the targeted graphic or frame from negative to positive values, or vice versa. Applied quickly over a small range of frames, the effect creates the impression of an explosion in the distance, especially one that is radiation based. Applied at 100% to an entire animation, the effect creates a solarized environment (like colored chrome), an effect that is often used in commercials to indicate a contemporary feel. This can be especially useful when the subject is a model who is dancing, or posed in aesthetically pleasing movements. (Perfume and hair care ads come to mind.)

Antimatter In Action

Open the Agric 1 animation on the companion CD-ROM. In this sample, Eye Candy Antimatter moves from 100 to 0% over the length of the animation. Other images move into the animation at different speeds. The central layer exhibits the Fur effect with Whirlpool Spacing set from 50 to 5 during the animation.

Chrome

The Chrome effect produces a polished metallic look with a wide range of variations. Chrome effects are generated from two colors. The Chrome effect does not blend with the selected graphic, so all image information, including color, is sacrificed to the Chrome look (see Figure 16.2).

Here are a few uses for applying Eye Candy Chrome:

- *Backgrounds*—Animated Chrome effects create two-color rippled animations. It's best to use lower band settings for this effect, because with higher settings backgrounds can become too busy and overwhelm other content.

- *Transitions*—Set the Bands from high at the start of a transition from one clip to another, to high at the end of the transition. The effect is rather like the transition between two scenes of the old television series *The Twilight Zone*.

Figure 16.2
From left to right, different Band settings are displayed. Softness, Variation, and Contrast are set at 100, with a direction of 60 degrees. Left: Bands at 2. Center: Bands at 8. Right: Bands at 30.

- *Text layers*—This is by far the best use for the Chrome effect. No animation is necessary, unless you want to emulate a glow in the Chrome. To do this, slightly animate over time the direction the Chrome is applied from.

Chrome responds to the following slider-controlled parameters:

- *Softness*—The slider ranges from 0 to 100. Softness mutes banding (described later). When set near zero, banding is pushed away from the center of the image toward the edges. When Softness is set at higher values, the banding is allowed to take over the center of the selected image or image area, although the bands are muted.

- *Variation*—The variation slider ranges from 0 to 100. Higher Variation settings produce more size variations in the Chrome Bands, while values closer to zero produce less. A Variation setting of zero creates a solid, nonbanded look, no matter what the other sliders are set at.

- *Contrast*—The lower the Contrast setting (0 to 100), the more apparent dithered colors will be in the banding. Higher Contrast settings create a two-color Chrome effect, with no apparent dithered smoothing between banded elements at a setting of 100.

- *Bands*—Banding settings range from 1 to 10 on the slider, but, by double-clicking on the number 10 above the slider control and bringing up the settings dialog, you can raise the upper limit to 30 in the numeric input area. Settings of 20 or higher tend to create moirés in the banded look, resulting in more of a striated texture than a chromed look.

- *Direction*—A radial control sets the direction from which the effect is applied. Rectangular looks are achieved by setting the direction at 90 degree increments.

Fire

This is by far the most popular effect in Eye Candy, and it is the single reason why many people purchase Eye Candy in the first place. With it, you can create tongues of flame that rise from your selected image components and layers. Fire works best with images that are dark, so you can appreciate the flames (see Figure 16.3).

Figure 16.3
From left to right, various flame settings are displayed. Left: Flames rendered against a dark background. Center: Patterned turbulence results when Edge Softness is maximized at a setting of 100. Right: Fire applied to a text block with Masking set to 100%.

Flame effects can be applied in a variety of ways. Here are a few:

- *Backgrounds*—Use flaming backdrops for text and other elements. Make sure there is a difference in the color cast of the other elements in the composition. Complementary colors are always a good choice. For instance, if you are using yellowish-red flames, give the other elements a green or blue cast.

- *Floating Layers*—Play with the Inside Masking settings for floating layers that are to exhibit flames. For realism, use masking setting parameters that cause the flames to overwrite the layer just a little. Try a setting of 80 to 90 for starters, and preview the results.

- *Text*—Use very high (from 90 to 100) Inside Masking settings for text. Lower settings may make the text unreadable. If you are combining the text with an Alpha channel, the flames can be seen as a bounded texture that never leaves the perimeter of the text.

Fire responds to the following slider-controlled parameters:

- *Flame Width*—The slider ranges from 5 to 50 pixels, but you can raise the upper limit to 600 pixels by double-clicking on the setting number above the slider. This brings up the numeric settings dialog. An average setting of 25 is recommended for realistic flames in most cases, but this depends on the size of the image area being affected.

- *Flame Height*—The slider ranges from 10 to 200 pixels, but you can raise the upper limit to a maximum of 3,000 pixels by double-clicking on the setting number above the slider. Take care not to set it too high, or you will see the flames bend as they reach the top of the frame (unless that's an effect you want). Very low settings cause the flame to remain at the bottom of the selected image area and flicker.

- *Movement*—How much movement do you want the flames to exhibit? A torch or candle shows little movement, while a forest fire shows a lot. The lower the Movement setting, the straighter the vertical flames become. Higher Movement settings create whorls and eddies in the flames. The slider ranges from 0 to 100.

- *Inside Masking*—Higher settings prevent the flames from being seen on top of the selected image area, while lower settings allow the flames to overwrite the image itself. Use higher settings for text flames, so the message won't be obliterated. The slider settings again range from 0 to 100.

- *Edge Softness*—At a Softness setting of 0, the edges of the flames become sharper. As the slider is moved to the right, the edges of the flames blend more into the background. When you are creating a fiery backdrop against which other elements are to be animated, use softness to mute the busy-ness of the background.

- *Color*—The two colors, Inner and Outer, that define the flame can be either "Natural" or "User Defined". Natural flames are yellowish-red, while user-defined flames can be any color you desire.

- *Random Seed*—The options range from 0 to 100.

- *Flow*—This control tells the flames how vociferous their actions are to be. Lower settings are good for fireplaces and candles, while higher settings lean toward cosmic conflagrations.

Playing With Fire

Open Electro 1 on the companion CD-ROM. This animation was created using the Eye Candy Fire and Glow effects. Fire was applied as a background, and the animated letters all exhibit a throbbing glow.

Fur

With the Fur effect, you can create looks that range from animal fur to sprinkles of dandelion fuzz. See Figure 16.4.

You can do many interesting effects with Fur, including:.

- Create furry titles for projects developed for children. Most of the time, the movement in a Fur-affected text block should be minimal (if used at all) to enhance the text's readability.

- Morph a background graphic into a Fur texture by adjusting Wave Spacing, Waviness, and Length from their lowest settings at the first frame to higher settings at the end of the animation. Explore the higher settings for the look you want to achieve. This is useful when the background has no overlayed graphics.

- Draw a simple teddy bear outline with the Bézier pen tool, and add fur to it with the Fur effect. If you use separate layers for the bear's appendages, you can use the rotation attribute to make it dance.

Fur responds to the following slider-controlled parameters.

- *Wave Spacing*—This is the most important parameter when it comes to developing different fur types. The slider ranges from 5 to 150, but the associated numeric dialog allows a maximum setting of 999. Settings less than 40 result in a spray of fur clumps, and this can be used to emulate such diverse effects as reflections on water. Larger settings, especially of 200 and above, result in closeups of realistic organic fur textures.

- *Waviness*—This controls the variance of the strands in a clump. Settings range from 0 to 100. A setting of at least 50 is recommended in most circumstances to emulate more-realistic fur textures.

Figure 16.4
Fur effects as displayed from left to right: Left: the original image. Center: Wave Spacing set to 100. Right: Wave Spacing set to 300. Waviness is set to 100 and length to 30 in both Fur examples.

- *Length (Pixels)*—This parameter controls the length of the hair strands in a clump. The higher the value, the more the underlying graphic is obscured. Value ranges from 3 to 30 on the slider, but the associated numeric dialog allows a maximum value of 100.

- *Shininess*—Higher values increase the number of white highlighted strands in a fur clump. To enhance realism, use a minimum value of 10, unless the underlying graphic has large areas of white. Slider values range from 0 to 100.

- *Random Seed*—Random values range from 0 to 100.

- *Flow Direction*—This radial indicator controls the direction of the fur's movement. Animating this attribute creates swirling clumps of fur.

- *Flow Speed*—This is a control for the rate of change. The slider ranges from 0 to 100, but the associated numeric dialog allows values as high as 999. Stay away from values over 200 unless you desire blurred speed effects.

- *Undulation*—This causes an expansion and contraction of the clumps in an animation. The slider ranges from 0 to 640, while using the associated numeric dialog allows you values as high as 6,400. Values higher than 100 are usually too fast and cause severe motion blur.

Glass

 The Glass effect can emulate overlays from plastic to glass, while warping the image in concert with refraction and opacity settings (see Figure 16.5).

Here are a few possible uses for the Glass effect:

- Use a rectangular area of color with a nonanimated glass texture in front of an animated backdrop. As the animated elements move behind the glass, they will warp realistically. (The glass layer must be somewhat transparent, so use the HSB Noise effect covered next.)

- Use low Speed and Undulation settings to emulate a rippling water effect.

 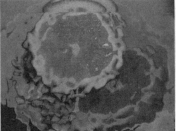 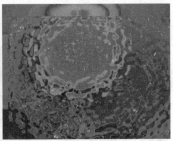

Figure 16.5
Left: With Highlight Brightness and Highlight Sharpness set to zero and Flaw Spacing set to 5, the overlayed glass warps the image very little. Center: Raising the Flaw Spacing to 50 warps the image more severely. Right: With a Refraction of 50, and Highlight Sharpness and Highlight Brightness set to 100, the glass overlay, rather than the underlying image, is emphasized.

Glass responds to the following slider-controlled parameters:

- *Bevel Width*—This sets the width of the surrounding frame, ranging from 0 to 300 pixels.

- *Flaw Spacing and Thickness*—Flaws warp the underlying image. The lower the spacing value—and the higher the thickness value—the more distorted the image becomes. The controls range from 5 to 300 for Spacing, and 0 to 100 for Thickness.

- *Opacity*—This ranges from 0 to 100% and sets the degree of opacity of the glass color. White glass does not respond at all to the opaqueness setting, while black glass responds very readily. With black glass, you can animate a fade-to-black simulation effectively.

- *Refraction, Highlight Brightness, Highlight Sharpness, Direction, and Inclination*—These settings determine the quality of the overlayed glass. You can look for an authorized refraction index table to set the refraction scientifically, or just experiment by moving the slider (0 to 100). Highlight Brightness and Highlight Sharpness settings (0 to 100) determine how light reflects off the glass flaws. The radial Direction setting determines which direction the light is coming from. Inclination sets the height of the incoming light (0 to 90 degrees).

- *Flow Speed and Undulation Speed*—These are animation settings that cause the glass to move over time. You would seldom use these settings at anything but zero if the targeted layer was a movie, since that would cause radical shifts and warps in the frames. Stick to animating the glass when the targeted image is stable. Flow Speed has a maximum setting of 999, and Undulation Speed can be set as high as 6,400. Use higher settings with care, or the resulting animation will be a meaningless and unpleasant jumble.

- *Random Seed*—The slider ranges from 0 to 100 for optional glass looks.

HSB Noise

HSB Noise alters hue, saturation, brightness, and transparency values, creating a noisy, or chaotic, texture effect (see Figure 16.6).

Here are a few possible uses for the HSB Noise effect:

- Set the Lump Width and Height to a maximum of 100, with a Brightness variation of 20, to create blobby washes of color over the image or frame. Keep the Opaque setting at zero.

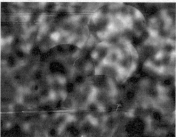

Figure 16.6
Left: The result of Hue, Saturation, and Brightness settings of 20, with Lumpiness of 5 x 5. Center: Lumpiness is increased to 30 x 30. Right: Hue, Saturation, Brightness, and Opacity Variation is pushed to the maximum of 100. Right: Blobby washes of color are the result of Lump Width and Height at 100 and a Brightness of 20.

- Create a chaotic cloud of particles on an oval graphic layer. Use all noise settings at their maximum, with Speed and Undulation also maximized over time. The look is similar to a disturbed nest of wasps.

HSB Noise responds to the following controls:

- *Hue, Saturation, and Brightness Variation*—All three of these controls are adjusted via the slider settings that range from 0 to 100. The result is a graphic that looks rather like a pointillist painting (as by Georges Seurat). The higher the settings, the more pixelated the result.

- *Opacity Variation*—This control parameter (0 to 100) allows you to adjust the transparency of the targeted graphic or frame, creating transparent areas that you can see through.

- *Lump Width and Height*—The Noise "lump" dimensions, in pixels, are set here. Smaller settings create pixelated looks, whereas larger settings result in more obliteration of the image data. Try setting the Width value to 20, and the Height at 100 for wormlike shapes.

- *Random Seed*—Set this slider from 0 to 100 for basic graphic variations.

- *Flow Direction, Flow Speed, and Undulation Speed*—These are your animation controls. Use them to create animated lumps that either undulate in place (Flow Speed = 0), or that move like nervous amoebas over the graphic or frame.

Jiggle

Jiggle breaks up the targeted graphic or frame according to the parameters of the control settings (see Figure 16.7).

Here are a few possible uses for the Jiggle effect:

- Use a Bubble Size of 0 at the first frame and a size of 20 at the final frame to create an amoeba that crawls across the frame. Move the shape from bottom left to upper right, with an Undulation setting of 60 and a Flow Speed of 7.

Figure 16.7
Left: The starting graphic before Jiggle is applied. Center: Bubbles, Brownian Motion, and Turbulence, all with size settings of 20 and Warp Amounts of 100. Right: Bubbles, Brownian Motion, and Turbulence, all with size settings of 50 and Warp Amounts of 199.

- Use the Brownian Motion type to emulate a swirling galaxy. Set the Bubble Size to 10, and the Warp Amount to 150. Over the length of the animation, keyframe the Flow Direction from 0 to 359. Set Flow Speed and Undulation to a steady 20. Do this against a starry backdrop with a white or light-blue targeted graphic.

- Use the Turbulence type to emulate a revolving star object. Make sure your targeted graphic layer is circular, and colored yellow or light blue against a starry backdrop. Set Bubble size to 10 and Warp Amount to 125. Rotate the targeted graphic clockwise two full times during the animation (Geometrics/Rotate), with Undulation set to 2,000 for the first and last frames. Set Undulation to 1,500 at a middle keyframe. Use a Twist of 215 throughout. This works very nicely if a lens flare is placed over the center (see Chapter 25 and the Knoll Software Lens Flare Pack).

The Jiggle effect is controlled by the following settings:

- *Bubble Size, Warp Amount, and Twist*—These three controls apply deformations to the selected graphic or frame. Bubble Size ranges from 1 to 999, with numbers above 100 only useful for very large image areas. Warp Amount (1 to 199) tells the target how much to break apart. Settings of 100 or less create a splat, while higher settings disintegrate the shape into disconnected bits. The Twist is controlled by a directional setting.

- *Flow Direction, Flow Speed, and Undulation Speed*—These are the Jiggle animation settings, creating splotches that crawl and undulate over time. Flow Direction is set by a radial control, while Flow Speed and Undulation Speed are set by sliders.

- *Movement Types*—There are three movement types: Bubbles, Brownian Motion, and Turbulence. Bubbles tend to keep the target cohesive, creating splats at settings from 0 to 100 and decayed splotches at higher settings than these. Brownian Motion breaks the target up into smaller pieces at all settings, with more decay at higher settings. Turbulence is similar to Brownian Motion, but attempts to keep the disintegrated elements flowing around a center.

Got The Jiggles?

Open Rotator2 from the companion CD-ROM. This animation demonstrates the Jiggle effect with Turbulence in rotation. A lens flare was added to the center of the turbulent swirl.

Smoke

 Smoke can be added to the Fire effect or used on its own. Effects range from realistic to abstracted patterns (see Figure 16.8).

A few possible uses for the Smoke effect include:

- *Flame reduction*—Use Smoke after you use a Fire effect, and the flames die down.

- *Animated smoke swirls*—Use Smoke with a high Breakup Amount and Roughness setting, and a low Masking setting, to add animated swirls inside an Alpha text block.

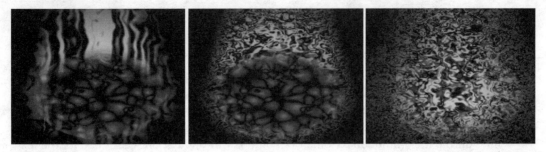

Figure 16.8
Left: Breakout Amount and Roughness of 20, with Inside masking set to 100. Center: Breakout Amount and Roughness of 100, with Inside masking set to 100. Right: Breakout Amount and Roughness of 100, with Inside masking set to 0.

- *Horizontal smoke flow*—Because there are no rotation controls to force the smoke to flow in any direction but up, it's hard to imagine how to cause the smoke to flow horizontally, or at an angle. I'll show you how.

If you understood the fire controls presented earlier in this chapter, you will understand Smoke controls. They are largely the same; only a few naming conventions are different. The following settings alter the character of the Smoke effect:

- *Wisp Width and Height*—This corresponds to Fire Width and Height. Settings for realistic smoke depend on the size of the targeted image.

- *Breakup Amount and Roughness*—Refer to the Fire settings of the same name. The more breakup, the more chance that cyclonic whorls will develop.

- *Inside masking*—The lower the setting, the more smoke will overwrite the selected image or frame.

- *Edge Softness*—The lower the softness, the higher the contrast of the smoke, and the more vertical the Smoke will appear when Inside masking is set low.

- *Inner/Outer Color*—Set these to your liking. The smoke is a blend of the two.

- *Random Seed*—Select a number from 0 to 100.

- *Flow Speed (in pixels)*—Select a setting from 0 to 999 to set the rate at which the smoke will move away vertically from the selected graphic. Usually, a setting between 10 and 50 will work best and allow you to see the intricate smoke patterns as they rise.

Making Smoke Flow

To make smoke flow horizontally or at an angle, perform the following steps:

1. Create an animation with the smoke flowing up as defaulted.

2. After saving the movie file, import it as a component, and place it in a new composition.

3. Use the rotation tool to turn the smoke movie in any direction you desire. That's the direction the smoke in the movie will flow. Use this method to add smoke trails to planes and rockets.

Swirl

Swirl is loosely related in appearance to the Fur effect, although it's more useful as a distortion than an environmental effect. Swirl can also be thought of as an impressionist painting method, not unlike Vincent van Gogh's "Starry Night" (see Figure 16.9).

Here are a few possible uses for the Swirl effect:

- Create an animated Van Gogh painting. Use a small amount of Undulation, a Whirlpool Spacing of 75, and a Smear Length settings of 125. Streak Detail should be set to 100, and the Twist should be set to two revolutions at 245 degrees.

- Create pointillist art by setting both Whirlpool Spacing and Streak Length to 5.

- To create a fur-like effect, use the following settings: Whirlpool Spacing = 777, Smear Length = 25, Twist = 15x +120 degrees. Turn Warp and Smooth off. An interesting animation results when you set the last frame at a Twist of 15x -120 degrees, as it makes the swirls reverse direction over time. Flow Speed is set at 15 with Undulation set to 0.

The following controls alter the look of the Swirl effect:

- *Whirlpool Spacing and Smear Length*—These two controls are responsible for the shape of the swirl. Whirlpool Spacing tells the swirls how far apart they are to become (5 to 999 pixels), while Smear Length (3 to 100) blurs the image more as values increase.

- *Twist*—By altering the direction of this radial control, or by inputting numerical data into the associated dialog, you can inform the graphic how much and in what direction the swirl loops will be painted down.

- *Streak Detail*—More-detailed swirls are created as detail increases by increasing the dark areas in the swirls.

Figure 16.9
Left: Very painterly effects can be achieved with low Whirlpool Spacing and Smear Length settings. Center: A Whirlpool Spacing of 50 and a Smear Length setting of 15 creates soft deformation loops. Right: Raising Whirlpool Spacing to 100 and Smear Length to 30 creates swirls that completely obliterate the targeted image data.

- *Warp and Smooth checkboxes*—When Warp is checked, the targeted image is deformed by the swirls. Left unchecked, the swirls overlay the image content like any overlayed texture. With Smooth on, the swirls blend any apparent graininess produced.

- *Random Seed*—Any number from 1 to 100 is accepted.

- *Flow Direction, Flow Speed, Undulation Speed*—These are the animation controls, determining how fast the components will move in the animation, from what direction they will come, and with what level of variance (undulation). Smoother animations result from lower settings.

Weave

The Weave effect creates an interleaved basket weave from the layer or background to which it is applied (se Figure 16.10).

A few possible uses for the Weave effect include:

- Use a Gap Width of 0 on a weave addressed to a stable background image to add an interesting texture. Keep Thread Detail and Shadowing set high to emphasize dimensionality.

- Animate the Gap Width over time on an animated movie layer placed over an animated background to create a transition effect from one movie to the next. (Professionals call this an A/B editing transition.) Set the Gap Width at 0 for the first frame, along with a Ribbon Width of 100. In the last frame, set the Gap Width to 50 and the Ribbon Width to 1. You'll see the background animation through a grid.

- Create smears of animated color across a weave, as shown next.

The following controls alter the look of the Weave effect:

- *Ribbon Width*—This sets the pixel width of the weave elements, from 1 to 600. The Ribbon Width that looks best depends entirely on the size of the targeted image or frame.

- *Gap Width and Color*—The Gap is the area between the ribbons, and it ranges from 0 to 50 pixels. The Gap Width that looks best depends entirely on the size of the targeted image or frame and the effect you are trying to achieve.

Figure 16.10

Left: A Weave with Smearing on and a high Shadow Depth. Center: A Weave with a Ribbon Width of 3 and a Gap Width at the maximum of 50 creates a grid (shadowing is off). Right: A Ribbon Width of 300 on a 320x240 frame creates large textured panels.

- *Shadow Depth*—The larger the Shadow Depth setting (0 to 100), the more 3D dimensionality the weave will seem to have.

- *Thread Detail, Length, and Smearing*—Each ribbon in the weave is textured with threads. You can heighten their contrast by increasing the Detail amount (0 to 100), their Length (3 to 100 pixels), and Smear them out altogether. Smearing creates a weave that looks as if it were painted with finger paints, obliterating the details of the targeted layer or background.

- *Flow Direction and Speed*—These are animation settings. Take care not to animate a weave that is targeting an animation, or you will make the viewer dizzy.

Smears Across A Weave

To create smears of animated color across a weave, perform the following steps:

1. Place an animation in the Comp area. A colorful one with lots of movement works best.

2. Create a weave that looks good to you in the Weave Effects Controls. Do not animate it. Turn Smear on by checking the Smear box.

3. Create the animation and save to disk. It will show a series of animated color washes moving across the weave.

Weave And Wash

Open Weaver from the companion CD-ROM. In this animation, the Weave effect is applied to an imported animation, and Smear is turned on. The effect creates a wash of color over the weave.

> **Note: AlienSkin Software is preparing to port their Xenofex Photoshop plug-ins to AfterEffects for animated use. This new volume of plug-in filters may be available by the time you read this book.**

Eye Candy II

Continuing with the Eye Candy AE plug-ins from AlienSkin presented in Chapter 16, this chapter details the rest of the Eye Candy plug-ins for After Effects.

The plug-ins covered in this chapter include Carve, Cutout, Gaussian Blur, Glow, Inner and Outer Bevel, Motion Trail, Perspective Shadow, Squint, and Star. I have separated the effects into two groups so that they can be described according to similar use categories, as indicated by the descriptive icons that accompany each effect.

Carve

 The Carve effect makes the solid areas of the selected layer appear chiseled. It is similar to the inner/outer beveled effects. The effect can be applied to the background image or a smaller floating layer (see Figure 17.1).

The following are some possible uses for the Carve effect:

- Create a fade up from black by using a Bevel Width in the first frame that covers the layer, and moves to disclose it on the last frame of an animation. Use a Shadow Depth of 0 in the first frame and 100 on the last frame. Reverse this procedure to fade out to black.

- Create outlines on a text layer by using a small Bevel Width, a Shadow Depth of 100, and a Darken Depth of 0.

Figure 17.1
Left: A 3D frame is placed around the entire layer by using a Shadow Depth of 30 on a frame sized to encase the image. Center: Using an Alpha mask, or drawing around a duplicate of a feature in the image, you can pop a selected figure out of the backdrop. Right: A small Bevel Width (in this case 8), a Shadow Depth of 100, and a Darken Depth of 0 create a dark outline around a selected floating layer.

You can use the following controls to adjust the effect's parameters:

- *Bevel Width*—This control sets the width of the beveled edge in pixels (0 to 600). The larger the image, the higher the setting will have to to be noticed.

- *Shadow Depth*—Lower settings (in the range of 0 to 100) allow you to see the image through the beveled shadow; higher settings make the beveled edge opaque. Use the higher settings to enhance the 3D effect.

- *Smoothness*—The edge where the frame meets the revealed image can be either sharp or blended with this setting (0 to 10).

- *Bevel Shape*—These options determine the shape of the framed edge of the selection. They are Button, Rounded, Flat, and Mesa.

- *Highlight Brightness and Sharpness*—In most cases, you will want to keep these settings at 100% in order to maximize the 3D nature of the effect.

- *Direction*—Direction determines which edges of the image will be cast in shadow. An interesting variation is to animate the direction, causing the beveled frame to spin around the layer.

- *Inclination*—This is the angle of the light, ranging from 0 to 90 degrees, with 0 akin to the sun below the horizon and 90 being high noon. A good default is around 15, causing the frame to be apparent on all sides of the layer, but more transparent on two of those sides.

- *Darken Depths*—Darken Depths (0 to 100) is best defaulted to around 20. Pushed higher, the image appears more 3D, but content is sacrificed.

Cutout

 The Cutout effect creates the opposite of the Carve effect, essentially creating a hole in the selected layer. The hole does not show the layers underneath, but is instead filled with a selected color (see Figure 17.2).

Here are a few uses for applying the Cutout effect:

- Create a "who is this" graphic by cutting out the shapes of individuals in a frame. You can imprint a question mark over the cutout to emphasize the mystery. This effect is often used in broadcast news and in magazines.

- Use Cutout to remove a background layer content, substituting a clean framed area.

Cutout responds to the following slider-controlled parameters:

- *Direction*—This determines the direction of the cutout's light source. The cutout will be darker directly opposite the direction set.

- *Distance (pixels)*—This setting (0 to 600) determines the perceived depth of the Cutout (Select it by exploring various settings, as it depends on the size of your composition.

Figure 17.2
Left: Using the maximum Blur setting and a Distance setting of 100, an interesting vignette is applied to the backdrop layer. Center: Altering the Distance to 20 softens the effect. Right: Using a Blur of 0 creates straight hard lines.

- *Blur*—This setting blurs the edges of the shadow. A setting of 0 creates a sharp edge.

- *Opacity*—This setting mutes the opacity of the selected Shadow Color.

- *Shadow and Fill Color*—Use the eyedropper or the color palette to determine each of these colors.

Gaussian Blur

Gaussian Blurs are useful for transition effects (see Figure 17.3). A couple of uses for the Gaussian Blur effect are:

- *Background Layer*—Blur the background to pop out the foreground layer(s).

- *Foreground Layers*—Blur the foreground layer at 100% at the start of an animation, and bring it into sharp focus with a 0% setting at the end. This is especially useful with text block layers.

A control slider with a range from 0 to 999 controls the Gaussian Blur. A setting of 50 blurs an image quite effectively, so it is doubtful you will experience a need to push the blur to a maximum setting of 999, or even anywhere close.

Figure 17.3
Left: The foreground layer blurred at 20%. Center: The background layer blurred at 10%. Right: The background layer blurred at 50%.

Glow

With the Glow effect, you can make your layers literally shine (see Figure 17.4). Here are a few suggested uses for the Glow effect:

- Create a throbbing glow by setting the Width value up and down at different keyframes in an animation. Use a Diffuse Glow.

- To outline a selected layer in any color, select the Thin Dropoff with Draw Everywhere unchecked.

- To use a Glow to blur the background layer, set the Width very high (500 or more), and Opacity to 50. Select any color to blur to that tint.

Glow responds to the following controls:

- *Width*—This is the width of the glow aura in pixels (0 to 999). Use larger values when selecting the Diffuse Opacity Dropoff and smaller values when using the other Opacity Dropoff options.

- *Opacity*—Ranging from 0 to 100 percent, this setting determines the visibility of the Glow around the selected layer.

- *Color*—This is the color of the Glow. It is selectable with the eyedropper or from the system color palette. Use a color that separates the selected layer from the backdrop(s).

- *Opacity Dropoff*—Opacity Dropoff has four options: Fat, Medium, Thin, and Diffuse. Diffuse is the more common setting because it displays a graduated haze instead of a sharp Glow perimeter, but your needs may warrant another option. Below this is a checkbox named Draw Everywhere. When checked, it bleeds the Glow into the layer itself.

Inner And Outer Bevels

Inner and Outer Bevels add frames around your layer that are shaped to the layer's perimeter. Bevels are best applied to layers that have a light color or muted image background, in order to appreciate the dimensionality of the rendered frame (see Figure 17.5).

Figure 17.4
Left: A Fat Glow with a pixel width of 50 and an opaqueness of 60%, applied to a foreground layer. Center: A Black Glow with a Medium Dropoff, Width of 100, and Opacity of 60. Right: Activating the Draw Everywhere checkbox causes the Glow—in this case with a Diffuse Dropoff—to render over the selected layer as well as beyond it.

Figure 17.5
Left: An Inner Bevel button with a Shadow Depth of 100 and a Highlight Sharpen of 10. Center: Enlarged Mesa Inner Bevel Width, so that the frame zooms in on the layer. Right: A Mesa Outer Bevel applied to the same layer.

Here are a few possible uses for the Inner/Outer Bevels effect:

- Use Inner Bevels when the layer has extra image information that is not essential to the content. Inner Bevels blur some of the surrounding image data next to the edge of the image.

- Use Outer Bevels when all of the image data in the layer is important because Outer Bevels minimize the overwriting of the layer's content.

Bevels respond to the following controls:

- *Bevel Width*—This sets the width of the surrounding frame, ranging from 0 to 300 pixels.

- *Shadow Depth*—This sets the overall opacity of the shadow. Set it high to emphasize the 3D frame.

- *Smoothness*—Set low for sharper transitions, and higher for blends between the frame and the rest of the layer content.

- *Bevel Shape*—Select one of four options: Button, Rounded, Flat, or Mesa. Explore each to see which best suits the image.

- *Highlight Brightness and Sharpness*—Use a high Highlight Brightness setting to emphasize the specular highlights. Set the Sharpness low to smear the specular reflections across a wider portion of the frame, and high to render sharper (but thinner) highlights.

- *Direction and Inclination*—These controls set the direction of the light source and its angle.

Motion Trail

 Motion Trails are also called "speed lines" by professional animators (see Figure 17.6).

Here are a few possible uses for the Motion Trail effect:

- Use Motion Trails on a layer that is placed over an animated background that is panning in one direction. A good example is an airplane as a foreground layer, with animated clouds flying by in the background. The direction of the motion trail should be the same direction as the movement of the background animation.

Figure 17.6
Left: A Length of 33 pixels and an Opacity setting of 60%, with Just Smear Edges on. Center: 200-pixel Length and 70% Opacity, with Just Smear Edges on. Right: Just Smear Edges on, applied to three different overlapping layers with different Motion Trail directions.

- "Fake 3D" is a good way to think of Motion Trails. By adding just a small amount of Motion Trail length with Just Smear Edges off, your flat layer takes on a 3D depth of its own. Keep Opacity at 100% for this effect.

Motion Trails respond to the following controls:

- *Length (pixels)*—The range is from 0 to 999, and the setting determines the observed length of the trail. If Just Smear Edges is unchecked, smaller Length settings produce clearer depth effects. When Just Smear Edges is checked, larger Length settings create more depth to the smear.

- *Opacity*—This is the opacity of the trails themselves. When compositing a Motion Trail layer over a background, adjust the opacity so that it is somewhat transparent and shows some of the background color. This enhances the effect. When used with a solid color backdrop, you can boost Opacity to 100%.

- *Direction*—This is the direction of the Motion Trail. It can be reconfigured at various keyframes in the animation to show the layer moving in a different direction.

- *Just Smear Edges*—When checked, this option adds a Motion Trail wherever there are holes in the layer. This can blur image content somewhat, so you may have to readjust the opacity accordingly. When left unchecked, Motion Trails are added to the perimeter of the object alone.

Mixing It Up

Open the ETMBlur animation on the CD-ROM. This title stands for "ET Motion Blur," and it features several Eye Candy effects in a stack. The original movie was rendered in Bryce 3D. I wanted to replace the original ET ship with something a bit more mysterious, so this was a perfect After Effects project. A number of Eye Candy effects were stacked on top of an oval shape that was used as the layer for the ET ship.

First, a Chrome effect was applied. The bands and colors were varied over time to create a shimmering surface. Then, a Glass effect was applied over the Chrome, blurring it out and giving it a more textured look. The Flaw Spacing of the Glass was also varied over the length of the animation, changing randomly to lower and higher settings. This created a material that seemed to throb. Finally, a Motion Trail was added with Just Smear Edges off. This blurred the back part of the ship even further, and added a speed blur to the back of it. The Length of the trail was varied over time to give a sense that the engines were pulsating subtly.

Perspective Shadow

 Perspective Shadows transform 2D footage into what is perceived as 3D (see Figure 17.7). Here are a few possible uses for the Perspective Shadow effect:

- Alter the direction over time to produce an animation that shows the shadow moving, as if a light were playing across its surface.

- Create a Perspective Shadow that is cast upon a background image or picture that displays a floor or other flat surface. Adjust the vanishing point to match the surface the shadow is being cast on.

The Perspective Shadow effect is controlled by the following settings:

- *Direction*—This is the direction the Perspective Shadow will point in, as set by the radial control. To emulate shadows on the ground, keep this setting between –70 to –40 (left-leaning shadow) or +40 to +70 (right-leaning shadow).

- *Vanishing Point*—The Vanishing Point control (0 to 100) emulates the sun's angle for the shadow. The lower the value, the higher the light source seems to be. A good default setting is 30.

- *Blur*—The higher the Blur setting, the less detail is in the shadow. The range of settings is 0 to 100. This also makes the light source seem farther away. It's best to add at least a little blur to address the jaggies in the shadow.

- *Opacity*—Decrease the Opacity when the shadow color conflicts with the image itself. Muted shadows also look more realistic. The range is 0 to 100.

Figure 17.7
Left: A Direction and Vanishing Point of 50, and Length of 60. Center: Changing Blur to 0 and Opacity to 50% mutes the shadow while making the details clearer at the same time. Right: Increasing Blur and Opacity to 100% creates a smudge for the Perspective Shadow.

- *Color*—Select a Perspective Shadow color with the eyedropper or from the system color palette. Impressionist painters discovered that the best shadow colors are the complements (red/green, orange/blue, violet/yellow) of a central color in the image.

Getting Some Perspective

Open the PerShad1 animation on the CD-ROM. This animation shows an animated Perspective Shadow, which seems to be cast by a moving light source.

Squint

Squint applies a blur and a distortion at the same time, just like the effect achieved when squinting your eyes (see Figure 17.8).

A few possible uses for the Squint effect include:

- Use Squint on a background layer to make the foreground image pop out.

- Use Squint on a text block. Start at the first frame with a radius setting of 100, and finish with a setting of 0. The text will emerge from nothing to be revealed in progressively sharper clarity at the end. You can also reverse this effect to make text disappear.

- Oscillate between no Squint and a setting of 50 to make layers vibrate in and out of focus.

Squint has one control, a Radius slider that ranges from 0 to 130. This tells the system how much of the effect to apply, although image resolution affects the look of any settings you apply. In most cases, a setting of 100 or higher will tend to erase the layer data altogether.

Figure 17.8
Left: The top text block has Squint applied at a setting of 100, while no Squint is applied to the bottom block. Center: The top text block displays a Squint setting of 4. Right: A non-Squinted text block is placed over a Squinted and enlarged duplicate, producing text with a strange glow.

Star

This Eye Candy plug-in creates star objects. They can be imprinted upon the selected layer, or the layer can be made invisible, leaving just the star (see Figure 17.9). Here are a few possible uses for the Star effect:

Figure 17.9
Left: With Erase Original Image on and Star Indentation settings of 95 for each star layer, stars with different numbers of sides look like gleams. Center: The same stars with Indentations of 40 appear very different. Right: With Erase Original Image off, you can see the shape of the original layers.

- Create star glints by selecting a high Indentation for your stars and fading them in and out of the animation. Pulse every star differently, so as not to bore the viewer.

- Use the stars to write a text message. Make them appear one by one to spell out the message, then fade out the stars and fade in the actual text.

- Use small, highly indented, four-point stars, with variable gleams over time, to create an interesting cosmic backdrop.

The following controls alter the look of the Star effect:

- *Number of Sides*—The number of sides a star can have ranges from 3 to 50. If the selected number is above 9, the Star begins to look like a burst, or even an explosion.

- *Indentation*—Indentation ranges from 0 to 95, with 30 as the standard setting. Settings below 30 make the star look like a polygon, while settings approaching 95 create thin, spokelike stars (great for "star glints").

- *Scale*—Scale can be set from 20 to 200%. Scaling in the control window scales the star as a component of the original image, so spokes can disappear beyond the image boundaries.

- *Position*—This sets the XY placement in the Composition window.

- *Opacity*—Settings range from 0 to 100% so stars can be set to appear and fade in an animation.

- *Orientation*—This is a rotation controller, allowing you to create animated spinning stars by setting the needed keyframes.

- *Inner/Outer Colors*—Select the inner and outer colors of the star, remembering that colors can always be animated over time with all the software's effects.

- *Erase Original Image*—You will probably want to erase the original image data most of the time, leaving just the star. But you can also explore what it looks like to leave the original image as a star background.

Sparkle Star Project

In this tutorial, we will create a sparkle effect from the Eye Candy Star filter. Do the following:

1. Load any graphic or animation you like to the Composition window. Darker footage works best.

2. Activate the Eye Candy Star effect from the filter list. Use the following settings for frame 1: Number Of Sides 50, Indentation 95, Scale 200, and Opacity 0. Leave the rest of the settings at their default values. Color the inside of the Star white, and the Outside dark blue.

3. Set the frame counter to the middle frame of your animation, and reset the following parameters as new keyframes: Number Of Sides 25, Opacity 100, and Rotation 2X. Leave the other settings as they are.

4. Set the frame counter to the end frame of your animation, and reset the following parameters as new keyframes: Number Of Sides 50, Opacity 0, and Rotation 4X. Leave the other settings as they are.

5. Record the animation. It will show a sparkle star appearing and rotating, and then disappearing at the end.

To see the result of the Sparkle Star project, open the SpklStr animation on the CD-ROM. Also take a look at Open StarBlur—Star glints and the Squint effect were used to create this animation.

> **Note: AlienSkin Software is preparing to port their Xenofex Photoshop plug-ins to AfterEffects for animated use. This new volume of plug-in filters may be available by the time you read this book.**

AE 2

BORIS

For After Effects users, Boris AE replaces Boris f/x. (Boris f/x continues as a separate plug-in collection for other applications, such as Adobe Premiere.) Boris AE has been revised and optimized for After Effects. A detailed look at all of the Boris AE version 2 filters is provided here and in the next chapter. The Boris AE version 2 Light filters can be found in Chapter 25. In this chapter, we detail the following Boris AE 2 filters: Blur and Sharpen, Color and Compositing, Keying, and Noise.

The PixelChooser Modifier

PixelChooser is not a separate Boris AE filter, but a modifier used to customize many of the Boris AE filters. For that reason, we are mentioning it first. The PixelChooser utility is included with the Boris AE Color, Blur, and Make Alpha Key plug-ins, so learning what it does and how to use it will enhance the quality of all your work with Boris f/x plug-ins. The PixelChooser allows you to select which areas of the image will be processed by the plug-in filter, and it can also be used to create blends between filtered and unfiltered parts of the image (see Figure 18.1).

The PixelChooser is controlled by the following options:

- *Choose Pixels By*—This control allows you to determine what pixels will be affected by the plug-in. You can choose from the following nine options:

- *All*—Selecting this option precludes the use of the PixelChooser.

- *Luma*—Pixels are selected by their luminance or brightness.

- *Red/Green/Blue/Alpha*—Each of these channels is chosen separately.

- *Saturation/Hue/Lightness*—Each of these channels is chosen separately. If you select Hue, then you can also influence the parameters by using the Angle Start/Angle End controls below.

- *RGB Difference*—Pixels are selected by the difference between their RGB values and the RGB value of a separate color that is chosen by the eyedropper or the system color picker.

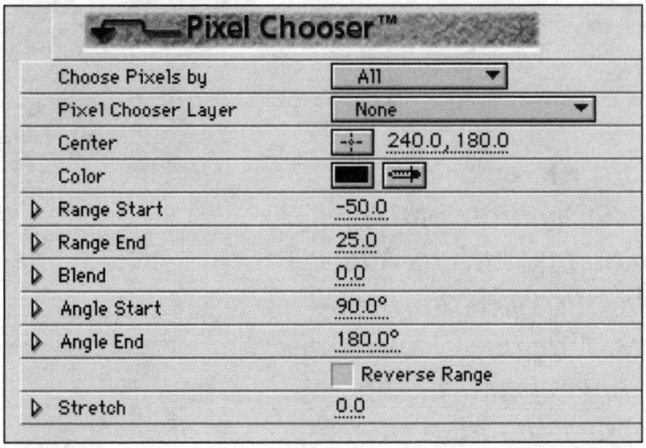

Figure 18.1
The PixelChooser controls are found in all of the Boris f/x Color, Blur, and Make Alpha Key plug-ins.

- *Distance*—Pixels are selected based on their distance from the PixelChooser center point (which can be moved). Selecting this option places a circle on the image. The circle can be stretched into an oval by using the Stretch control, detailed below.

- *Rectangle*—Pixels are selected based on their distance from the PixelChooser center point. Selecting this option places a square on the image. The square can be stretched into a rectangle by using the Stretch contro,l detailed below.

- *Edge Distance*—Pixels are chosen based on their distance to any edge of a layer.

- *Angle*—Pixels are chosen based on the angle (relative to the horizontal) of a line drawn from the pixel to the PixelChooser Center Point. This angle is adjusted with the Angle Start/Angle End controls.

- *PixelChooser Layer*—This control selects the layer to work on. This setting is ignored if you have selected one of the geometric settings via the Choose Pixels By control (Distance, Rectangle, Edge Distance, or Angle).

- *Center Point*—This control allows you to place crosshairs on the Composition window to determine the point from which all effects will originate. The Center Point can also be keyframe animated.

- *Color*—This control selects the color to be used when the RGB Difference is selected. Choose the color with the eyedropper or from the system color palette.

- *Range Start/Range End*—This control sets the pixel range values. You must thoroughly explore and experiment with this setting because the settings for range values are neither intuitive nor clearly describable. The best way to understand this control is to alter the range values and then preview the resulting effects.

- *Blend*—This control allows you to blend the effect with the original image or movie. At a setting of 0, none of the original graphic will be blended in. At a setting of 100, none of the effect will be blended in. Settings within this range blend both components to that proportion.

- *Angle Start/Angle End*—Use these settings when either Angle or Hue has been selected as the pixel parameters. Animating these settings creates spinning cones where the effects take place. Check Reverse Range to cause the effect to take place outside of the angled cone.

- *Stretch*—This control is used when either Distance or Rectangle is the pixel-choosing option. Circles and squares are stretched into ovals and rectangles according to movement of the slider.

The only way to truly understand how the PixelChooser works is to explore its use and to see what happens as you manipulate its control parameters. Also, note that the parameters of the PixelChooser *do not* affect any plug-in parameters except for the Boris f/x plug-ins that use it. A plug-in filter from another vendor will not use the PixelChooser parameters.

PixelChooser Animation

Open PixChuz on the companion CD-ROM. This animation shows an animated PixelChooser area that revolves like a lighthouse light. Pixels were chosen by Angle, and the start and end angles were then rotated around the center point. Everything in the beam is altered by the Boris AE Multitone Mix effect. The original animation was created with Photoshop and MetaCreations Ray Dream Studio.

Blur

Select All or Choose Pixels by one of the other PixelChooser options. This Blur plug-in differs from others that you may have run across from other plug-in vendors for After Effects. Blur allows you to work on the horizontal and vertical blurring separately (see Figure 18.2).

The following are some possible uses for the Blur effect:

- Animate the horizontal blur from 0 to 100 and the vertical blur from 100 to 0. This adds some interesting distortions to the blur.

- Start with 100 percent blur in either the horizontal or vertical directions, or both, and move toward no blur at the end. This makes an interesting focus animation.

Figure 18.2
Left: Original image. Center: 100% Horizontal Blur. Right: 100% Vertical Blur.

Note: The warping distortion seen in this animation is not a result of the applied After Effects filter, but was generated by MetaCreations Goo.

The following controls allow you to adjust Blur's parameters:

- *Lock To Horizontal*—This locks all blur effects to the horizontal of the footage. Moving the Vertical Blurriness control will have no effect if this is checked.

- *Horizontal And Vertical Blurriness*—These controls work in a range from 0 to 100, with increasing blurriness as the value increases.

- *Output Channels*—Most of the time the selection will be RGBA or RGB, but, depending on the color channels of your footage, you may want to explore the separate RGB channels to see what they look like.

- *Mix With Original*—This control mixes the original footage back into the composition.

Directional Blur

The Directional Blur plug-in allows you to select any rotational direction you need for the blur application. Because you can target different output channels, this filter also acts as an image modification tool (see Figure 18.3). Some possible uses for the Directional Blur effect include:

- Animate the Directional Blur dial from 0 to 360 to create a revolving blur, which is useful for animated tunnel effects.

- Use one of the Difference Apply Modes to create darker inverted imagery with integrated glows.

The following controls allow you to adjust Directional Blur's parameters:

- *Blur Amount*—The values range from 0 to 1,000, although a maximum setting of 50 is usually enough to blur out any detail in the footage.

- *Angle*—This radial dial is used to set the origin of the blur and can be animated.

Figure 18.3
Left: Original. Center: 135-degree Blur with Displace Pixels on. Right: 270-degree Blur with Displace Pixels on and a Difference Apply Mode.

- *Thin*—Select from a range of 0 to 500 to set the stroke thickness of the blurred lines. Settings from 0 to 20 produce streaky effects, while higher settings create more blocky, blurred lines.

- *Displace Pixels*—When checked, the image content is displaced in the direction of the blur.

- *Spread*—Ranging in value from 0 to 100, this setting controls the double vision effect. Settings higher than 0 increase this effect in the blur.

- *Blur Threshold*—(0 to 200) This is a setting you must explore to master. Increasing the value higher than 0 allows you to apply the blur only to areas of the footage that show rapid changes in color.

- *Apply Mode*—Select from 21 alternate modes to achieve different image effects. The Difference modes tend to create glows instead of blurs.

- *Apply Mix*—(0 to 100) This control allows you to blend the effect with the original source footage.

- *Output Channels*—Select from RGBA or other combinations of RGB and Alpha channel mixes for the output.

- *Alpha Blending*—Select either Faster or Better when the Alpha channel is targeted. Use Faster for previews and Better for final renders.

- *Mix With Original*—(0 to 100) Use this slider to mix the affected image with the original source footage. It's best to leave this set to 100 and use the Apply Mix control detailed above to achieve the composite mix.

Gaussian Blur

 The Gaussian Blur filter creates a smoother blur, but takes more time rendering it. The formula used in this blur applies a bell-shaped, or Gaussian, curve to each pixel in the footage (see Figure 18.4.)

The following are some possible uses for the Gaussian Blur effect:

- Apply a smoother blur to footage that demands higher output resolutions, especially for film.

- Keyframe animate a Horizontal Blur from 200 to 0 to create a transition that moves from black to multiple blurred images and then to a clear frame.

Figure 18.4
Left: Original. Center: Vertical Blur of 20, and a DifferenceX4 Apply Mode. Right: Horizontal Blur of 50 with a Lightness Apply Mode.

The following controls allow you to adjust Gaussian Blur's parameters:

- *Lock Blurriness*—Checking this option locks the blur to the horizontal. Uncheck it when you need to apply the effect to the vertical components of the footage.

- *Horizontal Blur*—(0 to 1,000) This sets the amount of blur applied to the horizontal elements of the footage. A setting above 200 tends to turn the footage black.

- *Vertical Blur*—(0 to 1,000) This sets the amount of blur applied to the vertical elements of the footage. A setting above 200 tends to turn the footage black. Note that this slider has no effect unless Lock Blurriness is switched off.

- *Spread*—Ranging in value from 0 to 100, this setting controls the double vision effect. Settings higher than 0 increase this effect in the blur.

- *Blur Threshold*—(0 to 200) This is a setting you must explore to master. Increasing the value higher than 0 allows you to apply the blur only to areas of the footage that show rapid changes in color.

- *Blur Quality*—Select from Low, Medium, or High. Use High only for final rendering.

- *Apply Mode*—Select from 21 alternate modes to achieve different image effects. The Difference modes tend to create glows instead of blurs.

- *Apply Mix*—(0 to 100) This control allows you to blend the effect with the original source footage.

- *Output Channels*—Select from RGBA or other combinations of RGB and Alpha channel mixes for the output.

- *Alpha Blending*—Select either Faster or Better when the Alpha channel is targeted. Use Faster for previews and Better for final renders.

- *Mix With Original*—(0 to 100) Use this slider to mix the affected image with the original source footage. It's best to leave this set to 100 and use the Apply Mix control detailed above to achieve the composite mix.

Unsharp Mask

The Unsharp Mask filter produces sharper images with greater contrast by blurring the source image and then subtracting it from the source image. This is a better alternative than using a Sharpen filter because it does not create the pixelated anomalies associated with standard sharpening (see Figure 18.5).

Possible uses for the Unsharpen Mask effect are:

- Apply the output to just the Alpha channel to sharpen an Alpha mask.

- Set both Radius and Amount to 100 to create saturated color footage.

The following controls allow you to adjust Unsharp Mask filter's parameters:

- *Radius*—(0 to 100) Settings other than 0 increase the sharpness of the effect, although settings of 50 and higher can cause halos around elements of the footage.

Figure 18.5
Left: Original. Center: Radius of 50 and Amount of 50. Right: Radius of 100 and Amount of 100.

- *Amount*—(0 to 100) This sets the amount of effect to apply.

- *Threshold*—(0 to 255) Default setting is 0, which means all pixels are affected. To apply the effect to only portions of the footage, explore altering this setting.

- *Output Channels*—Select from RGBA or other combinations of RGB and Alpha channel mixes for the output.

- *Mix With Original*—(0 to 100) Settings other than 0 mix in percentages of the source footage.

Artist's Poster

The Boris AE Artist's Poster filter is the best After Effects filter to use when you want to transform your footage into a look that resembles a color poster. It is also capable of providing excellent methods for creating rotoscoped footage from any photorealistic source (see Figure 18.6).

You can the Artist's Poster filter for the following effects:

- As basic settings for rotoscoped footage, apply a Pre Blur of 10 with no Post Blur. Adjust as your specific footage demands.

- To place a text block against a background without any Alpha channel compositing. Your footage should show a text block in a separate color from its background, and you should

Figure 18.6
Left: Original Center: Default Artist's Poster settings applied. Right: Default settings with a Pre Blur of 8 applied.

have a layer underneath the targeted layer with an appropriate texture. Use the Transparency Mode to target the text block's background color, and the textured layer will instantly replace the background.

The following controls allow you to adjust Artist 's Poster's parameters:

- *Mix Layer*—Select either None or any layer in the stack. The selection you choose sets the content of the Mix Layer for all other settings that target the Mix Layer.

- *Mode, Color, and Mix*—There are eight color groups that use these three settings. This allows you to select any hue for each of the eight colors. The Mode selected can be Color (the hue), Transparent (which displays the layer below the targeted layer), or Mix Layer (substitutes the Mix Layer in place of the hue).

- *Blend Mix*—Using this slider, ranging from 0 to 100, you can set the amount of hue, transparency, or mix layer associated with that color block in the footage. A setting of 0 means that the hue, transparency, or mix layer take command of that color block, while a setting of 100 indicates that the original image content replaces that color block. Intermediate settings mix the degree of the source image and selected Mode.

- *Color Soften*—(0 to 100) Using this slider at 0 allows the entire footage to be affected by the posterization, while at 100, no elements are affected. The default value is 0.

- *Pre Blur*—(0 to 200) This setting controls the amount of detail shown in the eight color areas. It's best to adjust this so that you lose some of the detail, or the resulting footage will lack a posterized style. A minimum setting of 25 is suggested, though exploring this value with specific footage is necessary. This is the most important control for creating good rotoscoped footage.

- *Post Blur*—(0 to 200) This control adds a blur after the posterization is accomplished. Usually, you will want to keep it at 0 to emphasize the posterization.

- *Blur Transparency*—(0 to 200) This control fades the Post Blur over the footage. Use it by exploring its affect on specific footage, after adding Post Blurring.

- *Mix With Original*—(0 to 100) Use this slider to mix the affected image with the original source footage.

Brightness And Contrast

 Select this effect for use on all pixels or on those defined by the PixelChooser. Altering brightness and contrast is a basic effect, but it can also be animated in After Effects (see Figure 18.7). Two possible uses for the Brightness and Contrast effects are:

- Set Brightness and Contrast to –100 at the start of an animation, and to 0 at the finish. This produces a fade-up from black. Reverse for fade-outs.

- Set Brightness and Contrast to 100 at the start of an animation, and to 0 at the finish. This produces a fade-up from white. Reverse for fade-outs.

Figure 18.7
Left: The original image. Center: Heightened brightness. Right: Heightened contrast.

The following controls allow you to adjust the effect's parameters:

- *Brightness*—The values for this control range from –100 to +100. Move the slider left or right to set the value.

- *Contrast*—The values for this control also range from –100 to +100, and the slider controls the setting.

- *Mix With Original*—This control allows you to blend the Brightness-Contrast settings with the original art. A good animation idea is to set this blend to 100 percent at the start of an animation and to 0 percent at the end, so that Brightness-Contrast settings will fade in.

Color Balance

Color Balance is the mixing of the red, blue, and green channels. You may use this effect on all pixels or on those defined by the PixelChooser (see Figure 18.8). Here are some possible uses for the Color Balance effects:

- Create fade-ups from color by moving one channel to -255 at the start of the animation and finishing as it reaches 0.

- Colorize a movie clip by altering the RGB setup.

Figure 18.8
Left: Blue channel data only. Center: Green channel data only. Right: Red channel data only.

The following controls allow you to adjust the effect's parameters:

- *Red, Blue, and Green Balance*—These three sliders allow you to alter the RGB mix by moving any of the RGB channels from their defaults of 0 to –255 or +255. These settings can also be keyframe animated.

- *Mix With Original*—With this control, you can blend the Color Balance settings with the original art.

Slowly Fading Away

Open the RGBfdup file on the companion CD-ROM. This is an RGB fade-up generated by the Boris f/x Color Balance plug-in. To do this, just fade the separate RGB channels from -255 to 0 at different rates. Fade one channel up so it reaches the 0 point at one-third of the animation. Fade the next channel up so it reaches the 0 point at two-thirds of the animation. Fade the last channel up so it reaches the 0 point at the end of the animation. This is much more interesting then a fade-up from black.

Color Correction

Color Correction can retouch layers whose content has been damaged by time or wrong film settings, and it can also be used to generate effects. It operates on all pixels or on those defined by the PixelChooser (see Figure 18.9). Following are some possible uses for the Color Correction effects:

- Apply a revolution of hues to a layer. The animation will move smoothly through all of the hue combinations. This effect is great when the targeted layer is a sky animation, as it makes the clouds subtly shift color. It's perfect for a sci-fi or mystery project.

- Create a grayscale clip from color data by simply moving the Saturation slider to -100 for the length of the animation.

The following controls allow you to adjust the effect's parameters:

- *Brightness, Contrast, Hue, and Saturation*—These are the four standard Color Correction options. In this plug-in, Brightness, Contrast, and Saturation can range from –100 to +100. Brightness at –100 turns the layer black, and at +100 gives the layer a washed-out

Figure 18.9
Left: The original layer content. Center: Brightness increased to 50. Right: Contrast at 75 and Saturation at 50.

appearance. Contrast at –100 turns the layer an even gray, and at +100 lowers the number of perceptible colors in the palette, removing all dithering between colors. Saturation at –100 gives you a perfect grayscale layer, and at +100 creates a psychedelic color range (usually too "hot" for video to handle).

The hue range is controlled by a radial dial that covers all possible hue ranges. This is great for quick control and also fosters the development of hue-based animations.

- *Output Black/Output White*—Output White (0 to 255) works on the white pixels in the layer. The default setting is 255. Decreasing this value will squeeze the whites in the image toward black. Similarly, Output Black (0 to 255) works on the black pixels in the layer, but the default setting is 0. Increasing it will squeeze the layer palette toward white. Moving both values to 127.5 creates a solid medium gray on the targeted layer.

- *Mix With Original*—This control allows you to blend the Color Correction settings with the original art.

Huey Animation

Open Huey on the companion CD-ROM. This animation was originally composed in MetaCreations Poser 2. It was then imported into After Effects, and the Boris f/x Color Correction filter was applied. The Hue control allowed for a complete revolution through the color wheel, producing a different color scheme for each frame. Brightness was enhanced by 10 for the whole clip.

Composite

The Composite filter allows you to combine the source footage with a Mix layer, either behind or in front of it. At the same time, a Gamma correction is applied to the selected Output, creating a better resolution (see Figure 18.10).

The following are some possible uses for the Composite filter:

- Use a Black Level of 140 and a White Level of 0 to create stark posterized footage with three or four colors.

Figure 18.10
Left: Source layer. Center: Mix Layer. Right: Composite filter applied with a Mix in Front of 40, a Lighten Apply Mode, and an Apply Mix of 80.

- With a Normal Apply Mode and Mix Behind set to 0, keyframe animate the Mix In Front values from 0 to 100 over the length of your animation. The Mix Layer will smoothly replace your target layer.

The following controls allow you to adjust Composite filter's parameters:

- *Mix Layer*—Select either None or any layer in the stack. The selection you choose sets the content of the Mix Layer for all other settings that target the mix layer.

- *Mix Behind and Mix In Front*—The selected mix layer can be placed behind and/or in front of the targeted layer, within a range from 1 to 100.

- *Black Level and White Level*—Adjusting either or both the Black and/or White Levels creates images that are either blacker or whiter. Each of these sliders has values ranging from 0 to 255.

- *Gamma*—(0 to 10) Increasing the Gamma level of the footage results in a brighter, but less contrasted footage.

- *Apply Modes*—Select from among the list of Apply Modes to create alternate composited looks for the way the mix layer is treated. Explore each before settling on the one you want.

- *Apply Mix*—(0 to 100) Adjust the degree to which the mix layer is composited with the targeted layer in the composite.

- *Alpha Channel*—This determines where the Alpha channel data is taken from to create the new Alpha Channel for the composited footage. Choices are the original layer, the mix layer, or a composited blend of the two.

Correct Selected Color

 The Correct Selected Color filter allows you to alter any color range in your footage associated with a specific hue. This can be for color correction or to introduce animated color effects.

Some possible uses for the Correct Selected Color filter include:

- Add muted color washes over any selected color region on any layer by keyframe animating the Hue control.

- With Show Mask checked, and your other settings decided on, render the graphic. You will have created a customized grayscale image to use as an Alpha mask for any project you have in mind.

The following controls allow you to adjust Correct Selected Color filter's parameters:

- *Color Matching*—In selecting a region of color to change, you can choose to select it according to its RGB, HSL, Chroma, or Hue parameters.

- *Color*—Select a color from the footage or from the system's color picker.

- *Color Range*—(0 to 256) The higher the Color Range value, the more neighboring colors will be added to the selection.

- *Blend*—(0 to 100) This controls the blending between the corrected and uncorrected regions. The higher the value, the more blending.

- *Blur Mask*—(0 to 200) This control blurs the mask between corrected and uncorrected regions.

- *Reverse Color Range*—This checkbox allows you to reverse the selected range.

- *Show Mask*—Checking this box allows you to see the grayscale mask, which is convenient when fine-tuning color correction values.

- *Brightness*—(–100 to 100) Increases or decreases the brightness of the selected region.

- *Contrast*—(–100 to 100) Increases or decreases the contrast of the selected region.

- *Hue*—This radial dial acts as a color wheel, allowing you to determine the new hue for the selected region. Keyframe animating it causes moving washes of color.

- *Saturation*—(–100 to 100) Increases or decreases the Saturation of the selected region.

- *Output Black and Output White*—(0 to 255) Tweaking these controls whitens or blackens the footage.

Hue-Saturation-Lightness

This effect can also be used to color-correct a layer, but with fewer options than the Color Correction effect. It operates on all pixels or those defined by the PixelChooser.

Here are two possible uses for the Hue-Saturation-Lightness effect:

- Apply a revolution of hues to a layer. The animation will move smoothly through all of the hue combinations. As with the Color Correction effect, this effect is great when the targeted layer is a sky animation, as it makes the clouds subtly shift color. It's perfect for a sci-fi or mystery project.

- Use the Lightness control to fade to (or from) black or white.

The following controls allow you to adjust this effect's parameters:

- *Hue, Saturation, Lightness*—In this plug-in, Saturation and Lightness both range from –100 to +100. Lightness at –100 turns the layer black, and at +100 turns the layer white. Saturation at –100 gives you a perfect grayscale layer, and at +100 creates a psychedelic color range (again, usually too "hot" for video to handle).

The hue range is controlled by a radial dial that covers all possible hue ranges. This is great for quick control and also fosters the development of hue-based animations.

- *Mix With Original*—This control allows you to blend the Hue-Saturation-Lightness settings with the original art.

Hue And Peter

Take a look at the Peter and Peter2 animations on the companion CD-ROM. These animations show what happens when Hue is animated over both an entire layer and a part of the layer.

Invert Solarize

This effect inverts the light parts of the image. It operates on all pixels or those defined by the PixelChooser. The effect is optimized when you use it in conjunction with the PixelChooser options (see Figure 18.11). Following are some possible uses for the Invert Solarize effect.

- Mix a stack of Invert Solarize effects, with each one having a different inversion channel option. Alter one or both over time to create colorful, abstracted animations.

- Follow these steps to add more red, blue, or green to a multicolored layer:

  1. Add a Boris f/x Invert Solarize effect that targets the layer.

  2. Go to the PixelChooser and select the color you want to emphasize from the Choose Pixels By list.

  3. Select the same color from the Invert Channels list.

  You will see that the color palette of the layer changes, and the dominating color will be the one you selected from the lists. To change to one of the other RGB colors, simply select it from the Select Channels list. PixelChooser tells the layer what pixels are to be selected for alteration, while the Invert Channels selection tells the pixels what color to become.

The following controls allow you to adjust the effect's parameters:

- *Invert Channels*—This control brings up the following list of possible channels to be targeted for inversion: RGB, RGBA, Alpha, Red, Green, Blue, Red and Green, Red and Blue, Green and Blue, Luminance, Hue, Saturation, and Lightness.

Figure 18.11
Left: Invert Solarize on Luminance with All selected. Center: Invert Solarize on Luminance with Luma selected. Right: Invert Solarize on RGB with Distance selected in PixelChooser, and a setting of 3 in the Stretch control to elongate the oval.

> *Note: Explore the possibility of inverting more than one channel. Simply select the effect again, as many times as you like. The layer will respond to the Invert and Solarize stack. For instance, in an Invert Solarize two-effect stack, try Saturation and Hue, Lightness and Red-Green, and RGB and Saturation.*

- *Mix With Original*—This control allows you to blend the Invert Solarize settings with the original art.

InSol Shines

Open the InSol file on the companion CD-ROM. This animation demonstrates one possible outcome when using the Invert Solarize effect. The red and green channels were inverted first, and then PixelChooser was used to target just the red channel. Mix With Original was set to 0 to maximize the effect.

Levels Gamma

 Gamma controls allow you to lighten the layer without the washed-out results that you often experience when using Lighten or Brighten. The Levels Gamma effect operates on all pixels or on those defined by the PixelChooser (see Figure 18.12).

The following are some possible uses for the Levels Gamma effects:

- Create a chrome effect by setting the Input Black level to 140 and Channels to Difference. Keep Gamma at 1.

- Create a yellow smog effect by setting Gamma and Output Black at 1.5 and selecting the Red and Green channel.

The following controls allow you to adjust the effect's parameters:

- *Input Black/Input White*—The input channels emphasize blacks and whites. Move the Input Black slider to add blacks to the layer. Move the Input White slider to emphasize the whites in the layer.

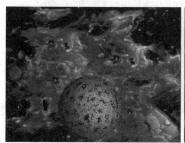  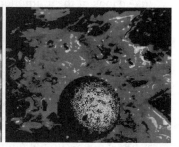

Figure 18.12
Left: Original image. Center: Gamma raised to 3.5. Right: Input Black at 100 and Gamma at 5.

- *Gamma*—The Gamma control (0 to 10) brightens the layer.

- *Output Black/Output White*—Output Black and Output White (0 to 255) are negative controls. Black, defaulted at 0, creates a white layer when the slider is pushed higher. White, defaulted to 255, creates a black layer when the slider is pushed lower. If both black and white are reversed, you will get a perfect negative image.

- *Channels*—This control allows you to target the following channels for the effects:

  - RGB

  - Red

  - Green

  - Blue

  - Red and Green

  - Red and Blue

  - Green and Blue

  - Difference

  - Alpha

  To target multiple channel options, simply add another Levels Gamma effect to the stack.

- *Mix With Original*—This allows you to blend the Levels Gamma settings with the original art.

Multitone Mix

Multitone Mix is the most variable of the Boris f/x color plug-ins. It creates toned images that have up to five fully toned colors. It can also grab color from pixels in any layer of the composition and place that color in a tonal range on another targeted layer. This effect operates on all pixels or on those defined by the PixelChooser. (Since a grayscale image that depicted these color effects would show nothing discernible, there is no associated figure.)

Take a look at the animations called Peter and Peter2 in the Movies folder on the book's CD-ROM. These animations use the Boris AE Multitone Mix effect to colorize a grayscale image. The alterations are controlled by altering the five specified colors (Black, Color 1, Midpoint, Color 3, and White).

Here are two possible uses for the Multitone Mix effects:

- Turn off Source 1 or Source 3 and apply the effect to a movie file. The result will be an animated tritone.

- Target one section of an image for Multitone Mix effects, like glasses on a face. One photograph can provide enough content for an interesting animation with this effect. The result resembles the animations from Monty Python's Flying Circus.

The following controls allow you to adjust the effect's parameters:

- *Source And Color*—The five paired source/colors are Black Source/Black Color, Source 1/ Color 1, Midpoint Source/Midpoint Color, Source 3/Color 3, and White Source/White Color. The sources can be any layer in the composition, which selects where the respective color is to be placed. The related color is then selected from either the source (if another layer has been chosen) or by using the eyedropper or the system color picker. You may also turn off one or more source/color pairs (except for Black or White). In this case, you would wind up with a duotone, tritone, or quadtone image.

- *Layers*—The three Layer Control slider options are Source 1 Level (0 to 100), Midpoint Level (0 to 255), and Source 3 Level (0 to 100). Each of these controls sets the thresholds of the respective layers, that is, how big a part each of the three layers will play in the final mix. The trick is to explore various combinations, keeping an eye on the visual feedback provided in the Composition window.

- *Input and Output Channels*—The Input Channel control selects the source for the toned or mixed image, while Output Channel selects the image that will be affected.

- *Mix With Original*—This control allows you to blend the Multitone Mix settings with the original art.

Posterize

The Posterize filter allows you to posterize footage based on the modification of its color palette. The Boris AE Artist's Poster filter is a better choice when you want to reallocate hues in the palette to those of your own choice (see Figure 18.13).

Some possible uses for the Posterize filter include:

- Create a dark red dreamlike posterization look for your footage by doing the following: Lock To Red unchecked, Red Levels 50, Red Scramble 50, and Maximum Scramble of 100.

- Use a Pre Blur value from 5 to 15 to remove the detail from an image or animation so it can be used as a nonobtrusive background for more detailed footage.

Figure 18.13
Left: Original. Center: Lock To Red, Red Levels of 2, and a Red Scramble of 15. Right: Lock To Red off, Red Levels 12, Green Levels 2, Blue Levels 8, Red Scramble 15, and Maximum Scramble 40.

The following controls allow you to adjust Posterize filter's parameters:

- *Lock To Red*—By checking this box, you can create a posterized look using the Red Level alone. Uncheck this box when you want to adjust the Blue and Green levels in the footage.

- *Levels*—(2 to 50) You can adjust each of the Red, Blue, and Green levels in the image separately. The value indicates the number of levels in that color channel. For instance, a setting of 6 for Red Levels would create six different reds for the Red channel.

- *Level Bias*—(–100 to 100) Settings below 0 push the levels toward black, while setting greater than 0 make the levels more white.

- *Color Soften*—(0 to 100) values greater than 0 soften the edges of the posterized areas.

- *Pre Blur*—(0 to 200) This control blurs the source image before the posterization is applied.

- *Post Blur*—(0 to 200) This control blurs the processed image after the posterization is applied.

- *Scramble*—(0 to 50) Each increment above 0 causes two levels in the selected RGB channel to be exchanged, creating unexpected image effects. In addition to Scramble controls for each RGB channel, there is also a Maximum Scramble control (1 to 100), which sets the maximum scrambles that each of the RGB Scramble controls can cause.

- *Random Seed*—(0 to 32,000) This sets a random seed number for the Scramble controls.

- *Mix With Original*—(0 to 100) This control allows you to blend the posterized footage with the original source.

RGB Blend

The RGB Blend filter allows you to create a composite from a source image's RGB Channels and those of a mix layer. All RGB channel properties can be adjusted separately (see Figure 18.14). A couple of possible uses for the RGB Blend filter are:

- Use a cloud image or animation as your mix layer to create a fog over your footage. Just set the Composite Order to Mix Over Original and make sure the Lock To Red option is

Figure 18.14
Left: Source layer. Center: Mix layer. Right: RGB Blend applied, with a DifferenceX2 Apply Mode, and all other settings left at their defaults.

unchecked. Then use a Red Mix of 8, and Green and Blue Mixes of 100, with everything else left at the default position.

- To create red-green posterized footage, use a Red Contrast setting of 100, and Green and Blue Contrast settings of 0. Leave everything else at the default settings.

The following controls allow you to adjust RGB Blend filter's parameters:

- *Mix Layer*—Select the layer in the stack to be used as the mix layer.

- *Composite Order*—There are two options: Mix Over Original or Original Over Mix. Explore both to see which one works best for your specific footage.

- *RGBA Mix*—(0 to 100) You can adjust each of the Red, Blue, Green, and Alpha levels in the image separately. The value indicates the comparative strength of that level in the total composite mix.

- *Lock To Red*—Checking this box locks the Brightness and Contrast settings to the Red channel only.

- *Brightness*—(–100 to 100) Each RGB channel's Brightness can be controlled separately, unless the Lock To Red option is activated.

- *Contrast*—(–00 to 100) Each RGB channel's Contrast can be controlled separately, unless the Lock To Red option is activated.

- *Apply Mode*—Select from among the listed modes for alternate image effects.

- *Apply Mix*—(0 to 50) This slider allows you to mix the selected apply mode with a normal apply mode.

- *Mix With Original*—(0 to 100) This control allows you to blend the altered footage with the original source.

Tint-Tritone

 Here's an easy way to get either a tinted layer or a tritone. This effect operates on all pixels or on those defined by the PixelChooser (see Figure 18.15). The following are some possible uses for the Tint-Tritone effects.

Figure 18.15
Left: Original image. Center: Midpoint at 75 with Luma Inverse. Right: Black Color is white, with a midpoint of 180 on a Luma Input Channel.

- Apply a nonanimated Repeats of 1.3 with a Back And Forth Repeat Mode to an imported movie. Set the Input Channel as Luma and the Output Channel to RGB. The result will be a tritone with pleasing highlights.

- Use a dark red Midpoint Color at the start of an animation, changing it to light blue at the end. Animate the Midpoint control from 100 to 170. Use Luma Inverse and RGB as Input/Output channels, and leave Repeats defaulted to 1. Set the Mix With Original to 50 percent at the end. The result is a negative image that moves toward a posterized blue tint at the end.

The following controls allow you to adjust the Tint-Tritone effect's parameters:

- *Colors*—With this control, you can configure the black, midpoint, and white colors in the image. Leaving Black and White as defaults, and selecting a midpoint color alone, will tint the image to that color. Altering either or both Black and White in addition will produce a tritone. Making Black and White the same color will produce a duotone. Unchecking Use Midpoint Color will also produce a duotone, using the Back and White color settings.

- *Midpoint*—This control (0 to 255) sets the threshold for the Midpoint Color.

- *Input/Output Channels*—The Input Channel control selects the source for the toned or mixed image, while the Output Channel chooses the image that will be affected.

- *Repeats*—This is an image-modifier control (1 to 10), associated with the Repeat Mode setting. Stay below 1.5 when using the Jump Repeat Mode, and 3.0 when using the Back And Forth Repeat Mode. Going above these settings breaks the image up into disconnected pixels. Of course, moving from high Repeats settings to low in an animation (or the opposite) would create an image that attains either clarity or chaos at the end, and that effect might be just what's wanted.

- *Repeat Mode*—Two options are activated when Repeats is set to anything but 1: Back And Forth, and Jump. Each alters the image in a different fashion, and should be explored.

- *Mix With Original*—This control allows you to blend the Tint-Tritone settings with the original art.

Using Tint-Tritone To Simulate Movement

 In this example, we will investigate the way that the Tint-Tritone effect can be used to simulate movement in a still graphic. Do the following:

1. Load any graphic that displays a wide array of hues into the Composition window. Select the Tint-Tritone effect from the Boris AE Color Effect menu.

2. Select either the Red, Blue, or Green Input Channel. Select the RGB Input Channel that represents a dominant color in your image.

3. For the first frame of your animation, set the Midpoint at 0. At a frame about two-thirds of the way toward the end, set the Midpoint at 255. For the last frame, use a keyframe midpoint of 0 again. This will make the animation loop.

See the animation TntTri on the companion CD-ROM.

Chroma Key

 Creating a keyed image that looks natural when composited over another image is an art, not a science. This is because no two images respond to exactly the same settings. It's also because when it comes to the finer details, no two individuals will have exactly the same view as to what looks good. The following, however, are general parameters that can be used for guidance:

- Unless specifically called for in a composite design, there should be no bleedthrough inside the foreground layer.

- No visible outlines should separate the foreground content when it is composited with the background layer(s). These outlines keep the composited image from looking natural.

- Whether the composite is a nonmoving montage or a multilayered animation, the components should not disturb each other. The whole is greater than the sum of the parts.

Boris AE Chroma Keying demands that the dropout color be red, green, or blue. This is usually accomplished by shooting the targeted layer against a blue or green screen (see Figure 18.16).

One way to use the Chroma Key effect is whenever the image has ambiguous areas that are difficult to drop out cleanly, like hair, smoke, or other partially transparent elements.

The following controls allow you to adjust Chroma Key's parameters:

- *Output*—The default is Composite, which displays the composited layers. To preview the Alpha matte, however, select Show Matte. This allows you to see any holes that shouldn't be present in the body of the matte.

- *Density, Balance, Lightness*—Density (0 to 200), Balance (0 to 200), and Lightness (0 to 100) control the density and threshold values of the matte. Play with the sliders until you attain the transparency that looks best to you.

- *Color*—Although you can select a color with the eyedropper or from the system's color palette, this plug-in automatically detects red, blue, or green backgrounds and drops them out. You may select another color, but that will radically change the expected dropout areas. It may, however, present unique and desirable effects.

Figure 18.16
Left: Background layer. Center: Foreground layer. Right: Composited with Chroma Key.

- *Red, Green, Blue*—Moving these sliders (defaulted to 100, with a range of 0 to 200) adjusts the density of each of the RGB channel colors in the targeted layer. It's always worth exploring these settings, because the resulting composite may exhibit more desirable results if one or more are altered.

- *Spill Suppression*—The Spill Suppression settings (Spill Ratio, Tone Mix, and Tone Range) alter the color parameters of the nondropout parts of the image. Explore their use.

Linear Color Key

 This key creates a matte based on the selected key color and the color of each pixel. Always use the Matte Cleanup effect after using Linear Color Key, since it removes any lingering edge anomalies (see Figure 18.17).

Use the Linear Color Key when the layer has no semitransparent elements, like hair or smoke. In those cases, use the Chroma Color Key.

The following controls allow you to adjust the effect's parameters:

- *Output*—The default is to show the composite, though you can also view the matte and inverted matte to check any anomalies. Another option is to show the gel, which is the matte colorized to your palette choice.

- *Color Matching*—The options are RGB (the default), HSL, Chroma (Hue and Saturation only), and Hue. Try all of the options to see which ones improve the selected layer matte.

- *Key Color*—This is the selected dropout color.

- *Similarity*—This is the most important control, as it allows you to fine-tune the dropout range. Although the range is from 0 to 255, a setting between 1 and 10 typically works best.

- *Weight, Softness, Post Blur*—Red-Green-Blue Weight, Softness, and Post Blur all fine-tune the dropout parameters of the matte. Post Blur is used mostly to blur the edges of the matte into the background. The Matte Cleanup effect is usually needed afterward to fine-tune the blurred edges.

Figure 18.17
Left: Computer graphic image (composed in Caligari trueSpace). Center: Photograph (pianist and composer, Andy Hildebrandt). Right: Linear Key composite on gradient background.

- *Region*—Placing these crosshairs blocks out large unwanted areas even before the matte is fine-tuned.

- *Gel Color*—Selecting a color of your choice adds the hue to the matte when Gel is selected as the Output Mode. This gives you the option of including solid-color silhouettes of the layer content. When animated, this can add interest to the composite image.

Linear Luma Key

 The Linear Luma creates a matte based on the luminance areas of the source. If you have content whose matte area differs in luminance (brightness) from its background, this key would be a good choice. For instance, you could use the Linear Luma key when your footage shows a distinct difference between the dropout and nondropout areas.

The following controls allow you to adjust the parameters of this effect:

- *Make Key From*—The key is usually made from Luma (brightness), although you can also use the Red, Blue, or Green channel for effect.

- *Output*—The default is to show the composite, although you can also view the matte and inverted matte to check any anomalies. Another option is to show the gel, which is the matte colorized to your palette choice.

- *Threshold, Similarity, Softness, Post Blur*—These are your fine-tuning controls. The most important ones are Threshold and Similarity because they produce preview results rather quickly. Post Blur may have to be followed up by using the Matte Cleanup effect to get rid of edge anomalies.

Make Alpha Key

 This effect automates the creation of the Alpha, dropping the background color. It can be fine-tuned with the additional controls, but you'll probably want to use the Matte Cleanup effect afterward. You can use this effect as an option to other Linear Alpha effects plug-ins (see Figure 18.18).

Figure 18.18
Left: Even with the best settings in Make Alpha, a line is still visible around the foreground layer. Center: Here is the matte view of the foreground layer after Make Alpha has been applied. Right: Adding a Matte Cleanup effect afterward removes the offending outline, as this matte view shows.

The following controls allow you to adjust the effect's parameters:

- *Output*—The default is Composite, although you may want to select a matte option to preview the Alpha channel.

- *Input Black/White*—These are fine adjustment controls. For a solid-color dropout of the image backdrop, try setting Input White at 0 and Input Black at 20. Adjust the controls from there.

- *Gamma*—Push up the Gamma (0 to 10) for a snappier image.

- *Output Black/White*—The control sliders for Output Black and Output White are best left at their default positions.

- *Post Blur*—If you increase Post Blur (range 0 to 100), you will still probably want to fine-tune in an added Matte Cleanup effect.

Matte Cleanup

MThis is an essential, final touch-up effect when creating mattes. It is not used to create mattes, but to do the final tweaking. Don't leave Alpha footage without it. When creating any matte with any plug-in, always consider using this effect as a final touch-up step to clean up edges and breakups (see Figure 18.19).

The following controls allow you to adjust the parameters of the Matte Cleanup effect:

- *Blend*—This control feathers the edges of the matte, especially to compensate for pixels created by the Choke option.

- *Output*—Composite is the default, but you can select Show Matte to see where any bleedthrough might exist.

- *Choke*—This control expands or shrinks the borders of the blend, but you may have to smooth out the pixelization afterward with a touch of Blend.

- *Black and White*—These controls set the thresholds for the levels of transparent and opaque areas.

Figure 18.19
Left: With Choke at –100, Black at 70, and Gain at a tiny 0.393, the targeted footage has just a tiny blur for blending into the background. Center: Setting Choke at +60, with none of the other settings altered, adds just a tiny outline. Right: Maximizing Gain and Choke at 100, with both Black and White set to 0, creates a thick black outline around the targeted footage.

- *Spread*—Use this in conjunction with Gain settings to adjust the thickness of the selected area and its smoothness.

- *Gain*—Increase this setting to create a thicker edge for the footage. Thick outlines look very contemporary, especially when used on animated footage.

Two-Way Key

 This plug-in is best used to generate Alpha-based special-effects footage, and also to target footage that has a definable dropout color backdrop and another color you want to keep under all circumstances (see Figure 18.20).

The following controls allow you to adjust the effect's parameters:

- *Output*—Composite is the default. Use Matte Output to see the matte clearly when you're trying to get rid of unwanted bleedthrough. Use Gel when you want to create a silhouette of the footage.

- *Key Color/Similarity*—This is the dropout color. Adjust the Similarity slider to include other colors in the dropout that are similar to the selected dropout color.

- *Keep Color/Keep Similarity*—This is the color you want to keep under all circumstances. Use the Keep Similarity control to widen the number of associated colors to keep.

- *Softness*—Increasing this value (range 0 to 255) will reintroduce the dropout color area at increasing opacity. In most situations, it's left at 0.

- *Post Blur*—Add blur to the edges of the targeted footage with this control. In many cases, it is set at the maximum, and the Matte Cleanup is used afterward to do the final touchup.

- *Gel Color*—Select a Gel Color when you want to create silhouetted footage.

Figure 18.20
Left: Two-way effect used to create a standard Alpha look, with Similarity set to 118 and Keep Similarity (from a facial color) set to 240. Center: Similarity raised to 165 to create dropout effects. Right: Gel output with a black Gel, and Similarity set to 185. Do not use the Matte Cleanup plug-in when creating Gel silhouettes.

Alpha Pixel Noise

The Alpha Pixel Noise filter allows you to transform the Alpha layer content into particles (see Figure 18.21).

Figure 18.21
Left: Source layer. Center: Alpha layer. Right: Composited layers with Alpha Pixel Noise applied. Percentage 65, Alpha Offset –200, and a Noise of 255.

The following are some possible uses for the Alpha Pixel Noise filter:

- Use this filter to create semitransparent overprints from Alpha layers.
- Animate the Perturbation values to create sparkling particles from Alpha channel data.

The following controls allow you to adjust Alpha Pixel Noise filter's parameters:

- *Percentage*—(0 to 100) This sets the percentage of pixels in the Alpha layer that are affected by Noise.
- *Alpha Offset*—(–255 to 255) Negative values make the affected pixels more transparent, whereas positive settings make the affected pixels more opaque.
- *Noise*—(0 to 255) This sets the amount of Noise applied to each pixel.
- *Noise Action*—You can Increase Transparency or Increase Opacity, or select Both to explore applying a combination of these effects.
- *Random Seed*—(0 to 32,000) The Random Seed Generator sets the initial pattern of the Noise.
- *Perturbation*—(0 to 500) This sets a random amount of movement to the Noise.
- *Perturbation Seed*—(501 to 32,000) This sets the pattern of the randomized movement of the Noise.

RGB Pixel Noise

 The RGB Pixel Noise filter applies noise to each of the RGB Channels of targeted footage independently (see Figure 18.22).

The following are some possible uses for the RGB Pixel Noise filter:

- Keyframe animate all of the RGB Noise settings from 255 at the start of an animation to 0 at the finish. This creates a transition from a noisy frame with no discernible image content to a clear image.
- Keyframe animate the Perturbation values to create moving particles over the footage content. Use RGB Noise settings of 50 and below.

Figure 18.22
Left: Original footage. Center: Clipping on, with a percentage of 70 and all RGB Noise values at 255. Right: The same settings with Clipping off.

The following controls allow you to adjust Alpha Pixel Noise filter's parameters:

- *Percentage*—(0 to 100) This sets the percentage of pixels that are affected by the Noise.

- *RGB Noise*—(0 to 255) These three controls set the RGB channels separately for the amount of Noise on each.

- *Link Noise Ratio*—This links the ratio of Noise in each channel together, so if one is altered they all are.

- *Clip Noise Values*—Without this checkbox on, the Noise can completely obliterate the image.

- *Random Seed*—(0 to 32,000) The Random Seed Generator sets the initial pattern of the Noise.

- *Perturbation*—(0 to 500) This sets a random amount of movement to the Noise.

- *Perturbation Seed*—(501 to 32,000) This sets the pattern of the randomized movement of the Noise.

Spray Paint Noise

The Spray Paint Noise filter allows you to render multicolored dots that emulate a spray nozzle (see Figure 18.23).

The following are some possible uses for the Spray Paint Noise filter:

- Use a text block as the Paint layer, and use a brick wall texture as the source layer with this effect. Create graffiti on a wall.

- Use the Difference Mode to create inverted composites.

The following controls allow you to adjust Spray Paint Noise filter's parameters:

- *Percentage*—(0 to 100) This sets the percentage of pixels in the layer that are affected by the Noise.

- *Paint Color*—Select the color with the eyedropper or by using the system palette.

- *Paint Layer*—Select any layer in the stack.

Figure 18.23
Left: Original footage. Center: Paint layer. Right: Composited with the Spray Paint Noise filter. Percentage is 65, with a Minimum and Maximum Opacity of 60, and a Subtract Paint Mode.

- *Opacity*—(0 to 100) You can both Minimum and Maximum Opacity separately, so you have an opacity range for the Noise.

- *Paint Apply Mode*—You can select from any of 21 different Apply Modes. It's best to explore each one to see how the images react.

- *Noise Seed*—(0 to 32,000) This Seed Generator sets the initial pattern of the Noise.

- *Perturbation*—(0 to 500) This sets a random amount of movement to the Noise.

- *Perturbation Seed*—(501 to 32,000) This sets the pattern of the randomized movement of the Noise.

PART 2

This is the second of three chapters that cover Boris AE 2 effects. In this chapter, you'll look at: Distortion (Bulge, Displacement Map, Polar Displacement, Ripple, Vector Displacement, and Wave), Particles (2D Particles and Scatterize), and Perspective (Cube, Cylinder, DVE, PageTurn, and Sphere). Note that the separate filters included here are listed alphabetically in the order of their headings, and not overall. Check out Chapters 18 and 25 for other Boris filters.

You can use the Boris AE Distortion effects to warp and twist your footage, the Boris AE 2D Particle filters to expand your options for creating particle effects in After Effects projects, and the Boris AE perspective effects to wrap footage around a selection of 3D forms.

Bulge

Bulge adds bloated effects to the selected footage, and can either bulge out or in (see Figure 19.1). Here are some possible uses for the Bulge effect:

- Create a rubberized surface animation by animating the center point in a circle over the length of the animation. Use center pinning, so the edges can wiggle. The content will look like it's being pulled from different directions as time passes. This can be very effective for underwater scenes, re-creating the effect of the water's refraction and distortion of the image.

- Animate the Stretch Angle for chaotic warps. Start with a revolution of 1 and an angle of 25 degrees, and end with a revolution of 87 and an angle of 25 degrees. Use footage that has a lot of color.

The following controls allow you to adjust Bulge's parameters:

- *Center Point*—Where you place the center point is vital because it controls the center for the effect's radius. You can make an eye wink or a mouth smile when it is placed in relation to these facial features.

Figure 19.1
Left: Bulge applied with a Height of 200 and a Radius of 75, with the center point over the left eye and no pinning. Center: A Height of –200 and a Radius of 125 pulls the whole image inward toward the center point. Right: "Brainy Mona" has the following settings: Height, 200; Perspective, 10; Radius, 200; Taper, 100; Stretch, –100 at 0 degrees; and Horizontal Pinning.

- *Height*—Height's settings range from –200 to +200, with 0 as the default. Values higher than 0 make the selected area bulge outward, while negative values cause the image to bulge inward.

- *Perspective*—The settings range from –1,000 to +1,000. This control moves you into or out of the image. Negative values tend to warp the edges of the image, even when they are pinned down. Decreasing the radius usually negates this.

- *Radius*—The range is from 0 to 200. A value of 100 covers the entire layer, so higher values stretch the effect beyond the layer's edges.

- *Taper*—Taper is associated with height. Height with no taper is like looking down on a sphere. The more Taper is applied, the more the effect is like looking down on a conical surface.

- *Stretch And Stretch Angle*—This control stretches (positive values) or squeezes (negative values) in the direction indicated by the Stretch Angle. Up to -88 or +88 revolutions can be applied to this angle, with utterly unpredictable results at very low or very high settings.

- *Pinning*—The image will not stretch or warp where it is pinned. The options are None, Edges, Center, Left, Top, Right, Bottom, Vertical, and Horizontal. Alternate pinning creates very different effects from the same control settings.

Battle Of The Bulge

Open MonaBulg from the companion CD-ROM. Check out Mona's strange wink and smile in this Boris f/x AE Bulge animation. The original animation was created in Kai's PowerGoo from MetaCreations. Now open MonaBlg2. This Bulge animation shows what happens when you move the center point in a circle on the footage with Center Pinning activated.

Displacement Map

The Displacement Map filter distorts the Source layer by taking information from the Map layer (see Figure 19.2).

Figure 19.2
Left: The Source layer. Center: The Map layer. Right: The resulting composite produced when a Displacement Map filter is applied.

Here are some possible uses for the Displacement Map filter:

- Explore various Horizontal and Vertical Displacement values to transform the Source layer into an abstract painting.

- Shrink the Map Layer to about one-quarter of the size of the Source layer, and place the Map layer in the upper left corner of the Composition window. Create a motion path for the Map layer so it moves to the lower right during the length of an animation. Apply a Displacement Map filter to the Source layer and watch as the Map layer creates displaced warping as it moves.

The following controls allow you to adjust Displacement Map's parameters:

- *Map Layer*—Select the Map layer from any layer in the stack.

- *Blur*—The amount of Blur can range from 0 to 200. The more Blur, the smoother the displaced areas of the Source layer become. You can also vary the Blur Threshold (0 to 200) to alter the way the Blur is applied. Explore for best use.

- *Map Black and White Levels*—(0 to 255) Increase the Black Level from its default of 0 to bend the Source layer downward. Decrease the White Level from its default of 255 to bend the Source layer upward.

- *View Map*—Click on this option to preview the Map layer. This is important when changing the Black and/or White Level settings.

- *Horizontal Channel*—Luma is the default. You may also apply the deformation to any of the RGB channels, or to White, Gray, or Black. Each creates a slightly different displacement. It's not a good idea to keyframe animate this setting.

- *Max Displacement*—Either or both the Horizontal or Vertical Displacement can be augmented in a range from –250 to 250. The farther these values are pushed away from 0 in either direction has a radical effect on the amount of distortion of the Source layer.

- *Map Behavior*—You can Center the Map layer, Stretch To Fit, or Tile It. Explore what is best for your particular project.

- *Region*—By using the Region settings, you may select to apply the entire Map layer in the distortion of the Source layer or only a portion of it.

- *Pinning*—The image will not stretch or warp where it is pinned. The options are None, Edges, Center, Left, Top, Right, Bottom, Vertical, Horizontal, and Point Pinning. Alternate pinning creates very different effects from the same control settings.

Sunset Lake

See the DispMap animation on the companion CD-ROM. The Source image was a sunset over a lake, and the Map layer was a group of trees. The Vertical Displacement was animated randomly to create the movement and the painted look.

Polar Displacement

 The Polar Displacement filter displaces pixels in the Source layer outward from a center point, as if you were looking down on a globe from the North Pole (see Figure 19.3).

Here are some possible uses for the Polar Displacement filter:

- Explore various White Radial Displacement values to transform the Source layer into an abstract painting, with the Source being used to colorize the Map layer's image content.

- Keyframe animate the White Angular Displacement value from 0 to 250 to create footage that has moving metallic textures mapped onto the Map layer footage.

The following controls allow you to adjust the Polar Displacement's parameters:

- *Mix Layer*—Select the Mix layer from any layer in the stack.

- *Blur*—The amount of Pre Blur can range from 0 to 200. The more Pre Blur, the smoother the displaced areas of the Source layer become. You can also vary the Blur Threshold (0 to 200) to alter the way the Blur is applied. Explore for best use.

- *Map Black and White Levels*—(0 to 255) Increase the Black Level from its default of 0 to bend the Source layer downward. Decrease the White Level from its default of 255 to bend the Source layer upward.

- *View Map*—Click on this option to preview the Map layer. This is important when changing the Black and/or White Level settings.

Figure 19.3
Left: The Source layer. Center: The Map layer. Right: The resulting composite produced when a Polar Displacement Map filter is applied with a White Radial Displacement of 150.

- *Center Point*—Place the centroid anywhere on the footage to determine the radial center of the Polar Displacement.

- *Radial Channel*—Luma is the default. You may also apply the deformation to any of the RGB channels, or to White, Gray, or Black. Each creates a slightly different displacement. It's not a good idea to keyframe animate this setting.

- *Radial Channel*—Luma is the default, but you may also explore other Channel settings.

- *White Radial Displacement*—(–250 to 250) The White pixels in the Map layer determine the warping of the Source layer, and this slider controls how powerful the White pixels are in this process.

- *Angular Channel*—This setting controls Angular Displacement. Luma is the default, but you should explore the other Channel settings as well to see what works best for each situation.

- *White Angular Displacement*—(–250 to 250) Either or both the Horizontal or Vertical Displacement can be augmented in a range from –250 to 250. The farther these values are pushed away from 0 in either direction has a radical effect on the amount of distortion of the Source layer.

- *Map Behavior*—You can Center the Map layer, Stretch To Fit, or Tile It. Explore what is best for your particular project.

- *Region*—By using the Region settings, you may select to apply the entire Map layer in the distortion of the Source layer or only a portion of it.

- *Pinning*—The image will not stretch or warp where it is pinned. The options are None, Edges, Center, Left, Top, Right, Bottom, Vertical, Horizontal, and Point Pinning. Alternate pinning creates very different effects from the same control settings.

> Note: Use this filter with care, since it commonly takes a lot longer to apply than a Displacement Map. Even on a 300 MHz system, a 150-frame animation can take several hours.

King Tut Lake

See the PolDisp animation on the companion CD-ROM. The Source image was a sunset over a lake, and the Map layer was a photo of King Tut. Radial Displacement was set to 150.

Ripple

 You usually see ripples when you toss a pebble in a body of still water, but the Boris f/x AE Ripple plug-in can create more varied effects than that (see Figure 19.4). The following are some possible uses for the Ripple effect:

- Use the Ripple effect to create multiple ripples (like raindrops) on the footage. Just stack three or more of the Ripple effects. Move the center point on each one, and stagger the Width and Speed of each ripple.

Figure 19.4
Left: A Ripple with Chaotic Wave set at 100. Center: Super Twirl applied. Right: Hyper Twirl applied.

- Use Hyper Twirl and Super Twirl to generate space-time warping effects. This is great for sci-fi titles and footage meant to replicate the effects of a ray gun on a surface.

The following controls allow you to adjust the effect's parameters:

- *Radius, Inside Radius, Falloff, and Center Point*—Radius settings range from 0 to 500, with 100 covering the image to the edges. The radius extends out from wherever the center point is placed. Moving the center point in an animation drags the Ripple with it. Inside Radius defines the central circle of the Ripple, and Falloff defines the speed at which the wave drops off beyond the Radius. Inside Radius is usually set to 0, with Radius having a value larger than that for Inside Radius.

- *Height and Perpendicular Height*—Height and Perpendicular Height define the amount of distortion applied to the rippling wave over time, as pixels are displaced. The only way to master these controls is to render a few animations with different settings and note the subtle changes.

- *Width*—Width is a very important control for Ripple effects. Lower settings create smaller and denser ripples, while larger settings produce wider and fewer ripples. Altering this setting over time creates ripples that move in or out from a center.

- *Speed and Phase*—These are animation controls. If Speed is set to anything but 0, it will automatically generate an animated Ripple over time on the footage.

Chaos Settings

The Chaos settings are modifiers for this effect. Explore them, and do test renders to get a better idea of how they alter the standard settings.

- *Twirl*—Twirl creates angular distortion on the Ripple. The four options are Off, On, Super, and Hyper, increasing the angular distortion with each succeeding selection. Super and Hyper are less for water effects than for more-bizarre warping.

- *Pinning*—Pinned areas do not react to distortions. Depending where the footage is pinned, very different effects result. The options are None, Edges, Center, Left, Top, Right, Bottom, Horizontal, and Vertical. Explore a few alternate pinning options before rendering your Rippled animation.

- *Waveform*—Waveform options determine the shape of the waves in your Ripple. Most differences are subtle unless magnified by other settings. Explore different waveforms to see which one fits the effect you're looking for. The options are Sine, Triangle, Square, Sawtooth, Circle, Semicircle, Uncircle, Half Sine, and 14 Spectrum waveforms unique to Boris f/x.

- *Chaos Wave and Chaos Blend*—Chaos Wave creates another waveform from two of the Spectrum waveforms, and it is added to the present waveform by the Chaos Blend settings. This creates interference patterns that add degrees of randomness to the wave.

- *Waveform Distortion and Intensity*—These settings apply a more random look to the waveforms. When used subtly, they create more natural-looking effects.

- *Stretch and Stretch Angle*—Stretch stretches (positive values) or squeezes (negative values) in the direction indicated by the Stretch Angle. Up to –88 or +88 revolutions can be applied to this angle, with utterly unpredictable results at very low or very high settings.

Creating A Chaos Ripple

You can apply chaotic parameters to a Boris AE Ripple to create some alternate ripple effects. All that is keyframe animated in this example is the Phase parameter. This effect is useful as a time tunnel. Do the following:

1. Load any animated or still footage. Activate the Boris AE Distortion Ripple filter from the Effects menu. Set the following parameters for the effect:

   - Radius 100

   - Height 9

   - Perpendicular Height 155

   - Width 1.3

   - Speed 33

   - Inside and Radius 0

2. In the Chaos settings, use the following values:

   - Twirl Off

   - Pin Top

   - Waveform Circle

   - Chaos Wave 14

   - Chaos Blend 0

   - Wave Distortion 100

   - Super Intensity

3. Keyframe the following settings for the Phase parameter: frame 1 equals –1X, and last frame +1X.

4. Render the animation and save it to disk.

Let 'er Ripple

Open MultRpl on the companion CD-ROM. The Ripple effect is created here using a stack of three Ripple plug-ins. Center points have been placed at different areas on the footage, and each ripple has its own timing and variants. Also see the ChsRip animation on the companion CD-ROM for a display of the Chaos Ripple tutorial.

Vector Displacement

The Vector Displacement filter distorts the Source layer by taking RGB information from the Map layer and distorting it in three different directions (see Figure 19.5).

Here are some possible uses for the Vector Displacement filter:

- Keyframe animate all three Rotation values to crate footage that looks like it is under water.

- Use a Limit Region of an Inside Rectangle, as defined by the Left and Right Corner Points to limit the effect to just a selected part of the footage. This works especially well when you need to affect just a face and not the surrounding environment.

The following controls allow you to adjust Vector Displacement's parameters:

- *Map Layer*—Select the Map layer from any layer in the stack.

- *Blur*—The amount of Blur can range from 0 to 200. The more Blur, the smoother the displaced areas of the Source layer become. You can also vary the Blur Threshold (0 to 200) to alter the way the Blur is applied. Explore for best use.

- *Map Black and White Levels*—(0 to 255) Increase the Black Level from its default of 0 to bend the Source layer downward. Decrease the White Level from its default of 255 to bend the Source layer upward.

- *View Map*—Click on this option to preview the Map layer. This is important when changing the Black and/or White Level settings.

- *RGB Direction*—Use the RGB radial dials to set the angle of the displacements for each of the RGB channels. Watch the preview in the Composition window, and make adjustments as necessary.

Figure 19.5
Left: The Source layer. Center: The Map layer. Right: The resulting composite produced when a Vector Displacement filter is applied.

- *RGB Displacement*—(–255 to 255) These sliders control the strength of the Displacements for each of the RGB channels. The only rule here is to explore the values, because each piece of footage will react differently.

- *Map Behavior*—You can Center the Map layer, Stretch To Fit, or Tile It. Explore what is best for your particular project.

- *Region*—By using the Region settings, you may elect to apply the entire Map layer in the distortion of the Source layer or only a portion of it.

- *Pinning*—The image will not stretch or warp where it is pinned. The options are None, Edges, Center, Left, Top, Right, Bottom, Vertical, Horizontal, and Point Pinning. Alternate pinning creates very different effects from the same control settings.

Wave

 Wave is similar to Ripple, except that you're seeing the Wave effects edge on. They do not originate from a center point that you set. Instead, they originate off the screen at an infinite distance, like cosmic rays or radio waves (see Figure 19.6).

The following are some possible uses for the Wave effect:

- Use Wave on a text layer with a very small Width setting to make the text shimmer.

- Use Wave on a solid-color background to add animated interest.

Waves are adjusted by the same controls used for ripples: Height, Perpendicular Height, Width, Speed, Phase, Wave Angle, and the Chaos settings. The only different control is Wave Angle. (For the rest of the control descriptions, refer to the Ripple section detailed above.)

- *Wave Angle*—Using this radial control, you can set the direction that the waves seem to be coming from on the footage. Animating this parameter is also possible.

Figure 19.6
Left: A Sine Wave applied at 90 degrees. Center: A Spectrum 8 waveform with a Width of 22, applied at a 45-degree angle. Right: With a Height of 33 and a Width of 40, applied from a 257-degree angle, Mona's personality changes.

Catch A Wave

Take a look at MonaWave on the companion CD-ROM. This animation displays a Wave displacement that moves on the vertical with a changing Width setting. Also see the Facewave animation for another variation of this effect.

2D Particles

 The 2D Particle filter is definitely the most complex and variable of all of the Boris AE filters because of the large number of controls involved (see Figure 19.7).

Here are some possible uses for the 2D Particle filter:

- Zoom in on the mouth or eye of a figure, and open it with the 2D Particle filter. Make sure you place the Center of Velocity centroid at the middle of the feature you want to open. Use a Particle Count and Density of 300, and the Centrifuge Velocity Type.

- Use the 2D Particle filter to dissipate the source layer to reveal the layer beneath. You do this to a bunch of layers in a stack to create a slide show. Set the Velocity to 5 to make the particles move out of the way faster.

- For creating rain: Use an XY Ratio of 60, a Particle Count of 25, Density of 200, Random Velocity Type, and a Straight Gravity with a strength of 50.

The following controls allow you to adjust the 2D Particle filter's parameters:

- *Scatter Amount*—(–3,200 to 3,200) At 0, the footage shows no effect. Moving the Scatter Amount lower or higher causes the breakup to occur in opposite directions, dependent on the Velocity Type setting.

- *Particle Count*—(1 to 300) This determines the number of particles the footage will break into. Values from 200 to 300 give the best results if you want to maintain some idea of what the footage looks like, especially for a Particle X value of 100 and 1,000 with a Scatter between –100 and 100.

  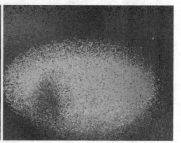

Figure 19.7
Left: Original footage. Center: Scatter Amount 256, Particle Count 100, Particle X 10, and Particle Density of 200, all with a Spiral CV Velocity Type. Right: Scatter 100, Particle Count 225, Particle X 1,000, Density 100, with a Random Velocity Type. There is also a Gravity setting of 5,000, causing the footage to break up and fall to the bottom of the frame.

- *Particle X*—(1, 10, 100, 1,000) The lower this setting, the larger and more blocky the particles are. At 1,000, the particles appear like grains of sand.

- *Particle Density*—(0 to 300) The more dense the particles are, the more cohesive and identifiable the footage will look.

- *Speed*—(0 to 5,000) This setting determines how fast the particles will move apart during an animation. A setting of 1,000 is a good default to start exploring from.

- *Speed Variance*—(0 to 100) A setting of 0 will cause all of the particles to move at the same speed, while higher settings introduce a randomness in the speed.

- *Move*—The most important here is the selection of a Velocity Type. You can select from Random, Straight, Centripetal, Centrifuge, Spiral CW (clockwise), and Spiral CCW (counter-clockwise). Each option causes a different global movement of the particles, so explore each option to see what's best for the effect you're looking for. You can also set the placement and rotation amount of the movement. If you select either of the Spiral types, you may select the Spiral Difference (strength of the spiral force from –75 to 75) and Radius (0 to 2,000).

- *Gravity*—Gravity causes the particles to fall or float (0 to 2,000), in response to the Gravity Type you set (Random, Straight, Centripetal, or Centrifuge). The higher the setting, the stronger the effect.

- *Scatter Wipe*—This is set to Off by default. If On, you can select from Top, Bottom, Left, or Right wipes. A wipe is used as a transition to another layer.

- *Use Alpha Only*—Checking this box applies the 2D Particle settings to the Alpha channel alone.

- *Keep Original*—Checking this box causes all of the effects to be overlaid on the Source footage.

- *Random Seed*—(–32,000 to 32,000) Values input here add variance to the effect.

- *XY Ratio*—(–100 to 100) A value of 0 creates particles that match the width-height ratio of the original footage. Values lower than 0 stretch the particles horizontally, and values higher than 0 stretch them vertically.

- *Size Tweak*—(1 to 20) Increasing this value forces the particles to overlap more.

- *Frame Size*—(0 to 600 percent) The default is 100, which allows the particles to occur within the current bounds of your frame. Lower settings reduce the size of the frame, so the particles, and your footage, become smaller. Sizes greater than 100 create larger frames, and larger particles as well. This setting acts to zoom the entire frame up or down.

- *Particle Shape*—Select from any shape in the stack for the particles. This is especially useful when the shape is an Illustrator file. Birds, stars, or any other shape you can think of can become that of the particles. This is an especially powerful feature of the 2D Particles filter.

- *Shape Use Alpha*—This addresses the Alpha channel alone.

- *Shape Invert*—The opaque areas of the shape are reversed if this is checked.

- *Shape Transformation*—(0 to 32,000) Settings above 0 increase the rate at which the standard rectangle shape is transformed into the selected shape over the length of the animation.

- *Opacity*—(0 to 100 percent) Defaulted to 100, lower settings cause the particles to become more transparent.

- *Z Order*—The Z axis runs in and out of your view screen. These settings determine how the particles look like when they are in front of or behind each other on that axis. Explore with each project you use.

2DPart

See the 2DPart animation on the companion CD-ROM. It was created by using the 2D Particle filter with a Centrifuge Velocity Type. The Scatter Amount ranges from 1 to 777. Particle Count is set to 300.

Scatterize

 Scatterize is a much simpler form of the 2D Particle effect, with far fewer controls (see Figure 19.8).

Here are some possible uses for the Scatterize filter:

- Use a Radial Style and keyframe animate the Variance values from 0 to 100 to make your footage look like it is exploding outward from wherever you have placed the Center Point.

- Use a Directional Style and keyframe animate the Directional Angle to cause the scattered particles to rotate around the Center Point location.

The following controls allow you to adjust the Scatterize filter's parameters:

- *Variance*—(0 to 100) This setting determines how scattered the footage will become.

- *Scatter Percentage*—(0 to 100) This setting determines what percentage of total pixels scatter over the footage.

- *Style*—You can select from Uncontrolled (random dots), Radial, or Directional.

Figure 19.8
Left: The original footage. Center: Radial Style with a Variance of 5. Right: Directional Style with an Angle of 130 degrees.

- *Directional Angle*—If you selected a Directional Style, this radial dial sets the angle.

- *Center Point*—The Center Point placement determines the place the scattering is focused on.

- *Center Bias*—When checked, the Center Point is emphasized.

- *Randomize*—Checking this option allows you to use the Random Seed slider.

- *Random Seed*—(–32,000 to 32,000) Each new setting creates a slightly different pattern of particles. If you keyframe animate this setting, the particles will seem to sparkle.

- *Apply Mode*—Select an Apply Mode that gives you the look you want from this list. Explore the possibilities.

- *Apply Mix*—This slider controls the mix of the composited footage with the uncomposited source. When set to 0, or when using a Normal Apply Mode, it has no effect. Explore various settings, and see what works best for your specific footage.

Cube

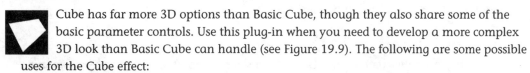 Cube has far more 3D options than Basic Cube, though they also share some of the basic parameter controls. Use this plug-in when you need to develop a more complex 3D look than Basic Cube can handle (see Figure 19.9). The following are some possible uses for the Cube effect:

- Spin the cube, with lights and shadows, over an animated background composed of solid colors that change hues.

- Create a rubber-sheet footage animation. Just set the X scale to 0 at the start, and the Y scale to 300. (Uncheck the Keep Proportional To X box.) At the end of the animation, X should equal 300, and Y should equal 0. Can you guess what this will look like? To make it even more interesting, tumble it one revolution from start to finish, keeping Spin and Revolve to 0 throughout.

For information on the standard controls, look at those just presented for Basic Cube. The following controls, specific to Cube, allow you to adjust the effect's parameters in ways that Basic Cube cannot:

Figure 19.9
Left: Using Shadow as a glow by maximizing intensity and softness with a bright color. Center: Adding light to the displaced cube adds more viewer interest. Right: Light and shadow give the cube increased dimensionality.

- *X Scale/Y Scale*—Instead of a simple Scale control like that contained in the Basic Cube plug-in, Cube allows you to separate the X and Y dimensions for scaling. Both can be locked together, however, by checking the Keep Proportional To X Scale box.

- *Shadow*—You can force the cube to cast a shadow by controlling the shadow's distance, intensity, softness, angle, and color. It's a good idea not to use too much softness, or the connection between the shadow and the cube will be lost as a shadow effect. It's also necessary to tone down the intensity to 75 percent at most if there is a background. That way, you'll see the background content through the shadow. Use a dark color so the shadow doesn't stand out over the image content.

> **Note: Shadow can become a glow for the cube by simply using a bright color, and setting the Intensity and Softness to 100, while keeping distance close at about 10. Angle doesn't matter in this case.**

- *Camera and Light*—Placing and adjusting lights is the main distinction between Cube and Basic Cube. The Camera controls are just placement controls for the cube, but the Light controls offer new and beautiful effects.

Animation Cubed

Open Cubey from the companion CD-ROM. This is an animation that displays a spinning basic cube, with semitransparent footage placed on its faces. Displace is another cube that shows a displacement on a cube with lights and shadows.

Cylinder

Cylinders make great receptacles for wraparound labels or any other art. When you look at a cylinder from the top, it becomes a hollow ring, just right for focusing on any image element (see Figure 19.10). The following are some possible uses for the Cylinder effect:

- Wrap a label around a partial cylinder, and spin it in space (Y axis) to advertise a product. Place a movie on the back face.

Figure 19.10
Left: You can generate cylinders from any layer in the composition. Center: By decreasing the Wrap Percentage, you create partial cylinders, perfect for labels. Right: Adjusting the Perspective setting from 100 to 1 gives the cylinder a tapered look.

- Use Axial Displacement in an animation, from -200 to +200, to fly a layer up from off the bottom of the screen to off the top. Use a Wrap Percentage of 1 to emphasize the perspective.

The following controls allow you to adjust the Cylinder effect's unique parameters:

- *Wrap Percentage*—Set to 100, this control produces a perfect cylinder. Set to anything less, it creates a partial cylinder. At a setting of 0, the 3D wrap becomes a perfect plane.

- *Axial Displacement*—Use Axial Displacement (–200 to +200) to simulate an object moving from the bottom off the top of the screen. Negative settings move the layer lower, while positive settings move it higher. When coupled with a low Wrap Percentage setting of 1, the wrapped layer takes on a cone-like appearance, further simulating a 3D object flying up and closer. Use this effect to simulate a sky camera watching a rocket taking off.

- *Alternate Back Face*—With this control, you can map a different footage on the back face of the cylinder. This is especially effective when Wrap Percentage is set between 40 and 60.

Cylindrical Animation

Open the Cylfire file on the companion CD-ROM. A spinning cylinder reacts to an explosion in the background. The explosion footage is from the REEL explosions collection from ArtBeats.

Now take a look at CylDbl. A partial cylinder spins with a graphic on the front and the same movie mapped to the back that is used as a background. Mapping a surface with the same animation that is used on the background makes the surface appear as a mirror. The background animation was created in MetaCreations Bryce 3D.

DVE

 A DVE is a digital video effect, which can be interpreted to mean a lot these days. Here, it refers to a planar surface that can be turned to any perspective and size. This effect is common when it comes to creating "flying logo" effects (see Figure 19.11). The following are some possible uses for the DVE effect:

- Create a logo that flies up from the background. If you like, use Alpha channel dropouts on the layer to emphasize the logo design. (Refer to the sections in this chapter on Alpha channel effects in Boris f/x AE).

- Map a series of images on stacked DVE planes and create a perspective slide show, allowing each one to fly into view at its own angle.

We have already covered the bulk of the control parameters present in the DVE effect. Refer to the previous Boris f/x AE perspective effects for a look at all of the control parameter details if you need to. The only unique controls offered by the DVE effect has to do with adding and customizing borders around the layer plane:

- *Border Width, Opacity, Softness, and Color*—This is the only perspective effect that allows you to add a border around the layer. It can be any width, opacity, softness, and color you like. Try to contrast the border with the background so the DVE layer pops out.

Figure 19.11
Left: The image layer can be turned to any angle. Center: Adding a border that contrasts with the background pops the DVE out. Right: Adding a shadow adds 3D depth.

REALISTIC SHADOWS

When it comes to selecting a color for the shadow, and you have background footage, select a dark color from that footage. (The shadow will look more natural.)

PageTurn

 Page turns have become commonplace as TV commercial effects. Boris f/x AE's PageTurn plug-in gives you all the control you need to produce smooth, high-quality page turns (see Figure 19.12). The following are some possible uses for the PageTurn effect:

- Use this effect to create a transition from one animated clip to another. This is especially useful when a storyline changes from one location to another.

- Use a page turn to flip the pages of a book. This can be a very effective way to animate the narrative of a storybook, even showing inset animated pictures on the revealed page, mixed with text.

The following controls allow you to adjust the effect's parameters:

- *Offset*—With a range from 0 to 100 percent, this control tells the top layer how much of the turn is complete. Commonly, a setting of zero would be used at the first frame and 100 at the last frame (or perhaps somewhere before the last frame). That way, the underlying layer would be displayed on the screen for some time.

- *Direction*—This is the direction the page will turn from. Animating it produces some strange results, as the page changes direction in the middle of a completed turn cycle. Most times, you'll want to stay away from settings divisible by 90, since they show less of the 3D nature of the turn. The exception would be the simulation of a scroll or window shade rollup, which are created very effectively at angles of 0, 90, 180, and -90 degrees.

- *Flap Radius and Opacity*—The Flap Radius sets the amount of layer area that will participate in the turn as the rollup occurs. A setting of 50 creates the turn with the most curvature. A setting of 0 creates more of a sharp flap movement than a turn.

Figure 19.12

Left: A standard page turn begins at one of the corners. Center: Stack as many page turns as you like to the same layer. This creates an animation that shows different corners or edges turning at the same time. Right: Page turns can be taking place on multiple layers, either at close to the same time or widely staggered.

- *Light And Shadow*—Most times you will want to maximize both of these settings because strong lights and shadows increase the 3D nature of this effect.

- *Alternate Back*—As the top layer goes through a page turn, the "back" of the layer becomes visible. This option allows you to map the back with another piece of footage. A subtly textured image or a solid color works best, since they don't detract from the content involved. You could map the back with a parchment texture, or one that looks like burlap, to give the impression that the active layer was made of these materials. Your project and design sense will determine the choice.

Turning The Page

The PageTurn file on the companion CD-ROM shows the PageTurn effect in action. Two clips from the ArtBeats REEL collections were used as the footage, and a smooth page turn accomplishes the transition.

Sphere

Spherical 3D effects are just becoming widely popular. Expect pretty severe image distortion when you use them (see Figure 19.13). The following are some possible uses for the Sphere effect:

- Wrap a Cartesian map on a sphere for a revolving globe.

- Create a beach ball by using the Sphere plug-in on a graphic with red and white horizontal stripes.

Details on the use of all of the Sphere controls have already been covered in this chapter related to the other Boris f/x AE perspective plug-ins. Refer to those previous details for understanding how the controls function.

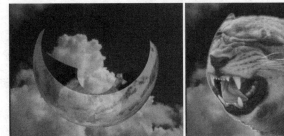

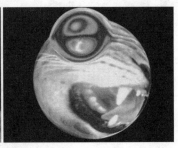

Figure 19.13
Left: Hollow crescent bowl-like objects can be produced with the Sphere effect by setting the Perspective control to 1 and the Wrap Percentage to 60. Then adjust size and rotation as necessary. Center: A cougar's face wrapped on a Sphere, and an Alpha two-way was used to drop out its background. Right: This strange result was created by first wrapping a graphic of a cougar's head on a sphere, and then applying a Boris f/x AE Bulge distortion to the eye.

Wild Stuff

Check out CougAlph on the comapanion CD-ROM. The image of a cougar is warped around a sphere using the Sphere plug-in. Then a two-way Alpha is applied, dropping out the cougar's background. The whole image revolves in front of one of the ArtBeats REEL Puffy Clouds stock animations.

> *Note: Some of the background images and animations used as layer content in the animations on this book's CD-ROM were provided by ArtBeats Software Inc. ArtBeats is a company dedicated to developing high-quality images and textures. ArtBeats offers the professional After Effects producer a wide array of image, animation, and texture volumes. For further information, contact ArtBeats at www.artbeats.com.*

BERSERK I

20

Starting with this chapter, and continuing for the next four, we'll look at the After Effects plug-in volumes from DigiEffects.

This chapter focuses on DigiEffects Berserk, a collection of plug-ins for creating new image looks and organic effects.

Blizzard

This plug-in creates a snowstorm over your footage. You can control its strength, from a gentle snow to a full-fledged blizzard (see Figure 20.1). The following are some possible uses for the Blizzard effect:

• Use a photo as a backdrop that shows a rural setting, perhaps a house nestled among the pines. Use Blizzard to place the scene in a deep winter environment.

• Color the Flakes red. Uncheck Brighten, and use a 70% Opacity setting. Set sizes at 0 to 10, and place the blizzard over a volcanic scene. Animate, displaying falling fiery debris.

• With Brighten off and a blue-green color, use the Blizzard plug-in to create underwater bubbles.

The following controls allow you to adjust the Blizzard effect's parameters:

• *Number Of Flakes*—The range is from 0 to 30,000. On 72dpi footage, more than 300 blots out the screen. You'd have to be working on a pretty large piece of footage to

Figure 20.1
Left: The original image. Center: 2,000 flakes ranging in size from 0 to 10. Right: 200 flakes sized 10 to 30 with Brighten off.

use anything over 1,000 or so, although you could animate large numbers of flakes down to smaller numbers to create an interesting wipe effect.

- *Wind and Gravity*—These are animation settings. Wind (–50 to 50) blows the flakes to the side, while Gravity (0 to 50) pulls them to the ground at faster rates as the values increase. A gentle snow might have a Gravity setting of 10, while a hard snow might have Gravity maximized. Changing Wind settings from negative to positive values during the animation would add horizontal shift to the flakes.

- *Lift Amount and Frequency*—Blowing snow tends to float up as well as down, especially when the storm is on the gentler side. Set the Lift Amount (0 to 100) and its Frequency (0 to 100) here. With flakes colored red and a high Lift Amount and Frequency, the flakes could be used as sparks.

- *Flake Color and Size*—For Color, do not use white, since it is not a good color for animated sequences or video. Use a light blue for snow, a darkish-red for fiery debris, or even a greenish-brown with a large flake size for falling leaves.

- *Brighten/Solid, Opacity and Blend*—If the flakes are solid, they appear as shaded spheres. If Brighten is selected, they blend as lightened areas over image content. Opacity and Blend is adjusted according to image content visibility.

BumpMaker

This effect is used to add a bump-like texture to the selected footage. The plug-in suffers from limited variables for customizing a texture (see Figure 20.2). Use this effect to texturize footage or to create a completely textured layer.

The following controls allow you to adjust the BumpMaker effects parameters:

- *Elevation and Height*—Elevation (0.1 to 100) determines the elevation of the assumed light source that affects the visibility of the bumpiness. Height (0.1 to 100) is the altitude of the bumps. Adjusting both controls in concert allows you to explore variations in the texture.

- *Grain, Random Seed, and Smoothness*—Grain (0 to 100) determines the visibility of the bumps, and is usually set from 80 to 100. Some colors can allow lower Grain settings, depending on

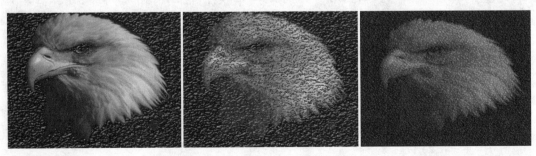

Figure 20.2
Left: A BumpMaker layer is used as a backdrop for an Alpha-masked image. Center: An Alpha-masked, BumpMaker layer is placed over another image. Right: The BumpMaker layer is blended with the original image, all on one layer.

the image's color palette. The Random Seed ranges from 1 to 32,000, though there is little change in the look of the bumps when this setting is altered. Smoothness (0.1 to 100) affects the clumpiness of the grains. Lower Smoothness settings lead to more-pixelated and smaller grains, while larger settings make the grains into elongated blobs.

- *Tint Color and Blend*—Use a tint color that suits the footage being affected. Blend in the original image, or leave Blend at 100 to get nothing but a texturized layer.

> **Note: This effect works much better when the Blend is set at 100 and the layer is used as an Alpha mask on another image.**

Contourist

Use this effect to flatten photographic footage and to create 2D cartoony results—see Figure 20.3. The following are some possible uses for the Contourist effects:

- Use Contourist to transform your real-world animations into rotoscoped animated comic-book art. Adjust the Tolerance control until you achieve the look you want.

- Create a one-color rotoscope of the image by setting all of the Contour Depth values to the same number.

The following controls allow you to adjust Contourist's parameters:

- *Blend and Tolerance*—Blend (1 to 100) sets the amount of blend with the original footage. At 0, you get no plug-in effect, and at 100 you get no original image. Tolerance is adjusted to achieve different looks. Explore different tolerances and preview the results.

- *Smoothness and After Smooth*—Smoothness (0 to 100) gets rid of pixelated areas as the values increase. After Smooth (0 to 100) adds a blur. For sharper rotoscoped art, keep After Smooth settings to 10 or lower.

- *Contour Depth and Color*—Contourist applies five colors in various strengths to the selected footage. You may select these colors with either the eyedropper or system color palette. Alter their respective intensity with the Contour Depth settings (0 to 255).

Figure 20.3
Left: With Smoothness and Blend set to 50 and Tolerance to 25, a photo becomes a symbol. Center: A blend of 20 and a Tolerance of 10. Right: Randomly altering the Contour Depth values creates an infinite number of looks.

Contouring Water

Open Contourist on the companion CD-ROM. This animation uses footage from the ArtBeats REEL water collection, which is altered with the Contourist plug-in from DigiEffects.

RotoToon Project

Do the following exercise to create a rotoscoped animation from photographic footage:

1. Import a photographic movie and place it in the Composition window.

2. Go to the Effects menu and select the DigiEffects Berserk Contourist filter.

3. Set the following parameters:

   - Blend 50

   - Smoothness 5

   - Tolerance 100

   - After Smooth 5

4. Select the five colors for the rotoscoping based on the palette you would like your animation to display. Selecting the separate Contour Depth varies their influence in the mix. You will have to watch the Composition window as you explore the variations in Color and Color Depth to achieve your desired palette.

5. There is no need for any keyframing, unless you want your palette to change over time. If you do, just vary the Colors and Color Depths to achieve a new look.

6. Render and save to disk. See the Cntr animation on the CD-ROM for a display of this exercise.

Crystalizer

This effect breaks your footage up into nodules or crystals (see Figure 20.4). The following are some possible uses for the Crystalizer effects:

- Use this effect to add warmth to nature scenes, like an out-of-focus camera. Bring things into focus again by moving Blend to 0.

- Use very low Size settings and check Randomize Every Frame to create swarms of pixels on the footage, which may act as an interesting transition between A/B footage.

The following controls allow you to adjust the Crystalizer effect's parameters:

- *Number Of Nodules, Size, and Falloff*—The number of nodules can range from 0 to 32,000. This effect renders very quickly, even at the higher numbers. It takes more nodules to define the image at lower Size settings, and fewer at higher sizes. A clearer image is produced by keeping the quantity high and the size low. Nodule Falloff adjusts the appearance of each nodule, with lower settings creating smoother crystals. Smoother crystals lead to a more blurry image, so if you want a sharper image, keep the Nodule Falloff set high.

Figure 20.4
Left: Setting Nodule Falloff high (90 to 100) allows the image to be defined. Center: Setting Nodule Falloff low (here, it's set to 20) blurs the nodules. Right: Decreasing the size of the nodules and blending the effect with the original image can create an interesting look.

- *Random Seed and Randomize Every Frame*—Random Seed (0 to 5,000) determines the nodule layout and creates a sparkling effect when animated. Checking the Randomize Every Frame box does just that, randomizing the effect on every frame in the animation.

- *Background Color and Blend*—Background Color allows you to choose the color with the eyedropper or the system color picker. Blend (1 to 100) sets the amount of blend with the original footage. At 0, you get no plug-in effect, and at 100, you get no original image.

CycloWarp

CycloWarp creates ripple-like effects that spread the image around the waves (see Figure 20.5). Use this effect when you want a ripple that looks more electronic than liquid based. Leave the Blend at 100 to emphasize the effect. Or, create a power wave that ripples out from the eye of your subject by simply placing the Power Centroid over the eye. Blend the image at about 60.

The following controls allow you to adjust the CycloWarp's parameters:

- *Strength*—The higher the Strength setting, the more the layer will be affected by the waves. Lower settings create mirrored effects, with image elements still intact.

Figure 20.5
Left: By placing the power centroid over the eye of this eagle, and using a Blend setting of 60, the wave is composited. Center: With the Wave Number set at 12, and a Blend of 100, the image is warped in a ripple-like fashion. Right: Pushing Number Of Waves and Wave Strength to 100 creates moiré patterns.

- *Power Centroid*—Placing the crosshairs on your footage determines the center for the effect.

- *Number Of Waves*—This is a frequency setting. The higher the value, the more waves will be generated. (The range is 0.1 to 100.)

- *Wrap Around*—It's good to check this box when you want to create seamless tiled textures for wrapping around objects in a later 3D application.

- *Phase*—With this radial control, you can adjust the wave phase by degrees and revolutions.

- *Blend*—Blend (1 to 100) sets the amount of blend with the original footage. At 0, you get no plug-in effect, and at 100 you get no original image.

EdgeX

 This effect is a cousin of the Contourist effect. It creates posterized footage based upon the RGB channels (see Figure 20.6).

To set the output to a two-color effect, do the following:

1. Select one color from the RGB options, and move its Edge control slider to 100. Set the Softness to 20.

2. Set the other two Edge control sliders to 255.

The following controls allow you to adjust EdgeX's parameters:

- *Edge and Softness*—Each of the RGB channels has a separate control for Edge (0 to 255) and Softness (0 to 128) settings. Edge settings determine value of that channel in the mix, and Softness sets the smoothness of the color blocks.

- *Mix With Original*—This is the same as a Blend parameter.

Figure 20.6
Left: A two-color image results from setting the colors you don't want to use to an Edge setting of 255. Center: Maximizing the Softness at 128 creates a more photographic-toned result. Right: Softness at 0, blended at 50% with the original.

Fog Bank

 When you need to alter the atmosphere to create a fog or haze, this is one effect that does the trick. This effect uses three layered planes so that each one can move against the other one (see Figure 20.7). The following are some possible uses for the Fog Bank effect:

Figure 20.7
Left: The unaltered photo. Center: With a Brightness of 100, the fog exhibits light and dark patches. Right: Raising the brightness level on all three planes of the fog intensifies the effect.

- Add to any outdoor footage, whether urban or rural, to create a smooth and realistic moving bank of fog or smog.

- With Brightness raised to maximum on all three fog planes, the effect can be applied to a blue color layer to simulate clouds.

The following controls allow you to adjust the Fog Bank's parameters for each of the three layered planes: Closest, Further, and Furthest:

- *Blend*—This control determines how much of the effect blends in the original footage. Use sparingly, since too much Blend will obliterate the effect.

- *Brightness*—This controls the brightness of the effect layer (from 0.1 to 100). Use more brightness on closer layers to enhance depth perception.

- *Offset*—Set the crosshairs to define the point, which the effect uses as a center. Use different offsets for each layer.

- *Seed*—Set a random Seed number.

- *Scale Horizontal and Scale Vertical*—This control stretches the fog bank vertically and/or horizontally. The settings range from 0.1 to 100. Larger scale numbers will make the fog look like it is receding from you.

Fog City
Open the FogBank file on the CD-ROM, and watch the fog roll gently across the bay.

GravityWell

GravityWell is a full-fledged particle system. It creates cosmic gravity wells, a form of black hole. It can swallow and/or emit particles. The following are some possible uses for the GravityWell effect:

- Use the GravityWell plug-in to create a particle storm being emitted from the eye or mouth of a character in your footage.

- Obviously, we would be remiss if we didn't suggest that you create black hole footage. Use a graphic that has a lens flare at the center, and make that the center of the action.

The following controls allow you to adjust the GravityWell's parameters:

- *Full Render*—Just say *no* to Full Render in the preview if you have over 200 particles. Full Render allows you to see the finished rendering in the preview, but at a time cost you will not enjoy. Instead, keep the particle count below 100 if you want to see particle rendering in the preview. You can increase the count just before rendering. With Full Render off, GravityWell renders just single pixels for the effect. With Full Render on, larger and more smeared particles are rendered.

- *Number Of Particles and Particle Life*—You can select between 0 and 32,000 particles, but values above 5,000 start to increase rendering times dramatically. Particle Life tells your system how long the particles should remain at full strength before fading out. The range is from 0 to 1,000, with 100 being a suitable default in most cases.

- *Show Streaks*—With Show Streaks on, you'll see motion trails as the particles revolve.

- *Min/Max Size*—Size ranges from 0 to 100. Explore the differences, since each project will require a new size for best results.

- *Wells: Source, Direction, and Strength*—There are three separate wells, with source locations for the particles to center on. A separate direction can be set for each according to revolutions and degrees with the standard rotational control. The Strength setting can be positive or negative (–500 to +500). Positive values cause the source area to repel particles, while negative values cause the source area to attract them.

- *Blend*—Blend (1 to 100) sets the amount of blend with the original footage. At 0, you get no plug-in effect, and at 100, you get no original image.

> *Note: GravityWell takes the color for particles from the targeted layer. Use footage with a lot of color, and the particles will attain multicolored aspects, too.*

Gravity Works

The effects created with this plug-in are too subtle to show in a grayscale picture. Instead, see the GravWell and GravWel2 animations on this book's companion CD-ROM. These two animations display the two types of GravityWell options. GravWell uses single pixels to display the effect, while GravWel2 uses particles.

Laser

 Lasers can be used to evoke many different situations in a project. They can be emitted from a ray gun, or used to simulate cosmic effects (see Figure 20.8). They can also be used to make a text block stand out or to point the way to another feature in the footage. The following are some other possible uses for the Laser effects:

- Create footage that shows someone holding a ray gun or a magic wand. Use the Laser effect in After Effects to animate the beam that is emitted.

- Use the Laser effect to show a beam being emitted from someone's eyes.

- Use a High-Energy laser beam as a meteor trail, streaking behind a skyline.

Figure 20.8
A lens flare is used to disperse (from left to right) a High-Energy laser beam, a Pistol laser beam, and a Stun laser beam. All have Spacing switched on.

DigiEffects Laser plug-in is really four plug-ins in one: High Energy, Pistol, Thin, and Stun.

The following controls allow you to adjust the Laser effect's parameters:

- *Beam Type*—You can choose from four Laser types: High Energy, Pistol, Thin, and Stun. Thin is a straight line, and is commonly used as a pointer to direct the eye to features in an image.

- *Start Point, Color and Size*—Crosshairs allow you to start a laser beam anywhere in the footage, with start color selectable. Size refers to the size of the beam at the start. (The range is 0.1 to 1,000.)

- *End Point, Color, and Size*—Crosshairs allow you to end a Laser beam anywhere in the footage, with end color selectable. Size refers to the size of the beam at the end. (The range is 0.1 to 1,000.)

- *Use Spacing*—Checking this box means the beam will be broken up into smaller segments, as indicated by the Spacing control settings. (The range is 0.1 to 1,000.)

- *Blend*—Blend (1 to 100) sets the amount of blend with the original footage. At 0, you get no plug-in effect, and at 100 you get no original image.

Sci-Fi

In the Laser animation on the companion CD-ROM, a Stun laser's fiery beam pierces the night sky.

Newsprint

The Newsprint effect simulates a halftone print seen close up. This effect is not as useful animated as it is for treating single images in your composition. For example, some possible uses for the Newsprint effect include:

- Use this effect on a text block to simulate a print closeup.

- Use this effect on an image you're zooming in on. Set the effect to 0 at the start, and increase the value as the zoom gets closer.

See Figure 20.9 for some examples of using Newsprint.

Figure 20.9
Left: Dot pattern at size 15. Center: Line pattern at size 20. Right: Square pattern at size 25.

The following controls allow you to adjust the parameters of this effect:

- *Halftone Shape*—Select Square, Line, or Dot. EachOne will act differently as far as clarity is concerned, depending on the image content. The best footage to use will have some solid color areas, as opposed to images packed with details from edge to edge.

- *Offset*—This control sets the center of the action, but doesn't seem to have much effect.

- *Size*—The size of the halftone elements is important (0 to 50). Size seems to work best from 15 to 25 as far as maintaining image clarity. The lower the values are set, the larger the simulated halftone blocks will be.

- *Angle*—For smaller details, use angles other than ones divisible by 90. Angles of 45 and 30 degrees work well.

- *Dark Color/Light Color*—The Newsprint plug-in renders in two colors, both of which you may select.

- *Blend*—Blend (1 to 100) sets the amount of blend with the original footage. At 0, you get no plug-in effect, and at 100 you get no original image. The effect looks best when applied at a Blend setting of 100.

> **Note: The halftone patterns themselves do not animate. If you set a keyframe at the start as a Dot pattern, and one at frame 100 as a Line pattern, the pattern will suddenly change to a Line at frame 100.**

BERSERK II

All the effects in this chapter center on image distortion, media looks, and environmental and organic effects.

DigiEffects

The ten DigiEffects Berserk plug-ins covered in this chapter are: NightBloom, Oil Paint, Pearls, Perspectron, Ripploid, Spintron, Squisher, Starfield, Still Noise, and VanGoghist.

NightBloom

NightBloom is a combination of the Blur and Media effects, with an emphasis on blurring. *Blooming* is a term used by printers to describe images or elements of an image that are flooded with so much light that they become blotchy. Here, blooming is used as a positive animation effect (see Figure 21.1).

Possible uses for the NightBloom effect include:

• Use NightBloom on a dark photo that shows lights in the distance. The lights will take on a blurry aura, as if seen through a mist.

• Use NightBloom with Blur set to 100 at the start of an animation, and 0 at the end. Used in this manner, NightBloom creates an interesting transition that moves from posterized blurriness to clarity.

The following controls allow you to adjust the parameters of the NightBloom effect:

• *Bloom Shape*—You can choose among five options that set the general NightBloom shape: Normal, Narrow, Hexagonal, Circular, and Flares. Use either Circular or Flares to emphasize lights in the distance in a night scene.

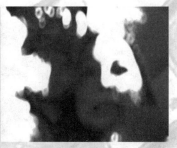

Figure 21.1
Left: The unaffected image. Center: A Flare Bloom sized at 10 with a Blur of 50. Right: A narrow Bloom of size 25 and a Blur of 100.

- *Bloom Size, Threshold, and Brightness*—Bloom Size (range 0.1 to 100) determines the areas of the footage to be affected, with lower sizes targeting the darker parts of the image. The Threshold value (0.1 to 255) determines the dividing line between affected and nonaffected parts of the footage, and Brightness (0.1 to 100) sets the amount of blotching that wipes the image with light.

> *Note: Keep Bloom Size at 25 or lower, since higher settings have an adverse effect on rendering times, increasing them by 10 times or more.*

- *Blur Amount*—Blur Amount (0.1 to 100) determines how much the source footage is affected. Set this value high if you are going to use NightBloom as a transitional fade between sequences.

- *Blend*—Blend (1 to 100) sets the amount of blend with the original footage. At 0 you get no plug-in effect, and at 100 you get no original image.

Oil Paint

 The Oil Paint plug-in gives your footage the effect of an oil painting. It is best used on nonanimated footage (see Figure 21.2). The following are some possible uses for the Oil Paint effect:

- Use Oil Paint to diffuse a backdrop that is too busy for foreground elements. Use Diameter settings of 30 and above.

- Create a soft, romantic look for your footage by setting the Diameter slider to 8, with Smoother Paint on.

The following controls allow you to adjust Oil Paint's parameters:

- *Diameter*—This is the main setting. It ranges from 1 to 50, although you should stay within the 8-to-12 range to make footage look like a true oil painting. Higher values tend to obscure image content.

- *Smoothing*—The two smoothness operators are the Smoother Paint checkbox and its Smoothness range (1 to 128). If Smoother Paint is unchecked, the Smoothness range setting is ignored.

Figure 21.2
From left to right, Diameter settings of 8, 30, and 45. Optimum settings for Oil Paint are from 8 to 12.

- *Blend*—Blend (1 to 100) sets the amount of blend with the original footage. At 0 you get no blend, and at 100 you get no original image.

Pearls

 This is a particle system that adds a pearled or cobblestoned look to your footage. Animated, it can create effects like molecules in motion. Use a +25 vertical speed setting with 200 small particles to create bubbles rising from a glass of champagne, with the footage source checked on.

Creating A Boiling Fibrous Mass

With the footage source off, follow these three steps to create a boiling, fibrous mass (see Figure 21.3):

1. Set all animation speed controls to 0. This stabilizes the framing of the effect.

2. At the start of the animation, set brightness (both minimum and maximum) to 90. Set the size to a minimum of 250 and a maximum of 400.

3. Randomly keyframe the maximum size to different values, from 300 to 500 during the animation. Force the maximum size to fluctuate up and down.

The following controls allow you to adjust the effect's parameters:

- *Include Source*—Checking this box includes the source image wherever the particles are absent.

- *Number Of Nodules*—You may select from 0 to 5,000 particles and animate the number over time. With No Source Image checked, use smaller numbers of larger particles to get a boiling-mud effect. Larger numbers of particles at a smaller size produces tiny, percolating bubbles.

- *Seed Value*—This is a random-seed generator that alters the particle pattern. It is best set and not keyframe animated in most cases because the particle pattern can look too erratic if the seed is animated.

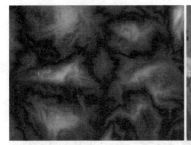

Figure 21.3
Left: 400 particles for a fibrous mass (ranging in size from 300 to 500). Center: 500 smaller particles are placed over the image with Include Source checked. Right: Increasing the number of particles to the maximum of 5,000 obliterates the underlying image.

- *Size and Brightness*—Particles can range in size from 0 to 500, and in brightness from 0 to 100. Use the settings that are best for the footage and the effect you are attempting to achieve. Stay away from brightness settings of 75 or higher since they pixelate the particles.

- *Animation Settings*—You can control the movements of the particles horizontally (left to – 100 and right to +100) and vertically (down to –100 and up to +100). Settings approaching 0 horizontally and/or vertically slow the particles down.

- *Tint Color and Blend*—Tint Color (the color between the particles) can be selected with the eyedropper or the system color picker. If Include Source is checked and you have selected a tint color of white, the source image will show through in its original palette colors. Blend (in a range of 1 to 100) sets the amount of blend with the original footage. At 0, you get no plug-in effect, and at 100 you get no original image.

Perspectron

This perspective effect is a combination of mapping and warping the perspective plane. The result is footage that acts as if it were reflected in a funhouse mirror (see Figure 21.4). The following are some possible uses for the Perspectron effect:

- Animated, this effect can be used to denote a dream sequence, or even a hallucination.

- If you use an area shaped like an amoeba's silhouette, the Perspectron effect can animate it over time. This is also useful for underwater scenes and liquid text effects.

The following controls allow you to adjust the effect's parameters:

- *Control Point Placement*—You can place four control points to control the warp of the footage: upper left and right, and lower left and right. It takes a few minutes of experimentation to realize how these control points affect the footage, but it soon becomes very intuitive. Place the upper points wider apart and the lower points closer together, and you have footage that is warped so that it is wider at the bottom than at the top. The control points can be placed according to keyframes, so the effect can be animated. The result is like footage mapped on a moving rubber sheet.

Figure 21.4
Left: The original image. Center: Control points placed far apart at the top and close together at the bottom. Right: Control points placed close together at the top, and far apart at the bottom.

Note: Consider switching the effect off as you place the control points. The control points act very fast, and, with the effect switched off, you can place all of them without being confused by the preview rendering. When they are all placed, switch the effect on again.

- *Include Source and Wrap Around*—Include Source results in a layered effect, with the source image as a background for the semitransparent Perspectron footage. Wrap Around allows the footage to completely cover the source image area.

- *Blend*—You can choose the background color with the eyedropper or the system color picker. Blend (1 to 100) sets the amount of blend with the original footage. At 0, you get no plug-in effect, and at 100 you get no original image.

Feeling Queasy?

Pspctron (found on this book's companion CD-ROM) shows the Perspectron effect in action. Don't get seasick watching it.

Ripploid

Ripploid combines a tiling and ripple effect, and, when animated over time, creates moving optical illusions (see Figure 21.5). The following are some possible uses for the Ripploid effect:

- Layer multiple Ripploids to generate very realistic—and surrealistic—multiple ripple effects.

- Start an animation with a strength setting of –100, and end it with +100. This creates a sequence that shows the footage starting as a ripple, moving toward the pure image, and then moving out as a ripple again. This could be a useful transition sequence.

Note: The spaces between the ripples are transparent, so placing multiple layers of your footage in the Composition widow and applying a different Ripploid effect to each one creates amazing multiple rippled overlays.

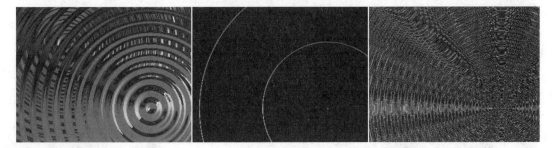

Figure 21.5
Left: Multiple Ripploid layers. Center: A low number of waves (five are used here) with a strength of 1,000 creates orbits that look like cloud-chamber traces. Right: 100 waves at a Strength of -100 produces interference patterns.

The following controls allow you to adjust the effect's parameters:

- *Strength*—Strength ranges from –1,000 to +10,000, with 0 applying no Ripploid effect. Very high strength values (1,000 and up) create dense backgrounds featuring few waves. Strength can be animated.

- *Power Centroid*—Placing the crosshairs on the footage determines the center of the Ripploid effect. This control can be animated.

- *Number Of Waves*—The range for this control is 0.1 to 100. Settings over 75 start to produce interference patterns when Strength is maximized.

- *Do Wrapping*—Checking this box forces the effect to cover the source image area.

- *Phase*—Set the dial to as many revolutions as needed to animate the wave phase over time.

- *Blend*—Blend (1 to 100) sets the amount of blend with the original footage. At 0 you get no plug-in effect, and at 100 you get no original image.

Ripploid In Action

Open Ripploid on the CD-ROM. In it, an animated Ripploid effect is applied at strengths ranging from –100 to +100.

Spintron

This effect is also known as Twist or Spiral in other applications (see Figure 21.6). The following are some possible uses for the Spintron effect:

- Use this effect on an animated starfield or a lens flare to create the feeling of a journey through a cosmic wormhole.

- Animate the placement of the Power Centroid to create a moving, animated spiral.

The following controls allow you to adjust the effect's parameters:

- *Strength*—Strength ranges from –10,000 to +10,000, but you will seldom need to use anything outside of the range of –500 to +500, unless you're looking to produce very small moiré patterns.

Figure 21.6
Left: With a Strength of –100 and a Spin of 333, fine-grained patterns start to appear. Center: With Strength and Spin set to 75 and a Blend value of 40, the effect is composited with the underlying source footage. Right: When Strength and Spin are set to 500 or more, interference patterns are generated.

- *Power Centroid*—The crosshairs determine the center for the spiral effect.

- *Spin Amount*—The settings for this effect range from –10,000 to +10,000. Although you will want to explore the values at each end of the range, the clearest spiral effects are achieved using settings in the range of –250 to +250.

- *Wrap Around*—As a default, leave this checked. Without it you are going to generate a lot of blank space.

- *Blend*—Blend (1 to 100) sets the amount of blend with the original footage. At 0 you get no plug-in effect, and at 100 you get no original image.

Take This For A Spin

Take a look at the Spintron file on the companion CD-ROM. This animation shows what happens when the strength goes from –555 at the start to +555 at the end, while the Power Centroid is moved from the upper left, to bottom center, to lower right.

SpinUp

To create footage that appears on the screen as a rippled and distorted image and moves to a clear image, do the following:

1. Place any still or animated footage of your choice in the Composition window.

2. Select the Spintron filter from the DigiEffects Berserk options in the Effects menu.

3. Set the following parameters:

   - Power Centroid at an interesting target of the footage

   - Spin Amount of 5,000

   - No Wrap Around

   - A Blend of 100

4. Keyframe the following settings with the Strength Slider: frame 1 to –100, and last frame to 0.

5. Render the animation and save it to disk. See the SpinUp animation on the companion CD-ROM.

Squisher

This effect is also called Pinch in other applications (see Figure 21.7). The following are some possible uses for the Squisher effect:

   - Use a Blend of 40 or less, and create Squished waves emanating from the eye of a character in your footage. Keyframe animate the Strength and Phase.

- Move the Squish Centroid over time to create wave patterns that move like photon torpedoes or bolts of power from a magic wand.

Figure 21.7
Left: Rays emanate from a candle, with a Blend value of 40. Center: 30 waves with a Strength of 15 generate a splash effect. Right: Raising the Strength to 50 creates an explosion.

The following controls allow you to adjust the effect's parameters:

- *Strength*—Although the range extends from 0.1 to 1,000, you probably will not use values much higher than 100 (due to the resulting interference patterns).

- *Squish Centroid*—Place the crosshairs where you want the footage to fold in on itself.

- *Number Of Waves*—You can set the number of waves anywhere from 0.1 to 500 waves. Higher wave amounts (200 and up) create interesting patterns that can be used for showing emanating rays of energy.

- *Wrap Around*—As a default, leave this checked. Without it you are going to generate a lot of crumpled space on the edges.

- *Phase*—Set the dial to as many revolutions as needed to animate the wave phase over time.

- *Blend*—Blend (1 to 100) sets the amount of blend with the original footage. At 0 you get no plug-in effect, and at 100 you get no original image.

Squishy

Squisher (found on the companion CD-ROM) is one of the best effects to use when you want an element in the footage to be emanating rays. In this example we've used a candle, but it could just as well have been a spaceship or an eye. A Blend value of 40 was used, and the Power Centroid was placed over the wick. Three keyframes were set: beginning, middle, and end. The following values were then keyframed: Strength (50, 100, 50), Number Of Waves (100, 133, 100), and Phase (0, 2X+0. 0).

Starfield

Starfield animations are very common and are used for everything from commercial product backdrops to movie effects. This effect has more options than most others, and so can serve a wider area of uses (see Figure 21.8). The following are some possible uses for the Starfield effect:

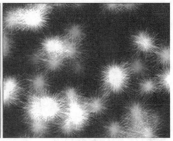

Figure 21.8
Left: Starfield acting as candle sparks. Center: Star shape types. Right: Explosion shape types.

- Place a ship against the Starfield. All you have to do is to animate the ship rocking from side to side. The animated Starfield will take care of the rest.

- Use the Starfield as the backdrop for a logo flung up from the background.

The following controls allow you to adjust the effect's parameters:

- *Star Shape*—There are six options for Star Shape: Single Dot, Soft, Glowing, Star, Explosion, and Alternate Star. Single Dot displays the stars as small points, much like the stars we see from Earth on a clear night. Soft displays them as smears of light, more useful for particle effects than as stars. Glowing shows the stars as central hot spots with glowing auras (whose colors you can also set). The Star option is the best for sky effects and also for glints around a selected element in your footage, because they are displayed with anamorphic streaks. Explosion displays the stars as bursts of light. The Alternate Star option displays the stars with more streaks than the Star option.

- *Number, Random Seed, and Speed*—You may have from 1 to as many as 32,000 stars over-laid on your footage. Lower numbers display animated effects more clearly, and usually a few hundred is quite enough. Select 500 or more only if you are using the Single Dot shape. Input a Random Seed value (1 to 32,000) to create unique patterns. Speed settings (0 to 2,000) determine how fast the animation will move through the field of stars. Unless you want to create a speed-of-light effect, a value of 300 or less should do fine.

- *Twist, Warp Center, and Streak Amount*—Twist (–32,000 to +32,000, or left to right bias) adds a cyclic motion to the animation, like stars being drawn into a black hole. A value of a few hundred in either direction will usually do the trick. The placement of the Warp Center determines where the point of the animation will unfold from. Streak Amount (0 to 30,000) sets the linear display of the star. Streaked stars make movements look even more real. Streak values over 100 take longer to render.

- *Birth Fadeup, Min/Max Size, and Color*—This control determines the number of frames to fade the star from nothing to maximum brightness (0 to 200). The higher the setting, the slower the star takes to brighten. A setting in the range of 20 to 30 is the default. Sizes can range from 1 to 5,000. (Don't bother with sizing single-dot star types.) Color sets the two-color range for the stars. Another color option is to check Random Color, which makes the star objects look more like confetti.

- *Blend*—Blend (1 to 100) sets the amount of blend with the original footage. At 0 you get no plug-in effect, and at 100, you get the full Starfield rendered over the original image.

Seeing Stars

Open the Starfld file on the companion CD-ROM. In this Starfield animation, a vortex of swirling lights beckons the adventurous explorer.

Still Noise

 This is random noise, just like static on a TV screen (see Figure 21.9). The following are some possible uses for the Noise effect:

- Animate the Amount from 100 to 255 at random keyframes to create static on a TV screen.

- Add this effect at an Amount value of 255 to a backdrop to create a media look of stippled ink.

The following controls allow you to adjust the parameters of this effect:

- *Amount*—This is the only setting that adjusts the noise quantity. Its range is 0.1 to 255.

- *Seed*—Select a seed value from 0.1 to 100.

- *Contrast*—Blend (1 to 100) sets the amount of blend with the original footage. At 0 you get no plug-in effect, and at 100 the noise overwrites the image.

Figure 21.9
Left: The original image. Center: Noise setting of 50. Right: Noise setting maximized at 255 and a Blend of 80.

VanGoghist

 Like Oil Paint, this effect is meant for use on nonanimated backdrops, although you may explore this rather blobby effect in motion (see Figure 21.10). The following are some possible uses for the VanGoghist effect:

- An interesting but strange animation results when you set the horizontal/vertical stroke size to 4/35 at the start of an animation, and reverse it to 35/4 at the end. The brush strokes are animated from a vertical to a horizontal bias.

- Use VanGoghist to add painterly effects to a scenic background layer.

Figure 21.10
Left: A Droplet brush type, with a size setting of 4 horizontally and 36 vertically. Center: The Swirl brush type.
Right: The Block brush type.

Note: Leave Include Source checked if your footage is on a solid-color backdrop, and un-checked if the backdrop is complex.

The following controls allow you to adjust the parameters of the VanGoghist effect:

- *Brush Type*—This is the most important control in VanGoghist. You will choose from a list of 15 brush types, each one of which adds a new media look to the footage. Included are Dabble, Swirl, Water, Block, Droplet, Shard, Dunes, Swish, Softer, Mesh, Stroke, Pyramid, Arrow, Cylinder, and DE (actually the abbreviation for DigiEffects, a crafty marketing ploy). Explore each brush type before rendering the final output.

- *Stroke Size and Quantity*—The settings for stroke size range from 0 to 100 for both the horizontal and vertical axes. You must have a setting greater than 0 in both the horizontal and vertical values to create a brush effect. The number of strokes ranges from 0 to 32,000, with anything over 10,000 tending to obliterate the content of the image.

- *Blend*—Blend (1 to 100) sets the amount of blend with the original footage. At 0, you get no plug-in effect, and at 100 you get the full value of the effect.

Aurorix 1

22

This is the first of three chapters dealing with the Aurorix effects collection from DigiEffects.

We'll start with the following effects: Aged Film, Bulgix, Chaotic Noise, Chaotic rainbow, Earthquake, Electrofield, and Flitter.

Aged Film

If film sits around for too long in an unprotected environment, it begins to deteriorate. Dust, hair, and other particles begin to collect on its surface, and the telltale damage becomes irritatingly visible when the film is projected. This plug-in duplicates those negative artifacts. Some interesting uses for the Aged Film effect could be to take current footage to be used in a documentary, and give it a vintage look. Or, you could use this effect to make recent home movies look like they were taken 50 years ago (see Figure 22.1).

> **Note: For even more options to mimic the look of damaged film, (see Chapter 37 for the DigiEffects CineLook and Film Damage plug-ins.**

The following controls allow you to adjust the parameters of the Aged Film effect:

- *Film Response*—This sets the brightness of the footage, from 0 to 100. At 0, you see no footage but all of the damage marks. It's interesting to fade this in and out in an animation, so the footage looks even more damaged.

Figure 22.1
With the original footage displayed on the left, the next two images display different Aged Film looks, achieved by exploring the amount and extent of the defects applied.

- *Grain, Dust, Hair, and Scratches*—The amount and size of these attributes can be adjusted, In addition, you may select the color for Dust and Hair artifacts. All controls work in the range 0 to 100.

- *Animation Controls*—Scratch Velocity, Lifespan, and Opacity can be keyframe animated, all in a range from 0 to 100. Use a Lifespan value of no more than 50 so there isn't a constant scratch running through the footage. I prefer an Opacity setting of 100 so the damage can be seen clearly. Different footage will require adjusting these settings to suit the image content. You may also animate annoying Frame Jitters, points at which the damaged film seems to leave the sprockets. You can set the amount of the offset and also the probability that this anomaly will occur, both on a scale of 0 to 100. An offset between 30 and 50 is a good default. The speed and amount of film flicker can also be animated (again in ranges from 0 to 100).

- *Convert To Gray*—This should read "Convert to Monotone," since you can select the tint used in the conversion. Select an orange-brown for an antique sepia look.

- *Random Seed*—This control sets optional probability patterns, ranging in value from 0 to 6.5536e+08.

- *Blend*—Blend (in a range of 1 to 100) sets the amount of effect blend with the original footage. At 0, you get no plug-in effect, and at 100 you get 100 percent of the effect.

Bulgix

 Bulgix is a combination of image tiling and punch effects. A selected area of the image is enlarged as through a magnifying glass, and a tile is applied to it at the same time (see Figure 22.2). The following are some possible uses for the Bulgix effect:

- Place a Bulgix distortion over footage that shows a panned animation left/right or right/left. The footage will seem to be warped under a magnifying glass.

- Create a tiled animation that moves from a Bulgix size of 2,000 to 5,000 over logo footage to generate an animated background of the tiled logo.

Figure 22.2
Left: Size of 100 and Strength of –100. Center: Size of 100 and Strength of 40. Right: Size of 5,000 and Strength of –100.

The following controls allow you to adjust the parameters of the Bulgix effect:

- *Size and Strength*—The Size of the bulge (0 to 31,000) is the size of a spherical area on the footage. At sizes over 50 or so, the area of the bulge starts to move beyond the limits of the frame. At sizes over 5,000 or so (depending on the size of the original footage), the bulged area fills the entire frame. Strength values (–100 to +100) determine the amount of warping inside the bulging sphere. A setting of –100 will display the tiled area with less distortion, while a setting of +100 will show the area in greater magnification, but with more
distortion.

- *Bulgix Centroid*—Placing the Bulgix Centroid determines the center of the bulge.

- *Scale*—Horizontal and vertical scale adjustments stretch the spherical bulge into an oval on either bias. Settings above 60 on either axis will cause wraparound distortions on the footage.

- *Blend*—Blend (1 to 100) sets the amount of blend with the original footage. At 0, you get no plug-in effect, and at 100 you get no original image under the centroid bulge.

Battle Of The Bulge

Open the Bulgix file on the companion CD-ROM. This animation shows what happens when just the Strength control values are altered from –100 to +100 over a selected part of the footage. This animated footage was originally created in NewTek's LightWave application. Bulgix2, also found on the companion CD-ROM, shows another variation of a Bulgix animation, using just the Bulgix size control to move between a setting of 2,000 to 15,000. Strength remains set at –100.

Chaotic Noise

This effect is generated by applying different areas of interest to the red, blue, and green channels. Composited, this produces a look that emulates a multicolored sky. You could also use Chaotic Noise to colorize text block layers (see Figure 22.3).

  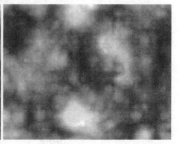

Figure 22.3
Left: Chaotic Noise is applied to a text layer. Center: Chaotic Noise makes a great animated sky. Right: Chaotic Noise also creates interesting, muted-color backdrops for After Effects animations.

Creating A Chaotic Noise Sky

To create a Chaotic Noise sky, do the following steps:

1. Import a graphic that depicts a scene with a background sky. Use the lasso tool to outline the sky.

2. Copy and paste the outlined sky, which will place it on a second layer.

3. Save the graphic in Photoshop format, which preserves the layers for After Effects.

4. In After Effects, import the graphic as a Photoshop Comp, and place it in the Composition window.

5. Select the outlined sky layer, and activate the DigiEffects Aurorix Chaotic Noise effect.

6. Animate the Chaotic Noise effect by altering the Red, Green, and Blue settings over time. Render and save the animation.

The following controls allow you to adjust the Chaotic Noise effect's parameters for each of the red, blue, and green channels:

• *Zoom*—The Zoom control allows you to change the mix of each RGB channel. Higher settings, in a range from 0.1 to 100, lessen the overall mix of the channel in the composite.

• *Offset*—Placing the crosshair on the footage sets the center point for the channel mix.

• *Time Variance*—The Time Variance control allows you to vary the amount of change that the selected channel will exhibit over either the length of the animation, or from keyframe to keyframe. Its range is from 0.1 to 100.

• *Blend*—Blend (1 to 100) sets the amount of blend with the original footage. At 0, you get no plug-in effect, and at 100 you get no original image.

Bring On The Noise

Look at CNoise1 on the companion CD-ROM. In this animation, the Chaotic Noise effect is targeted to a text layer. The CNoise2 animation shows the Chaotic Noise effect applied to a layered sky, which was generated using Photoshop.

Chaotic Rainbow

This effect can be substituted anywhere you might apply the Chaotic Noise effect. The shapes of the color areas are a bit more cohesive than Chaotic Noise (see Figure 22.4). The following are some possible uses for the Chaotic Rainbow effect:

• Use this effect on an Alpha channel layer to create a multicolored fog over a backdrop.

• Use Chaotic Rainbow on a circular layer to simulate an energy orb. This is a great effect for chaotic gas planets in the sky over a science-fiction landscape.

The following controls allow you to adjust the parameters for each of the RGB channels, except for Blend, of the Chaotic Rainbow effect:

Figure 22.4

Left: Chaotic Rainbow can simulate a multicolored fog layer. Center: The orb is on a separate layer and addressed by the Chaotic Rainbow effect. Right: A completed scene adds a horse on another layer (also mapped with the Chaotic Rainbow effect).

- *Zoom*—Zoom controls how much of the channel is present in the mix; its settings range from 0.1 to 100. The lower the Zoom setting, the smaller the shapes related to that channel.

> **Note: Set the Zoom value to 0.1 for all three channels to create tiny sparkles on the targeted layer.**

- *Frequency*—Frequency controls the strength of the channel in the mix. Its range is from 0.1 to 32,000.

- *Phase*—The Phase control relates to the wave shape in the mix. Its range is also from 0.1 to 32,000.

- *Offset*—Place the crosshairs to determine where the channel is centered in the Composition window.

- *Time Variance*—This setting determines how much change will take place over time. The settings range from 0.1 to 100.

- *Blend*—Blend (1 to 100) sets the amount of blend with the original footage. At 0, you get no plug-in effect, and at 100 you get no original image.

Psychedelic Rainbows

On the CRnbow file on the companion CD-ROM, Chaotic Rainbow is applied on a second layer over a scenic backdrop, for a super-psychedelic electric fog.

Earthquake

 Earthquake is a finely controllable directional blur (see Figure 22.5). Use the Earthquake effect whenever you need to show the footage being affected by an unseen shock wave. Just set and keyframe the directional variance over time.

The following controls allow you to adjust the Earthquake's parameters:

- *Horizontal and Vertical Vibration*—The variation values (0 to 100) determine the amount of either or both horizontal and vertical shudder in the footage.

Figure 22.5
Left: The original footage. Center: Horizontal Vibration at 100 and Vertical Vibration at 0. Right: Horizontal Vibration at 0 and Vertical Vibration at 100.

- *Blend*—Blend (1 to 100) sets the amount of blend with the original footage. At 0, you get no plug-in effect, and at 100 you get no original image.

Electrofield

Electrofield is a concentric energy vortex effect (see Figure 22.6). The following are some possible uses for the Electrofield effect:

- Center all three channels on any point of energy flow, like an eye or the barrel of a weapon.

- Center the RGB channels separately to create a rippled energy effect, or emanations from three sources in the footage.

The following controls allow you to adjust the Electrofield parameters for each RGB channel:

- *Field Strength*—The strength of the field (in a range from 0.1 to 31,000) determines how much of that channel shows in the mix.

- *Field Center*—The center of each RGB channel determines the position from which that ring will emanate.

Figure 22.6
Left: Electrofield waves with Strength at 700 and Field Brightness at 60. Center: Strength of 10 and Brightness of 500. Right: RGB Field Centers placed at three different locations.

- *Field Brightness*—The brightness of the selected RGB channel determines the width of the rings that flow out from the center point.

- *Blend*—Blend (1 to 100) sets the amount of blend with the original footage. At 0, you get no plug-in effect, and at 100 you get no original image.

Flitter

 Flitter adds a disintegration component to a blur, causing the targeted footage to break up into chaotic pixels (see Figure 22.7). The following are some possible uses for the Flitter effect:

- Use Flitter to disintegrate image content, perhaps after an energy beam strike.

- Blend in the Flitter at 50% to add pixelated elements to the edge of the content. This is an effective way to add interest to a text layer.

The following controls allow you to adjust Flitter's parameters:

- *Size*—Flitter Size determines how far the disintegrated pixels range from the image elements. Settings of 0 cause no flitter, while larger values start to disintegrate the image content. Its range is from 0 to 100.

- *Squeeze*—Squeeze is set separately for horizontal and vertical directions, causing the flitter to be spread along either or both the horizontal and vertical axis. Its range is also from 0 to 100.

- *Blend*—Blend (1 to 100) sets the amount of blend with the original footage. At 0, you get no plug-in effect, and at 100 you get no original image.

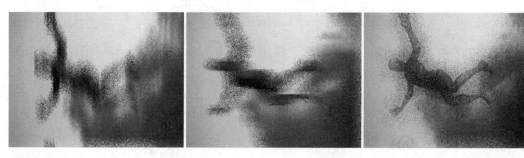

Figure 22.7
Left: A Flitter with a Horizontal Squeeze of 0 and a Vertical Squeeze set to 100. Size is 75. Center: With the same size value, the Horizontal Squeeze is now 100 and the Vertical is 0. Right: Size, Horizontal Squeeze, and Vertical Squeeze set to 100, with a Blend of 70.

Aurorix II

23

This is the second of three chapters about the DigiEffects Aurorix collection of AE plug-ins, which adds fractal, warp, interference waves, and other effects to your creation.

Here you'll read about Fractal Noise, Infinity Warp, Infinity Zone, Interferix, Interpheroid, Interpheron, Noise Blender, and Soap Film.

Fractal Noise

 This effect is in the same category as Chaotic Noise and Chaotic Rainbow, covered in Chapter 22 (see Figure 23.1 for examples). The following are some possible uses for the Fractal Noise effect:

• Use Fractal Noise for clouds. The Photoshop Difference Clouds effect is based on this same algorithm.

• Use Fractal Noise on an Alpha layer to create fog and haze in the foreground over the footage.

The following controls allow you to adjust the Fractal Noise effect's parameters:

• *Seed*—The Seed control sets the pattern generator, in a range of 0.1 to 100. Seed does not keyframe animate very well, except if the values are far apart. When values are far apart from one keyframe to the next, expect a very fast moving animation.

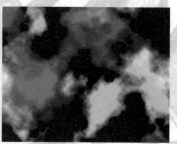

Figure 23.1
Left: Fractal Noise placed on footage with a Blend of 40. Center: Fractal Noise mapped to an Alpha channel. Right: Fractal Noise as a standalone background.

- *Scale*—Scale is determined separately for the horizontal and vertical axes. Scale movements cause the Fractal Noise to change size. Its range is also from 0.1 to 100.

- *Brightness*—The range of Brightness values is from 0.1 to 100. Low settings shrink the Fractal Noise when it is mapped to an Alpha channel; higher values expand it.

- *Offset*—Changing the Offset values in an animation causes the Fractal Noise to pan.

- *Blend*—Blend (1 to 100) sets the amount of blend with the original footage. At 0, you get no plug-in effect, and at 100 you get no original image.

Fun With Fractals

Take a look at the FracNoiz file on the companion CD-ROM. In this example, in which blue fractal globs move across the footage.

Infinity Warp

 This effect zooms in on a selected area of your footage, warping the footage at each step. It is one of the most dynamic effects you can apply (see Figure 23.2). The following are some possible uses for the Infinity Warp effect:

- Set the Blend to 40 with an animated Warp that moves from 0 to 100, and the resulting effect can be made to emanate from any point in the footage. You can also skip the Blend setting if the Infinity Warp is targeting an Alpha channel.

- Use this effect on a background whenever you need to show a foreground layer traveling through a time tunnel or a cosmic wormhole.

The following controls allow you to adjust the parameters of Infinity Warp:

- *Warp Strength*—Two controls determine the warping of the footage: Fine (0 to 100) and Rough (–1,000 to 10,000).

- *Warp Centroid*—Place the centroid crosshairs wherever you want the warp to emanate from.

Figure 23.2
Left: With a Blend of 40, the Infinity Warp becomes transparent enough to display the underlying image. Center: Using Repeat Edge Value Tiling results in a squarish warp. Right: Combining horizontal Tile and vertical Repeat Edge Value creates this effect.

- *Tiling*—Tiling is set separately for the horizontal and vertical axes, for which you determine three types: Repeat Edge Value, Tile, and Mirror. Repeat Edge Value creates a very square, tiled look, while Tile and Mirror display the best warping for tunnel effects.

- *Blend*—Blend (1 to 100) sets the amount of blend with the original footage. At 0, you get no plug-in effect, and at 100 you get no original image.

To Infinity, And Beyond

Take a look at InfiniWrp on the companion CD-ROM. The Warp Strength of the Infinity Warp effect was applied in this animation, moving from 0 to 100 and back to 0. For InfnWrp2, Horizontal Tiling was set to Tile, and Vertical Tiling was set to Repeat Edge Value.

Infinity Zone

 This effect is also known as Vortex Tiling in other applications. It is a combination of tiling and spiraling in a fractal dimension, where the longer you look the more detail there is to see (see Figure 23.3). The following are some possible uses for the Infinity Zone effect:

- Use Infinity Zone as an alternate tunnel effect, but use it sparingly, since its look is so identifiable.

- If your footage contains a close-up of an eye, use Infinity Zone on a layer that addresses just the pupil of the eye to create footage of hypnotic power. This works best if the targeted footage is not animated.

Note: This effect is too complex to work well with any blend.

The following controls allow you to adjust the parameters of the Infinity Zone effect:

- *Infinity Color Mode*—There are two options: RGB Together and RGB Separated. If you need to blend the effect with a background target, use RGB Together, and also set each of the RGB centroids at the same location. Do not blend with the background if RGB Separate is your choice.

Figure 23.3
Left: The original footage. Center: RGB Separated. Right: RGB Together.

- *Strength*—Adjust the relative strength (0.1 to 100) for each of the RGB channels separately to control the RGB mix.

- *Centroid*—Place the centroid crosshairs for each of the RGB channels on the footage where you would like the center of the vortex.

- *Brightness*—Set the brightness (0.1 to 100) of each of the RGB channels separately to determine their relative brightness in the mix.

> *Note: Turn all RGB Brightness channels to the lowest setting, 0.1, if you want a tinted effect. The channel with the highest Strength value will determine the tint.*

- *Blend*—Blend (1 to 100) sets the amount of blend with the original footage. At 0, you get no plug-in effect, and at 100 you get no original image.

In The Zone

The InfnZone animation on the companion CD-ROM should get your attention. Hold onto your chair for this one. Based on the Infinity Zone effect, it demonstrates what happens when the Red Strength setting moves from 0.1 to 100 over 120 frames.

Cloud Tunnel Project

This exercise creates an animated cloud vortex. Do the following:

1. Import a graphic or animation of clouds to the Composition window.

2. Leave all of the Centroid pointers at their default position and make sure that the Infinity Color Mode is set to RGB Together.

3. Do the following settings:

    - Red Brightness to 100.

    - Green Strength and Brightness to 0.1 and 100, respectively.

    - Blue Strength and Brightness to 0.1 and 100, respectively.

    - Blend to 100.

4. Keyframe the Red Strength at frames 1, 80% of the way toward the end, and at the last frame with the following settings: 100, 0.1, 100, respectively. This will create a looping animation.

5. Render the animation and save it to disk. For an example of what this looks like, see the CldTun animation on the companion CD-ROM.

Interferix

 Interferix creates interference waves, with control over the placement and strength of each RGB channel (see Figure 23.4). The following are some possible uses for the Interferix effect:

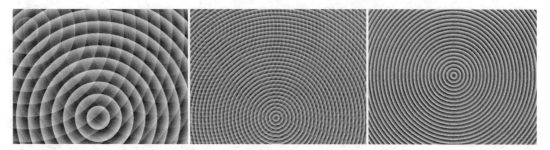

Figure 23.4

Left: Three waves with separate centers and Brightness values of 15. Center: Raising the channel values to 50 thins out the waves. Right: Placing the centers at the same location creates a single wave source.

- For a colorful backdrop, place the wave centers at separate locations for each RGB channel.

- If you are going to use Blend, or intend to target this effect to a component layer in your footage (Alpha layers are recommended), then set the center of each RGB channel at the same location. This creates one energy source for the waves.

The following controls allow you to adjust the effect's parameters:

- *Channel*—The thickness of the waves emitted by each RGB channel can be controlled within a range of 0.1 to 100. Lower settings produce thicker waves.

- *Center*—This crosshair determines the center of each RGB channel.

- *Brightness*—The settings of the Brightness control (0.1 to 100) determine the dominance of each separate RGB channel in the mix.

- *Blend*—Blend (1 to 100) sets the amount of blend with the original footage. At 0, you get no plug-in effect, and at 100 you get no original image.

Interpheroid

 This effect becomes intense at channel settings above 1, so realize that your use of it will probably have to incorporate interference patterns that are small and complex. The effect is emphasized when RGB channel centers are placed at different locations (see Figure 23.5). If you're looking for simple interference patterns, it's best to selec Interferix.

The following are some possible uses for the Interpheroid effect:

- Use this effect as a background-pattern generator when you want a chaotic backdrop for foreground layers.

- Use this effect on text block layers to internally animate the text.

The following controls allow you to adjust the parameters of the Interpheroid effect:

- *Channel Strength*—If you want simple uncluttered interference patterns, use the Interferix effect. Setting Channel Strength to more than 1 (in its range of 0.1 to 100) creates instant complexity.

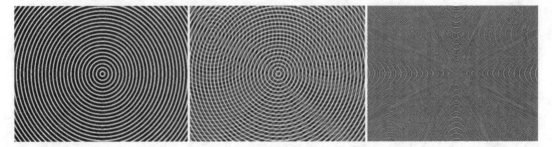

Figure 23.5
Left: Even with strengths set to 1, the pattern gets pretty tiny. Center: Multiple interference is created by placing each RGB channel center at different locations. Right: Raising the strengths to as little as 2 creates an interference tangle and moirés.

- *Channel Center*—This control lets you place each RGB channel center at a desired location on the footage.

- *Channel Brightness*—With this control, you can determine the brightness of each RGB channel in the mix.

- *Blend*—Blend (1 to 100) sets the amount of blend with the original footage. At 0, you get no plug-in effect, and at 100 you get no original image.

Interpheron

Interpheron is an interference-pattern generator like Interpheroid, but it is much more gentle. Use this effect when you want something that acts like Interpheroid, but with less interference and complexity. Think of the Interpheron plug-in as a moderate, middle-of-the-road interference wave effect. For instance, you could use this effect on an Alpha layer to create semitransparent interference patterns (see Figure 23.6).

The following controls allow you to adjust the parameters of the Interpheron effect:

- *Channel Strength*—Unlike Interpheroid, this effect doesn't get complex until you set the Strength for RGB channels over 90.

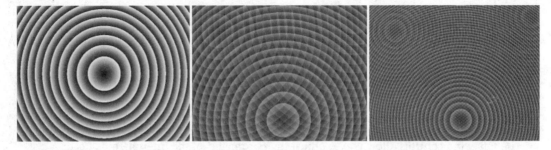

Figure 23.6
Left: Sharing a common center with strengths of 90, the RGB channels create a pleasing wave. Center: Staggering the RGB channel centers produces the expected interference results. Right: Increasing the strength of each RGB channel to 100 generates finer detail, but without the chaos as in the Interpheroid effect.

- *Channel Center*—This control lets you place each RGB channel center at a desired location on the footage.

- *Channel Brightness*—With this control you determine the brightness of each RGB channel in the mix.

- *Blend*—Blend (1 to 100) sets the amount of blend with the original footage. At 0, you get no plug-in effect, and at 100 you get no original image.

Noise Blender

At low settings, the Noise Blender shapes look like stippled daubs of paint, or like a blurry circuit board at maximized settings.

Creating A Power Cycling Circuit Board

To create footage that looks like a power cycling circuit board, do the following:

1. Set all of the RGB Zoom values to 30.

2. Place all of the RGB centers at the same location in the center of the footage.

3. Set the Green and Blue Time Variance to 0.1, and do not animate them.

4. Animate the Red Variance from 0.1 at the start of the animation to 50 at the end. The result will be a circuit board-like footage with the red components flashing subtly over time.

Another way in which to use the Noise Blender is to set all of the RGB Zoom values to 0 and all of the RGB Time Variance values to 100. Use a Blend of 50 to apply this texture to the footage. The result is footage that looks as if it has a sand material applied to it (see Figure 23.7).

The following controls allow you to adjust the parameters of the Noise Blender effect:

- *Channel Zoom*—This control sets the relative sizes of each of the RGB channels (in a range of 0 to 100). At low settings, the elements look very pixelated, and at higher settings they resemble a circuit board. A good display setting is around 30.

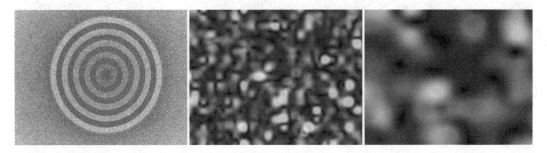

Figure 23.7
Left: Blended at 50, the footage takes on a sandy texture, with Zooms set to 0 and Time Variance set to 100. Center: Setting the RGB Zooms to 30 generates a pattern like that of a circuit board. Right: Raising the RGB Zooms to 100 produces a blotchier look.

- *Channel Offset*—With this control, you place the crosshairs to determine the center of the effect for each of the RGB channels.

- *Channel Time Variance*—The settings (0.1 to 100) for this control vary the animating pattern for each of the RGB channels over time.

- *Blend*—Blend (1 to 100) sets the amount of blend with the original footage. At 0, you get no plug-in effect, and at 100 you get no original image.

An Intriguing Blend

Take a look at the NoizBlnd animation on the companion CD-ROM. This animation was created using the technique described in the Suggested Uses for the Noise Blender effect.

Soap Film

 The result of using this effect can vary the look from blobs of shadowed elements to a structure composed of symbolic blocks. It all depends on what the settings are. The name "Soap Film" may be due to the way the patterns undulate when you zoom in (see Figure 23.8).

The following are some possible uses for the Soap Film effect:

- Use a nonanimated Soap Film effect to texture a background that will have a text layer placed on it. Set all RGB frequency values to 1,000.

- Create a temple wall with symbols on it by setting the Overall Zoom to 4 and all of the frequency values to 175. Change each Channel Offset value over time by only five from start to end of the animation to make it slowly undulate.

The following controls allow you to adjust the parameters of the Soap Film effect:

- *Overall Zoom*—There is only one Zoom control for all channels. Its range is 0.1 to 100. A value of 0.1 zooms you as far away as possible, while 100 brings you as close as you can get.

Figure 23.8
Left: With all RGB frequency values raised to 6,000, more detail is added to each component in this close-up. Center: With an Overall Zoom of 4 and all RGB frequency settings at 175, the footage looks like a wall with strange symbols on it. Right: With an Overall Zoom setting of 2.5 and all RGB frequency values set at 77, the footage begins to look like melted capacitors or alien candy.

- *Channel Offset*—The settings for Channel Offset (0.1 to 32,000) control the placement of the selected RGB channel in the mix.

- *Channel Frequency*—Channel Frequency values (0.1 to 32,000) determine the amount of detail that is shown in each RGB channel. Higher values produce greater detail, which can be seen at high Zoom settings.

- *Channel Phase*—Altering the phase of each RGB channel changes the placement of the pattern for that channel.

- *Channel Time Variance*—This is an animation setting. Higher intervals between keyframes create more movement in the footage.

- *Blend*—Blend (1 to 100) sets the amount of blend with the original footage. At 0, you get no plug-in effect, and at 100 you get no original image.

Clean Animation

In the SoapFilm file on the companion CD-ROM, undulating patterns zoom into view thanks to the Soap Film effect.

AURORIX III 24

This is the last of three chapters covering the Aurorix plug-ins from DigiEffects.

In this chapter we explore Strange Nebulae, Tilos, Turbulent Flow, VideoLook, Warpoid, Whirlix, and WoodMaker.

Strange Nebulae

This effect creates a smeared group of rays that appear to be floating in space (see Figure 24.1). The following are some possible uses for the Strange Nebulae effect:

- Use this effect on an Alpha channel to superimpose the rays over a background. This works very well when the background is a starfield image or animation.

- Zoom in on the nebulae while panning to produce an interesting flyover.

The following controls allow you to adjust the parameters of the Strange Nebulae effect:

- *Render Smoothness*—This control applies a smoothness to remove the pixelated appearance of the streaks. A default value of 20 usually works well.

- *Nebulonic Seed*—This is a random-seed generator that produces different patterns. The range of its settings is 0.1 to 32,000.

- *Zoom*—Zooming in brings the whole view closer.

Figure 24.1
Left: As a standalone effect, you can fly over the nebulae using the Zoom controls. Center: Used on an Alpha layer, the nebulae can be composited with underlying imagery. Right: As you zoom around the composition, the nebulae shifts and shimmers.

- *XY Offset and Zoom*—Set the X and Y offsets to move the rays around the view. Zoom them to bring you closer to the nebulae (make it appear larger).
- *Blend*—Blend (1 to 100) sets the amount of blend with the original footage. At 0 you get no plug-in effect, and at 100 you get no original image.

Tilos

Tilos is a basic but powerful tiling effect (see Figure 24.2). The following are some possible uses for the Tilos effect:

- Move animated footage from maximum tiling to no tiling in an animation. This is useful as a segue between clips.

- Use a nonanimated Tilos setting on a background to emphasize a targeted feature.

The following controls allow you to adjust the parameters of the Tilos effect:

- *Tile Size*—Tile Size (0 to 100) determines how many replicated images will be created.
- *Tile Offset*—The Tile Offset control determines where the center of the tiling will be placed. Depending on the images in your footage, the center has to be adjusted each time for the best symmetry.
- *Blend*—Blend (1 to 100) sets the amount of blend with the original footage. At 0 you get no plug-in effect, and at 100 you get no original image.

Turbulent Flow

This plug-in applies warped area maps to the selected footage, based on a selection of warping styles or other image footage. The ability to control the warp of one image with the content of another leads to some spectacular results, and has to be one of the most variable effects available from any developer (see Figure 24.3).

The most spectacular results from this effect are achieved by the Use Image mode. In most cases, the target footage should be an animated sequence and the controlling footage a stable graphic. Portraiture works very well as the controlling footage.

Figure 24.2
Left: The original footage. Center: A Tilos setting of 10. Right: A Tilos setting of 30.

Figure 24.3
A selection of Turbulent Flow modes. Left: Strange, Center: Flow Around. Right: Using an underlying image to control the effect, in this case, a portrait of the author.

To create interesting warped sequences from single-image footage, use any of the modes except Use Image. Apply it in a keyframed animation that targets the single-image graphic.

The following controls allow you to adjust the Turbulent Flow effect:

- *Flow Mode*—The Flow Mode control comprises 10 options. Nine are warping brushes: Noisy Swirls, Simple Swirls, Outward Butterfly, Outward Burst, Square Burst, Circular, Flow Around, Flow Around Alternate, and Strange. The most intriguing effect, though, is saved for the tenth option, Use Image. With this choice, you can control the footage using another image or animation, and apply the controlling footage from either its X and Y axis, or both. You might even use one control footage to alter the targeted footage on the X axis, and another to control the Y axis. The results are always surprising, so there are no exacting rules, just an exploration of the possibilities.

- *Field Time Vary*—This slider sets the variance (in a range from 0.1 to 100) over time of field alterations, and is best thought of as a keyframe animation option. Large amounts of variance are to be avoided since the animation will tend to jump around too chaotically.

- *Flow Distance*—Set this slider (0.1 to 100) all the way to the left at the lowest setting if you are using the Use Image mode. This allows the controlling footage to show through, and creates astounding composites. If you are using other mode options, this control can be explored to create the best warping needed.

- *Zooms and Offsets*—Adjust the XY Zooms (–32,000 to +32,000) and Offsets (0 to 32,000) in conjunction with keyframe controls to create an infinite number of results. You'll have to play around here, since there is only one hard and fast rule: Do not use keyframe changes with these controls if the main footage is animated, as they produce too much complexity and far too much chaotic movement for most desired results.

- *Blend*—Blend (1 to 100) sets the amount of blend with the original footage. At 0 you get no plug-in effect, and at 100 you get no original image.

Turbulence Ahead

Open the TurbFlow animation on the companion CD-ROM. The Turbulent Flow effect, in Noisy Swirls mode, is applied to an animated sequence in this example. It's not necessary to keyframe the effect, since there is more than enough movement caused by the way it is applied over time to the changing frames. Now open TurbFlw2. This time, we are using the Turbulent Flow effect in the Use Image mode. An underlying image is used as the control mechanism for the footage. It is especially useful for documentary production, where you have both a portrait of a historical person and some animated footage of an event they have participated in.

VideoLook

 This effect creates a video look similar to that of early television broadcasts, complete with visible scan lines (see Figure 24.4). The following are some possible uses for the VideoLook effect:

- Use this plug-in when you need to create footage that has an old-time video look, especially useful in some documentary situations.

- Used with a greenish cast, this plug-in is also useful for creating what might be seen on a green-screen computer monitor, or a surveillance camera. This is useful for film productions that feature footage playing on a monitor in the background.

- You might try to use this effect as a way to fix bad video footage, trying to balance scan line problems in the original footage. This is tricky, however, because you can address only a certain range of anomalies digitally. It may be worth a try.

The following controls allow you to adjust the VideoLook effect. Most of these effects are targeted to each of the scan lines present in a video display, odd and even. These artifacts are more noticeable on a TV set than on a computer monitor. A TV displays both odd and even scan lines at a refresh rate that usually prevents their being noticed, at 30 frames x 2 or 60 "fields" a second. This effect allows you to control and generate all sorts of noise effects, making the footage look as if it were captured on a video camera or transmitted from a source that has problems:

- *Even and Odd Scanline Problems You Can Introduce and Control*—You can set separate odd and even scanline parameters for each of the following video anomalies in VideoLook:

Figure 24.4
Left: Video signal with colorized noise. Center: Video signal with horizontal shift problems on the odd scanlines. Right: Video signal with odd and even noise-blending problems.

Blend, Brightness, Noise (including colorized noise), Size, Decay, Bleed, Distortion, Shift, and Comb masking.

- *Blend*—Blend (1 to 100) sets the amount of blend with the original footage. At 0 you get no plug-in effect, and at 100 you get no original image.

Warpoid

This plug-in is very useful at lower values for controlling the warping and morphing of foreground footage (see Figure 24.5). The following are some possible uses for the Warpoid effects:

- Use subtle warps to change facial expressions and personalities.
- Warp selected areas of your footage by copying a second layer of the same footage to the Composition window, and masking out unwanted material with the pen tool.

To warp a foreground target, like a face, without warping the background as well, you have two options. The first is to use the pen to cut out the image area of interest, so that it sits on the background color. The second is to create an Alpha mask of the footage, as long as its natural backdrop is a solid color. Of course, you can always Alpha mask the area of interest against complex footage in the background, moving or still.

The following controls allow you to adjust the effect's parameters:

- *Horizontal Phase and Strength*—These controls are used to warp the footage on the horizontal axis. Although its range is –32,000 to +32,000, increasing the values of Phase beyond about 100 or Strength (0.1 to 100) beyond about 15 introduces wave anomalies at the edges of the footage.

- *Vertical Phase and Strength*—These controls are used to warp the footage on the vertical axis. Again, increasing the values of Phase (–32,000 to +32,000) beyond about 100 or Strength (0.1 to 100) beyond about 15 introduces wave anomalies at the edges of the footage.

- *Blend*—Blend (1 to 100) sets the amount of blend with the original footage. At 0 you get no plug-in effect, and at 100 you get no original image.

Figure 24.5
Left: Horizontal Phase of 35 and Horizontal Strength of 11. Center: Horizontal Phase of –35 and Horizontal Strength of 15. Right: Vertical Phase of 60 and Vertical Strength of 8.

Phase Waves Project

Using this example, you can create interesting patterns over footage that resemble textured blocks. Do the following:

1. Load a colorful image or animation to the Composition window.

2. Under the Effects menu, select the DigiEffects Aurorix Warpoid filter.

3. Set the following parameters: Horizontal and Vertical Strength to 100, Blend to 100.

4. Keyframe both Horizontal Phase and Vertical Phase to –22 at frame 1 of your animation.

5. Keyframe both Horizontal Phase and Vertical Phase to 22 at the last frame of your animation.

6. Render the animation and save it to disk. The result will be a shimmering textured effect that shows the original footage at the middle of the animation. See the PhzWav animation on the companion CD-ROM.

The Time Warp

The Warpoid file on the companion CD-ROM shows an interesting effect. The Warpoid plug-in is used to put the author's countenance through a horizontal and vertical squeeze play.

Whirlix

Whirlix is a vortex effect with controllable area vortex warping (see Figure 24.6). The following are some possible uses for the Whirlix effect:

- Use Whirlix to generate the vintage "spinning newspaper" effect, often seen in the movies. Just use a graphic of a newspaper with a bold headline.

- Use the Whirlix effect to warp the footage subtly, by keeping Strength to values between –2 and 2.

Figure 24.6
Left: The original footage. Center: With the centroid placed at the center of the footage, a Size of 100, and a Strength of –4, the footage starts to vortex warp. Right: Placing the centroid over the eye of the figure on the left, and raising the Strength to –5, alters the footage in a different way.

The following controls allow you to adjust the Whirlix effect:

- *Whirlix Size and Strength*—The settings for Whirlix Size (0 to 31,000) determines how much coverage will be addressed, while Strength (–100 to +100) adjusts the power of the vortex warp. Sizes over 100 reach farther out to include parts of the footage not in the Composition window. Negative Strength values spin the vortex counterclockwise, while positive Strength values force it clockwise.

- *Whirlix Centroid*—Place the centroid at the pivot point for the effect, whether inside or outside the Composition window.

- *Blend*—Blend (1 to 100) sets the amount of blend with the original footage. At 0 you get no plug-in effect, and at 100 you get no original image.

WoodMaker

 WoodMaker is a texture generator that uses a mix of the RGB channels to create patterns that look like wood grain under red, blue, and green lights (see Figure 24.7). You could use the WoodMaker effect to texturize a backdrop for footage. Or, use the WoodMaker plug-in on an Alpha layer, and drop out one of the channels to reveal the footage below.

The following controls allow you to adjust the WoodMaker effect:

- *RGB Zoom*—Using this control, you can adjust the zooming in or out for each RGB channel (0.1 to 100), so the whorls in the wood can be seen more clearly at higher zooms. The lower the Zoom value for the channel, the more pixelated that color will be in the mix.

- *RGB Offset*—Adjusting the Offset crosshairs determines where the selected RGB channel colors will be centered in the mix.

- *RGB Time Variance*—This is an animation controller that allows you to adjust the amount of pattern variance between keyframes (0.1 to 100) for each RGB channel.

- *Blend*—Blend (1 to 100) sets the amount of blend with the original footage. At 0 you get no plug-in effect, and at 100 you get no original image.

Figure 24.7
Left: A WoodMaker texture used as a potential backdrop for footage. Center: WoodMaker texture used on an Alpha layer. Right: Footage on an Alpha layer showing the WoodMaker textured backdrop below.

With The Grain

Take a look at the WoodMakr animation on the companion CD-ROM. Using the WoodMaker plug-in, this animation displays the way the texture responds to alterations in the RGB channels zooms over time.

LIGHT EFFECTS 25

The AE plug-ins covered in this chapter center on lighting effects. They are DigiEffects Aurorix's Spotlights, Color Spotlights, LightZoom, and 3D Lighting; ICE, Inc.'s Final Effects Complete's LightBurst, LightRays, LightSweep, and Spotlight; Knoll Software's Lens Flare Pack; and Boris AE 2's Alpha Spotlight, Light Sweep, Reverse Spotlight, and Spotlight.

Aurorix Spotlights

 These three spotlights are white, and can be animated over the footage (see Figure 25.1). The following are some possible uses for the Aurorix Spotlights effect:

- Add roving spotlights to point out elements in still footage. This is a good effect for documentary stills.

- Add spotlights to target a logo in an animation.

The following controls allow you to adjust the parameters of the Spotlights effect:

- *Spotlight Size*—Spotlight Size can be animated, so you could start off with no light and over time light up the entire footage. Its range is 0.1 to 100. Make sure to dim the spotlights when the size is set to over 50, so you don't wash out the footage.

Figure 25.1
Left: Original footage. Center: Footage illuminated by a single spotlight. Right: Footage illuminated by three smaller spotlights.

- *Spotlight Center*—This control allows you to place the crosshairs anywhere in the composition window for Spotlights 1, 2, and 3.

- *Spotlight Brightness*—Spotlight Brightness works best when set higher for smaller areas than for larger areas, although maximum settings should be avoided unless you plan to lower them fairly quickly. (Its range is from 0.1 to 100.) Use a setting of 50 to 60 for smaller areas, and a setting of 30 to 40 for larger areas. When spotlights cross, dim the brightness of each. Assigning a value of 0.1 to all spotlights forces the footage to black.

- *Blend*—Blend (1 to 100) sets the amount of blend with the original footage. At 0 you get no plug-in effect, and at 100 you get no original image.

Aurorix Color Spotlights

 The Color Spotlights feature acts very differently than the Spotlights effect just covered. Turning them all off does not turn the footage black, but instead displays it with its original palette and brightness (see Figure 25.2). The following are some possible uses for the Aurorix Color Spotlights effects:

- Set the size of one color spotlight to 15, and its strength to 32,000. Voila! You have a laser pointer. Use it to point out targeted aspects of the footage, or even as a bouncing ball for sing-along lyrics.

- Create a subtractive color wheel by using a size of 50 for each spotlight, with brightness values of 32,000. Place them in an overlapping triad. You will see the three primary colors and their secondaries, with pure white where they all cross. This is a nice effect for logos.

The following controls allow you to adjust the Color Spotlights effect:

- *RGB Size*—Size (0.1 to 100) controls the separate RGB channels' coverage of the footage. Be aware that at a setting of 100, edges are left in the footage that are not covered.

- *RGB Center*—Place the crosshairs anywhere in the composition window for each of the RGB spotlights.

Figure 25.2
Left: Placing the three color spotlights in an overlapping triad, with Brightness values of 32,000, creates a subtractive color wheel. Center: Reducing the Brightness value to 100 mutes the edges of the lighted areas. Right: Reducing Size of any spotlight to 15, with the others switched off, and increasing Brightness to 32,000, creates a great laser pointer.

- *RGB Brightness*—The RGB Brightness value (0.1 to 32,000) determines the saturation of the color for that channel. Values above 200 start to wash out the image data. The higher the brightness setting, the harder the edge of the spotlight.

> **Note: Be aware that for lower brightness settings, the blue channel may have to have a brightness value twice that of the other channels, because blue is always the weakest channel to see. This is not the case, however, at settings above 500.**

- *Blend*—Blend (1 to 100) sets the amount of blend with the original footage. At 0 you get no plug-in effect, and at 100 you get no original image.

In The Spotlight

Open the ColrSpot file on the companion CD-ROM. Using the Aurorix Color Spotlights plug-in, this animation displays the way crossing spotlights create subtractive overlays on the footage.

Aurorix LightZoom

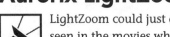

LightZoom could just as well have been called "LightSpeed." It creates the effect you've seen in the movies when a spaceship jumps to lightspeed. Just start an animation with Zoom set to 0, and increase the value to 100 at the end (see Figure 25.3). You can also create some scary footage by leaving the Zoom at about 30, but increasing the Brightness to 500. This is great if the subject is also scary, like a vampire bat.

The following controls allow you to adjust the LightZoom effect:

- *Zoom Amount*—Unless you plan to go on vacation while your footage is rendering, do not use a Zoom setting higher than 100. (You can go as high as 32,000, but don't dare.) Usually, a setting of 50 will suffice quite nicely.

- *Brightness*—Brightness values can range from –100 to +32,000, with negative Brightness values creating some interesting posterizing effects. As a default, Brightness works best in the range –100 to +600. If you use higher values the footage washes out dramatically.

Figure 25.3
Left: Original footage. Center: Zoom at 5 and Brightness at 400 creates an eerie, posterized effect. Right: Increasing the Zoom to 100 starts to show the telltale lightspeed streaking.

- *Light Center*—Place the center point anywhere you want to zoom to. Try to make it a point of focal interest, like an eye or a star.

- *Blend*—Blend (1 to 100) sets the amount of blend with the original footage. At 0 you get no plug-in effect, and at 100 you get no original image.

Spooky Stuff

Take a look at the LiteZoom animation on the companion CD-ROM. It's a scary animation that uses the LightZoom effect to zero in on a bat's eye.

Aurorix 3D Lighting

 This plug-in produces an embossed effect, colorized by the pseudo-3D light settings (see Figure 25.4). The following are some possible uses for the Aurorix 3D Lighting effects:

- You can create interesting 3D embossed animation by moving the light across the footage. Set Relief at values around 3,000 and Light Height at 10,000. Do not use Smoothness values above 10.

- For embossed background (nonanimated footage), blend the original with the altered footage. Use a Blend value of 25. Do not set Smoothness above 10.

The following controls allow you to adjust the effect's parameters:

- *Light Color, Position, and Height*—You may select any color for the light you need, either with the eyedropper or from the system palette. Its position is set by the crosshairs. The Height is set by imagining that the footage has a Z dimension, an axis that runs perpendicular to the screen. The higher the setting (in a range of 0.1 to 10,000) the more you are moving the light away from the footage. Closer lights produce more glare; the farther away the light is, the more subtle the effect. To prevent pixelization, set the Height in the upper ranges.

- *Gloss, Diffuse, and Specular Colors*—The Diffuse color is taken to be the overall tint of the footage. Gloss and Specular colors are highlights. Generally, set the Diffuse color to a medium-bright color, and give the Gloss and Specular colors a different hue.

Figure 25.4
Left: The original footage. Center: A Light Height and Relief of 50 create an interesting embossed effect. Right: Light Height of 7,777 and a Relief of 2,200 creates an entirely different look, especially when blended with the original footage at 25.

- *Relief*—The relief of the image is its imagined depth. The settings range from 0.1 to 32,000, and should be set lower in most cases than the Light Height, so that the light shines down on it. As a rule, a Relief setting of around 3,000 usually suffices, with the Light Height anywhere above that.

- *Smoothness*—Smoothness gets rid of pixelization, but with a corresponding increase in rendering time. Though the range of this control is from 0.1 to 500, settings above 10 increase rendering times dramatically. This may be acceptable if you are creating a single image, but it is annoying when you are rendering an animation. Do what you can to avoid high Smoothness values.

- *Blend*—Blend (1 to 100) sets the amount of blend with the original footage. At 0 you get no plug-in effect, and at 100 you get no original image.

FE LightBurst

 Use this effect on an Alpha channel. It creates bursts of light that seem to emanate from the footage (see Figure 25.5). The following are some possible uses for the FE LightBurst effects:

- Create footage that seems to glow from a strange inner light. This is very effective for fantasy and mythical productions.

- For surprising effects, alter the content of the Alpha channel in an animation. For instance, if you created the Alpha channel by using BorisFX Linear Key, change the values over time, so the Alpha image displays different visible and invisible elements.

The following controls allow you to adjust the parameters of the FE LightBurst effect:

- *Source Position*—Place the crosshairs to select the light's center. (Remember that you may also explore placing the light center outside the Composition frame.) Everything depends on the look of your Alpha layer.

- *Light Factor*—This is an intensity setting with a range of 0 to 100. The softest rays are produced at lower values, usually below 5.

Figure 25.5
Left: The Alpha channel of the targeted footage, created with the BorisFX Linear Key. Adjust the Alpha until you can discern the image. Center: A Light Factor of 7 and a Ray Length of –3, with Halo Alpha enabled, creates this third-eye ray. Right: In this example, the Alpha Halo is off, Light Factor is 33, and Ray Length is 0.4.

- *Ray Length*—This control sets the length of the light rays (–50 to +50). Experiment with negative values to create bursts that have less effect on the surrounding footage.

- *Burst Type*—There are three Burst Types: Fade, Straight, and Center. Fade is the default, and it creates normalized bursts. Straight creates harder line bursts with no fades, and Center creates bursts that fade as they reach the center point.

- *Halo Alpha*—With this checkbox enabled, the Alpha mask is basically ignored.

- *Color/Replace Colors*—Select a color of your choice, and check the Replace Colors option to tint the entire footage with the selected color.

See The Light Animation

LiteBrst, found on the companion CD-ROM, is an amazing little animation that shows some of the power of the LightBurst plug-in. The light is not animated in any way, nor is the targeted footage. Instead, the content of the Alpha layer is altered over time to mask and unmask the contents. The LightBurst was applied with a Light Factor of 33 and a Ray Length of 0.4 with a Fade Burst type.

FE LightRays

 This may be one of the strangest light effects available. It is a combination of light rays and image warping, and always creates strange and unexpected results. The best target footage is a face, and the effect can be applied to an Alpha layer or directly to the footage. You can also use this effect on an image or animation of a lens flare. The result will be a fast cosmic journey. Just vary the Radius values, from small to large, over time. A good default is in the range of 0 to 3,000 (see Figure 25.6).

The following controls allow you to adjust the parameters of the FE LightRays effect:

- *Shape*—With this control, you choose between a Radial (circular) or Rectangular (squarish) shape for the effect.

- *Radius*—Set the radius as needed. Its range is 0 to 10,000. As the values near 10,000, the effect on the image is the same, regardless if you chose either Radial or Rectangular shapes.

Figure 25.6
Left: LightRays can warp any footage from a center point outward. Center: Using the Rectangular Shape option, the footage is confined to a squarish appearance. Right: Radial Shape option explodes the footage in a more circular fashion.

- *Center*—Center the crosshairs on a targeted feature in the footage.

- *Direction*—Rotate the light with this dial and keyframe it. The resulting light will spin on its center. Use this effect on footage of a lens flare (like the Knoll LensFlare covered later in this chapter).

- *Color/Color From Source*—Select any color with the eyedropper or from the system color palette. If Color From Source is not checked, an orb of that color will appear on the footage, obliterating the image. If Color From Source is checked, the footage will be warped along the ray lines.

Ray Of Light

Start by taking a look at LiteRayz on the companion CD-ROM. The FE LightRays plug-in was used to generate this animation by applying the effect to an Alpha layer. Compare this animation to LitRayz2, which shows the same setting applied directly to the footage. A radial light ray was animated from a Radius of 0 to 1,234, with an Intensity value of 2,000 throughout. LitRayz3 has the same settings as LitRayz2, but uses a rectangular instead of a radial shape.

FE LightSweep

This effect allows you to place a revolving beam of light on your footage. Place its center where the light should be coming from, like a lighthouse tower or a star (see Figure 25.7). The following are some possible uses for the FE LightSweep effects:

- Use this effect to generate a light beam from footage of a flashlight. No need to do this in 3D since After Effects can handle it quite effectively in many cases.

- Use a thin-beamed light in Add mode, with a high intensity, to create a laser or other high-energy beam. Let it sweep across a logo.

The following controls allow you to adjust the FE LightSweep effect:

- *Light Center*—Center the light anywhere on the element of the footage that is to act as the light source.

Figure 25.7
Left: A Sharp beam with a Cone Intensity of 22 and a Sweep Intensity of 70 is centered in the sky in this footage. Center: Here, the beam is changed to a Smooth Composited type, and the Sweep Intensity is left the same. Right: A Sharp Cutout beam obliterates the rest of the footage. This LightSweep type is best applied to an Alpha channel and composited into an underlying layer.

- *Light Angle*—The Light Angle is controlled by a radial dial, and can be keyframe animated to perform whatever sweep angle you need.

- *Light Cone and Light Cone Width*—The options are Sharp, Smooth, and Linear. Sharp is a standard cone that widens as it gets farther from the source. Smooth is all one width and blurs out over the length of the beam. A Linear light is best used to emulate a laser or some other narrow beam.

- *Light Sweep Intensity*—Sweep Intensity (0 to 200) controls the brilliance of the light on the footage. In general, Composited lights need more intensity than ones that use the Add mode to be seen clearly. (See the explanation under Light Reception.)

- *Light Edge Intensity*—This controls the amount of embossing applied, if the light is being targeted to an Alpha layer.

- *Light Color*—Select the color of your light to fit the effect you need and the footage you're using.

- *Light Reception*—The three options are Add, Composite, and Cutout. The light can be added to the footage, in which case it stands out from the footage content and color. It can be composited, in which case it blends into the footage, or you may select Cutout. If Cutout is selected, the rest of the footage is dropped, and only the light remains.

More Light Effects

Take a look at LtSweep on the companion CD-ROM. A sharp light beam sweeps across this footage from a star above—or perhaps it's a spaceship.

FE Spotlight

 Here's another Spotlight effect. With this one you can place an image layer in the spot and use it as a projected Gel, or create a spotlight that illuminates only that part of the footage you want to expose (see Figure 25.8).

The following are some possible uses for the FE Spotlight effects:

- Use an Intensity and a Height of 100 and an animated target to move a light across a logo in the footage. Adjust the Cone Angle as needed to frame the image, and use the Light Shadow mode.

- Use the Light Only mode with an Edge Softness of 100 and keyframe the target position at different locations to create footage to use later as an Alpha layer.

The following controls allow you to adjust the FE Spotlight effect's parameters:

- *From/To*—This allows you to set the source and target for the spotlight.

- *Height*—Height (0 to 100) allows you to see the source of the light at a value of 0, but at higher values, the source is hidden. (All you see at higher values is the lighted area.)

- *Cone Angle*—At low Cone Angle values, the size of the area of light is smaller. At higher values, the light area is larger. The range is from 0 to 360.

Figure 25.8
Left: Using a Height of 0, you can pinpoint the location of the light source. Center: With height set to a value of 100, the light source is somewhere off-camera. Right: Raising the Intensity to 100 obliterates everything except what is seen under the beam.

- *Edge Softness*—Always use a little Edge Softness (0 to 100) to blur the boundary where the light meets the rest of the image. A good default is 50.

- *Color*—You can set the color of the light, but you'll see this color only when you select the Light Only or Light Add Render types.

- *Intensity*—Intensity is light brightness. You can see the intensity change only when you use a Render type other than Light Shadow.

- *Render*—You can choose among the four standard Render types and four Gel types. The standard types are Light Only, Light Add, Light Add+, and Light Shadow (the most common for realistic lights). Light Only drops all image content. Light Add and Light Add+ allow you to see the Light Color. The Gel types are Gel Only, Gel Add, Gel Add+, and Gel Shadow. Gel Only shows the Gel image you have selected in the lighted area, with no other image data. Gel Add and Gel Add+ composite the Gel image with the original footage. Gel Shadow places the source image in shadow, and shows the Gel image in the spotlight. Using Gel selections is a way to create projected composites.

- *Gel Layer*—Select the Gel image from any resident footage in the project. Projected Gels are best used against solid-color layers or other colorful footage.

Rotating Image Spotlight

Here's a way to add a spotlight that projects a rotating image on top of your targeted footage. Do the following:

1. Set the Composition window size to 480×360 pixels. Load any two images to two different layers in the Composition window.

2. Open the FE Spotlight filter in the Effects Lights menu.

3. Set the parameters as follows: Height 75, Cone Angle 25, Edge Softness 75, Intensity 100, Render Gel Only, and your top layer as the Gel Layer. Set the From Centroid to 403, 318.

4. Set up five equally spaced keyframes for the To Centroid (which includes the first and last frame): 403/231, 305/320, 405/395, 510/315, and back to 403/231.

Render the animation and save it to disk. Take a look at the FESpot animation on the companion CD-ROM for an example of this effect.

In The Spotlight, Part 2

Open FESpot from the companion CD-ROM. By using the FE Spotlight and keyframe animating the cone angle from 0 to 70, a progressive display of the footage is revealed.

Knoll LensFlare Pack

 The Knoll LensFlare Pack is a vital plug-in for anyone who needs to create lens flares in After Effects. As you are no doubt aware, you can access the Photoshop lens flare plug-in, but, as useful as that may be, it pales in comparison to the Knoll LensFlare Pack option. The Photoshop lens flare plug-in offers you very few customizing or animating features. The Knoll LensFlare Pack allows you to design lens flares for your projects that ensure variable and high-quality effects. The following are some possible uses for the Knoll LensFlare Pack effects:

- Create multiple Knoll LensFlare plug-ins on a dark-blue backdrop to create a starry space project with different animated lens flares. Rotate or resize each in a different manner to maintain viewer interest.

- Target an Alpha layer with one or more colored lens flares to tint and posterize the composited footage.

The following controls allow you to adjust the basic Knoll LensFlare parameters. However, you should see the following Options section to acquaint yourself with the more customizable features:

- *Brightness*—The Brightness settings (in a range of 0 to 200) affect the entire environment of the footage. At values above 100, the footage starts to become washed out with the intensity of the lens flare. At 200, that result is maximized, and the entire footage displays whatever color the lens flare is set at, as long as the Scale setting is above 0.8.

- *Scale*—Think of the lens flare scale (0.09 to 5) as the dimension of the central lens flare orb. If the Brightness value is kept at 150, you can see and grow the elliptical orb within a value range of 0.1 to 0.8. At levels higher than that, the orb becomes so dominant that it washes out the footage. You use the orb at controllable levels to create energy flashes and explosions.

- *Light Source Location*—Set the source of the lens flare with the standard crosshairs.

- *Color*—Here is where you'll select an overall color for the aura of the flare, but realize that the central orb will remain white and opaque. Use white for the look of a standard lens flare, red for fiery explosions, and green, blue, or violet for more-cosmic effects.

- *Angle*—Setting an angle for the lens flare makes sense only if the flare has some streaks or spokes protruding from it. Otherwise, you won't notice any changes. Set the angle to animate the lens flare around its own center point.

- *Layers*—The location layer of the lens flare can be none, or any other layer in the stack. None is the default, since it allows you to interactively place the lens flare location point. You can, however, also select to target the lens flare to an Alpha layer for interesting tinting effects. In the same way, you may select an obscuration layer. Select Alpha if the lens flare is to be targeted to the Alpha mask layer; otherwise, leave it at the default of None. The only time to select another layer, other than None or Alpha, is if the layer you want to target has some degree of transparency, so the effect of the lens flare can be appreciated. Choosing the type of obscuration layer has to agree with the layer being targeted for a lens flare.

- *Source Size*—The size of the lens flare source is set here.

Mastering The Knoll LensFlare Options

This is where the Knoll LensFlare plug-in literally shines. By clicking on Options, you bring up the LensFlare design environment, where every parameter of the lens flare can be modified (see Figure 25.9).

Here's where you can see a preview image of the lens flare and also a list of all the elements of which it is constructed. Highlighting any element in the list brings up that element's parameters, any of which can be altered by using the control sliders. Alterations are displayed immediately in the Preview window. You may choose to delete elements by dragging them from the list into the trash. You may also want to add elements not included in the lens flare under modification. To do that, click and hold (Mac) or just click (Windows) on the downward-pointing arrow next to the trash can. You'll bring up the Element Types list shown in Figure 25.10.

Any element you select is immediately displayed in the Preview pane. In just a few explorations, you'll get the idea of what each element represents. Elements can also be added as many times as you like and rotated to different orientations on the lens flare. One last point of interest is that you can tap the library of basic lens flares, located in the AE Plug-ins directory in the Knoll LFP Custom Flares folder in the Knoll folder. Here you'll find a selection of basic lens flares to modify (see Figure 25.11).

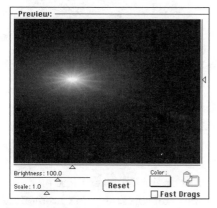

Figure 25.9
The primary Knoll LensFlare design screen.

Figure 25.10
The Element Types list. You can add any of these lens flare elements to your lens flare design.

Applying A Knoll LensFlare To An Alpha Layer

Normally, you would apply a lens flare directly to the footage to create artifacts like sparkles or cosmic bodies. At times, however, you might want to explore applying the lens flare to an Alpha layer. My favorite method for creating a suitable Alpha layer from the footage content is to use the BorisFX Linear Color Key, and to adjust the Similarity slider while viewing the matte. (This is covered in Chapter 18.) Once you create the Alpha layer, you can apply your choice of Knoll lens flares to it and animate it as you like (see Figure 25.12).

> *Note: When a Knoll lens flare is applied to the Alpha layer and its color is changed, that color will tint all of the nonmasked parts of the composited footage. This is a good method to use for the selective tinting of posterized footage.*

Contrast Figure 25.12 with Figure 25.13, in which the lens flare is applied directly to the footage layer.

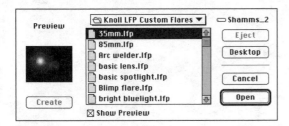

Figure 25.11
A list of basic lens flare designs is open for you to import and customize.

Animation With Flare

The companion CD-ROM has a series of animations based on the Knoll LensFlare plug-in (Mac only). Start with LnsFlr1, which shows a spinning SpikeBall lens flare with Chroma Hoop and Sparkle components. Then move on to LnsFlr2. In this example, an Alpha layer was used

Figure 25.12
Left: Alpha layer of footage created with BorisFX Linear Color Key. Center: The Alpha layer displayed with the lens flare applied. Right: The finished composite shows that the lens flare altered the luminance balance of the footage, creating a posterization effect.

Figure 25.13
Left: The original footage. Center: A Bright Blue Light lens flare, from the Knoll library, is added in the footage. Right: The saved footage from the center figure is reloaded into the Composition window, and another Knoll lens flare is applied (a Vortex Bright).

on top of the lens flare footage. The Alpha layer was generated from the Clouds graphic in the After Effects mask folder. Using the BorisFX Linear Color Key, with the Similarity control, the Alpha layer is gradually decreased in size, and the lens flare dominates the scene.

Now take a look at LnsFlr3. This animation, created in Bryce 3D, already had a flare effect included. I wanted to give it a double-whammy. At the moment the ship hits the dimensional doorway, I introduced a Knoll lens flare with a Scale of 5 and a Brightness of 0.01. A few frames later, Brightness is increased to 105, causing an explosive glare over the entire footage. Then Brightness dissipates to 0 at the end. Finally, in LnsFlr4 I stacked four separate Knoll LensFlare plug-ins over the same footage to create this multiple-flare animation.

Boris AE Alpha Spotlight

This Alpha Spotlight filter affects only the layer's Alpha channel. If the layer has no Alpha channel, use of this filter creates one based on the shape and attributes of the Alpha Spotlight (see Figure 25.14).

Figure 25.14
Left: Original footage. Center: Alpha Spotlight applied so that just a portion of the footage is affected. Right: Using a Matte allows the Alpha Spotlight to create a composite.

The following are some possible uses for the Alpha Spotlight filter:

• Use this filter as a quick way to create an Alpha channel for the layer. Then you can use any of the other filters on the same Alpha channel to modify it.

• Use the Invert Apply Mode to create a black oval on the layer's Alpha channel, which is perfect for a white text block shape.

The following controls allow you to adjust the Alpha Spotlight effect's parameters:

• *Centroids*—You can place three separate Centroids on your footage: Near Corner, Far Corner, and Displace Light. Near Corner and Far Corner set the longest diameter of the Spotlight cone. Displace Light allows you to move the light cone by small increments, so you can place it exactly where it is needed. Animating the Displace Light Centroid allows you to keep the same light shape as it moves.

• *Light Elevation*—(0 to 100) Any value of Elevation higher than 0 creates a larger lighted area.

• *Light Squeeze*—(0 to 100) A value of 100 creates a circular lighted region, while lower values create an ellipse.

• *Intensity*—(0 to 2,000) This value increases the strength of the light. Note that at a value of 2,000, the edge of the lighted area will look less blurred out.

• *Center Falloff*—(–100 to 100) Settings above 0 tend to dim the intensity of the light. Settings that fall below 0 create a dropout area at the center of the light.

• *Edge Falloff*—(0 to 2,000) At 0, the edge of the light cone is sharp. The higher you push this setting, the more the edge fades out gradually.

• *Apply Mode*—There are six Apply Modes: Normal, Invert, Add, Subtract, Multiply, and Screen. Explore each before selecting the one that works best with your footage needs.

• *Gel Matte Layer*—Select either None or a layer from the stack.

• *Gel/Matte*—Select None, Gel, or Matte. A Gel is a projected image or animation, and a Matte is a layer that interferes with the light source, creating dropout areas.

• *Best Quality Gel*—Checking this box gives you the highest-quality Gel projection. Always use this for finished renders that contain a Gel.

Boris AE Light Sweep

 The Light Sweep filter allows you to create a beam of light, which can either be configured to shine from any 2D direction or animated to twirl around its center (see Figure 25.15).

The following are some possible uses for the Light Sweep filter:

- Use the Light Sweep filter to create heavenly rays streaming down from cloud footage. Keyframe animate the Direction and Color for additional mystery. For a more complex version of this effect, use several Light Sweep Effects on top of each other, each with different colors.

- To use this filter to create a thin laser light, set the following parameters: Cone Width 15, Shape 100, and Intensity 80.

The following controls allow you to adjust the Light Sweep effect's parameters:

- *Light Center and Direction*—Use the centroid to determine the center of the beam and the radial dial to determine its direction.

- *Falloff Distance*—(0 to 100) This value sets the length of the beam. At 0, length equals 0. Higher settings increase the length.

- *Cone Width*—(0 to 1,000) At a width of 0, the light is invisible. Higher settings widen the beam.

- *Center Percentage*—(0 to 100) This value effects the spread of the center of the beam. At 0, the center remains away from the edges, whereas higher values spread the center to overlap the edges.

- *Shape*—(0 to 200) At 0, the Shape is fuzzy, and it becomes more coherent (edges defined with no fuzziness) at higher settings.

- *Intensity*—(0 to 2,000) This value increases the strength of the light. Note that at a value of 2,000, the edge of the lighted area will look less blurred out.

Figure 25.15
Left: Footage displaying laser Light Sweep (Cone Width 15, Shape 100, and Intensity 80). Center: Heavenly Stream (Cone Width 220). Right: Using a Subtract Apply Mode with an Intensity of 200 at an angle of 50 degrees creates an inverse light effect.

- *Edges From*—There are five channel options: Alpha, Luma, Red, Green, and Blue. Explore each before selecting the one that works best with your footage needs. Luma causes glows on the footage.

- *Edge Intensity*—(0 to 100) A value of 0 creates the fuzziest blended edge, and higher settings create more opaque edges.

- *Edge Threshold*—(0 to 100) This setting adjusts the range of the Edge Intensity parameter. Explore its use while watching the Composition window.

- *Blurs*—(0 to 200) You can add either or both Pre Blur and Post Blur to soften the effect.

- *View Edges Only*—View only the edges of the light.

- *Light Color*—Select any hue you want. Animating hues creates interesting variations.

- *Ambient Light*—(0 to 100) Setting this value lower than 100 darkens the source footage. Use it to increase the contrast between the source footage and the Light Sweep.

- *Apply Mode*—Explore the use of these alternate Apply Modes to see which works best.

- *Apply Mix*—(0 to 100) Don't bother using this control if you are using a Normal Apply Mode. With any other Apply Mode, using a Max value of less than 100 tones down the Apply Mode look.

- *Shadow Transparency*—Checking this box makes the layer transparent to whatever is below, except in those areas illuminated by the Light Sweep.

- *Gel/Matte Layer*—Select a Gel or a Matte from any layer in the stack.

- *Gel/Matte*—Select None, Gel, or Matte. A Gel is a projected image or animation, and a Matte is a layer that interferes with the light source, creating dropout areas.

Beam Me Down

See the LtSwp animation on the companion CD-ROM, which displays an animated multicolored beam coming down from above.

Boris AE Reverse Spotlight

The Reverse Spotlight filter is just an alternative version of the Spotlight filter. The main difference is the way the light is placed with the centroids (see Figure 25.16).

Use the Reverse Spotlight when its placement controls are more to your liking than those found in the Boris AE Spotlight filter.

The following controls allow you to adjust the Reverse Spotlight filter's parameters:

- *Centroids*—You can place three separate Centroids on your footage: Near Corner, Far Corner, and Displace Light. Near Corner and Far Corner set the longest diameter of the Spotlight cone. Displace Light allows you to move the light cone by small increments, so you can place it exactly where it is needed. Animating the Displace Light Centroid allows you to keep the same light shape as it moves.

Figure 25.16
Left: Original footage. Center: Elevation and Squeeze of 100, Intensity of 30, and an Edge Falloff of 1 creates a spotlight with a defined edge. Right: Increasing the Intensity to 40 and the Edge Falloff to 100 generates a very different Reverse Spotlight.

- *Light Elevation*—(0 to 100) Any value of Elevation higher than 0 creates a larger lighted area.

- *Light Squeeze*—(0 to 100) A value of 100 creates a circular lighted region, while lower values create an ellipse.

- *Intensity*—(0 to 2,000) This value increases the strength of the light. Note that at a value of 2,000, the edge of the lighted area will look less blurred out.

- *Light Color*—Select any hue from the System Palette or with the eyedropper.

- *Ambient Light*—(0 to 100) This is the amount of light that illuminates the entire footage. When set to 0, the footage content will be invisible, but you will see a smudge of light where the spotlight falls. Set at 100, the footage content is the clearest.

- *Center Falloff*—(–100 to 100) Settings above 0 tend to dim the intensity of the light. Settings that fall below 0 create a dropout area at the center of the light.

- *Edge Falloff*—(0 to 2,000) At 0, the edge of the light cone is sharp. The higher you push this setting, the more the edge fades out gradually.

- *Apply Mode*—There are six Apply Modes: Normal, Invert, Add, Subtract, Multiply, and Screen. Explore each before selecting the one that works best with your footage needs.

- *Apply Mix*—(0 to 100) This works with all Apply Modes except Normal. It remixes the Apply Mode effect with the original Source footage content. Default is 100.

- *Shadow Transparent*—Checking this box removes all footage content except that seen in the light. It's an interesting way to focus attention only on the content that is illuminated by the spotlight.

- *Gel Matte Layer*—Select either None or a layer from the stack.

- *Gel/Matte*—Select None, Gel, or Matte. A Gel is a projected image or animation, and a Matte is a layer that interferes with the light source, creating dropout areas.

- *Best Quality Gel*—Checking this box gives you the highest-quality Gel projection. Always use this for finished renders that contain a Gel.

Boris AE Spotlight

The Boris AE Spotlight filter is the most standard spotlight in the group of Boris AE light filters (see Figure 25.17).

The following are some possible uses for the Spotlight filter:

- Select a Subtract Apply Mode to create a negative image area wherever the spotlight shines.

- Select a Transparency Apply Mode, and the layer beneath your source layer will show through wherever the spotlight shines.

The following controls allow you to adjust the Spotlight filter's parameters:

- *Centroids*—There are three centroids to place: Light Source, Light Target, and Displace Light. Light Source sets the direction the light is coming from. Light Target sets the place on the footage that is the center of the light cone. Placing both Source and Target over each other tends to create a circular cone. Displace Light allows you to move the light cone by small increments, so you can place it exactly where it is needed. Animating the Displace Light Centroid allows you to keep the same light shape as it moves.

- *Light Elevation*—(0 to 100) Any value of Elevation higher than 0 creates a larger lighted area.

- *Cone Width*—(0 to 120) A value of 120 creates the largest lighted area, whereas 0 shows no light cone at all.

- *Intensity*—(0 to 2,000) This value increases the strength of the light. Note that at a value of 2,000, the edge of the lighted area will look less blurred out.

- *Light Color*—Select any hue from the System Palette or with the eyedropper.

- *Ambient Light*—(0 to 100) This is the amount of light that illuminates the entire footage. When set to 0, the footage content will be invisible, but you will see a smudge of light where the spotlight falls. Set at 100, the footage content is the clearest.

Figure 25.17
Left: Source footage. Center: Layer under the Source layer. Right: Composite, created with the Transparency Apply Mode. Wherever the Spotlight shines, the layer underneath it shows through.

- *Center Falloff*—(–100 to 100) Settings above 0 tend to dim the intensity of the light. Settings that fall below 0 create a dropout area at the center of the light.

- *Edge Falloff*—(0 to 2,000) At 0, the edge of the light cone is sharp. The higher you push this setting, the more the edge fades out gradually.

- *Apply Mode*—There are six Apply Modes: Normal, Invert, Add, Subtract, Multiply, and Screen. Explore each before selecting the one that works best with your footage needs.

- *Apply Mix*—(0 to 100) This works with all Apply Modes except Normal. It remixes the Apply Mode effect with the original source footage content. Default is 100.

- *Shadow Transparent*—Checking this box removes all footage content except that seen in the light. It's an interesting way to focus attention only on the content that is illuminated by the spotlight.

- *Gel Matte Layer*—Select either None or a layer from the stack.

- *Gel/Matte*—Select None, Gel, or Matte. A Gel is a projected image or animation, and a Matte is a layer that interferes with the light source, creating dropout areas.

- *Best Quality Gel*—Checking this box gives you the highest-quality Gel projection. Always use this for finished renders that contain a Gel.

AFTER EFFECTS 4 STUDIO

This studio's purpose is to showcase the myriad special effects from filters built into After Effects 4 and from third-party developers, which are available as plug-ins.

These images build on the content presented in this book's chapters.

Examples of footage altered with the internal After Effects Blur and Sharpen filters.

Channel Blur. The original footage, followed by two variations with alternate Blurs applied.

Compound Blur. The original footage, followed by two Compound Blur variations.

Gaussian Blur. The original footage, followed by a Gaussian Blur of 10 and 60.

Sharpen. The original footage, followed by applications of 10 and 4,000.

Examples of the internal After Effects Channel filters.

Alpha Levels variations.

The Arithmetic filter.

The Set Channels filter, displaying different channel combinations.

Using the Shift Channels filter, the RGB channels in these examples were referenced to themselves, but the Alpha channel draws its data from other sources.

A collection of internal After Effects Distortions filter examples.

Displacement Map alterations.

The Mirror filter.

The Spherize filter applied.

The Wave Warp filter can radically alter image content.

Examples of the After Effects internal Image Control and Perspective filters.

Brightness and Contrast effects.

Change Color effects. The original footage, followed by the results of a Hue Transform and a view of the Color Correction Mask.

Variations using the Tint filter.

The Basic 3D filter applies DVE operations to the footage.

Examples of the internal Stylize filters.

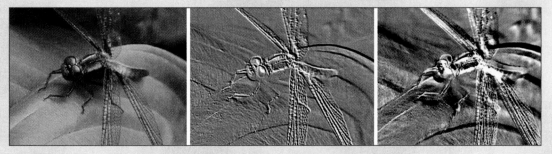

Applications of the Emboss effect.

The Mosaic filter transforms the footage into horizontal and vertical blocks.

The Strobe Light creates a disco dance-floor effect.

Texturize, using one layer to add texture to another. The original footage, the texture layer, and the result.

Examples of the After Effects 4 internal Synthesize, Text, and Time filters.

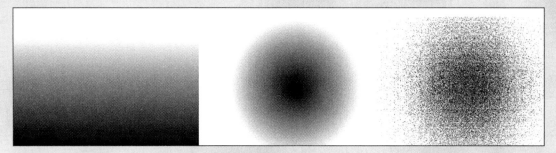

Synthesize Ramp creates alternate graduated content.

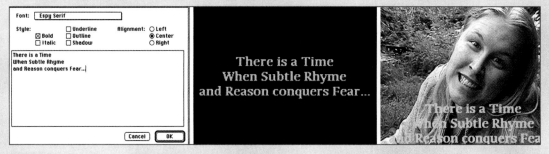

With Basic Text, a variety of composited designs can be achieved.

Using the Numbers filter, you can add Timecode, Long Date, and Short Date data to the layer.

Time Echo can add a composited look based on past or future frames in an animation layer.

Examples of the Transitions, Video Options, and Text filters.

The Transitions shown are Block Dissolve, Radial Wipe, and Venetian Blinds.

This Gradient Wipe example displays a progression from Source to Target footage.

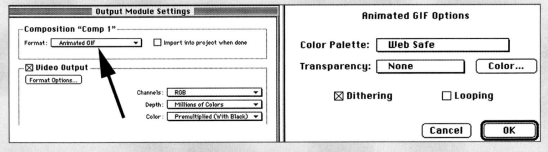

GIF Animation saves begin by accessing the Output Module Settings dialog box, selecting the Format options button, and moving to the Animated GIF Options dialog box for final computations.

Text On A Path is one of the most useful text filters in After Effects.

Examples of the Keying and Matte Tools filters, used to composite footage layers.

With the Color Key, the cat's background is dropped out to reveal the flowers. One result is that the flower pattern can be superimposed on the fur.

Three layer composites are altered with the Extract filter.

With the Luma Key, composites are created based on the brightness of selected footage content.

These examples of the Simple Choker filter display a Matte layer with Choke Matte values of 0, 1, and 2.

Examples of how the Distortion filters warp and distort layer content.

The Bulge filter bloats selected footage areas.

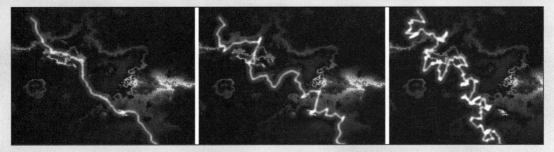

A series of frames from an animation created with the Lightning filter.

Various Ripple filter effects.

Three results of using the Wave filter, displaying Circle, Triangle, and Sine wave effects.

Examples of Alien Skin Eye Candy filters.

The Antimatter Filter applied at percentages of 0, 35, and 100.

Fire effects are a favorite of After Effects users. Here you see flames rendered against a dark background, patterned turbulence, and Fire applied to a masked text block.

These Fur effects display the original image, Wave Spacing set to 100, and Wave Spacing set to 300.

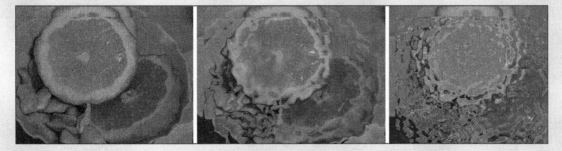

The Glass filter creates areas that look as if they are made from layers of transparent and opaque glass.

Alien Skin Eye Candy filters, continued.

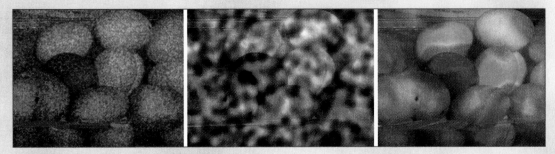

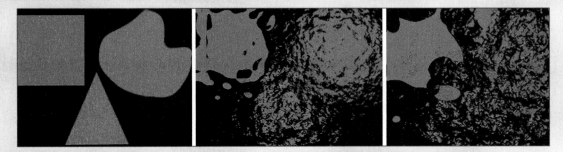

HSB Noise creates a variety of chaotic elements in the layer.

The starting graphic before Jiggle is applied followed by two variations of Bubbles: Brownian Motion and Turbulence.

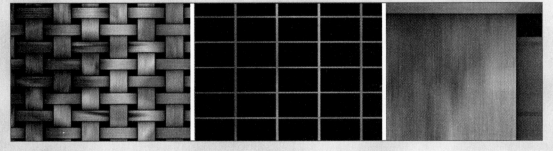

Three variations using the Smoke filter.

The Weave filter makes your footage look as if it were printed on a woven mat.

Alien Skin Eye Candy filters, continued.

Carve can add a 3D carved frame around selected footage areas.

You can select a number of options when applying a Glow effect.

  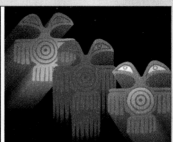

Motion Trail filter adds a smeared trail of image content in any direction.

  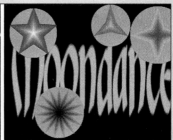

Using the Star filter, you can add a wide variety of star types to your footage.

Examples of the Boris AE filters, which add more professional effects to your After Effects productions.

Color Correction adjusts hue in a variety of ways.

Tint-Tritone can be applied to any layer channel.

The Linear Color Key can composite selected multiple layer content on any background.

The Two-Way Key is great for generating drop-out effects.

Boris AE filters, continued.

The Bulge effect can warp your footage in interesting ways.

Using the Ripple filter, you can apply Chaotic Wave Distortion, Super Twirl, and HyperTwirl.

Wave filter displays, showing Sine Wave and two variations of the Spectrum 8 waveform.

With the Cube filter, you can wrap your footage on a 3D resized cube.

Boris AE filters, continued.

Another use for the Cube filter is to add shadow, glow, and a 3D light source.

You can generate 3D Cylinders from any layer in the composition.

Selecting the DVE filter, the content layer can be turned to any angle, adding a shadowing and 3D depth.

The Sphere filter, displaying a hollow crescent bowl-like effect, spherical mapping, and a combination effect combining the Boris f/x AE Bulge distortion to the eye of the figure afterwards.

Examples of the Berserk filters, from DigiEffects, which give you a large variety of radical image distortion and particle tools.

The Blizzard filter adds snowflakes of various sizes.

The Contourist effect reshapes image content.

The Fog Bank filter adds a user-selected density of fog to the selected layer.

Examples of the Laser filter include a High-Energy Laser beam, a Pistol Laser beam, and a Stun Laser beam.

DigiEffects Berserk filters, continued.

With NightBloom, your footage can be transformed into an abstract painting.

Oil Paint adds another media effect.

With the Perspectron filter, you can create a combination of perspective plane mapping and warping effects.

Ripploid combines a tiling and ripple effect, and when animated over time, creates moving optical illusions.

Examples of DigiEffects filters, which create new media looks.

The Squisher filter is also called Pinch in other applications, and allows you to pinch selected areas of the footage.

Starfield effects are always in high demand and are used for everything from commercial product backdrops to effects for the movies.

The Still Noise filter creates random noise, just like static on a TV screen.

Like the Oil Paint filter, The VanGoughist filter is meant for use on non-animated backdrops, although you may explore this rather blobby effect in motion.

Examples of DigiEffects Aurorix filters, which add another huge collection of options.

If film sits around for too long in an unprotected environment, it begins to deteriorate, and the Aged Film filter is perfect for emulating this condition.

The Bulgix filter creates a combination of image tiling and punch effects. A selected area of the image is enlarged as through a magnifying glass, and a tile is applied to it at the same time.

The Chaotic Noise filter applies transformed areas of interest to the Red, Blue, and Green channels. Composited, this produces a look that emulates a multicolored sky.

The Electrofield filter creates a concentric vortex effect.

DigiEffects Aurorix filters, continued.

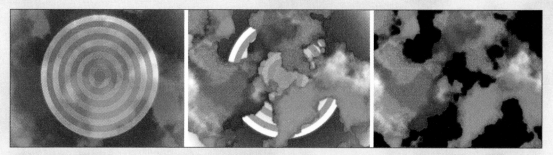

The Fractal Noise filter is in the same category as the DigiEffects Chaotic Noise and Chaotic Rainbow filters, and adds another Noise look to the footage.

Infinity Warp zooms in on a selected area of your footage, warping the footage at each step. It is one of the most dynamic effects you can apply.

The Infinity Zone effect is also known as Vortex Tiling in other applications. It is a combination of tiling and spiraling in a fractal dimension, where the longer you zoom in, the more detail there is.

The Noise Blender shapes look like stippled daubs of paint at low settings, and like a blurry circuit board at maximized settings.

DigiEffects Aurorix filters, continued.

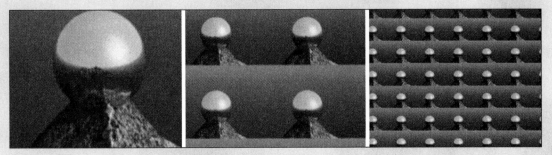

The Tilos filter creates basic but powerful tiling effects.

The Warpoid plug-in is very useful for controlling the warping and morphing of the foreground layer.

Whirlix is a vortex effect with controllable area vortex warping.

WoodMaker is a texture generator that uses a mix of the RGB channels to create patterns that look like wood under red, blue, and green lighting.

Examples of After Effects filters from a number of developers that create Light effects.

The Final Effects Lightburst filter is especially effective on an Alpha channel. It creates bursts of light that seem to emanate out from the footage.

Final Effects LightRays is one of the strangest light effects available. It is a combination of light rays and image warping, and always creates strange and unexpected results.

The Final Effects Spotlight allows you to pinpoint the location of the light source and the target.

Using the Knoll Lens Flare filter, a Bright Blue Light and a Vortex Bright Lens Flare, from the Knoll library, is added in the footage.

A collection of Final Effects filters.

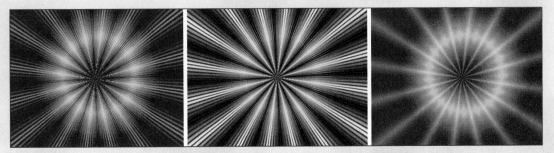

The FE Alpha Map filter should be applied to an Alpha channel in the footage stack. It works best when used to target an already formulated Alpha map (like those in the Masks folder in your After Effects folder).

FE Composite is useful when you want to achieve a blended image on one layer that includes a mix of the original footage and the footage effected by any other plug-in choice.

With FE Color Offset filter, you can rotate the color of each RGB channel separately.

The FE Threshold filter is useful for creating singular or multiple Alpha masking channels.

Final Effects filters, continued.

The FE Threshold RGB filter gives you the ability to colorize your threshold associated footage.

The FE Toner filter uses three different values of one hue to address the Highlights, Midtones, and Shadows of a selected layer.

The FE Wire Removal filter comes in handy for removing wires or other layer elements. Hollywood producers often need to use wire removal software to get rid of puppet rods and strings and cables used to support actors.

Seven wipe types are included in FE Transitions. These include: Grid, Image, Jaws, Light, Radial Scale, Scale, and Twister.

Examples of Final Effects Distortion filters, which add over a dozen new ways to alter your footage.

The FE Bend filter performs a taper on your footage.

Flo Motion is a vortex well effect, with a complex set of controls.

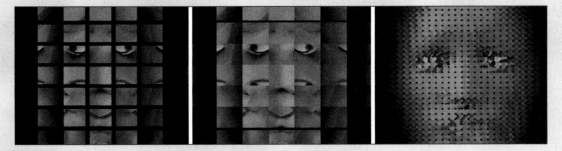

Griddler creates spectacular grid effects, either distortion or tile based.

The FE Lens effect is like looking through a glass lens, concave or convex, at your footage.

Final Effects Distortion filters, continued.

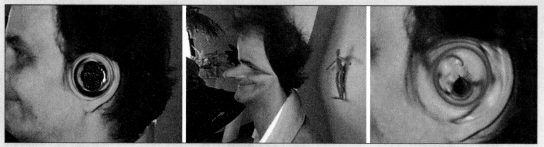

The Ripple Pulse filter can create ripples in ripples, each revealing a repeated zoom on the footage content.

The basic Slant effect tilts the footage. It can also create basic perspective planes.

The Smear effect is capable of creating both subtle and radical footage warps.

The Tiler filter creates a basic tiling effect and is also excellent for creating footage zooms.

Examples of what can be accomplished with the FE Particle filters.

The FE Bubbles filter creates bubble particles that move from the bottom of the footage upward and reflect the background layer.

The FE Drizzle filter creates rippled puddles.

The Hair filter generates stable or animated hair that targets the layer or selected area.

The Star Burst filter takes the star color from the footage and the space color from the background layer to create a wide range of particle effects.

FE Particle effects, continued.

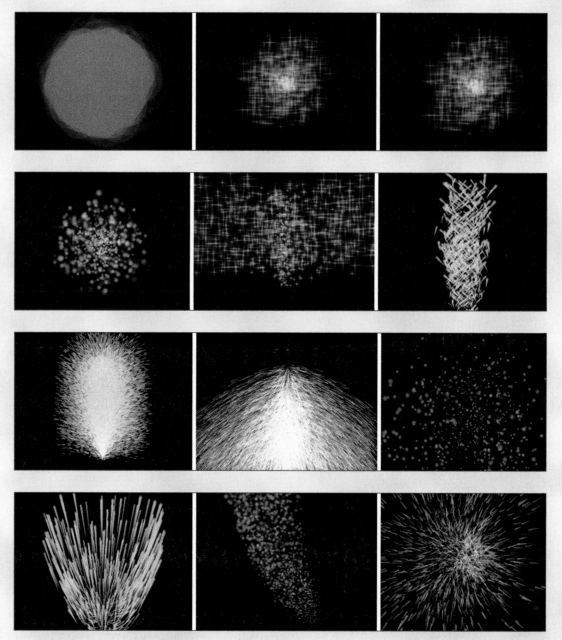

FE Particle Systems II is an extensive particle animation system with unlimited effects capabilities.

Examples of the Final Effects Stylize filters.

The Blobbylize filter allows the Alpha channel of targeted footage to create a cutout of footage on another layer.

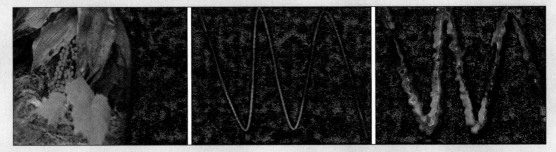

Using the Glue Gun filter, you can create animated writing on a layer that takes its color and content from the footage.

The Kalieda filter will take you and your audience back to your childhood, to the time when you were first mesmerized by seeing the world through a kaleidoscope.

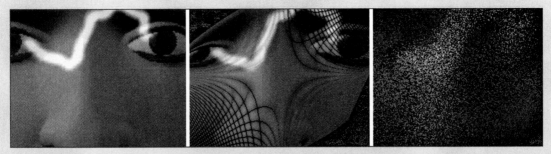

Scatterize is a very complex marriage between two effects: a twist warp and a particle system.

Examples of the results of the Intergraph VisFX filters.

The Blur filter creates blurred footage.

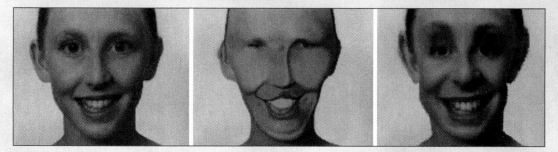

Using the Bump filter, the footage is warped by either referencing itself or by referencing another footage layer in the stack.

The Raindrop filter creates multiple ripples on any selected layer.

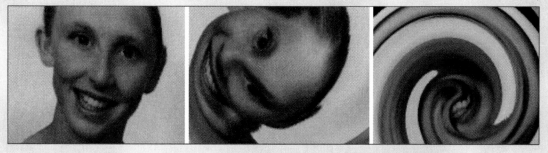

The Whirl filter creates a vortex effect, spinning and warping the selected footage.

Hollywood FX, from Synergy International, offers the After Effects user the highest quality and variety of 3D effects available.

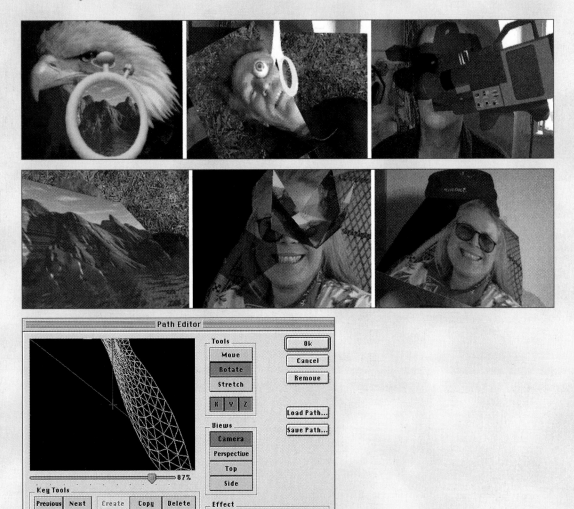

Instead of deform mapping a 2D effect, Hollywood FX generates real 3D objects and maps the footage to them. Outside of DVE hardware costing thousands of dollars, there is nothing to compare with these AE transition effects when you need to segue from one layer to another.

FE MIX

This chapter details the following ICE FE (Final Effects) Complete AE plug-ins, which represent quite a mix of effects: Alpha Map, Color Offset, Composite, Threshold, Threshold RGB, Toner, Simple Wire Removal, and Transition.

FE Alpha Map

The FE Alpha Map plug-in should be applied to an Alpha channel in the footage stack. With it, you can customize and modulate the contents on an Alpha channel. The plug-in works best when it's used to target an Alpha map that is already formulated, like those in the Masks subfolder in your After Effects folder (see Figure 26.1).

The following are some possible uses for the Alpha Map effect:

- Use the Output Level slider to adjust the transparency of the Alpha over time, to create animated glows and other subtle effects. This effect is useful for logos and for groups of footage objects, such as a school of fish, moving against a color or mixed-footage backdrop.

- Use the Output Level slider to control animated fades, especially in conjunction with a Custom transition.

Figure 26.1
Left: SunRays Alpha mask from the After Effects Masks drawer. Center: Customized FE Alpha Map applied using the 5 Waves option at the maximum level of 511. Right: Using a SoftIn option at a level of 120.

The following controls allow you to adjust the parameters of the effect:

- *Alpha Map Type*—You can select from Triangular, Smooth, and Custom. Although Triangular and Smooth offer some subtle differences that you will want to explore, it's the Custom setting that allows you to control the effect by altering an Alpha graph.

- *Output Level*—This slider adjusts the extent to which the effect alters the Alpha layer. Its range runs from 0 to 511.

- *Options*—When the Custom type is selected and you employ the Options trigger, you are presented with a graph of the Alpha Map. You can either draw a new curve on the graph or use one of the optional settings listed to alter both the graph and, consequently, the way the Alpha Map creates transparencies (see Figure 26.2).

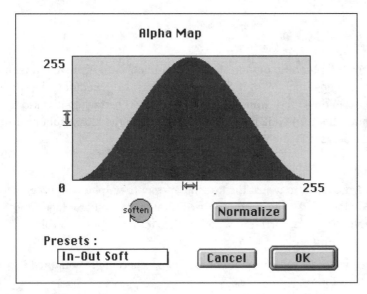

Figure 26.2
The Alpha Customize Curve can be interactively shaped, affecting how the Alpha layer is treated.

FE Color Offset

With FE Color Offset, you can rotate the color of each RGB channel separately (see Figure 26.3.) The following are some possible uses for the FE Color Offset effect:

- Create shimmering sepia- to blue-toned effects by keyframe animating just the red channel. Set the value of each keyframe to a multiple of 180, with a Solarize Overflow Behavior.

- Using a Wrap Overflow behavior, keyframe an animation with all channel values at 90 at the start of an animation, and ending with all set to 270. The result is a contemporary, highly posterized look, which is great with any moving footage.

Figure 26.3
Left: Original footage. Center: Wrap Overflow behavior with a setting of 270 on each RGB channel control. Right: The same settings as the center image, but with the Solarize Overflow Behavior applied.

The following controls allow you to adjust the FE Color Offset parameters:

- *Red/Green/Blue Offset*—Using these three separate radial controls, you can offset the RGB color channels.

- *Overflow Behavior*—The three options are Wrap, Solarize, and Polarize. Wrap tends to create footage that looks highly posterized with fewer colors than the original footage. Solarize emphasizes a more muted look, and, with values greater than one revolution on all channels, creates interesting colorized negatives. Polarize can be used to create wispy duotone and tritone effects.

FE Composite

This effect is useful when you want to achieve a blended image on one layer that includes a mix of the original footage and the footage affected by any other plug-in. Normally, you would achieve this by using a Blend function. By using this Composite plug-in, you can keep the blended result separate from the applied effect (see Figure 26.4).

The following controls allow you to adjust the parameters of the FE Composite effect:

- *Opacity*—This slider allows you to control the blending of the original image with the altered image. Its range is from 0 to 100.

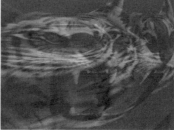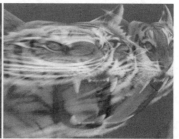

Figure 26.4
Left: Original footage of Aurorix CycloWarped tiger. Center: FE Composite using the InFront option at an opacity of 50. Right: FE Composite, using the Screen option at an opacity of 100.

- *Transfer Mode*—Select a Transfer Mode from the list to decide what the blended footage will be based on. You can explore among 22 different modes.

- *Channel Option*—If the original footage has an Alpha layer that you want to keep in the new blended mix, leave this option checked.

FE Threshold

The Threshold plug-in is useful for creating singular or animated Alpha masking channels (see Figure 26.5). The following are some possible uses for the FE Threshold effect:

- Use a Luminance Threshold type, blended with the original at 50 percent, with a Threshold value of 40 to create footage that looks like pen-and-ink outlined wash media. This can be used on either stable or moving footage. Checking the Invert option alters the look to a more dreamlike sequence.

- Use a Threshold of 100, with RGB blended with the original moving footage at 50 percent to create a posterized animation that still allows the content of the footage to be appreciated.

- Create an animated Alpha channel by following these steps:

  1. Set Blend to 0 so that none of the original footage is blended in.

  2. Set the type to Luminance and adjust the Threshold value to 0 at the start of an animation and 256 at the end.

  3. Render, then save the file as Alpha channel mask footage. Load the finished animation as an Alpha layer over the original footage.

  4. Apply any effect you like to the Alpha layer. As the animation progresses, it will show the effect applied first to the entire footage and then decreasing to 0 at the end. This is an interesting method using any of the Aurorix effects.

The following controls allow you to adjust the FE Threshold effect:

- *Threshold*—Threshold allows you to adjust the extent to which the image will be affected. Its range is from 0 to 256. At 0, the maximum amount of the image is affected, and at 256, none of the image is affected.

Figure 26.5
Left to right: The Luminance Threshold type with values set at 25, 50, and 75 with a Blend at 0.

- *Threshold Type*—You can choose between two threshold types: Luminance and RGB. The Luminance type is essential for creating Alpha masks, while the RGB option is useful for creating posterized effects on the selected footage.

- *Invert*—Checking Invert reverses the effect of the Threshold value.

- *Blend*—Blend sets the amount of blend with the original footage, with a range of 1 to 100. At 0, you get no original image; at 100, you get no Threshold effect.

FE Threshold RGB

Similar to the FE Threshold effect described in the preceding section, the Threshold RGB version gives you the ability to colorize your threshold footage as well (see Figure 26.6). The following are some possible uses for the FE Threshold RGB effect:

- Use the Invert command on any or all RGB channels in an animation to make the light source appear to reverse direction.

- Use any two RGB Threshold settings to create posterized four-color footage.

The following controls allow you to adjust the parameters of the Threshold RGB effect:

- *Red/Green/Blue Threshold*—These controls set the visibility levels of each selected channel.

- *Invert Red/Green/Blue Channel*—When checked for any or all RGB channels, this option reverses the channel content.

- *Blend*—Blend sets the amount of blend with the original footage, in a range of settings from 0 through 100. At 0 you get no original footage, and at 100 you get no plug-in effect.

On The Threshold

Look at ThrshRGB on the companion CD-ROM. This animation shows how an FE Threshold RGB effect can be used to created either a footage effect or an effect that targets saved Alpha footage. Note that an Invert was applied to the animation halfway through, so that the light seems to suddenly switch directions, adding more interest. ThrsRGB2 is a variation on the ThrshRGB animation. In this example, a red channel was added with a value of 100 to the mix, resulting in more image definition and the addition of red and yellow to the palette.

Figure 26.6
Alternate blends of different RGB Threshold settings. Left: Red at 100 and Green at 50, with both inverted. Center: All channels set to 140 with inversions applied. Right: Same settings as the center image, but with a 70 percent blend of the original.

FE Toner

Toned images use three different values of one hue to address the highlights, midtones, and shadows. The most common toned images use brown for the middle tones, and are called sepia tones (see Figure 26.7). The following are some possible uses for the FE Toner effect:

- Use the FE Toner effect to create sepia-toned footage for an antique look. Sepia toning is also a good first step before applying any film-damage effect.

- Use a solid black on all the tonal ranges, and use the blend slider to fade up from black for footage transitions. Use a solid white on all tonal ranges to fade up from white.

The following controls allow you to adjust the parameters of the FE Toner effect:

- *Tone Palette*—Select the three tonal values for highlights, midtones, and shadows. These are usually three values of the same hue, although you may select three hues for more experimental results.

- *Blend With Original*—Blend sets the amount of blend with the original footage. Its range of settings is from 0 to 100. At 0, you get no original footage; and at 100 you get only the original footage with no set tonal components.

Figure 26.7
Left: A standard toned image has white highlights, midvalue midtones (color or gray), and black shadows. Center: Create an instant negative by setting highlights and shadows to white and midtone to black. Right: Using white highlights and black midtones and shadows with a 50 percent blend creates a dramatic lighting effect.

FE Simple Wire Removal

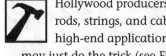

Hollywood producers often need to use wire removal software to eliminate the puppet rods, strings, and cables that are used to support actors or other screen elements. For high-end applications, this effect may not suffice, but for multimedia productions it may just do the trick (see Figure 26.8). The following are some possible uses for the Simple Wire Removal effect.

- Use a stack of this effect to remove multiple wires and cables, or any other selected anomalies.

- If you shoot a frame at the start of your footage that has only the background and not the wired or cabled image, you can use the Frame Offset type to select it as the replacement area. Later, during post-edit, the frame with the replacement content can be deleted.

Figure 26.8
Left: Original footage showing the guitar strap. Center: Strap partially removed with a Thickness value of 12 and a Slope of 27.5. Right: Strap removed by increasing the Slope value to 65.

The following controls allow you to adjust the FE Simple Wire Removal effect:

- *Point A And Point B*—Set Point A at one end of the offending element and Point B at the other to identify it.

- *Removal Style*—You may select from four removal styles: Fade, Frame Offset, Displace, and Displace Horizontal. Fade shows the background through the foreground layer. Frame Offset brings in pixel data from a previous or subsequent frame within a range of –60 to +60. Displace replaces the selected wire with data from outside of the selected area. Displace Horizontal samples only the horizontal for replacement of the wire area.

- *Thickness*—Thickness sets the area to be affected. Its settings range from 0 to 100. Alter the values while watching the preview.

- *Slope*—Slope controls the softness of the removal edge. Its range of settings is also from 0 to 100; as the Slope settings increase, the edge becomes more abrupt. Solid-color backdrops can use a higher Slope value, whereas complex backdrops will demand lower values and more blending.

- *Mirror Blending*—Mirror Blending is used to fine-tune the removal of artifacts around the replaced area. Its settings also range from 0 to 100.

- *Frames To Offset*—This control is used when you select the Frame Offset style, allowing you to set the frame from which the replaced area is taken. Its settings range from -60 to +60.

FE Transitions

FE Transitions features seven wipes: Grid, Image, Jaws, Light, Radial Scale, Scale, and Twister. A wipe is used to get you from one layer to another in a patterned fashion (see Figure 26.9).

FE Radial Light Wipe

The FE Light Wipe allows you to reveal a layer beneath the selected footage by using a glowing shape. Do the following:

Figure 26.9
Left: A Grid Wipe reveals footage B by breaking up footage A into a grid. Center: A Radial Light Wipe reveals footage B by creating a circle of light through footage A. Right: An Image Wipe uses footage A as a semi-transparent pattern to reveal footage B.

1. Place two content layers in tour Composition window, each containing either an image or animated footage.

2. Select the top layer, and load the FE Light Transition from the Effects menu.

3. Use an Intensity of 35%, and a Radial Transition Type.

4. Set the Color to a hue that compliments the dominant color in your top layer. For example, if you have a blue sky that dominates the image, use an orange or green Color. The Color indicates the hue of the glow around the selected Transition Type shape.

5. Keyframe animate frame 1 to a Transition Completion of 0, and the last frame to a Transition Completion of 100.

Render the animation and save to disk. See the FELtWp animation on the companion CD-ROM. The following controls allow you to adjust the Transition effect:

- *Grid Wipe*—You control the size of the grid blocks and whether the effect displaces footage A in a Radial, Rectangular, or Doors fashion. Animation is controlled by the percentage of completion of the effect on a keyframe basis.

- *Image Wipe*—You control which layer in a stack is used as the gradient fill, as well as its softness in the mix. Animation is controlled by the percentage of completion of the effect on a keyframe basis.

- *Jaws Wipe*—Jaws open like doors with teeth. You control the opening angle (which can be animated), the tooth number and height, as well as placement center. The teeth can be Blocks, Robo Jaws, or Spikes. Animation is again controlled by the percentage of completion of the effect on a keyframe basis.

- *Light*—A light opening in footage A slowly opens to reveal footage B. You control the center, direction, intensity, and color of the light. The opening type can be Doors, Radial, or Rectangular. Animation is controlled by the percentage of completion of the effect on a keyframe basis.

- *Radial Scalewipe*—Transition Complete and Center are the only two parameters. This effect creates a warping footage A revealing footage B via a circular, lens-like opening. Used with a more complex footage A, it can be quite beautiful.

- *Scale*—A Scale Wipe rotates around a center, creating an image smear. This works on one layer only, although that layer can be an Alpha channel.

- *Twister*—Twister is the most complex FE Transition effect. You select the starting footage A and the footage B to be revealed (which is on the reverse side of footage A). Set the center point, and use the percent completion to set the keyframes. Clicking Shading on gives the transition a more 3D appearance. You can also keyframe animate the direction of the warp. This transition is best appreciated over a third layer, with stable or animated background footage.

A Good Transition

There are four Transition examples on the companion CD-ROM. ImgWipe was created by using a Saturation type FE Image Wipe Transition. RadScale is a Radial Scale Wipe animation, created with FE Transitions. ScaleWip is an example of an FE Transitions Scale Wipe in animated action. Finally, Twister creates complex animated warps that flip and warp footage A to reveal footage B.

FE DISTORT

This chapter covers the following ICE FE AE plug-ins, all of which are distortion effects: Bend It, Bender, Flo Motion, Griddler, Lens, Power Pin, Ripple Pulse, Slant, Slant Matte, Smear, Split, and Tiler.

> **Note: You should already understand common AE terms and processes (such as layer or mask) before attempting to use these plug-ins. Related terms and processes are adequately explained in the AE documentation and tutorials.**

Bend It

The effect of Bend It is similar to performing a taper on your footage. Depending on the footage content and the placement of the start and end points, it can warp the footage into a tapered shape or bend it so that is spherical. Each case is unique, so there are no hard and fast rules that determine what you will get (see Figure 27.1). The following are some possible uses for the Bend It effect:

• Use this effect on a logo layer to animate it, starting at a bend and ending with no warping. Set the start point in the center of the logo and the end point to the right center of the screen. Use Bend/Extended, and start the animation at a bend value of either -100 or +100. End the animation with a Bend value of 0.

• Create a slide-on from the background color by following these steps:

1. Place your footage on a layer over the background.

2. Place the start point off the screen, centered on the vertical, and to the right.

3. Place the end point off the screen at the same height as the start point, but farther right by about the width of the footage. These are the settings for the start of the animation.

4. At the end of the animation, keyframe-move the start point left to the edge of the footage. In the animation, a vertical line will reveal the footage from right to left.

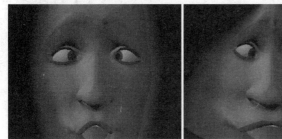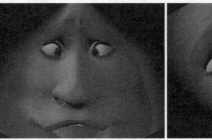

Figure 27.1
Left: The original footage. Center: A bend of -100, with the start point in the middle of the footage, and the end point off screen to the right. Right: A bend of +100, with the same start and end point values.

The following controls allow you to adjust the Bend It effect:

- *Start/End Points*—The start and end points determine the angle and focal points for the bending warp.

> **Note: If your footage looks too vertically squashed at the start, place the start point at the center of the footage and place the end point off the screen to the right, adjusting its exact placement until the footage renders full frame in the preview.**

- *Bend*—The Bend control adjusts the extent of the bending warp that is applied. Its settings range from -100 to +100. In general, negative values warp the footage so that it is narrow at the top and wide at the bottom, and positive values do the reverse.

- *Render Prestart*—You can render the region before the start point by selecting one of these options: Static, Bend, Mirror Bend, or None. Static renders before the start point with no bend, so the start point retains the power of the bend. Bend renders before the start point with a bend, so the start point has less control over the warp. Mirror Bend renders before the start point with a bend mirrored horizontally around the start point as the center. Selecting None will not render any frames before the start point region. Explore each alternative to see what works best for the footage you are working with.

- *Distort*—You can continue the distortion beyond where the end point is placed by selecting Extended, or cut it off at the end point by selecting Legal.

Bender

 This effect is a much more standard warp than Bend It because it warps the footage without the Bend It taper. Everything depends on the placement of the control points (see Figure 27.2).

The following controls allow you to adjust the parameters of the Bend effect:

- *Point A, Point B*—The placements of the A and B points determines how the bend distorts the footage. Point B should always be placed to the right of Point A. The closer it is to Point A on the right, the more powerful the distortions. Placing Point B to the left of Point A will have no effect on the footage.

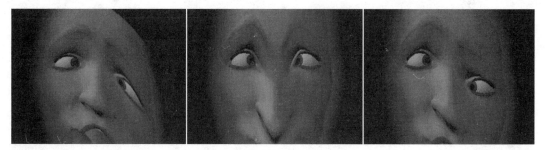

Figure 27.2
In each example, Point A was placed over the right eye of the figure and Point B over the left eye at a Bend value of 100. Left: The Empire State style. Center: The Marilyn style. Right: The Boxer style.

- *Bend Style*—There are four bend styles: Empire State, Marilyn, No. 5, and Boxer. There is little discernible difference between Marilyn and No. 5, as each pulls the footage downward from a point halfway between the A and B points. Empire State warps the image and bends it, based on the placement of point B. Boxer bends the image in the same manner, but leaves the horizontal data more intact.

- *Bend*—The Bend slider adjusts the strength of the bend distortion. Its settings range from –250 to +250.

- *Absolute Value*—Checking Absolute Value lengthens the pull of the distortion.

Flo Motion

 This is a vortex well effect, with a complex set of controls. Use this effect wherever you want a finely controlled vortex gravity-well effect. Or, you could create a double effect by alternating the Amount value of each knot over time (see Figure 27.3).

The following controls allow you to adjust the Flo Motion effect:

- *Knots*—You can place two control points or "knots" on the image. The one with the lowest Amount value acts as a pin, and the one with the highest value acts as the center for a vortex well distortion.

Figure 27.3
Left: Knot 1 has a setting of 0 and is placed over the right eye. Knot 2, with a setting of 3, is placed over the left eye. Center: Knot 2 value increased to 6. Right: Knot 2 value at –3.

- *Amount*—Each knot is set for an Amount value between –16 and +16. Negative values produce holes in your footage. Positive values create vortex warps that distort the image at the placement point of the most powerful knot. If you check Fine Controls, the sensitivity of the Amount sliders is multiplied by 20.

- *Edge Behavior*—Checking Wrap Edges creates seamless symmetrical tiling.

- *Antialiasing*—Use antialiasing to get smoother output. Select Low, Medium, or High.

- *Falloff*—The lower the value (in its range of 0 to 10), the more concentrated the vortex effect.

Griddler

Griddler creates spectacular grid effects, either distortion or tile-based (see Figure 27.4). The following are some possible uses for the Griddler effect:

- To zoom footage from upside down to right side up while it is also being resized from 100 percent to 0 percent back to 100 percent, simply set the Tile Size at 200. Then create an animation that has both horizontal and vertical scales moving from –100 to +100.

- For an animated effect that makes your footage look as if it were being seen through a collection of glass prisms, set the horizontal and vertical scales to 110 and Tile Size to 3. Leave Cut Tiles unchecked. Now animate the rotation so that it completes a full revolution in either direction from start to end of the animation.

The following controls allow you to adjust the Griddler effect:

- *Scale*—These controls (horizontal and vertical, in a range from –2,000 to +2,000) scale the footage. Negative values invert the footage vertically in addition to scaling it.

- *Tile Size*—Tile Size controls the dimensions of the tiles. The settings range from 1 to 200, and smaller values yield a halftone effect, especially with Cut Tiles checked.

> *Note: Leaving the Tile Size set at its maximum value of 200 allows you to use the Scale settings to resize the footage with no distortion.*

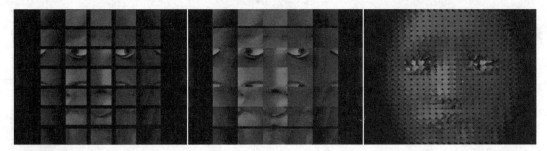

Figure 27.4
Left: With both scales set to 80, a Tile Size of 20, and Cut Tiles checked, a visible grid covers the distorted footage. Center: The same settings with Cut Tiles unchecked. Right: Cut Tiles checked with scales set to 100 and a Tile Size of 5.

- *Rotation*—Use the Rotation control to angle the tiles.
- *Cut Tiles*—With this option checked, "grouting" appears between the tiles. When off, the effect is like tiled glass.

Griddle Me This

For examples of using the Griddler effect, check out the two Griddler files on the companion CD-ROM. Griddler shows the effect with Cut Tiles unchecked, applied to moving footage. Tile Size is animated from 200 at the start to 1 at the end. In Gridler2, Tile Size is left at 200. The horizontal and vertical scales are keyframe animated from –300 at the start to +300 at the end.

Lens

The FE Lens effect is like looking through a glass lens, concave or convex, at your footage (see Figure 27.5). The following are some possible uses for the Lens effect:

- Set Convergence to 100 to animate just the Size attribute.
- Use this effect as an alternative to Spherize at settings below 0.
- With a Size value of 40 or less and a Convergence of –200, moving the center point in an animation creates a spherical distortion in motion.

The following controls allow you to adjust the Lens effect:

- *Center*—Place the crosshairs at the center of the area of the footage that you want to use.
- *Size*—Size determines the radius of the lens power. Its settings range from 0 to 500.
- *Convergence*—Lower Convergence values (in its range from –200 to +100) simulate a convex lens, and higher settings simulate a concave lens. A setting of 0 applies no lens effect.

BubbleFly

Here's a way to use the FE Lens filter to create a bubble that has your footage wrapped on it, and then flies away. Do the following:

1. Import the image or animation footage you want to use as the target of this effect, and place it in the Composition window.

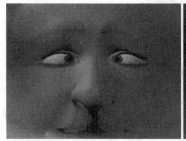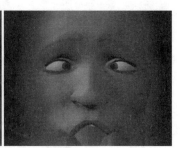

Figure 27.5
With a Convergence of 100, the Size value is altered from (left to right) 110 to 150 to 200.

2. Keyframe your footage layer's Geometrics so that the footage is displayed in the Composition window at frame 1, and moves out of the window at the upper right for the last frame.

3. Open the Distort FE Lens filter in the Effects menu.

4. Set the Convergence to 100.

5. Keyframe the Size to 250 for the first frame, and 30 for a frame close to halfway through the animation.

Render the animation and save to disk. See the FELnsBub animation on the companion CD-ROM.

Warping With Lens

Check out FELens on this book's companion CD-ROM. The FE lens effect was used to warp this footage, keyframe animated from a Size of 110 at the start to 175 at the end.

Power Pin

  Power Pin is both a distortion effect and a perspective effect, depending on how you apply it (see Figure 27.6). The following are some possible uses for the Power Pin effect:

- Use Power Pin when you have footage on a top layer that must be configured to fit on a perspective plane or the side of a box or wall on an underlying layer. Placing each of the corner pins allows you to fine-tune footage placement.

- Use Power Pin as an alternative when creating flying logo effects. Remember that you can adjust the perspective (by realigning the four corner points) and also move the footage interactively with the Move and Scale options.

The following controls allow you to adjust the parameters of the Power Pin effect:

- *Scrubbers*—Two interactive scrubbers move and scale the selected footage layer. By moving the mouse and watching the preview screen, you can move and scale footage for keyframe positioning.

Figure 27.6
Left: Target footage. Center: Perspective footage created by moving the four points. Right: Footage showing the effect of Unstretch.

- *Points*—The four points determine the corners of the footage, so it's easy to configure perspective planes. Reversing left/right and top/bottom point placement also reverses the footage, either horizontally or vertically, or both.

> **Note: For a triangular perspective plane, just place the top left/right or bottom left/right points in the same position. Use a Perspective setting of 100 to warp the footage accordingly.**

- *Perspective*—Perspective controls how much the footage content will warp inside of the perspective. Its settings range from 0 to 100. When set to 0, the content does not warp; when set to anything higher than 0, the content stretches like taffy.

- *Unstretch*—Checking the Unstretch option distorts the footage using the pin positions as a center point. Use this option when you need to emphasize the distortion capabilities of Power Pin, while negating its perspective effects.

Ripple Pulse

This effect can create ripples in ripples, each revealing a repeated zoom on the footage content (see Figure 27.7). The following are some possible uses for the Ripple Pulse effect:

- Use multiple Pulse values at random points in your animation to create a zoom that repeats the footage content, but distorts it inside the expanding ripple. Use random Time Span and Amplitude keyframes at the same points, previewing the results until you achieve something interesting.

- Create a unique background image by saving a single interesting frame from a Ripple Pulse animation. You can also multiply this effect by using several stacked Ripple Pulse filters on the same footage, making each one different.

The following controls allow you to adjust the effect's parameters:

- *Center*—Place the crosshairs where you want the effect to be centered.

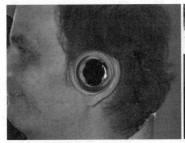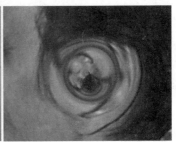

Figure 27.7
From left to right, a Ripple Pulse animation seen at different frames.

- *Pulse Level*—If you don't keyframe this value (its range of settings is from –10,000 to +10,000), you will not see any effect on the footage. You can keyframe it from a lower setting at the start of the animation to a higher setting at the last frame, but more varied effects can be achieved by keyframing it several times over the length of the animation, increasing or decreasing the values each time. Keep the values between –100 and +100 for your initial explorations.

- *Time Span*—Time Span sets the speed of the ripple outward. Keyframe the Time Span values whenever you keyframe a Pulse value.

- *Amplitude*—This setting controls the extent of the warp for the footage, controlling the ripple crest. Its settings can range from –10,000 to +10,000. Negative values tend to flip the footage vertically. Start your explorations by keeping the values between –5 and +5. Higher settings create a sharp line between the ripple and the footage content.

- *Bump Map*—Checking this on creates a bump map from your footage, which can then be applied to any plug-in filter that requires bump map layers.

> **Note:** As far as the FE Documentation is concerned, this is the most sparsely described plug-in filter. The FE CD does have an FE Ripple Pulse AE project, but even that fails to give any helpful details for easy use, although you can study the settings. You're going to have to do some serious exploration to understand how this plug-in filter can best serve your needs.

Rippling Pulse

Open the RiplPuls file on the companion CD-ROM. All the controls were keyframed several times during the duration, within the ranges mentioned previously in this section.

Slant

  This is a basic effect that slants the footage and can also create basic perspective planes (see Figure 27.8). The following are some possible uses for the Slant effect:

- Use this effect anywhere you need a basic perspective plane, with the footage mapped to it. It is not as variable as the FE Power Points plug-in filter, but it may serve you well where less variance isn't a problem.

- Animate Slant footage by using the Height control alone, and input a value of 0 at the start of an animation and 100 at the end. The result is a footage plane that rises from the ground. Leave Slant set at 0, and set the floor at the bottom of the frame. This also acts like a vertical wipe transformation. You can also warp the image vertically by setting the end frame to a height value of 200 or more.

Figure 27.8
Left: Original footage. Center: Footage slanted at –0.7. Right: Height of 50 and a Slant of 0.3.

The following controls allow you to adjust the effect's parameters:

- *Slant*—Slant controls the angle of the vertical orientation of the footage, in a range of settings from –100 to +100.

- *Height*—The height control (settings values from –1,000 to +1,000) adjusts the vertical dimension of the image. A perspective plane seen at a low height looks flattened. As height increases, footage content becomes more discernible.

- *Floor*—The floor (set by placing the crosshairs) refers to where the bottom of the image is to be set. This can be inside or outside the Composition window.

Slant Matte

 The best use for this plug-in is to target a text block Alpha layer that is used for a shadow effect, with the same Alpha footage on top of it (see Figure 27.9). The following are some possible uses for the Slant Matte effect:

- Create a matte shadow by placing two copies of an Alpha layer (based on a text block) in the Composition window. Use Slant Matte on the underlying Alpha to create the shadow.

- Create a ground shadow by keeping the Height value between 10 and 20. Place the top Alpha above it so it looks real.

Figure 27.9
These three examples were produced with different Slant and Height values. The footage consists of two Alpha layers of the same content, with the background layer, which has the Slant Matte effect, colored lighter to emulate a shadow. Left: A Height value of 20 creates a ground shadow with text in the air above it. Center: A Height of 100 with no Slant creates a wall shadow. Right: A Height of 50 and Slant of 20 places the text on the ground.

The following controls allow you to adjust the parameters of the Slant Matte effect:

- *Slant*—The angle of the slant is configured here, within a range of –100 to +100.

- *Floor*—Set the base of the Alpha layer with the crosshairs.

- *Height*—Set the height by adjusting the slider within a range of –1,000 to +1,000.

- *Matte Color*—Colorize the underlying Alpha as the shadow color.

A Different Angle

Look at the file called Slant on the companion CD-ROM. The Slant Matte effect was used at a Height value of 0 for the start of the animation, and changed to a Height value of 250 at the end. Slant was kept at 0.

Smear

Smear is capable of creating subtle or radical footage warps (see Figure 27.10). Some ways to use the Smear effect include the following:

- Use Radius values from 10 to 25 when you want to widen a smile or an eye, and set the completion of the animation at 100.

- Use Radius and Completion values above 100 when you want the entire footage to smear more radically.

The following controls allow you to adjust the Smear effect's parameters:

- *From/To*—The From point starts the smear and the To point determines the end of its effect.

- *Completion*—This is a percentage of completion control for animating the Smear, although its range of –400 to +400 exceeds the anticipated range of 0 to 100. Values outside the 0-to-100 range create more radical smears that affect footage beyond the From/To points, especially at higher Radius settings. Negative values move the smear from the To point to the From point, reversing it.

- *Radius*—Radius sets the area of the footage to be incorporated in the smear. Its settings range between 0 and 400, but keep the radius value in the range from 10 to 25 for subtle alterations.

Figure 27.10
Left: Original footage. Center: Radius of 25 and Completion of 100, with the From point on the lips and the To point above and to the right. Right: Radius of 10 and a completion of 50, with the From point on the tip of the nose and the To point on the chin.

Getting Smeared

The Smear file on the companion CD-ROM shows a warping face animation created by adjusting the From/To points with the Smear effect.

Split

This plug-in filter performs a tear of the footage to reveal the next layer below (see Figure 27.11). The following list shows some possible uses for the Split effect:

- Use the Split effect to show the content of a layer beneath. You can target a small area, like the screen of a TV in your footage. This might be called a "peekaboo" effect as well.

- Use the Split effect as a transition from footage A to footage B. Just make sure that the points are set wide apart so nothing of footage A remains at the end of the transition.

The following controls allow you to adjust the Split effect:

- *Points*—The area of the split is determined by setting the two control points. A split is shaped like a double teardrop, and warping of the footage takes place on both sides of the split, as if it were being pushed aside.

- *Split*—The Split control sets the amount of the split completed. Its range is from 0 to 250. Use the maximum value with widely spaced control points to completely remove the split layer.

Figure 27.11
Left: The original footage. Center: A small split shows the layer beneath. Right: A large split obliterates the split layer.

Tiler

This is a basic tiling effect, good for creating a footage zoom (see Figure 27.12). The following are some possible uses for the Tiler effect:

- Create an animation with Scale set to 0 at the start and 100 at the end. Use it to transition to the footage from other footage.

- Set the Scale at any value you want, and leave it there. This creates a series of footage clones. Consider this as a step before wrapping the footage on a 3D object (as with BorisFX Cube, Hollywood FX, or MetaCreations 3D effects).

Figure 27.12

Left: Tiles set at a Size of 0 do not disappear, but are very tiny. Center: Tiles set at a Size of 50. Right: The tiled footage is wrapped on a BorisFX Cube.

The following controls allow you to adjust the effect's parameters:

- *Scale*—This sets the scale of the tiles from –1 to 100.

- *Scale Center*—The Scale Center allows you to place the point on your footage from (and to) which the tiles will zoom.

- *Blend With Original*—Blend sets the amount of blend with the original footage. Its range is from 0 to 100. At 0, you get no original footage; at 100; you get no Tiler effect.

F/X I

This is the first of two chapters to detail the FE Particle f/x AE plug-ins. In this chapter, you'll read about FE Ball Action, Bubbles, Drizzle, Hair, Mr. Mercury, Pixel Polly, Rain, Snow, and Star Burst and all of the animated magic that only particle systems can provide.

FE PARTICLE

Ball Action

This particle system is based on spherical ball elements, and serves animations from or to chaotic states (see Figure 28.1). The following are some possible uses for the Ball Action effect:

- Use Ball Action to move from chaos to stability by creating an animation that starts with a random collection of balls and moves toward a reconstruction of the footage. Use Ball Action to move from stability to breakup by creating an animation that starts with the footage and ends with a random collection of dispersed balls.

- The "beam me up" effect: Target footage on its own Alpha layer (preferably a person, on the deck of a spaceship on a background layer). Use a Ball Size of 0.5 and a Grid Spacing of 0 at the start of an animation, with a Scatter of 0. At the end of the animation, set the Scatter to the maximum of 1,024 and move the footage up and off the screen.

Figure 28.1
Left: Original footage. Center: A Scatter of 5 and a Grid Space and Ball Size of 2. Right: Scatter increased to 500 and Ball Size reduced to 1. Notice that by increasing the Scatter rate, the Ball Sizes become more randomized because some are seen as "closer" to the eye, as long as a Z axis is selected.

The following controls allow you to adjust the parameters of the Ball Action effect:

- *Scatter*—This control sets the perceived distance and space between particles. Its settings range from –1,024 to +1,024.

> **Note: If you need to use Scatter values above 500, make sure that you have an animation long enough for the audience to appreciate the ball movements (at least 8 to 12 seconds at 30 fps). Shorter animations show the balls moving too quickly from frame to frame.**

- *Rotation*—Particles can rotate any number of degrees as they move, on either single axis or double axis choices. The Rotation axis, combined with the Rotation angle value, sets the footage on a perspective plane. You can see the perspective only at angles other than 0.

- *Twist Property and Twist Angle*—The Twist Property and Angle set the pattern for the particles to follow when animated. You can select either an X or a Y axis, or you can select the Center, Random, or Radius option. Selecting Red, Green, or Blue makes the particles follow that particular channel. Brightness, Diamond, Regular, and Fast Top are other options to explore. The Diamond pattern resembles animated beadwork when the particle size remains at 1 or lower.

- *Grid Spacing*—This is a size setting, in that it determines the layout or grid that the particles are referenced to. Its range is 0 to 50, and the higher the value you set, the larger the ball particles are. With a Scatter of 0, the result is a grid pattern over the footage, which is good for mosaic effects. The grid starts to warp toward a collection of spheres as the Scatter value increases to more than 0.

- *Ball Size*—Ball Size works with Grid Spacing to create the ball particles. Its settings can range from 0 to 100. The lower the Grid Spacing value, the more balls will be seen, as long as the Ball Size is set above 0. At a Ball Size of 0, the footage goes black.

- *Antialiasing*—Antialiasing can be set low or high. For tiny particles, keep it low. For large particles, use the high setting.

- *Instability State*—This is a control it's best not to animate. Set it and leave it for the length of the animation. Instability State creates a movement pattern that is targeted to a specific direction. Too much randomness results in a jumble of actions that obliterates the sense that these are ball particles. An Instability State of any number of degrees that remains constant will allow other controls more power.

Fur Balls

Atomized felines on parade! Just open the BallActn file on the companion CD-ROM. Watch as the cats evaporate into particle dreams, as one example of the Ball Action plug-in filter. Scatter moves from 0 to 999, Grid Spacing from 1 to 6, and Ball Size from 1 to 0.3 over the length of the animation.

Bubbles

Bubbles move from the bottom of the footage upward and reflect the background layer (see Figure 28.2). The following are some possible uses for the Bubbles effect:

- This is the particle plug-in to use over sea footage, or even when the footage content is a fish tank.

- If the targeted layer is a cutout element, the Bubbles effect will be limited to the parameters of the cutout. This can produce strange bubble warps inside of an object. Make sure that the Bubble Size ranges from values of 5 to 20 to maximize this effect.

The following controls allow you to adjust the Bubbles effect's parameters:

- *Bubble Amount*—The settings for Amount range from 0 to 5,000. The higher the amount, the smaller the size.

- *Bubble Speed*—This is the speed at which the bubbles rise upward (positive values) or downward (negative values). Its settings range from –30 to +30. A good default range is from –5 to +5, since speedier bubbles are harder to appreciate.

- *Amplitude and Frequency*—Amplitude controls the side-to-side motion of the bubbles. Its range is from 0 to 600. Set this value according to the effect you need. Bubbles from an air tank shimmy less than bubbles from an underwater volcano. Frequency (0 to 50) sets the compactness of the bubbles, with higher settings moving the bubbles apart. There is very little discernible difference when using this setting.

- *Bubble Size*—Size settings range from 1 to 50. At a Size of 50, one bubble more than covers 320x240 footage. Increase the size by at least a small amount as the number of bubbles increases.

- *Reflection Type*—Select from either Inverse or World Reflection. Inverse magnifies the background that it passes over, whereas World Reflection contains a reflection of the whole image area of the background layer.

- *Shading Type*—Shading Type is chosen based on the palette of your footage. For light footage select Darker, and for darker footage select Lighter. Choosing None will create flat bubbles, while fading the bubbles inward or outward somewhat lessens the 3D effect. In most situations, Lighter is the best option.

Figure 28.2
Left: Original footage. Center: 200 Lighten Bubble types at a Size of 1.0. Right: Size changed to 8.0.

Bubble, Bubble

Check out Bubbles on the companion CD-ROM. This animation shows the Bubbles effect in action. The Bubble Amount moves from 0 to 250 and back to 0. Size is constant at 4.5.

Drizzle

 Use this effect over footage content that is either landscape or cityscape oriented (see Figure 28.3). The following are some possible uses for the Drizzle effect:

- Use this effect on an Alpha text block layer to create rippling text over a background layer.

- Use this effect on a solid-color backdrop, or on a foreground that partially covers a background image. You will have an instant foreground water effect. Note that by shrinking footage vertically, the ripples from the Drizzle plug-in filter automatically become ovals, convenient for enhancing this effect on a foreground layer.

The following controls allow you to adjust the Drizzle effect's parameters:

- *Birth Rate*—The Birth Rate control determines how much rain is falling. Its settings can range from 0 to 1,024. For a true drizzle, keep this value below 10. For a real downpour, use values above 500. For variety, always adjust it a little over time so a constant rate is avoided.

- *Longevity*—Longevity is how long it takes the ripple to go from birth to death over time, and to reach its full Radius setting. Its range of settings is 0 to 3,000. Normal Drizzle settings are at values between 1 and 2. Very high values are good when the ripple is caused by a cosmic object hitting a watery or muddy surface.

- *Rippling*—This setting determines how many rings the ripple is to have. One full revolution is equal to an added ring.

- *Displacement*—If the underlying imagery is to distort, then add a Displacement value in the range of –1024 to +1,024. If the footage receiving the drizzle is pictorial, then adjust the Displacement to make the drizzle appear more real. If the footage is just a color layer, no Displacement is necessary.

Figure 28.3
Left: Drizzle applied to a color layer that overlaps the bottom of the background footage with nine rings per ripple. Center: The same settings at four rings per ripple. Right: The Drizzle effect is applied directly to the background footage, with a rippled Displacement set at 44, and a Ripple height of 60.

- *Ripple Height*—You can set shadows for the ripples' edges when needed. Water evidences fewer shadowed ripples than mud or lava. The Ripple Height settings range from 0 to 100.

- *Ripple Radius Grow*—This setting determines the size the ripple reaches at the end of its life. Its settings range from 0 to 1,024.

Hair

This is one of the more interesting effects offered by any developer of plug-in filters (see Figure 28.4). The following are some possible uses for the Hair effect:

- Grow hair on any model that needs it. Make sure that the model's head remains stable during the animation. If not, you need to adjust the placement on a frame-by-frame basis.

- Create a field of grass or grain. Just target a vertically reduced color layer that sits on top of a sky or other appropriate backdrop. Create long strands and allow it to vary in Thickness and Length values over time. Use a negative Weight value so it rises up.

The following controls allow you to adjust the parameters of the Hair effect:

- *Hairfall Map/Base Hairfall On*—The Hairfall Map allows you to select a layer in the stack to apply the hair to. Base Hairfall On has a list of choices. The default is Luminance, but you may also select an RGB color channel; Lightness, Hue, and Saturation; or an Alpha. Each option alters the look of the hair pattern, so it's best to explore before settling on one.

- *Map Softness and Post-Noise*—Increasing the Softness value (in its range of 0 to 511) forces the hair to fall more uniformly. Map Post-Noise adds randomness as the value increases. Its range is 0 to 100. For neater hair, set Softness high and Post-Noise low.

- *Length, Thickness, and Weight*—Hair Length sets the length in a range of settings from 0 to 500. Values between 1 and 30 are usually enough, unless you want the entire footage to look overgrown. Thickness values range from 0 to 4, with higher values beginning to look like feathers rather than hair. The Hair Weight (–100 to +100) tells the hair which way to grow. Negative values grow upward, and positive values force it to obey gravity and fall downward.

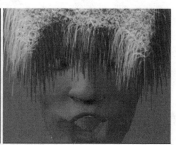

Figure 28.4
Left: Hair Length at 13, Weight at 0, and a Thickness of 1. Center: Length at 20 and Thickness at 4 create a feathery look. Right: A Weight of 1 forces the hair to hang down.

- *Spreading and Density*—Spreading, wrongly called "Extrude" in the FE documentation, sets the Z axis depth of the hair. Its settings range from –1,000 to +1,000. Density (in its range of 0 to 10,000) sets the XY amount.

- *Color Controls*—Use these settings to set the hair color and other parameters that determine the way it looks in light and shadow.

A Hairy Situation

Open the Hair1 file from the companion CD-ROM. As the character's countenance changes, his hair responds in kind. Using the Hair particle filter, the hair in the footage grows longer and changes color. Length values change from 13 to 68 as Weight goes from –0.4 to 0.2.

Mr. Mercury

This effect is guaranteed to hypnotize. Watch as a gelatinous mass writhes through the animation. For the best effects, make sure your background layer has a lot of color (see Figure 28.5). The following are some possible uses for the Mr. Mercury effect:

- Use a Jet Influence Map of 1 and a Birth/Death Size of 0.9 (stable during the animation) to create a stream of nonsticky blobs. This can be targeted to (pardon me) a sneeze that emanates from the mouth of an animated head. (Use Poser 3 to create the character.) This would suffice for commercial footage for a cold-relief capsule.

- Use Mr. Mercury to create the effect of a drinking glass leaking its contents on a surface, as in the following steps:

1. Get some footage of a glass sitting on a colorful tablecloth, shot from above at a 45-degree angle. Place it in the Composition window twice, and cut out the glass for the top layer. Create a negative mask for the glass, so it is not affected by Mr. Mercury.

2. On a separate, third layer over this background (it can be a simple color layer), position the Producer coordinates under the cutout and masked glass. Use an XY Radius of 0 at the beginning frame and 100 at the end frame. Use a Fire Animation System and the Come-In Influence Map. Set the Birth Size to 0.4 and the Death Size to 0.9, with a blob Influence Map of 20. For a slow leak, set the velocity to 2.

Figure 28.5
Left: An XY Radius of 3 creates a small puddle of blobs. Center: Increasing the Radius of X and Y to 60 enlarges the coverage. Right: Increasing the blob Birth/Death Size unifies the blobs into a single mass.

The following controls allow you to adjust the effect's parameters:

- *Producer*—The Producer is the effect center, the place the blobs are born. The coverage the blobs eventually reach is set by the values in the X and Y Radius controls (within a range of 0 to 1,024). Keep the Radius settings at 10 or lower to confine the blobby mass to a swirling colony. Higher settings cover more of the footage.

- *Direction and Velocity*—These are animation settings. Set the Direction via the radial dial. Velocity (in a range from –1,024 to +1,024) tells the blobs how fast to travel before their life ends. Negative values force the blobs to travel in an opposite direction from the one set.

- *Birth Rate and Longevity*—How many blobs need to appear at one time? Set that value (from 0 to 1,024) in the Birth Rate control. It's a good idea to set the Birth Rate lower at the start of an animation and higher in the middle, producing an increasing rate of expulsion from the Producer coordinates. Longevity determines their lifespan. Its settings range from 0 to 3,000. Set it lower at the last frames of the animation than at the beginning, even at 0, so that you clear the footage.

- *Gravity, Resistance, and Extra*—Gravity interferes with the blob flow, fighting the Direction setting. Its possible settings are between –1,024 and +1,024. Positive values drag the blobs down, while negative values force them upward. Resistance values (–1,024 to +1,024) are a friction coefficient, which slows down their movement and fights velocity. The Extra option sets a mystery component, adding more anomalies to the movement.

- *Animation System*—These selections offer different global patterns that set the blob movement. Although their names are very informative, the only way to appreciate and understand their differences is to explore them all. The different systems are Explosive, Fractal Explosive, Twirl, Twirly, Vortex, Vortex Fire, Direction, Direction Normalized, Bi-Directional, Bi-Directional Normalized, Jet, and Jet Sideways. Also see the FE documentation for a description of these options.

- *Blob Influence and Influence Map*—Blob Influence determines how prone the blobs are to gather together to form larger entities. The higher the setting, the more likely they will commingle. Influence Map options are Go Out, Come In, Come In&Out, Go Out Sharp, and Constant. These options represent the blobs' behavior during their short lifespans. See the FE documentation for a description of each option.

- *Birth Size/Death Size*—The size of a blob (from 0 to 1,024) can vary from its birth to its death or it can remain constant, depending on the effect you want to achieve. You can also keyframe it to alternate as many times as you like during the animation.

The Blob

FE Mr. Mercury is one of the most spectacular effects offered for After Effects. First look at the MrMerc1 on the companion CD-ROM. In this example, a blob uses the Fire Animation System and the Come-In Influence Map. The Producer is set at the bottom center. Watch this baby do its stuff! Then take a look at MrMerc2. This Mr. Mercury example uses the Fractal Explosive Animation System and a Constant Influence Map. Blobs are born tiny at 0.23 and die at 1.23, so they have a chance to intermingle.

Pixel Polly

 Pixel Polly acts to break the footage into polygons, as if it were made of glass and shattered. The strongest operator is Gravity, and a setting as low as 1 is sufficient to drag the footage shards downward. There's not much reason to include a series of figures for this effect, so it is suggested that you take a look at the PixPoly animation in the Chapter 28 Movies folder on the companion CD-ROM to appreciate the effect.

Gravity Works

Take a look at the PixPoly file on the companion CD-ROM. This example shows the PixelPoly FE Particle Systems II plug-in filter in action. Footage is broken into polygons, and gravity brings it down. Gravity values range from 0 at the start of the animation to 1 at the end, causing the footage to respond increasingly to gravity's pull as the animation progresses.

Rain

 Rain does what it says. It simulates animated raindrops over the footage (see Figure 28.6). Or, by increasing the Drop Size to its maximum of 30 and the Amount to 500 or more with Speed set to 5, you can create an interesting textured static effect that can be used as a backdrop for a text block.

The following controls allow you to adjust the Rain effect's parameters:

- *Rain Amount*—Although the Rain Amount settings range from 0 to 10,000, the effect works best when set to values ranging from 10 to 50. More than that and it looks less like rain than an animated whiteout.

- *Rain Speed*—The Rain Speed is an animation setting. Its settings range from 0 to 10, but keep it below 5 so the rain doesn't become a blur.

- *Rain Angle*—Rain Angle determines the angle at which the rain is falling. Its settings range between –60 and +60; negative values slant it to the left and positive values slant it to the right. The harder the rain falls, the more slant it should have.

Figure 28.6
Left: Original footage. Center: A light drizzle. Right: Sleet, created by increasing the Drop Size to 20.

- *Drop Size*—This is the size of the rain streaks. Although its settings range from 0 to 30, values below 3 produce the most believable results.

- *Source Depth*—The Source Depth creates the illusion that the rain has depth. Its settings range between 0 to 100, and a value of 50 is a good default.

- *Opacity*—Opacity determines the transparency of the raindrops. Its values can be from 0 to 100. A setting lower than 20 makes the rain hard to see, while values above 40 give the impression of ice rather than rain.

Snow

Just in time for the holidays, you can create an animated video postcard and post it on a Web site. Or, to get an interesting depth effect, apply the Snow effect to several stacked layers, adjusting the amount of the snow on each. Make the flakes larger on the closest layer, and very small on the back layer. Set the speed so that the faster values are on the back layer(s) (see Figure 28.7).

The following controls allow you to adjust the Snow effect's parameters:

- *Snow Amount*—The values for Snow Amount (0 to 32,000) set the season. Early winter uses a lower value (200 is fine), while midwinter blizzards need values of 500 or higher. Values above 1,000 start to obscure the footage and should be avoided in most instances.

- *Speed, Amplitude, and Frequency*—The Speed settings (from –30 to +30) set the animation speed and work best in a range from 2 to 8. Higher values move too fast for most footage. If you need the snow to fall upward, use negative values. Amplitude adds a wobble to the snow. Its settings are from 0 to 50, and a good default is 15. Frequency sets the speed of the wobble, so keep this rather low (from 5 to 10 out of its overall range of 0 to 50) or you'll just get a shake in the flakes that's too strong.

- *Flake Size, Source Depth, and Opacity*—Although the Flake Size settings can range between 0 and 50, they are best defaulted to a value between 2 and 6 in most cases. Source Depth sets the depth effect for the snow from 0 to 100 percent. A value of 50 works best

Figure 28.7
Left: A Snow Amount with an Opacity of 50 gives the impression of a light dusting (Flake Size of 4). Center: Change the Amount to 2,000, and it's time to get off the road. Right: Reducing the Flake Size to 1 and increasing the Amount to 5,000 create a more granular look.

for most situations. Although Opacity settings can range from 0 to 100, they should never be set above 50, because the partial transparency of a snowflake is what gives it its definitive charm.

Let It Snow

Open the Snow file on the companion CD-ROM. This animated sequence shows the Snow effect in action. The most important setting is speed, which underlines the reality of the effect. In this case, Speed is set to 4, making the flakes float down moderately slowly. This is, however, a blizzard.

Star Burst

 This is another star field journey-maker. It takes the star color from the footage, and the space color from the background layer (see Figure 28.8). The following are some possible uses for the Star Burst effect:

- Set the Size at 15 and the Scatter at 5, with a Grid Spacing of 1, for an animated trip through a molecular froth.

- Set the beginning Size at 1 and the end Size at 7, with a Grid Spacing that ranges from 1 to 32 over the length of the animation. This creates an effect like a speed-of-light journey that is just completed, delivering you to the other side of the universe.

The following controls allow you to adjust the Star Burst effect:

- *Scatter Amount*—The Scatter Amount introduces a chaotic element into the Star Burst appearance. Its settings can be between –10,000 and +10,000. At a value of 0, you see the rectangular grid. The higher the value, the more random the star field will appear. Selecting a value between –100 and +100 is usually sufficient. Scatters below –200 and above +200 make the star field very sparse.

- *Speed*—This control sets the velocity of the journey. Settings range between –5 and +5, with maximum values creating faster trips.

Figure 28.8
Left: With the Scatter Amount at 0 you see the grid of your footage. Center: A Scatter of 10 and a Size of 1 creates thousands of individual particles. Right: A Size of 15 (at the same other settings) creates a collection of spheres.

Note: The FE documentation is wrong as far as the Speed settings. It claims you can set the value between –50 and 50.

- *Phase*—This is not an animation control. It is meant to set the phase of the star field relative to the original footage.

- *Grid Spacing*—Grid Spacing adjusts the packing of the stars and is best seen by first setting the Scatter Amount to 0. Settings range between 1 and 32, and lower settings produce more stars per unit area. A moderate default is 4.

- *Size*—Size sets the dimensions of the star particles. Its settings range between 0 and 25, and anything above a value of 5 starts to look like planets or large molecular clusters. A value of 22 fills the screen with single orbs.

- *Blend With Original*—Blend sets the amount of blend with the original footage. Its range is from 0 to 100. At 0, you get no footage; at 100, you get no effect.

F/X II

This chapter is the second in a series of two chapters dedicated to ICE FE Particle f/x. Here, you'll look at Particle Systems II and Particle World.

> **Note: For all Particle f/x II and Particle World effects, make sure that you have a background footage layer and a foreground layer placed in the Composition window. The foreground layer can be a simple color layer, another piece of footage, or duplicate footage from the background layer. Note that you won't see any results of particle effects until you move away from the first frame of the animation.**

FE Particle Systems II

 FE Particle Systems II is an extensive particle animation system with unlimited effects capabilities. For that reason we will detail only the basic options, illustrating several. It is then up to you to explore further by experimenting with various settings to achieve more-customized results. Table 29.1 shows some suggested uses.

Table 29.1 Some suggested uses for FE Particle System II particle animation types.

Particle Animation Type	Suggested Uses	Best Related Particle Object
Explosive	Besides explosions, use for brush fires (Gravity at –2); sun (Particle Death Size 6x, Birth Size and Fade Out, Bubble).	Pixel and Drop for explosion; Shaded Sphere for globular cluster (Birth Rate 20); Bubble at High Death Rate and Death Sizes (Figure 29.1, left).
Fractal Explosive	Use as a more controllable alternative to Explosive. Spokes of explosion altered by Direction values.	Antialiased Pixel for explosions; Star for smeared sky object; Shaded Shaded Faded Sphere for lumpy looks (Figure 29.1, center).
Twirl	Pinwheel galaxy (Shaded Faded Sphere); pinwheel fireworks (Drop); hypnotic Whirlix (Birth Rate 6 and Longevity 2).	Shaded Faded Sphere for pinwheel galaxy; Drop for pinwheel fireworks; Star for blurry sky object (Figure 29.1, right).

(continued)

Table 29.1 Some suggested uses for FE Particle System II particle animation types *(continued)*.

Particle Animation Type	Suggested Uses	Best Related Particle Object
Twirly	Use as a more controllable alternative to Twirl. Spokes of twirl altered by Direction values, creates interference patterns or electric explosions	Pixel/Antialiased Pixel for explosive Twirls; faded Sphere for atoms—Direction is animated (Figure 29.2, left).
Vortex	Black hole vortex (X Radius 3, Y Radius 40, Shaded Faded Sphere, oscillate, Birth to Death).	Bubble for undersea bubbles; Cuby for cubic array; Star for spinning galaxy in distance (Figure 29.2, center).
Fire	Flames (Pixel); air-tank bubbles (Bubble); magic sparks (Star); tornado (Drop, X Radius 3, Y Radius 40).	Pixel; Bubble; Star; and Drop. The best Fire particle is Pixel (Figure 29.2, right).
Direction	Ground explosion (Direction to 0, Drop); water spray (Direction at 0, Antialiased Pixel, X Radius 3, Y Radius 40).	Antialiased Pixels (Water f/x); Star (Ground Fireworks). See Figure 29.3, left.
Direction Normalized	Use as an alternative to Direction f/x. Spreads particles more evenly than Directional.	Pixel for rocket flame (Gravity at 2, Direction at 180 degrees) See Figure 29.3, center.
Bi-directional	Spark showers from torch (Star or Drop); cosmic and sea journeys (particles spread evenly in both directions).	Shaded Faded Sphere (cosmic journey); Drop (sparks from a power source); Bubbles (journey over sea floor). See Figure 29.3, right.
Bi-directional Normalized	Alternative to Bi-directional effects. Spreads particles more evenly than Bi-directional	Antialiased Pixel (symmetrical particle fire); Drop (Ground Emitter, X radius 3, Y radius 16, longevity of .3, Gravity –7). See Figure 29.4, left.
Jet	Fire from a smokestack (Antialiased Pixel, Gravity –7); comet headed downward (Pixels, throbbing tail by altering Velocity values).	Drops (shooting ground fire); Shaded Faded Sphere (bubbles from underwater heat vent). See Figure 29.4, center.
Jet Sideways	Use as an alternative to Jet. Spreads particles related to the animation of the Producer point.	Motion Polygon (Spiked Fire); Pixel (Streaking Fireball). See Figure 29.4, right.

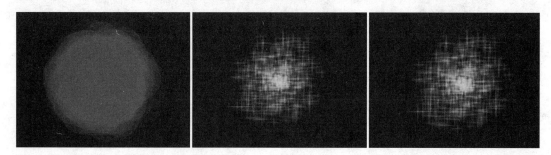

Figure 29.1
Left: Sun, with Death Rate of 20 and Birth Rate of 0.4, Explosive, Bubble, Fade Out, and Birth To Death. Center: Fractal Explosive with Shaded Faded Sphere creates a lumpy cluster. Right: Twirl with Star creates a blurry sky object.

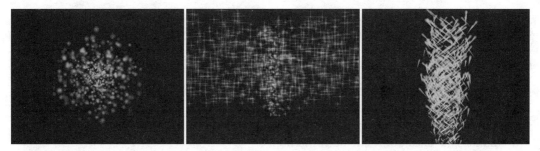

Figure 29.2
Left: Twirly with Faded Sphere creates an atom. Center: Star Vortex. Right: Fire Tornado (Drop, X Radius 3, and Y Radius 40).

Figure 29.3
Left: Directional Water Spray (Direction at 0, Antialiased Pixel, X Radius 3, Y Radius 40). Center: Direction Normalized Rocket Flame (Pixel, Gravity at 2, Direction at 180 degrees). Right: A cosmic journey, enhanced by Bi-directional Shaded Faded Spheres.

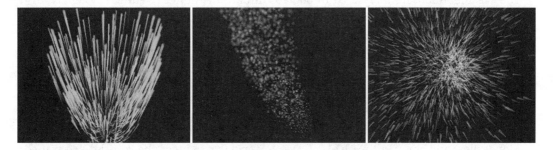

Figure 29.4
Left: Bi-directional Normalized bowl of sparks (X Radius of 3, Y Radius of 10, Gravity at –7). Center: The jet option with a Shaded Faded Sphere creates bubbles from an undersea vent (Velocity at 2, Gravity at –2). Right: A Motion Polygon object was used in this Jet Sideways example to create a spiked fireball.

> *Note: The FE, 3D Polygon, 3D Squares, Tetrahedron, Textured Poly, and Cuby Particle Objects aren't mentioned in the above table because, although experimental options, their use is negligible. They serve a very limited purpose in creating viable particle-system effects and animations. Also note that the Lens Objects aren't detailed here. They all work in a similar fashion to blur and warp the image content under the Producer placement. They are useful in simulating effects caused by unseen agents.*

Except for the controls listed in this section, the rest were adequately covered in Chapter 28. If you need clearer details for the rest of the control options, refer to Chapter 28 and to the FE documentation.

- *Particle Animation Type*—The types (as shown in Table 29.1) include Explosive, Fractal Explosive, Twirl, Twirly, Vortex, Fire, Direction, Direction Normalized, Bi-directional, Bi-directional Normalized, Jet, and Jet Sideways. You will find these briefly detailed in the FE documentation. Most important, you will find six of these types to be the focus of animations, detailed at the end of this section.

- *Air Resistance*—Here's a setting we haven't run into before. Air Resistance creates a drag on the velocity of particle movements, which increases with higher values. Its settings can range from –1,024 to +1,024.

- *Particle Objects*—These 21 objects are the actors in an FE Particle System II animation. Some look authentic and some look silly, but you should explore them all. Also, see the animations on the companion CD-ROM, which are detailed at the end of this section.

- *Opacity Map*—Fades, Oscillation, and a Constant setting are listed here. Oscillation is best for explosions, whereas fades also add realism by allowing sparkle to fade out as they die. The Constant setting is useful for effects like a beam of sparks.

- *Color Map*—The options are Birth To Death, Original To Death, Birth To Original, and Original To Original. ("Original" refers to the colors under the particles on the targeted footage, leading to subtler effects.)

Putting It Into Practice

The five animations from Psys2_01 through 05 display alternative FE Particle System II Particle Animation options: Twirl, Explosive, Vortex, Fire, and Jet Sideways. The rest of the settings, and even the footage, remain the same (unless indicated otherwise) so that you can clearly compare these four Particle Animation types.

The settings are as follows: X and Y Radius set to 0.6, Producer moves from off-screen upper left to off-screen lower right (creating a meteor-like fireball), Birth Rate of 2, Longevity of 0.4, Velocity and Gravity of 0.5, Air Resistance of 0, Direction of 312 degrees (creating the tail effect for the meteor), Extra setting of 1.4, An Oscillate Opacity Map, a Birth To Death Color Map (yellow and blue), Birth Size of 0.4, Death Size of 0.5. In order, the Particle Objects used are Star, Drop, Shaded Sphere, Motion Polygon, and Lens Bubble. So keep an eye on two things when you play with these animations: the Particle Animation System Type, and the Particle Objects used.

- *PSys2_01*—This animation uses the settings detailed in the preceding paragraph with the Twirl Particle Animation System and the Star Particle Object.

- *PSys2_02*—This animation uses the settings detailed in the preceding paragraph with the Explosive Particle Animation System and the Drop Particle Object.

- *PSys2_03*—This animation uses the settings detailed in the preceding paragraph with the Vortex Particle Animation System and the Shaded Sphere Particle Object.

- *PSys2_04*—This animation uses the settings detailed in the preceding paragraph with the Fire Particle Animation System and the Motion Polygon Particle Object.

- *PSys2_05*—This animation uses the settings detailed in the preceding paragraph with the Jet Sideways Particle Animation System and the Lens Bubble Particle Object.

One More Time

Here's one more Particle System II animation. FracExpl shows a multiple Fractal Explosion, with the Producer set in one place in the sky. X and Y Radius is set to 4.7, Birth Rate and Longevity are at 3 and 0.5. Velocity is set to 1.4 for the first three-fourths of the animation, then dwindles to 0. Max Opacity ranges from 100 to 0 during the animation. Gravity also plays an important role. At the start, and for 75 percent of the animation, Gravity is set to 0, which allows the explosion to continue unhindered. The Gravity value is set to 22 at the end frame.

The explosions take place behind the trees because the top layer duplicates the footage. It is cut so that only the trees remain, with the sky invisible. Because the explosion takes place on three underlying layers at different times, the top layer of trees acts as a mask to prevent the sparks from being seen in front. Experienced After Effects users will recognize this as a standard way of utilizing a layer stack.

All of this results in a spectacular series of starbursts that fade into the air at the end, with a shower of sparks that headed earthward behind the trees.

FE Particle World

 What distinguishes FE Particle World from the previously described FE Particle Systems II plug-in filters? The effects you produce with FE Particle System II filters are really 2D effects, meant to be appreciated from a distance, like fireworks in the sky. Effects created with FE Particle World filters are meant to be moved through, offering a wide variety of 3D possibilities. You have already been introduced to 3D particle effects such as Ball Action and Star Burst in Chapter 28.

Unlike FE Particle System II's controls (most of which are covered in Chapter 28), FE Particle World is a whole new ballgame. This is a 3D particle system, complete with cameras and other specific 3D parameter controls. That being the case, it's best to give some detailed comment upon Particle World controls, before moving ahead with suggestions for their use. It's strongly suggested that you study the FE documentation, rereading as necessary, to get a better understanding of the FE Particle World operations. Also make sure that you view the animations on this book's CD-ROMs, detailed at the end of this section.

- *Scrubbers*—Scrubbers are a new concept for AE control interface dialogs. There are three Scrubbers: Screen/World Positional, Radius, and Camera orientation and Z-axis zoom (see Figure 29.5).

  - *Interactive Screen/World Controls*—Each of these options contains both a "+" crosshair icon and a "Z" icon, controlled by mouse movements. They differ in that Screen moves your

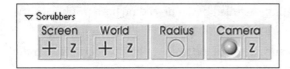

Figure 29.5
Scrubbers are interactive controls at the top of the FE Particle World Controls dialog box.

viewpoint relative to the current camera position and angle, whereas World moves your viewpoint in relation to the absolute coordinates of the Particle World 3D environment. The good news is that if you keep your eyes on the numerical display that pops up, you'll see exactly what the coordinate readout is, and the Composition window will instantly reflect the changes. Remember, this is a real 3D environment, not the 2D environment that AE users have come to expect. Both Screen and World make the same use of the "+" and "Z" icons, with "+" altering your position along the XY coordinates, and "Z" moving you along the Z axis (into or out of the screen). Before doing anything else in Particle World, explore the use of these positional alternatives.

- *Interactive Radius Control*—Placing the cursor over this icon and click-holding it while moving reveals a 3D cube that grows smaller or larger on an XY orientation, telling you that you are altering the Producer's Radius. This allows you to enlarge or reduce the size of the particle system effects, just as you would do if inputting XY scaling numerically. Experienced AE users will get used to this control in minutes because of the instant feedback in the Composition window.

- *Scrubber*—This tool is devoted to altering the rotation (XYZ) and Z distances of the camera. It is highly visual in that as you click-hold and move the mouse on the camera sphere, you will see a 3D cube that displays X, Y, and Z faces. Setting the orientation of the cube translates into Camera Rotation coordinates, and the particle system effects in the Composition window are reoriented accordingly. Next to this is the Z icon, which allows you to interactively zoom in on the particle effect on screen.

- *Producer XYZ/Radius XYZ*—These are simply numerical equivalent controls that substitute for the respective Scrubbers already mentioned, for users not comfortable working in the interactive 3D Scrubber environment.

- *Animation System*—We have already detailed Explosive, Twirl, Twirly, Vortex, Fire, Jet, and Jet Sideways in the Particle Systems II section and Table 29.1. However, Particle World has a few new listings that need to be examined. They are Direction Axis, Cone Axis, Viscous, Fractal Omni, and Fractal Uni:

  - *Direction Axis*—The particles are controlled by the Extra Angle setting, which adds randomness. The result is a 3D cone-shaped particle environment. This is a good selection for meteors and comets.

  - *Cone Axis*—This is an alternate cone-shaped particle environment. Details on the differences between it and the Direction Axis selection can be found in the AE documentation.

  - *Viscous*—This is probably my favorite selection because it creates a more natural-looking effect. Setting higher values on the Extra control slider slows the Particles' initial speed.

- *Fractal Omni*—This selection is best used for realistic explosions, and works well with Pixels or Drops.

- *Fractal Uni*—This selection forces the particles to erupt in a stream, and so is the one to use when you need to animate volcanic detritus.

- *Velocity, Birth Rate, Longevity, and Gravity*—These controls have been adequately covered previously in other chapters.

- *Extra/Extra Angle*—These controls are modifiers to Animation Systems, including Cone Axis, Viscous, and the Fractal-based systems. Their primary purpose is to introduce randomness.

- *Max Opacity*—This is a standard opacity control that can be animated over time. As a most-cases rule, keep Opacity no higher than 75%.

- *Color Map*—Set the Color Map options from the four standard items: Birth-Death, Original-Death, Birth-Original, and Original-Original. The particles are colorized in accordance with their Lifespan setting. Birth and Death colors are selected separately.

- *Particle Objects*—The standard Particle Objects previously detailed in the Particle System II section are also available in Particle World. Also refer to Table 29.1 in the Particle Systems II section for further details.

- *Camera Controls*—For those individuals a bit hesitant about using the Camera Scrubber interface to control the 3D camera, standard AE slider controls accomplish the same task.

Rules For Effective Use Of FE Particle World Effects

Keep the following in mind when using the FE Particle World effects:

- Be careful about mixing standard footage with Particle World effects. Particle World effects are created in a true 3D environment, much as if you were using a separate, high-end 3D art and animation application. As such, think of the rest of your footage as a background in a 3D application, whether it's static footage or animated. With careful attention to the placement and orientation of the 3D particles you create, you might even use footage created in a 3D application as the background, adjusting your Particle World effects to display correctly by changing the orientation to match the background footage.

- By moving the Producer Z control into negative values, you will be able to actually zoom in and through the particle stream, just as though you were flying in a 3D visual environment. This leads to all manner of flythroughs. When you move far enough on the negative Z axis, you will have moved through the particles to the other side, and they will be "behind" you. If you want to see them again, you'll have to either back up through them or rotate the Scrubber Camera 180 degrees.

- The Options item at the top of the Particle World list brings up a number of additional interactive controls: Opacity Map, Color Map, Grid, Rendering; Gravity, Direction, Light Direction, Rotation; Load, and Save. Except for Load and Save, which allow you to save your settings for use in other Particle World projects, the other options give you interactive visual control over parameters normally adjusted through slider and numerical manipulations. If you are an experienced 3D artist and animator, it will make more sense for you to work visually and to access this Options list (see Figure 29.6).

- The power of Particle World can be greatly enhanced when you remember that, after configuring your 3D particle movements, you still have the option of adding another effect on top of it. For example, using an Eye Candy AE Glow effect causes all the Particle World elements to glow as they move through 3D space. It is, in fact, the possibility of always stacking another effect in the mix that gives After Effects its awesome power (see Figure 29.7).

> **Note: Make sure that you turn off the Grid option before you render the animation, or it will be rendered along with the footage.**

- The final thing to remember concerning the application of Particle World effects has to do with the fact that 3D manipulations must be seen to be appreciated. The background you use Particle World effects with is very important. If you use a background footage whose 3D viewpoint is constantly changing, the Particle World effects will seem like they are out of sync with the background footage. If you use just a solid color, the fact that the particle

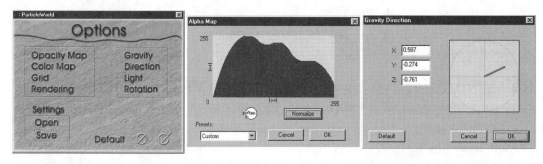

Figure 29.6
Accessing the Options for Particle World brings up a set of dialog boxes that allow you more interactive control over the parameters. Left to Right: The Options interface; control dialog box for Map and Rendering options; and control dialog box for Gravity, Direction, and Rotation options.

Figure 29.7
Added effects enhance the power of Particle World's 3D options, like these generated by Eye Candy on top of Particle World effects. Left: Glow. Center: Motion Trail. Right: Fire.

stream is a 3D rendering will be lost on the viewer, since it will appear that the particle stream is just rotating in some strange 2D manner. The best background footage to consider when using Particle World animated 3D effects is either a straight-on view of an animated piece of footage (like a journey through a star field that is coming straight at you), or a single frame with some image content (like a room or a cloud shot). This way, the viewer will become aware that the stream is moving in a 3D environment and will be all the more impressed.

Using Particle World

PW-1 on the companion CD-ROM shows a Particle World animation that displays footage created in Bryce 3D, overlain with both a Particle World Viscous Animation System and an Eye Candy AE Fire effect on top of it.

PW-2 displays a shower of multicolored sparks that emanates from a sun. Pixel Objects were used with a Viscous Animation System, with Gravity values moving from 0.1 to 0 to 0.1 again at the end.

FE PERSPECTIVE

The following ICE FE Complete AE plug-ins are covered in this chapter: Advanced 3D, Cylinder, Sphere, Force Motion Blur, Time Blend, Time BlendFX, and Wide Time.

> *Note: The FE perspective filters (Advanced 3D, Cylinder, and Sphere) are good for basic wraparound projects, but are less full-featured than other effects packages that do similar things. For more advanced options, see BorisFX Perspective f/x (Chapter 19) or Hollywood FX (Chapter 34).*

Advanced 3D

The most novel aspect of this Perspective Plane effect is that you have control over the Z axis, or dimension in and out of the screen, expanding your AE world into a real 3D universe (see Figure 30.1). The following are some possible uses for the Advanced 3D effect:

- Use this effect on a logo layer to create flying-logo animations.

- Import any footage you want to use as a proxy. Check Show Grid on, and create an animation using only the grid. Save the animation as a series of single frame files. Open them in MetaCreations Painter 5, and paint on the grid. This is a way to create new and unique footage.

> *Note: Thanks to the sculptor David Huber of Burlington, Vermont, for allowing the use of this image of his work.*

The following controls allow you to adjust the parameters of the Advanced 3D effect:

- *Scrubbers*—Scrubbers give you interactive control of the X, Y, and Z position of the perspective plane, as well as its rotation. Refer to "FE Particle World" in Chapter 29 for a more detailed overview.

- *Anchor Point Z*—This sets the central point for the Z axis, the axis that represents a line perpendicular to the surface of your monitor's screen. The default value is 0, which places it in the center of the Composition window.

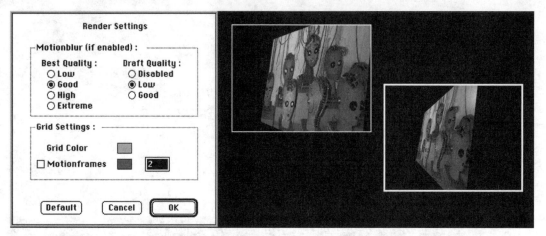

Figure 30.1

Left: The Render Settings dialog box, where you can set Motionblur and Grid options. Center: A standard perspective orientation with the Camera Lens Angle set to the default of 45. Right: A more radical warping of the perspective plane, caused by changing the Camera Lens Angle value to 90.

- *Position XYZ/Rotation XYZ*—If you are uncomfortable using the Scrubbers to achieve these operations interactively, or if you find you need to tweak these settings numerically, then access these sliders and numeric dialogs.

- *Alternative Rotation*—This is a checkbox to activate if you plan to use Advanced 3D along with the Particle Systems II effects (detailed in Chapter 29). Particle Systems II isn't a true 3D generator, so compensations need to be made to have your position and rotation settings match. Leave this unchecked if you don't plan to use any Particle Systems II effects in the composition.

- *Camera Lens Angle*—This control allows you to set the camera lens for fisheye effects and zooms. This control works in conjunction with the Z Position setting. The possible settings range from 0 to 179. When the value of the Z Position is 0, altering the Camera Lens Angle settings will have no effect. At Z Positions less than 0, Camera Lens Angle settings will zoom in on the footage the higher the value is set. At Z Positions higher than 0, Camera Lens Angle settings will zoom out on the footage the higher the value is set.

- *Render*—You can select to render the full plane, just the front, or just the back. If the plane has a separate color and you render just the front or back, the color will be seen on the side of the plane where no image appears.

- *Light*—Because Advanced 3D sets up a 3D environment, light acts on the footage as it would be expected to act in the real world. There are no Light settings for color, but there are for setting the Ambient, Diffuse, and Specular components. A Roughness setting controls the spread of the Specular highlight. Metals will have lower Roughness settings, and more absorbent materials will have higher ones.

- *Show Grid*—If this box is checked, the footage will disappear and be replaced by a reference plane. This allows you to set the keyframes for your footage without the redraw times necessary when working with viewable footage.

Cylinder

This is a hollow cylinder effect that wraps the footage around its vertical axis (see Figure 30.2).

The following are some possible uses for the Cylinder effect:

- Create a camera lens warp effect using the following steps:

  1. Set the footage to a straight-on view of the footage-mapped cylinder from the top (X and Z rotations of 90).

  2. Start the animation at a Camera Lens Angle value of 0, and change the value to 179 for the last frame.

- Start at a Radius value of 1 and end the animation at a Radius value of 5 to fly through a cylinder (facing the camera and mapped with your footage).

All of the controls mentioned for the Advanced 3D effect apply here as well. There are only a few differences. There is a radius setting that adjusts the relative diameter of the cylinder. The Render options list Full, Outside, and Inside for the cylinder. There is no Show Grid option. There is also no Options dialog for customizing Motion Blur options.

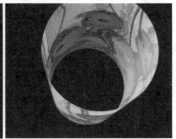

Figure 30.2
Left: Original footage. Center: A cylinder mapped with footage, showing the effect of light placed on the left side. Right: With careful manipulation of the Z axis in the negative value range, you can fly right through your cylinder-wrapped footage.

Cylinder Effects

Look at the CyLensFX file on the companion CD-ROM. Here the cylinder remains motionless, but the Camera Lens Angle value is adjusted from 0 at the start of the animation to 179 at the end. The result is a zoom on the entrance to the cylinder, while the other end takes up less and less space, for a hallucinogenic outcome. Use this effect on time tunnels and space warps.

Now, contrast the CylFly animation with the CyLensFX one. Here, it seems as if you actually enter the cylinder and exit the other side. Altering a few settings makes this possible. The Radius moves from 1 to 5, enlarging the footage in your view. The X placement value starts at 3, placing the cylinder obliquely to the right, and ends at 0, centering it in the view. Last, the Camera Lens Angle value changes from 50 to 35.

Sphere

This is a basic Sphere-wrap effect, placing your footage around a sphere on the Y axis (see Figure 30.3). The following are some possible uses for the Sphere effect:

- Use a Reflection map that has alternate footage, and fade it in and out of a revolving sphere by adjusting the Reflection Amount control. This works well for logos wrapped on a sphere, and it adds viewer interest.

- Alter the radius from 0 to 2 to zoom in on the footage content. Doing this while the Sphere rotates slowly is like zooming in on a planet, especially if you're using a Reflection Map of animated clouds.

The following controls allow you to adjust the Sphere effect's parameters:

- *Rotation XYZ*—Use these radial controls to inform the sphere how it is to be oriented as seen in the Composition window at keyframe points on the Timeline.

- *Radius*—This control sizes the sphere with setting values from 0 to 100.

- *Offset*—Set the crosshairs to place the sphere in your workspace.

- *Render*—The options are Front, Back, or Both. Use Front or Both when applying footage to a sphere. If the footage is to drop out the sphere itself (Alpha channel footage), you might want to explore the Back option. Alpha channel footage wrapped to a sphere curves the footage, but the sphere is invisible.

- *Lights*—All the Light options, detailed at the start of the chapter for the Advanced 3D effect, also apply here.

Sphere, Sphere

Open Sphere1 from the companion CD-ROM. In this example, the sphere rotates 360 degrees on its Y axis. An image is mapped to the sphere, and another animated piece of footage (a cloud animation from the ArtBeats REELs collection) is set as the sphere's reflection map. The Reflection Map value is 0 at the start of the animation, 0.85 in the middle, and 0 again at the end. This is an interesting way to create composite fades mapped to a 3D object.

  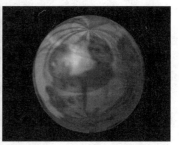

Figure 30.3
Left: Original footage. Center: Footage wrapped on sphere. Right: Same footage wrapped as in center image, but with Reflection Map of another image added.

FE Time Blurs

The following four effects transform footage with motion blurs. Motion blurs add a touch of realism to moving footage, adding a smeared edge that follows the movements of animated elements. Cartoonists often call motion blurs "speed lines," because they suggest in illustrations that something is moving too quickly for the eye to discern all its edges. Taking a snapshot of something moving very fast with a camera also shows motion blur. Add any of these options to emulate that same effect.

Very Important Procedures To Follow For FE Time Blurs

The FE documentation is extremely unclear when it comes to telling you what to do and in what order with Time Blurs. The following steps should be taken in order before you apply any of these effects:

1. Always use animated footage for these effects. The frames of the footage have to be interpolated in order to create the effect. The first thing to do is to add the animated footage to be time blurred into the Composition window.

2. Next, check the Enable Motion Blur checkbox in the Time window, and select the Motion Blur Switch from the Layers menu (or simply place a check in the "M" on the layer's timeline).

3. Pre-compose the layer. This is important. Without it, the FE Time Blurs cannot do their work.

4. Only after the layer is composed and the Motion Blurs are activated as detailed can you add the required FE Time Blur effect. All this must take place because these effects do not obey the strict guidelines After Effects suggests, and for other reasons detailed in the FE documentation.

Forced Motion Blur

 Forced Motion Blur is one of the blur options you can select from. Blur effects add speed lines to moving elements in animated footage, and different ones treat the footage in unique ways. See the Forced Motion Blur animation and project on the FE Complete CD-ROM.

The following controls allow you to adjust the effect's parameters:

- *Motion Blur Levels*—This control sets the number of frames that will determine the blur. Its setting can range from 0 to 256, but using a value below 10 is usually sufficient. Higher values create a blur that obliterates the content.

- *Overwrite Shutter Angle*—Keep this option checked. It allows the effect to negate the AE standard settings, which is required in most cases.

- *Shutter Angle*—With settings from 0 to 360, this control adds another effect, using camera lens setting to composite with the original blur.

- *Geometric Motion Blur*—Select Compensate to apply the effect. Switched Off disables the effect, and Preferences Settings returns control of the settings to AE Preferences.

Time Blend

 This is probably the easiest motion blur to apply, and is especially useful for adding blurred trails to other effects plug-ins, like particle systems effects. Blur effects add speed lines to moving elements in animated footage, and different ones treat the footage in unique ways.

The following controls allow you to adjust the Time Blend parameters:

- *Buffer Transfer*—You can choose Blend With Original, Composite Under Original, or Composite Over Original. Working with solid footage that has no transparent areas forces you to choose the Composite Over Original option to see the blur effects. Working with Alpha channel footage allows you to explore the other settings.

- *Buffer Opacity*—A good default is 50, although the range is from 0 to 100.

Changing Time

Look at TimeBlnd on this book's companion CD-ROM. Here's an example of the Time Blend effect applied to animated footage. It was created with an 85 percent Buffer Opacity and the Composite Over Original option.

Time Blend FX

 This effect is a little more complex than Time Blend because it allows you to copy the footage from one layer and use it as a blended composite on another layer. You don't have to pre-compose the two footage layers in this case. Use Time Blend FX when you have two pieces of footage that will work to create an interesting blended composite.

The following controls allow you to adjust the Time Blend FX parameters. You have to use two separate layers in the Composite to apply this effect:

- *Instance*—Select each layer in turn, and determine whether it is to be copied or pasted to the buffer for rendering. The pasted layer receives the image content of the copied layer.

- *Paste Transfer*—As with Time Blend, you have three options for blending the data: Blend With Original, Composite Under Original, and Composite Over Original. Explore each option, moving ahead in the Timeline to see what looks best.

FE STYLIZE

This chapter details the following ICE FE AE plug-ins: Blobbylize, Burn Film, Glass, Glue Gun, Kaleida, Mr. Smoothie, Page Turn, RepeTile, and Scatterize.

Blobbylize

 Blobbylize allows the Alpha channel of targeted footage to create a cutout of footage on another layer (see Figure 31.1). You can use the Blobbylize effect, for example, to alter the solarization of the Alpha layer over time.

The following controls allow you to adjust the Blobbylize effect:

- *Smoothness*—The Smoothness value (1 to 511) controls the roundness of the effect. Set it high to achieve mercurial blobs. Settings higher than 50 increases rendering time dramatically.

- *Light Source*—Place the crosshairs to center the Blobbylize light source.

- *Light*—You control Ambient, Diffuse, Specular, and Roughness settings for the light.

- *Boost Depth*—Enhance the depth perception of the effect.

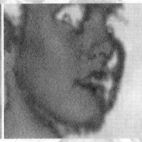

Figure 31.1
The Blobbylize effect, showing the result of different Diffuse values. Left to right: 0, 0.5, and 1.

Burn Film

 If you are old enough, you may remember sitting in the theater and watching the dark burn splotches eat away at a film. Well, if not, here's your chance to see it in action anyway (see Figure 31.2). The following are some possible uses for the Burn Film effect:

- Use this effect as an A/B roll transition. When you're through applying the effect to one sequence of footage, use that recorded sequence as an Alpha layer, so that the "burns" reveal the underlying layer.

- Use this to denote terror in wartime newsreel footage, like the burning of European cities.

The following controls allow you to adjust the parameters of the Burn Film effect.

- *Burnt*—By adjusting the control slider from 0 to 500, you influence the amount of burned splotchiness of the film. For general use, a setting of 50 is usually sufficient to black out the entire footage.

- *Center*—Place the crosshairs where you want the burns to start.

- *Random Seed*—This is a random-number generator that decides the shape of the burned areas.

Figure 31.2
From left to right, the burned film progresses.

Glass

  This effect creates the look of bumpy glass over the footage (see Figure 31.3). As an option, look at the Glass effects from Alien Skin in Chapter 16. The following are some possible uses for the Glass effect.

- Use this effect to add a blobby overlay to your footage.

- Alter the Light Direction over time to animate the Glass effect.

The following controls allow you to adjust the Glass effect.

- *Light Type and Position*—Select from either Distant or Point Light. The Distance option creates a more global aura of light. Set the Position crosshairs for the Point effects, since this control has no effect on Distant Light effects.

Figure 31.3
Left to right, the Glass effect as applied to the red, blue, and green channels of selected footage.

- *Light Angle and Height*—Adjust these controls as needed to cause the light to reflect off the Glass blobs. The greater the light angle, the brighter the overall footage will be. For darker footage, increase the height value.

- *Light Quality*—You can adjust the light's Ambient, Diffuse, Specular, and Roughness values. Explore different settings until you achieve the best look for your footage.

- *Bump*—You may select any footage layer in the stack as the source for the glass bumps. The Bump Map itself can be based on Red, Blue, Green, Alpha, Luminance, or Lightness channels. Explore the option that best suits your footage and desired effect.

- *Displacement*—Displacement adjusts the quantity of glass bumps. Its settings can range from –500 to +500, with values lower than –100 and higher than +100 increasing the bumps.

- *Softness*—This control mutes the hardness of the bumped edges the higher the value is set. The range of settings is from 0 to 511.

Glue Gun

The Glue Gun filter is used to add an animated paint effect to the footage. You have to keyframe the position of the paint to see this in the Composition window (see Figure 31.4).

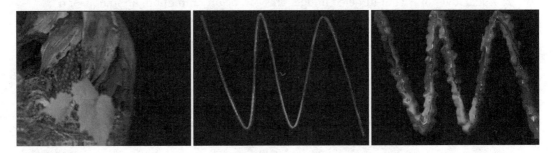

Figure 31.4
Left: The effect of wide Glue Gun strokes. Center: Thin, nonwobbly lines are good for ornate letter strokes. Right: Adding a wiggle gives the stroke a living personality.

The following are some possible uses for the Glue Gun effect:

- Create the title for a horror movie by using this effect over a solid red image or even over a frame taken from the film.

- Use the Plain option with a thin brush to create detailed and ornate text. This is a good option for soap operas or other romance-oriented content.

The following controls allow you to adjust the Glue Gun effect.

- *Brush Position*—The Brush Position crosshairs are used to trace a path for the Glue Gun output.

- *Stroke Width and Density*—Width adjusts the width of the Glue path. Its range is from 0 to 1,024, with large widths acting as wipes over the entire footage. Think of the Density control as the nozzle on a real glue gun. Its settings range from 0 to 200, with lower densities creating small globs of glue, while higher values create a continuous path.

- *Time Span*—Glue Gun is a particle system, so each of the globules can have a lifespan in seconds (0 to 3,000). A lifespan of 0 creates a permanent glob on the footage.

- *Reflection*—Reflection Amount allows you to adjust how each glob reflects the entire source footage. The settings can range between 0 to 200, with a setting of 0 showing the footage beneath and higher values showing the entire footage reflected in each globule.

- *Blob Influence*—Blob Influence sets the viscosity, or thickness, of the glue. Its settings are percentages (0 to 100). A default of 100 is recommended because this setting will enhance the 3D nature of the globs.

- *Paint Action*—Paint action can be Plain or Wobbly. Wobbly action makes the globs wiggle, depending on the Wobble settings.

- *Wobbliness*—You can control the wobble by adjusting its width, height, and speed. Higher values create a living shuddering substance.

Glue Line

Do the following to use the Glue Gun filter to outline any part of an image layer:

1. Import an image to the Composition window that has a feature you want to outline.

2. Add a layer over your targeted image. This can be an animation, an image, or a color layer. The glue line takes its color information from this layer.

3. Activate the FE Glue Gun filter from the Stylize list under the Effects menu.

4. Set the following parameters: Width 4, Density 25, and the rest of the parameter values at their default settings.

5. The next step is to keyframe animate just the position centroid to outline your area of interest. Depending on the complexity of your outlined area and the degree to which you want to outline each curve, you may wind up with a large number of keyframes. The approach is to advance the keyframe on the timeline and to reset the position of the glue each time, until the outline is finished.

Render the animation and save it to disk. See the GluLin animation on this book's CD-ROM.

Gluey

As you run the Glue Gun animation, watch as the wobbly line moves across the footage. You can find Glue Gun on this book's companion CD-ROM.

Kaleida

 Here's an effect that will take you and your audience back to childhood, to the time when you were first mesmerized by seeing the world through a kaleidoscope (see Figure 31.5). The following are some possible uses for the Kaleida effect:

- Animate this effect from a Size value of 3 to 1,000 to zoom in on the footage.

- Animate both the rotation and the center placement to maximize the Kaleida effect.

The following controls allow you to adjust the Kaleida effect's parameters:

- *Set Center*—This control sets the center of the Kaleida action.

- *Size*—The Size value (in its range from 1 to 1,000) increases the amount of the footage included in each Kaleida slice. Smaller values create a more tiled look.

- *Kaleida Type*—Each Kaleida type creates a new tiled possibility. Select from Unfold, Wheel, Fish Head, Can Meas, Flip Flop, Flower, Dia Cross, Flipper, and Star Fish. Explore all the options before selecting one.

- *Rotation*—Just as you turn a real kaleidoscope to reveal new patterns, so you can animate the rotation of the Kaleida effect.

- *Floating Center*—With this attribute checked, you can move the center of the effect over time, just as you can move a real kaleidoscope to look in a new direction.

Figure 31.5
Left to right: The Wheel, Flower, and Starfish Kaleida types.

Kaleida Fish Head

The Kalieda 1 example on this book's CD-ROM is the first of two animations that demonstrate the Kaleida effect. In this example, the Size value is altered from 30 to 60 and back to 30. This is the Fish Head type.

Kaleida Starfish

In the second Kaleida animation, Kaleida 2 on the companion CD-ROM, Rotation is the operator. Settings move from 0 to 360. This is a Starfish type.

Mr. Smoothie

 The Mr. Smoothie filter posterizes the footage based on your selection of two representative colors (see Figure 31.6). The following are some possible uses for the Mr. Smoothie effect:

- This effect is good to show the flash of an explosion. Just move the Sample A position over time to get different palettes.

- Use this effect on a text block floating over a background layer. Use an ABA color loop and animate the rotation from 0 to 360. The result will be like reflected chrome.

The following controls allow you to adjust the Mr. Smoothie effect.

- *Flow Layer*—Select the layer to be used as the source footage. The more color, the better.

- *Use*—Select the channel type to use.

- *Smoothness*—Increasing the Smoothness values defines the smoothed areas as less connected to the original footage content and increases the chrome effect. Its settings range from 0 to 511.

- *Samples*—Mr. Smoothie works by blending two color selections from the footage, Sample A and Sample B. For a maximum chrome effect, make sure these are different from each other.

- *Revolve*—Revolving the values with this radial control alters the phase of the samples, creating interesting whorls.

- *Color Loop*—These options set the direction of the gradation from Sample A to Sample B. Explore each one: AB, BA, ABA, BAB.

That's Mr. Smoothie To You

Mr. Smoothie works his magic on the Smoothie animation on the companion CD-ROM. Moving the "A" position to different points on the footage created the effect.

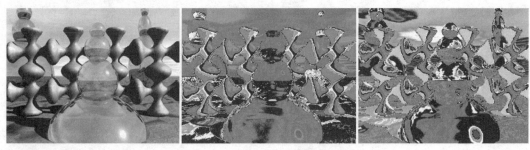

Figure 31.6
Left: Original footage. Center: AB Color Loop. Right: ABA Color Loop.

Page Turn

This is a basic Page Turn effect (see Figure 31.7). For other Page Turn options, see BorisFX Distort and Perspective (Chapter 19) and Hollywood FX (Chapter 34). The following are some possible uses for the Page Turn effect:

- Set this effect to several layers in a stack, to create a book whose pages turn one by one.
- Set different moving footage on both the front and back side of the Page Turn to emphasize the magical nature of the effect.

The following controls allow you to adjust the parameters of the Page Turn effect.

- *Fold Edge Position*—Set the starting and ending positions of the turn by moving the crosshairs.
- *Fold Direction*—Set the direction of the fold. Animate this control for more-bizarre effects.
- *Fold Radius*—The Fold Radius values (in their range from 4 to 100) set the curvature of the fold. A value of 4 creates a sharp crease.
- *Light Direction*—The light reflects off the underside of the footage.
- *Backside And Paper Color*—The backside of the footage is revealed as the page turns. If it is set to None, then it will show the paper color.
- *Render*—You can render the Full Page Turn (most common), or either the Front or Back alone.

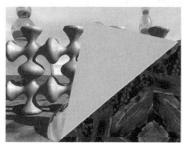

Figure 31.7
Left: A Fold Radius of 4 creates a sharp crease. Center: The larger the radius, the larger the curvature of the turn. Right: Using the same footage front and back is effective in simulating the 3D nature of the effect.

A Real Page Turner

The FE PageTurn effect is animated in the FE-PgTrn file on this book's CD-ROM.

RepeTile

This is an excellent tiling effect, not repeated by other AE tiling filters, that allows you to control the tiling sizes in all four directions from the original footage (see Figure 31.8). The following are some possible uses for the RepeTile effects:

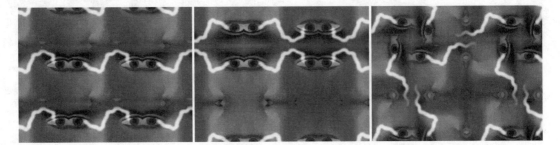

Figure 31.8
Three tile types. Left: Repeat. Center: Unfold. Right: Rosette.

- Use this effect when you need tiles with a different look. Blending the edges gives your footage a very dreamlike appearance.
- Use a Random Type with a Blend value of 100 to simulate a bad hangover.

The following controls allow you to adjust the RepeTile effect:

- *Expand*—You may expand the footage in any or all of four directions: left, right, up, and down. The range for each is 0 to 200. The footage should first be reduced so that you can see the tiles that are created. As a start, try reducing the footage to one-half its size, and centering it in the Composition window.
- *Blend Tile Borders*—Rather than harsh borders, you may want to blend the borders of the tiles. Its values range from 0 to 100. A blend of 50 is a good place to start.

Mosaic Tile

The effect animated in the RepeTile file on the companion CD-ROM with the FE RepeTile filter is that of an animated mosaic tile. The RepeTile Type here is the Rosette option.

Scatterize

 This is a very complex marriage between two effects—a twist warp and a particle system (see Figure 31.9). The following are some possible uses for the Scatterize effects:

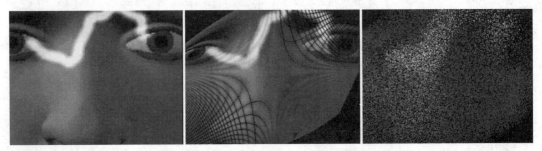

Figure 31.9
Left: Original footage. Center: Left and right twists added. Right: Scattering added.

- Apply only the Twist settings to an Alpha text block layer to twist or untwist a title or a logo.

- Apply both the Twist and Amount values to a piece of sci-fi footage to show a space warp and a following explosion. Don't start the Scatterize amount until the twist warp is about three-fourths completed.

The following controls allow you to adjust the Scatterize effect's parameters:

Note: You can apply the Amount control alone to achieve an exploding-particle effect, or the Twist controls alone to warp the footage. Or, you may elect to apply them together for more-complex effects.

- *Amount*—This simple control sets the amount of scattering that takes place (its settings range between –1,024 to +1,024). As the value is increased, the particles fly farther apart.

- *Right Twist/Left Twist*—Although these radial controls appear very basic, they are powerful. They each add a twist to the plane on which the footage rests, and can be applied together or singly. A grid is superimposed on the footage so you can appreciate the twist.

Scatter Basics

This animation displays the basic Scatterize effect, moving from 0 to 100. See the ScatRize animation on the companion CD-ROM.

When Ships Fly

The SCATIZE animation on this book's CD-ROM shows a far more complex use of the Scatterize effect. In this animation (the original footage was created in Bryce 3D), two ships fly over a city. As the journey progresses, one of the ships crashes into a building, and the whole scene starts to warp, thanks to the Right and Left Twist alterations. Then a Scatter is performed, exploding the entire footage into nothingness.

VIZ<small>FX</small> I

Intergraph's VIZfx AE is only for users of Windows NT (4 or higher). This chapter covers the VIZfx plug-ins that concern color (Blur, Convolve, Dye, Noise, and Posterize); geometry (Bump, Deform, Emboss, Raindrops, and Whirl); and masks (Balloon, Combine Alpha, and Compare).

Blur

 This is a basic Blur filter. This effect has just one control, which is enough to evoke quality blurs (see Figure 32.1). The following are some possible uses for the Blur effect:

- Use any of the types you want. Animate footage that starts with the intensity set high enough to obliterate the footage (0.75 or above) and end the animation with the footage in full, clear view. The Blur effect makes a great fade-in.

- Place footage of a face in your composition twice. On the top layer, outline only the eyes. Now, use the VIZfx Blur filter on the bottom layer to animate a blur from 0 to 0.5. The resulting animation shows just the eyes remaining while the rest of the face blurs. Whatever you leave untouched will be the new focus of the footage.

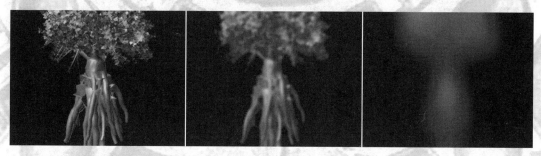

Figure 32.1
Left: Original footage. Center: Cubic Spline blur of 0.15. Right: Cubic Spline blur of 0.5.

The following controls allow you to adjust the Blur effect's parameters.

- *Blurring Filter*—These four options create blurs that are slightly different: Triangle, Mitchell, Bell, and Cubic Spline. Explore each to see which works best for you.

- *Intensity*—The Intensity settings range from 0 to 1. Higher values increase the Blur effect.

Convolve

 Convolves are created by altering how groups of pixels in an image affect neighboring pixels. This results in effects like blur, sharpen, and embossing, among others. Convolves are common effects in desktop publishing work, and, with this collection, Intergraph brings them into animated usage for AE (see Figure 32.2). The following are some possible uses for the Convolve effect:

- Apply the Laplacian Diagonal preset to transform the footage into a look that's suitable for a dream sequence.

- Use the Edge Detection preset at full intensity to create footage that appears to break up into pixelated dots.

The following controls allow you to adjust the parameters of the Convolve effect.

- *Preset Filter*—You may explore 32 preset filters. Also, a User Defined option allows you to use the nine control sliders to experiment with setting up your own convolution matrix.

- *Use Alpha Channel*—By checking this option, the Convolve is applied to the Alpha channel of the selected footage.

- *Intensity*—With this control you adjust the amount of Convolve applied to the footage. Its settings range from 0 to 1.

- *User Defined Controls*—If you have selected User Defined from the Presets list, these nine sliders allow you to create your own convolution filter, selecting from a range of –99 to +99.

Figure 32.2
Convolve presets applied from left to right: Laplacian Diagonal, Edge Detection, and Gradient East.

Dye

This filter transforms your footage into a duotone by applying any color you desire over the selected image area. The following are some possible uses for the Dye effect:

- Stack several Dye effects on top of each other, and animate the color over time to create muted washes of color.

- Animate the Intensity values over time to create footage that moves from its color palette to a single color. This is also useful in night scenes, where colors lean toward the blue end of the spectrum.

The following controls allow you to adjust the Dye effect's parameters.

- *Intensity*—This control allows you to adjust the strength of the selected hue. Its settings range from 0 to 1. Lower values tint the footage, while higher values transform it entirely into the selected color.

- *Saturation*—By default, this option is left checked. Deselecting it removes the saturation value of the image, and creates an even but featureless tone.

- *Alpha*—Checking this option applies the Dye effect to the Alpha channel.

Noise

Noise adds squares of color or gray over the footage (see Figure 32.3). The following are some possible uses for the Noise effect:

- Simulate static by animating just the X Noise value over time, which creates horizontal bands.

- Create blocks of noise 3x3, and animate their value from 0 to 1 with the Distribution set at a constant 100. Use the same settings, but in reverse on another piece of footage, creating a transition from color blocks to a clear content. This results in a transition for the first footage from the image to a color-block screen, while the second piece of footage moves in the opposite way. Combining them is useful in moving from one sequence to another.

Figure 32.3
Left: Original footage. Center: A Level of 0.5 and a Distribution of 40 creates noise that still shows the image. Right: Increasing the Level to 1 and the Distribution to 100 replaces the image with the noise.

The following controls allow you to adjust the Noise effect's parameters.

- *Block Size X, Y*—Block Size values (in a range of 0 to 100) determine the horizontal (X) and vertical (Y) sizes of the noise block. Setting one at 0 emphasizes the other, creating horizontal or vertical bands.

- *Level*—The Level settings (from 0 to 1) determine the transparency of the blocks, with lower values showing more of the original image. A value of 1 obliterates the footage in areas with noise blocks.

- *Distribution*—The Distribution settings (0 to 100) control the number of noise blocks placed on the footage. A setting of 100 covers the footage with noise.

- *Noise Color*—The noise blocks can be a random color or gray.

Posterize

 Posterizing removes most of the hues from selected footage, replacing the palette with a limited number of colors (see Figure 32.4).

The following are some possible uses for the posterize effect:

- Posterized footage changes photography into a more graphic look, trading wide palettes for larger color block areas. Use it for this purpose.

- Animate the Transparency setting to move in and out of posterized looks. This can be an interesting effect when applied to title footage.

The following controls allow you to adjust the Posterize effect:

- *RGB Output*—Use these three controls to adjust the RGB levels in the footage. Each one effects the color palette of the footage. The range of settings for the RGB Output is from 2 to 256.

- *Alpha Output*—Alter the Alpha channel in the mix. High values mute the footage.

- *Transparency*—Transparency sets the amount of the original footage seen through the posterized effect. Its settings range from 0 to 1, with a setting of 0 showing no effect, and a setting of 100 showing no original footage.

- *Use Alpha Channel*—Checking this alternative limits the effect to only the Alpha channel.

Figure 32.4
Left: Original footage. Center: Posterized footage. Right: Transparency added to show through original footage.

Bump

This is an effect whose results cannot be predicted. The footage is warped either by itself or by another footage layer (see Figure 32.5). The following are some possible uses for the Bump effect:

- This effect is geared toward warping portraiture, so select footage that shows a front view of a human face. Animate the offset center by moving it from the top center to the bottom center.

- Animate the Smoothness setting from 0 to 0.3 and back again to create a moving contorted image. Leave the Intensity at 1.

The following controls allow you to adjust the effect's parameters:

- *Secondary Image*—You may select any footage in the stack. You can even select the same image, although if you do, it's best to offset it.

- *Intensity*—Intensity controls the strength of the effect. Although the settings can range from 0 to 1, keep 1 as the default.

- *Smoothness*—To keep the footage recognizable, yet still see the warping that takes place, the best default for this setting is around 0.3. (Its range is from 0 to 1.) Settings much lower than 0.3 tend to make the footage ripple, and higher settings reduce the effect.

- *Secondary Image Offset*—This is the most important setting for animating the effect. Placing the offset at different areas on the footage creates warps based on the placement.

- *Wraparound*—Explore checking this on and off because it can either smooth out the footage or have no effect at all, depending on the content and the placement of the offset.

- *Antialias*—The footage can be antialiased at settings from 1 to 5, with 2 as the default. Higher values require more rendering time.

- *Use Alpha Channel*—When checked, the effect is applied to the Alpha channel.

The Bump

Bump is an animation of the Bump effect, created by animating the offset center from top center to bottom center. The Intensity value was 1, and the Smoothness was set to 0.32.

Figure 32.5
Left: Original footage. Center: Intensity at 1 and Smoothness at 0.25. Right: Smoothness of 0.3, with the offset moved out of the frame to the center bottom.

Deform

VIZfx Deform is a perspective plane effect (see Figure 32.6). For alternate perspective plane effects, see BorisFX (refer to Chapter 19), FE Advanced 3D (refer to Chapter 30), and Hollywood FX (see Chapter 34). The following are some possible uses for the Deform effect:

- Warp the content of the footage by placing the bottom corners far apart and the top corners close together, or vice versa.

- Use this effect to create flying-logo effects simply by altering the size and orientation of the perspective plane.

The following controls allow you to adjust the Deform effect's parameters:

- *Place Corners*—Place the four corners of the perspective plane to warp the footage.

- *Antialias*—Set antialiasing from 1 to 5.

Figure 32.6
A selection of VIZfx Deforms.

Emboss

Embossing creates a 3D effect while also limiting the color palette (see Figure 32.7). The following are some possible uses for the Emboss effect:

- Make any two colors white and the other one black, and use Directional Light Sources to create a neon look.

Figure 32.7
A selection of embossed treatments.

- Use the VIZfx Emboss effect to create living woodblocks by applying it to moving footage. Use Point Light Sources, and make the color red, blue, and yellow, all with high intensity.

The following controls allow you to adjust the Emboss effect's parameters:

- *Depth Criterion*—You can select an RGB channel, Luminance, or Alpha as the target of the effect. Luminance is the default and creates the most variety.

- *Emboss Intensity*—This control determines the power of the effect on the footage. Its settings range from 0 to 1, but it's usually set to the maximum of 1.

- *Softening*—Softening blurs the edges of the effect. Its settings can range from 0 to 1, but 0.1 is usually sufficient, with higher values blurring the effect dramatically.

- *Antialias*—Set antialiasing from 1 to 5.

- *Color Settings*—The emboss effect is created by treating the footage as if it were being lighted by three different sources. You can set the color, direction, intensity, height, and azimuth of these three light sources. Everything you do will alter the targeted footage, so experimentation is a must. The only ground rule is to adjust combinations of settings until you achieve something you like.

Raindrops

  This is an excellent effect for simulating drops falling on a liquid surface (see Figure 32.8). The following are some possible uses for the Raindrops effect:

- Use this effect on a solid-color layer, or a frame from production footage, to create a backdrop for text.

- Use the Fixed Point Drop Location to place a ripple at the center of an eye, with a high speed setting, to create energy waves emanating from an eye.

The following controls allow you to adjust the Raindrops effect:

- *Drop Location*—The options are Random and Fixed Point. You'd want to use Random for a pond effect and Fixed Point when you want the ripple to emanate from a specific point on the footage.

  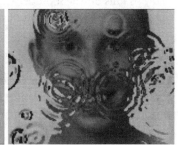

Figure 32.8
Selected frames from a VIZfx Raindrop animation.

- *All Drops Fall On Image*—By unchecking this, some of the drops will fall outside of the image, and you may or may not catch an edge of their ripple.

- *Fixed Point*—If the Drop Location is Fixed Point, then use this crosshair to place it.

- *Time Dampening*—Time-dampened ripples are affected by the passage of time and gradually diminish and disappear.

- *Maximum Ring Size*—Although settings for this control can range from 0 to 10,000, they usually are kept between 15 and 25. Higher values break up the footage into wavelets, with extreme values (above 200 or so) causing no apparent effect at all, except on very large footage sizes.

- *Random Seed*—This is a random seed generator.

- *Frequency*—This control determines how many rings are produced. Its range is from 0 to 10,000, but 5 is usually sufficient for falling drops, with settings above 10 starting to wreak havoc on the footage.

- *Ring Speed*—This setting sets the speed of the ripple rings as they move outward from the center. Settings for this control can range from 0 through 100. A value below 10 is a good default, with values above 20 creating energy waves instead of liquid ripples.

- *Drop Force Minimum/Variance*—The higher the Drop Force setting (in a range from 0 through 100), the more the ripples will affect and warp the footage underneath. Variance adds a random factor.

- *Output Type*—The selections are Input Image (the default) or Grayscale. Selecting Grayscale creates a 256-gray-level footage, perfect for transforming into an Alpha layer.

- *Fill Spaces*—Leave this control checked on. Checking it off places dark patches in the spaces between the ripples.

- *Antialias*—Select a setting from 1 to 5.

- *Amplitude Adjustment*—If you want stronger waves, increase this value.

Raindrops Keep Falling

Check out the RainDrps file on this book's companion CD-ROM. Watch as a gentle series of drops falls on the footage. This is a beautiful environmental effect and could be used as a backdrop for a title or credit sequence.

Whirl

 This is a vortex effect (see Figure 32.9). The following are some possible uses for the Whirl effect:

  - Use just a slight variation of the inner/outer angles to alter the personality of a face.

- Spin the inner/outer angles several times in the opposite directions to create a ripple effect.

Figure 32.9
Left: A slight vortex warp, caused by setting the inner and outer angles at 5 and –5, respectively. Center: A more emphatic vortex, centered on the right eye. Right: Increasing the inner and outer angles to a full turn, and centering the vortex on the mouth. The following controls allow you to adjust the Whirl effect's parameters:

- *Rotation Center*—This control places the center of the vortex.

- *Inner and Outer Angle*—Set each of these angles separately, or use only one. Using only one will distort the image in whatever direction is selected, while using both tears the image as well as rotating it.

- *Antialias*—Settings for this control range from 1 to 5.

- *Fill Spaces*—Leave this on as a default to fill the vortex with image content.

Balloon

 This is a channel effect that allows you to enlarge or reduce each channel separately, and then composite all channels back in the mix. The following are some possible uses for the Balloon effect:

- Use Deflation at a Radius of 10 at the start of an animation, with all RGB channels selected, and a radius of 0 at the end to make your footage begin in darkness and end as a clear image.

- Use Inflation at a Radius of 50 at the start of an animation, with all RGB channels selected, and a Radius of 0 at the end to make your footage begin in washed-out light and end as a clear image.

The following controls allow you to adjust the Balloon effect's parameters:

- *Type*—Select either Inflation or Deflation.

- *Channels*—Activate the red, blue, green, or Alpha channel in any combination to explore this effect. As far as the RGB channels, it's best to leave at least one deactivated to appreciate what this filter does, or else everything will go too dark. Used on the Alpha channel, this effect reduces or enlarges it in one-pixel increments.

- *Radius*—Increasing the Radius value (1 to 10,000) increases the power of the effect. Increasing the value beyond 100 tends to turn the footage black.

Trial Balloon

Look at the Balloon animation on the companion CD-ROM. It uses Inflation at a Radius of 50 at the start of an animation, with all RGB channels selected, and a Radius of 0 at the end to show footage beginning in washed-out light and ending as a clear image.

Combine Alpha

 This filter allows you to combine the Alpha channels of two selected layers into one. The following are some possible uses for the Combine Alpha effects:

- Use Combine Alpha to make the best use of two layers of footage to be composited against a separate background.

- Animate the combination to alter the Alpha layers over time, creating effects for both layers.

The following controls allow you to adjust the Combine Alpha effect:

- *Secondary Image*—This control selects the secondary layer from the stack.

- *Combination Type*—You may select Union, Intersection, or Subtraction. Each will create a unique Alpha channel that you can preview.

- *Output Image*—The resulting Alpha combination can be based on either the primary or secondary data, or just the Alpha. Your choice depends on your footage content, your purpose, and how it looks when you preview the results.

- *Alpha Intensity*—Set the Alpha Intensity values of both the primary and secondary selections with these two sliders. As you adjust the intensity, keep an eye on the Composition window to preview the effect.

- *Secondary Input Offset*—You may want to offset the secondary footage to alter the combined Alpha image. Place the crosshairs to achieve this effect.

- *Secondary Input Wraparound*—Selecting this attribute forces the secondary image to be added completely, without being affected by the Combine Alpha operation.

Compare

 Compare is the opposite of Combine Alpha. It subtracts one layer from another to create a mask. Use the Compare effect as an alternative to the Combine Alpha effect.

The following controls allow you to adjust the effect's parameters:

- *Secondary Image*—This control selects the secondary image from a layer in the stack.

- *Comparison Criterion*—These four controls allow you to toggle the red, blue, green, or Alpha channels on or off to determine what channels will be targeted in the mix.

- *Output Type*—You may select either Binary (black and white) or Grayscale output. Grayscale is the more common for Alpha channels with multiple levels of transparency, but you may run into situations where a basic mask is desired.

- *Secondary Input Offset*—Offsetting the secondary image creates unique blends. Experiment with different positions for the secondary image, and watch the Composition window for the previewed results.

- *Secondary Input Wraparound*—Selecting this attribute forces the secondary image to be added completely, without being affected by the Compare operation.

VIZfx II

INTERGRAPH

33

This chapter covers the Intergraph VIZfx AE plug-ins that include particles (Blast, Erode, Melt, Mosaic, Pulverize, Scatter), shines (Color Glow, Edge Shine, Foggy Glow, Glow, Outline, Shine), and transitions (Concentric Blinds, Radar Blinds, Tokyo Blinds, Venetian Blinds).

Blast

The Blast effect pulverizes the footage with animated pixels (see Figure 33.1). The following are some possible uses for the Blast effect:

- Use the Blast effect anywhere that the footage needs to be obliterated.

- Use it for explosion effects that require squarish particles.

The following controls allow you to adjust the effect's parameters:

- *Offset*—With this control you can place the center of the effect, the point from which the particles will emanate.

- *Particle Size*—Size can be anywhere from single pixel points to squarish blocks at large values. Its settings range from 1 to 100.

- *Particle Speed*—Speed sets the rate at which the particles fly apart. Its settings range from 0 to 100.

- *Gravity*—Gravity's settings range from 1 to 100. The higher the value, the more gravity pulls the particles downward.

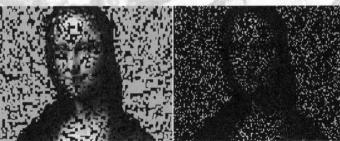

Figure 33.1
Left to right: Progression of the Blast effect.

- *Minimum Delay*—Minimum Delay acts as a drag on the particle movements. Its range of settings is 0 to 1,000, with the drag increasing as the value does. Typically, the delay would be higher at the start of the animation than at the end.

Blaster

To use the Blast filter to remove your footage content from the screen, take these steps:

1. Import any still or animated footage to the Composition window.

2. Activate the Intergraph VIZfx AE Blast filter.

3. Place the Offset centroid anywhere on the footage that you want the blast to be centered on.

4. Set Particle Size to 20 and Particle Speed to 50.

5. Set Gravity to 100 and Delay to 0. This makes the particles fall downward.

Render the animation and save it to disk.

Blast At Last

Look on the companion CD-ROM for an example (Blast.mov) of the VIZfx Blast particle effect.

Erode

 Erode adds blotches to the footage until it is obliterated (see Figure 33.2). The following are some possible uses for the Erode effect:

- Use as an alternative to obliterate the footage.

- Use this effect along with the FE Burned Film effect (refer to Chapter 31) to add film damage.

The following controls allow you to adjust the effect's parameters:

- *Activation Speed*—Speed determines how fast the blotches spread across the surface of the footage. Its range of settings is 1 to 10,000.

- *Minimum Spread Delay*—The Spread Delay acts as a drag on the spread of the blotches. Its range of settings is also 1 to 10,000.

Figure 33.2
Left to right: A progression of the Erode effect.

- *Pixel Fade Duration Minimum*—This control fades the blotches. The higher the value (in its range of 1 to 10,000), the more the blotches are faded.

- *Pixel Fade Variance*—You can add a random factor to the fades with Pixel Fade Variance. Its range is also from 1 to 10,000.

- *Use Alpha Channel*—When checked, the effect is applied to the Alpha channel.

Erosion

Look on the companion CD-ROM for an example (Erode.mov) of the VIZfx Erode particle effect.

Melt

This is a great footage-melting effect that is not found in other effects volumes (see Figure 33.3). The following are some possible uses for the Melt effect:

- Melt a series of opening credit layers in any direction to bring in the next credits.

- Melt a footage component that has been shot with a death ray.

The following controls allow you to adjust the parameters of the Melt effect:

- *Activation Controls*—You can apply this effect to melt the footage up, down, left, or right, either singly or with all directions activated at once. In each case, you can control the starting position and speed of the melt.

- *Blast Area*—Select Union or Intersection to determine how the melted pixels will interact.

- *Melt Direction*—This is the dominant direction that moves the melt globally.

- *Particle Size*—Set the Width and Height values separately (both in a range from 1 to 200 pixels).

- *Minimum Delay (in Frames)*—The delay sets a drag on the melt movement in the direction indicated, but not on the melt itself. Its settings can range from 1 to 10,000.

- *Length Minimum and Variance (in Pixels)*—Length Minimum and Variance work in concert to add a more random look to the melt. Settings for both controls range from 1 to 10,000.

- *Speed Minimum and Variance*—Speed Minimum and Variance work in concert to randomize the speed at which different areas of the footage melt. Settings for both controls range from 0 to 100.

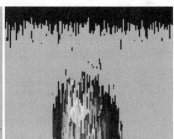

Figure 33.3
Left to right: The progression of the Melt effect.

Melt Away

Look on the companion CD-ROM for an example (Melt.mov) of the VIZfx Melt particle effect.

Mosaic

 This effect breaks the image into blocks that eventually overcome the footage content (see Figure 33.4). The following are some possible uses for the Mosaic effect:

- Start an animation at an XY Mosaic size of 100, and end it at a size of 1. This reveals the content from a series of blocks.

- Start an animation at an XY Mosaic size of 100 with Transparency set to 0, and end the animation with a Transparency value of 1. This reveals the content from a series of blocks by the transparency method.

The following controls allow you to adjust the parameters of the Mosaic effect:

- *Block Size*—Configure the X (horizontal) and Y (vertical) block sizes individually, within a range of settings from 1 to 100.

- *Transparency*—At 0, the Mosaic effect dominates, while at 1 the footage remains unaffected.

- *Alpha*—When checked, the effect is applied to the Alpha channel.

Figure 33.4
Left to right: A progression of the Mosaic effect.

Pulverize

 Pulverize is another particle-explosion effect. It is unique in the way it breaks up the footage (see Figure 33.5). The following are some possible uses for the Pulverize effect:

- Use this effect as an alternate particle explosion.

- This effect works particularly well as a gravity-based particle explosion, so use it with that intent in mind.

The following controls allow you to adjust the Pulverize effect:

- *Activation Controls*—You can apply this effect to melt the footage up, down, left, or right, either singly or with all directions activated at once. In each case, you can control the starting position and the speed of the pulverization.

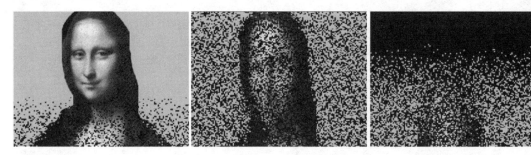

Figure 33.5
Left to right: A progression of the Pulverize effect.

- *Blast Area*—Select Union or Intersection to determine how the pulverized pixels interact.

- *Melt Direction*—This is the dominant direction that moves the Pulverize effect globally.

- *Particle Size*—Set the Width and Height values separately (from 1 to 200 pixels).

- *Minimum Delay (in Frames)*—The delay sets a drag on the pulverize movement in the indicated direction, but not on the melt itself. Its settings can range from 1 to 10,000.

- *Length Minimum and Variance (in Pixels)*—Length Minimum and Variance work in concert to add a more random look to the Pulverize effect. Settings for both controls range from 1 to 10,000.

- *Speed Minimum and Variance*—Speed Minimum and Variance work in concert to randomize the speed at which different areas of the footage pulverize. The range of settings for both is from 0 to 100.

Scatter

 Scatter breaks up the image into a random series of dots (see Figure 33.6). The following are some possible uses for the Scatter effect:

  - Use the circle type to create a more 3D explosion of the footage.

- Use the square type to emphasize the 2D nature of the footage.

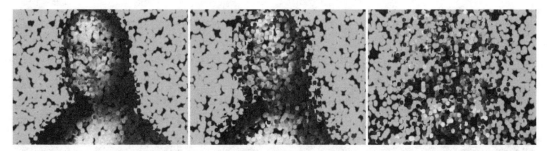

Figure 33.6
Left to right: A progression of the Scatter effect.

The following controls allow you to adjust the effect's parameters:

- *Particle Type*—This control is the core difference between this VIZfx effect and the other VIZfx particle systems. Here, you may select either circles or squares as the type. Circles make the effect look more 3D.

- *Particle Size*—The Size values range from 1 to 100.

- *Intensity*—The Intensity value (0 to 1) sets the amount of force applied. The higher you set the value, the more space you'll get between the particles.

- *Delay*—Delay acts as a drag on the speed the particles fly away from each other. Its settings range from 0 to 1.

- *Apply Matte/Alpha*—When selected, the effect is applied to either or both a matte or Alpha layer.

Scatter

Look on the companion CD-ROM for an example (Scatter.mov) of the VIZfx Scatter particle effect.

Color Glow

 This effect must be applied to the Alpha channel. It adds a dark glow to the selected image, based on the color of the edge of the footage (see Figure 33.7). The following are some possible uses for the Color Glow effect:

- Use this effect when you want a darker glow that blends the image edge into the background footage. This is not, however, a good choice for applying a glow to a text block or a logo.

- Use this effect to add a component of mystery and foreboding to the composition.

The following controls allow you to adjust the Color Glow effect:

- *Display Glow*—Remember that all of these settings refer to targeting the Alpha channel. You may select to display the glow along with the image or without it. Selecting to display without the image creates a Glow map that is not image based.

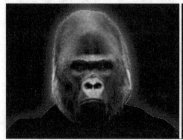  

Figure 33.7
Left to right, color glows of 2, 4, and 6, applied at full intensity to the Alpha channel.

- *Place Glow*—The glow may be placed behind the shape (which is the more common alternative) or in front of the shape. If you have selected to display the glow without the image, and then select to place the glow in front of the shape, an interesting effect can be achieved by targeting not the Alpha channel but the RGB image itself. The result is a blurry, light-soaked image layer, like a fog lit from the inside. This is an alternate effect that can be achieved with this filter.

- *Speed*—The speed of the effect sets the way the animation will show it progressing. Its settings range from 0 to 1.

- *Intensity*—The intensity of the effect sets the strength of the glow. Its range is also 0 to 1.

Edge Shine

This effect adds a moving shine to the footage, based on the Angle setting. It must be applied to the Alpha channel. This effect is also known as a glint (see Figure 33.8). The following are some possible uses for the Shine effect:

- Animate an edge shine by rotating its angle from 0 to 360, producing a revolving shine on a backdrop.

- Alternate the edge radius from 5 to 20 (with a constant angle of 90 degrees) to create a glowing halo shine at the center top of the footage.

The following controls allow you to adjust the Edge Shine effect:

- *Display Shine*—The shine can be displayed along with the image (the default), or without it. Selecting to display the shine without the image creates a blurred shine over the background layer.

- *Starting Position*—This control sets the point at which the shine becomes visible, or you might think of it as a wave-phase setting. This control ranges from –100 to +100.

- *Edge Radius*—The radius of the shine is a line that moves outward from the image. Its settings range from 0 to 100, and higher settings make the line longer.

- *Shine Width*—The width of the shine is the thickness of the radial line. Its range is also 0 to 100. Set the control at a default of 50, and adjust it from there.

Figure 33.8
From left to right, edge shines applied to the Alpha channel at different angles: 0, 90, and 230 degrees.

- *Decay Region*—This setting (with values between 0 to 100) determines the blend at the edges of the shine. Low values create bands, and high values blur out the shine stroke.

- *Shine Angle*—The angle of the shine stroke is set here. Note that some angles may not show up in the composition, so explore the angles carefully.

- *Shine Speed*—The speed of the shine determines how fast it moves in the animation. Settings can range from –10,000 to +10,000, and negative values move the shine opposite to that of positive values.

- *Multiple Shines*—This multiplies the shines during the animation, so that more than one moves across the footage. Exactly how much is determined by their Width, Speed, and Separation settings.

- *Separation*—Separation sets the distance between multiple shines. Its range is from 0 to 100.

- *Shine Color*—Set any color you like for the shine. The wisest choice for most footage is a color that stands out against the background.

- *Transparency*—The range for this control is 0 to 1. Set it to 0 to maximize the opacity of the shine.

Foggy Glow

This is the best all-around glow option from VIZfx. You must apply it to the Alpha channel (see Figure 33.9). The following are some possible uses for the Foggy Glow effect:

- Use this effect around a text block to make it pop out.

- Use this effect around a space vehicle reentering the atmosphere, as it heats up from friction.

The following controls allow you to adjust the effect's parameters:

- *Display Glow*—The default for this control is to display the glow along with the image. If you select Without The Image, the image will stand out as a color silhouette, which is useful for some effects.

- *Place Glow*—The more common option is Behind The Image, but selecting In Front Of The Image creates interesting, ghostly aura effects.

Figure 33.9
From left to right, a Foggy Glow of 0.2, 0.4, and 0.7.

- *Direct Glow*—The most common choice is Away From The Center, but selecting Towards The Center can create interesting alternate effects, especially with the Place Glow In Front Of Image option.

- *Glow Color*—This control allows you to set the color for your glow.

- *Speed*—Set the speed (in a range from 0 to 1) of the effect for the animation.

- *Intensity*—Set the opacity of the glow (in a range from 0 to 1).

Glow

 The difference between this effect and the Foggy Glow effect is that the Glow effect can be applied to either an Alpha channel or to the RGB footage. The footage should be a smaller element than a full-screen image however, so the glow can be seen (see Figure 33.10). The following are some possible uses for the Glow effect:

- Set a Glow effect around a jewel in a treasure chest, or a fuel rod in a nuclear reactor.

- Use the In Front Of option to create a ghostly apparition.

The following controls allow you to adjust the Glow effect:

- *Display Glow*—The default for this control is Along With The Image. If you select Without The Image, the image will stand out as a color silhouette, which is useful for some effects.

- *Place Glow*—The most common option is Behind The Image, but selecting In Front Of The Image creates interesting ghostly aura effects.

- *Direct Glow*—The most common choice is Away From The Center, but selecting Towards The Center can create interesting alternate effects, especially with the Place Glow In Front Of Image option.

- *Glow Color*—This control allows you to set the color for the glow.

- *Radius*—This value sets the spread of the glow in a range from 0 to 100.

- *Transparency*—Transparency determines the opacity of the glow. Its range is 0 to 1.

Figure 33.10
Left: Original footage. Center: A glow added with 20 percent transparency and a Radius value of 30. Right: A Glow in front of the footage.

Sci-Fi Glow

The VIZfx Glow effect on the companion CD-ROM is perfect for your next sci-fi or horror project. It also works well to pop a text block out of a backdrop. This file is named Glow.mov.

Outline

This effect creates a color border around the footage (see Figure 33.11). The following are some possible uses for the Outline effect:

- Use the Outline effect, with a thin border, to pop dark text out of a dark background.

- Use the Outline effect anywhere you need to call attention to a layer. Use the effect several times on the same layer, with different thicknesses and colors, to create a multicolored outline.

The following controls allow you to adjust the effect's parameters:

- *Display Outline*—The default for this control is Along With The Image. If you select Without The Image, the image will stand out as a color silhouette, which is useful for some effects.

- *Place Outline*—The most common option is Behind The Image, but selecting In Front Of The Image creates washed-out aura effects.

- *Direct Outline*—The most common choice is Away From The Center, but selecting Towards The Center can create interesting alternate effects, especially with the Place Outline In Front Of Image option.

- *Outline Color*—This control lets you set the color for the glow.

- *Radius*—This value sets the spread of the outline. Its settings range from 0 to 100.

- *Transparency*—Transparency determines the opacity of the outline. Its range is 0 to 1.

Outline Color Shrink And Grow

Go to the companion CD-ROM for an example (Outline.mov) of the VIZfx Outline effect. In this example, the outline color shrinks and grows several times during the animation.

Figure 33.11
Left to right: Frames from an Outline animation.

Shine

This is the companion effect to Edge Shine, with the difference being that it adds the shine (glint) to the footage instead of around it (see Figure 33.12). The following are some possible uses for the Shine effect:

- Add a shine to any surface that is supposed to be metallic.

- Add a shine to your logo or logo text.

The following controls allow you to adjust the Shine effect:

- *Starting Position*—This control sets the point at which the shine becomes visible. You might think of it as a wave-phase setting. Its settings can range from –100 to +100.

- *Shine Width*—The width of the shine is the thickness of the radial line. Set it at a default of 50, and adjust it from there. Its range is from 0 to 100.

- *Decay Region*—This setting determines the blend at the edges of the shine. Its range is from 0 to 100. Low values create bands, and high values blur out the shine stroke.

- *Shine Angle*—The angle of the shine stroke is set here. Note that some angles may not show up in the composition, so explore the angles carefully.

- *Shine Speed*—The speed of the shine determines how fast it moves in the animation. Its settings can range from –10,000 to +10,000, and negative values move the shine opposite to that of positive values.

- *Multiple Shines*—This control multiplies the shines during the animation, so that more than one moves across the footage. Exactly how many is determined by their Width, Speed, and Separation values.

- *Separation*—The Separation control (with its range of 0 to 100) sets the distance between multiple shines.

- *Shine Color*—Set any color you like for the shine. The wisest choice for most footage is a color that contrasts with the background.

- *Transparency*—Set this value to 0 to maximize the opacity of the shine. The range is 0 to 1.

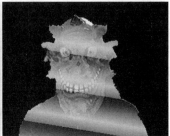

Figure 33.12
Left: Original footage. Center: Shine added. Right: Multiple shines added.

Shiny Chrome

The Shine effect is commonly used with a logo layer to make the logo appear to be made out of chrome. The file on the companion CD-ROM is named Shine.mov.

Transitions

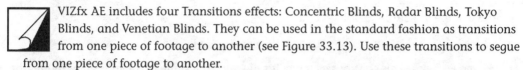

VIZfx AE includes four Transitions effects: Concentric Blinds, Radar Blinds, Tokyo Blinds, and Venetian Blinds. They can be used in the standard fashion as transitions from one piece of footage to another (see Figure 33.13). Use these transitions to segue from one piece of footage to another.

Figure 33.13
Left: Concentric Blinds. Center: Radar Blinds. Right: Tokyo Blinds.

34

HOLLYWOOD FX

This chapter covers the Hollywood FX AE Transition plug-in. Hollywood FX, from Synergy International, offers After Effects users the highest quality and variety of 3D effects. Rather than deform mapping a 2D effect (which is how other 3D effects are designed), Hollywood FX generates true 3D objects and maps the footage to them. Outside of DVE hardware costing hundreds of thousands of dollars, nothing compares with these AE effects when you need to transition from one footage layer to another.

> **Note: Although we will look at the general way that individual Hollywood FX effects are applied in After Effects, the quantity of potential effects far exceeds our ability to detail their looks or uses in this book. I also suggest that if you want to learn more about Hollywood FX, you should access the Club Hollywood Web site, where additional volumes of Hollywood FX filters can be previewed and purchased. The URL for Club Hollywood is www.hollywoodfx.com.**
>
> **Once at the site, simply click on the Club Hollywood logo. You must register for access, so have your Hollywood FX serial number ready, and apply for membership. Make sure that you read the Hollywood FX documentation and work through the tutorials.**

Hollywood FX Controls

Hollywood FX works very differently from other AE plug-in filters. It is a real 3D application, nested into After Effects as a plug-in. Because of this, its controls remain outside the After Effects controls dialog box. The Hollywood FX Controls dialog box allows you to control only two parameters: the completion of the effect over time, and the content of additional layers (see Figure 34.1).

The real action in customizing and controlling Hollywood FX filters is found in its own control pages, accessed by clicking on the Option key in the Effects Controls dialog box.

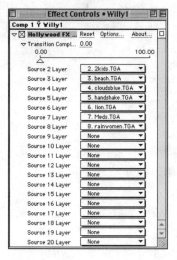

Figure 34.1
The Hollywood FX Controls dialog box displays only two parameters: the Completion Percentage slider, and room for targeting 20 layers to incorporate into the effect.

The Hollywood FX Control Environment

Once you click on Option in the Effects Controls dialog box, you enter the detailed control environment of Hollywood FX. The first window you see is the FX Group tab in the Hollywood FX-Selection dialog box (see Figure 34.2).

This is where you actually select which of the Hollywood FX effects to apply to the selected footage. This is accomplished by accessing a pull-down list of FX groups (see Figure 34.3).

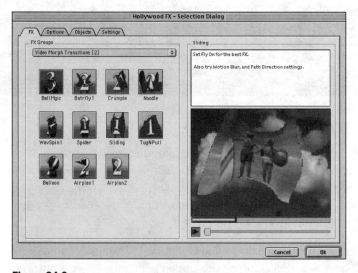

Figure 34.2
The first window displayed when you click on the Option item in the Hollywood FX Effects Controls dialog box is the FX Groups in the Hollywood FX-Selection dialog box.

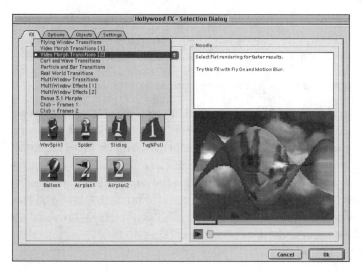

Figure 34.3
The FX Groups list.

After an FX group is visible in the leftmost window, clicking on any particular effect starts the preview rendering on the bottom right. When the preview is finished, it plays back so that you can see exactly how the effect will accommodate the footage layers.

Having selected the effect you want from one of the FX groups, it's time to move on to the effect's options by clicking on the Options tab (see Figure 34.4).

Here is where you select whether the layer will fly off or on, its rendering quality, how lights will play on its surface, and whether motion blur will be added. (Motion Blur has to be

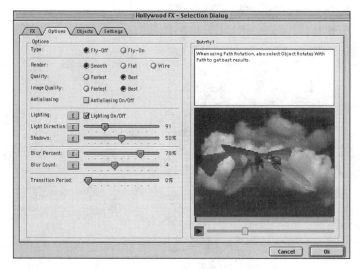

Figure 34.4
Clicking on the Options tab brings up the Options page.

switched on in the After Effects Timeline window). Every change you make starts the rendering preview again, so you can always see exactly how the rendered animation will look. Hints always appear on the upper right to suggest basic settings you may want to try.

Next, it's on to the Objects page by clicking its tab (see Figure 34.5).

Remember that, in working in Hollywood FX, you are working with 3D objects, not just flat, 2D footage planes. All targeted layers in the effects stack are 3D objects that have properties that 2D planes lack, and here is where you adjust those properties. This includes luminosity, shine, transparency, and path rotation along the XYZ coordinates. You can also add movement trails (speed lines) to the effect as it moves, making the movement seem much more realistic. At the bottom of the Objects page are control buttons for the Path Editor and Morph Envelope, items we will cover under Advanced Topics later in this chapter. Also covered under the same heading are the Editing options, accessed by clicking on the "E" buttons next to the Object Attributes sliders on this page.

The last tab, Settings, brings up the Settings page. Here, you are presented with more ways to customize your Hollywood FX work. Items here have to do with how the Selection dialog box looks and works, and how rendering of the effects will take place (see Figure 34.6).

At the top are FX Page Settings options. Below the Setting options are options for customizing how the previews will render. You should uncheck the Automatic Preview render box to prevent the preview from rendering all the time. That way, when you've made a few changes, you can click the Render button manually. You will see that Hollywood FX uses an OpenGL rendering engine on both Windows and Mac platforms. (It actually installs this engine on the Mac.) All of your preference settings can be saved as the default for future Hollywood FX sessions.

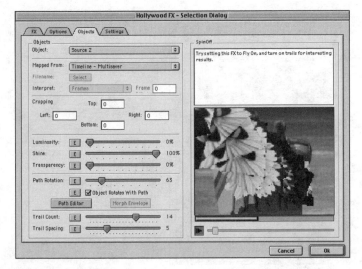

Figure 34.5
The Hollywood FX-Selection Dialog Objects page.

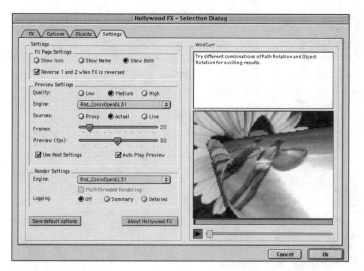

Figure 34.6
The Settings page.

Advanced Topics

At the start of your Hollywood FX interactions, you'll be satisfied to apply a canned effect from one of the FX Groups to your footage. As time passes however, you'll want to take more specific control over each effect's movements and other parameters. When that happens, you will want to learn how to maneuver in the Path Editor, the Morph Envelope Editor, and the other attributes editors located on the Hollywood FX Objects page.

Path Editor

As with any professional 3D application, Hollywood FX allows you to edit the path that the footage object moves on. You can rotate, resize, and move the path, and preview the results, all in the Path Editor (see Figure 34.7). Because you are really working in 3D, you can view the 3D environment from Camera, Perspective, Top, and Side viewpoints. Paths can be saved and loaded as well.

Morph Envelope Editor

A number of effects choices in Hollywood FX morph from one state to another. A 3D plane may roll up, or turn into another shape. For these effects, customization of the object morphing is possible in the Morph Editor. Effects that do not morph show the Morph Editor as ghosted out. The Morph Editor shows the morphing transition as a line in time. You can select any point on the line and reshape the curve, although this may reverse the effect for a number of frames in the animation. For example, an object that transforms a plane into a cube may show it morphing back and forth if you have reshaped the Morph curve to force it to do so. Working in the Morph Editor gives you very fine control over the timing of the morphing effect (see Figure 34.8).

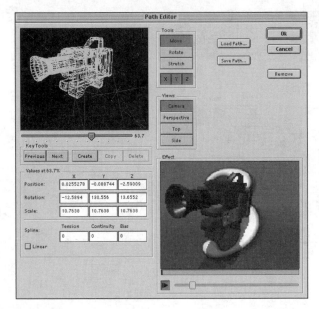

Figure 34.7
The Hollywood FX Path Editor.

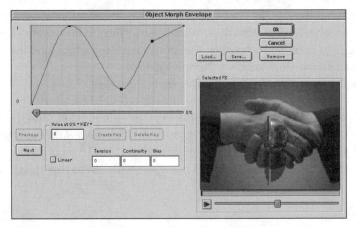

Figure 34.8
The Morph Editor dialog box.

Other Attribute Editors

All the attributes that have an "E" button next to them have Envelope Editors, so by adjusting the envelope curves, you adjust the time in which events take place. You can flash lights and reverse movements by adjusting the envelope curves (see Figure 34.9).

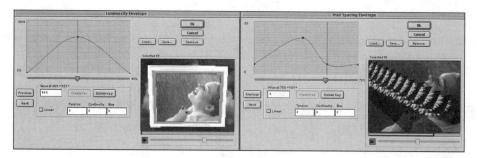

Figure 34.9
These Luminosity and Trail Spacing dialog boxes are two examples of Envelope Editors in Hollywood FX.

Highest Quality 3D Effects

Unlike other effects filters that you will run across for After Effects, the Hollywood FX collection offers a true 3D solution. Each effect can be customized, as we have seen, to produce hundreds of alternate effects with the same 3D-object result (see Figure 34.10).

Animations On The CD-ROM

Look on the CD-ROM in the Movies folder, and open the CH-34 folder. You will find six original animations that display some of the effects from this chapter.

Figure 34.10
From left to right and top to bottom, the following Hollywood FX options are displayed: Real World Transitions/Clocker, Real World Transitions/Scissor 1, Real World Transitions/48-Hours, Curl and Wave Transitions/Rock and Roll, VideoMorph Transitions 1/Pyramid, and VideoMorph Transitions 2/Airplan 1.

HFX1

This animation was created with the help of Real World Transitions/Clocker from Hollywood FX.

HFX2

This animation was created with the help of Real World Transitions/Scissor1 from Hollywood FX.

HFX3

This animation was created with the help of Real World Transitions/48-Hours from Hollywood FX.

HFX4

This animation was created with the help of Curl and Wave Transitions/Rock and Roll from Hollywood FX.

HFX5

This animation was created with the help of VideoMorph Transitions 1/Pyramid from Hollywood FX.

HFX6

This animation was created with the help of VideoMorph Transitions 2/Airplan 1 from Hollywood FX.

SpiceRack

35

The Pixelan Video SpiceRack volumes are not plug-ins for After Effects, but a large collection of over 300 gradient transitional effects. The collection is separated into five volumes: CoolWipes, Organix, Pure & Simple, WonderBands, and Standards Plus.

Having already detailed Synergy's Hollywood FX 3D effects volumes in Chapter 34, it follows suit that you would want to avail yourself of the largest collection of 2D transitional effects available for After Effects. In situations where applying a 3D transition might detract from, rather than enhance, your composition, the Pixelan volumes come in quite handy.

It's also important to stay in touch with Pixelan through their Web site: **www.pixelan.com**. Pixelan is constantly developing new volumes of gradient transition effects, and free samples are offered through their Web site.

Working With Gradient Wipes

If you are an experienced After Effects user, you will already be aware of how to assign a gradient wipe to your footage. For those of you who have never done this before, or who need a gentle reminder, the following steps are presented:

1. Select the source and target footage elements, and add them to the composition.

2. Add one of the Pixelan Gradient images to the composition.

3. Select your source footage in the timeline, and under the Effects menu, select Transition|Gradient Wipe.

4. Move the gradient frames in the timeline so they show a few frames of the source image before the gradient wipe begins, and a few frames of the target image after the wipe is complete.

5. In the Gradient Wipe Effects Controls, select your Pixelan gradient graphic from the Gradient Layer list. Set the Softness value to your requirements. (The Pixelan wipes look best with softness set to a default of 50.) Keyframe animate the Percentage Completed control. This is commonly set to 0 at the start of the gradient footage and 100 at the end. You may also want to explore inverting the wipe to achieve the opposite effect.

How A Gradient Wipe Works

A gradient wipe is a 256-level grayscale image. It is read by After Effects as a luminance (light/dark) image: 0 is black and 255 is white, and this is the order that the gradient is read in, with the black pixels of the gradient being first to replace the source footage with the target footage. You can even try your hand at painting your own gradient wipes in a bitmap painting application such as Photoshop or Painter.

Gradient Wipe Options

As an option in working with gradient wipes, you may elect not to use a specific gradient wipe image, but to use footage in the stack as the gradient wipe. You can even select the source or target footage as the gradient wipe image, creating interesting fades from the source to the target. You must explore these options to appreciate them because all compositions require a unique treatment.

SpiceRack Volumes

The SpiceRack collections come in five flavors: CoolWipes, Organix, Pure & Simple, WonderBands, and Standards Plus. Each of these flavors has a number of separate Gradient Wipe SpiceRack collections.

CoolWipes

The four CoolWipes collections include Patterns, Progressions, Transactive, and Videogami (see Figure 35.1). Taken as a whole, the CoolWipes Gradient Wipes are contemporary, in that they progress in unexpected ways to reveal the target footage.

Figure 35.1
This is the Videogami Revolva gradient wipe from the CoolWipes collection.

Organix

The four Organix collections include Kaleidos (see Figure 35.2), Live Irises, Live Wipes, and Textures. Organix Gradient Wipes appear like real-world images, drawn from the natural realm.

Figure 35.2
This is the Kaleidos Spiral 3 gradient wipe from the Organix collection.

Pure & Simple

The five Pure & Simple collections include EdgeToEdge, IrisEssentials, Splits, Thirds, and TruQuads (see Figure 35.3). The Pure & Simple Gradient Wipes are perfect when you want to tone down the fancy nature of the wipe so you won't detract from the footage. These wipes are very useful for documentary compositions.

Figure 35.3
This is the TruQuads Twisty gradient wipe from the Pure & Simple collection.

WonderBands

The three WonderBands collections include Radiant (see Figure 35.4), Uniform, and Variable. Use WonderBands as alternatives for the Pure & Simple collection.

Figure 35.4
This is the Radiant Seisma gradient wipe from the WonderBands collection.

Standards Plus

The two Standards Plus collections include Irises and Wipes (see Figure 35.5). Organix Gradient Wipes appear like real-world images, drawn from the natural realm.

Figure 35.5
This is the Wipes Inset H gradient wipe from the Standards Plus collection.

Animations On The CD-ROM

Look on the companion CD-ROM in the Movies folder, and open Chapter 35. You will find five original animations that display some of the effects from this chapter.

Spice1

To create this Pixelan gradient wipe transition:, this animation uses the CoolWipes/Videogami/Revolva selection.

Spice2

To create this Pixelan gradient wipe transition, this animation uses the Organix/Kaleidos/Spiral3 selection.

Spice3

To create this Pixelan gradient wipe transition, this animation uses the Pure & Simple/TruQuads/Twisty selection.

Spice4

To create this Pixelan gradient wipe transition, this animation uses the Standards Plus/Wipes/Inset H selection.

Spice5

To create this Pixelan gradient wipe transition, this animation uses the WonderBands/Radiant/Seisma selection.

AND QTVR MATTE

AutoMasker

This chapter explores two third-party tools: AutoMedia's AutoMasker and QTVR Matte from ElectricFish. AutoMasker is a multiplatform plug-in application that allows you to create complex masks in After Effects, and QTVR Matte is a Mac-only application that lets you use any QTVR panorama movie as footage in After Effects.

AutoMasker

MWith AutoMasker, you can create a mask on one frame of an animation and have that mask applied to succeeding animation frames. AutoMasker uses automated processes and customization tools to interpolate your mask so that your "Traveling Matte" changes shape over time to accommodate targeted footage elements. You access AutoMasker from the Effects menu, just like other plug-ins.

To apply AutoMasker to a layer, do the following:

1. Import an animation, placing it in the composition window. (AutoMasker can be used to remove very complex backgrounds from your footage, so explore its use with footage that features complex backgrounds.)

2. In the After Effects Composition, make sure that the layer is selected. From the Effects menu, choose AutoMedia/AutoMasker. The Effect Controls window is displayed, indicating the name of the layer (see Figure 36.1).

3. This is quickly followed by the display of the AutoMasker Stage window (see Figure 36.2). This window is used to create, modify, and view the mask. The AutoMasker Stage window displays the source of the frame that is currently displayed in the Composition window. The display is rendered through an Alpha channel, if one exists, and the size of the window reflects the actual dimensions of the layer's source. If the Composition window is closed, you can click on Options in the Effect Controls window to manually open the Composition window.

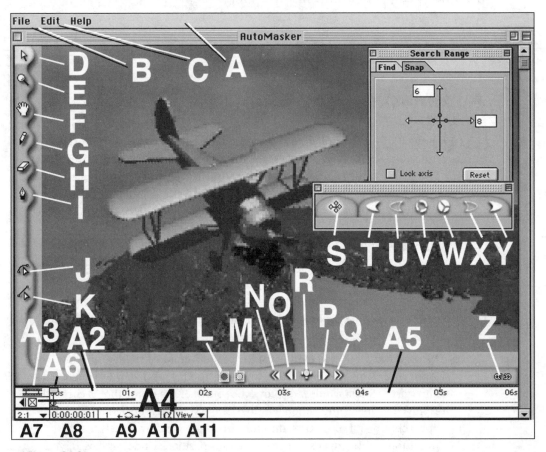

Figure 36.1
AutoMasker's Effect Controls window has controls for fine-tuning the masked areas after you create them in the AutoMasker Stage window.

Figure 36.2
The AutoMasker Stage window, with key letters indicating tool options.

Note: The size of the window reflects the actual dimensions of the source of the layer. AutoMasker uses only the source (and Alpha channel, if one exists). AutoMasker doesn't take into consideration other effects that are applied to the After Effects layer, unless the source footage has been composed in After Effects.

AutoMasker Stage Window Tools And Controls

This section describes AutoMasker's tools and controls (refer to Figure 36.2).

Menu Bar

The AutoMasker Menu bar (A) provides the usual File and Edit functions, as described in Table 36.1.

Table 36.1   The Menu Bar's File and Edit tools.

Menu	Selection
File Menu (B) Quit	Closes the AutoMasker Stage window and quits the AutoMasker plug-in application
Edit Menu (C) Undo	Lets you reverse the last 10 actions
Edit Menu (C) Cut and Copy	Cuts and copies the selected item. Becomes active only after you select an entire border or path

Toolbar

The AutoMasker toolbar provides more controls and functionality, as described in Table 36.2.

Table 36.2   The Toolbar's tools and controls.

Tool	Description
Pointer (D)	Selects/deselects segments, borders, and paths
Zoom (E)	Magnifies or reduces an area of the object
Hand (F)	Scrolls the window to reveal areas beyond its edges
Freehand Pencil (G)	Marks freehand segments
Eraser (H)	Deletes part of a freehand segment
Pen (I)	Marks Bézier segments
Convert (J)	Converts the type of segments (freehand to Bézier, or vice versa)
Straighten (K)	Straightens Bézier and freehand segments

The Selection Buttons

With the Set Selection and Load Selection buttons, you can save a set of selected segments so you can reload them later. This lets you save the currently selected segments, edit or compute different segments, and then reload the saved selection. The Set Selection button (L) saves the current selection so it can be activated later. The Load Selection button (M) activates the selection that was saved by Set Selection.

Time Control Buttons

AutoMasker's Time Control buttons are described in Table 36.3. Note that navigation between frames in AutoMasker is synchronized with After Effects (so that the navigation buttons navigate to frames within AutoMasker accordingly). The opposite is also true, so that AutoMasker always shows the current After Effects frame.

Table 36.3 AutoMasker's Time Control buttons.

Button	Description
Go to Beginning (N)	Navigates to the first frame in the layer
Step Backward One Frame (O)	Navigates to the previous frame in the layer
Step Forward One Frame (P)	Navigates to the next frame in the layer
Go to End (Q)	Navigates to the last frame in the layer

Border Machine

The Border Machine provides various options to compute borders. The buttons on the Border Machine palette are described in Table 36.4.

Table 36.4 The Border Machine's buttons.

Button	Description
Activation (R)	On/Off
Search Range (S)	Specifies the size and direction of margins to compute within
Find Previous (T)	Navigates to the preceding frame and activates Find Border on the entire path
Selective Find Previous (U)	Navigates to the preceding frame and activates Find Border for the segments that were selected in the source frame
Find Border (V)	Computes the border for the selected segments according to the data of the preceding and current frames
Snap to Image (W)	Computes the border for the selected segments according to the data of the current frame
Selective Find Next (.)	Navigates to the succeeding frame and activates Find Border for the segments that were selected in the source frame
Find Next (Y)	Navigates to the succeeding frame and activates Find Border on the entire path

Update Mode

The After Effects Composition window can be set to automatically refresh while using the AutoMasker effect. (By default, there is no automatic refresh in AutoMasker.) Whenever you navigate, the After Effects Composition window is refreshed regardless of the state of the Update mode (Z). Note that use of the Update mode may adversely affect speed.

Time Bar

The Time Bar (A2) represents the duration of the layer and enables you to navigate and set keyframes. Table 36.5 describes the Time Bar buttons.

Note: Whenever the border is created, a keyframe is created for that frame, even if the Keyframe box is unchecked. A keyframe can be deleted only when it appears in the current frame. (A marker will be situated on this frame in the Time Ruler.)

Table 36.5 The Time Bar's buttons.

Button	Description
View Button (A3)	The View button, by default, zooms out the Time Ruler to display the entire duration of the layer in seconds. The number and existence of frame marks that fit into the ruler depend on the current size of the AutoMasker stage window.
Keyframe Box (A4)	The Keyframe box enables you to select or deselect the currently displayed frame to be a keyframe. Check the box to set the frame to be a keyframe. Whenever the checkbox is checked, the keyframe indicators let you navigate between keyframes. (Deselect the Keyframe checkbox to remove the keyframe status from the keyframe.) The Keyframe navigation arrow(s) enable navigating between keyframes. Keyframes created in AutoMasker are internal and can be viewed only in the AutoMasker Time Bar.
Time Ruler (A5)	The Time Ruler represents the duration of the layer, zoomed in or out, as set by the View button. The diamond-shaped markers indicate the set keyframes. If you navigate to frames that are located beyond the length of the Time Ruler, it will scroll accordingly.
Current-Time Marker (A6)	The Current-Time Marker marks the frame you are currently viewing. Drag the marker to navigate forward or backward, and the ruler scrolls accordingly. Stop dragging to display the current frame on the screen.

View Bar

The View Bar enables you to manipulate the view while working with borders and viewing effects in the AutoMasker Stage window. Table 36.6 describes the tools available in the View Bar.

Table 36.6 The View Bar's tools.

Button	Description
Magnification Ratio Popup (A7)	Lets you select a magnification ratio.
Current-Time Indicator (A8)	Indicates the location in the layer in time units and enables navigation.
Onion Skin Mode (A9)	Displays the borders of neighboring keyframe(s), and the border of the current frame by toggling the button on/off. Use this mode to detect and eliminate jittering.
View Alpha State (A10)	When the button is pressed, the matte is displayed in black and white. When the button is released, the key returns to the current view mode. To see a grayscale Alpha affected by the current render attributes, hold down Option (Macintosh) or Alt (Windows) and click on View Alpha State.
View Popup (A11)	Provides several view modes, as well as the option to view the effect of the rendering attributes in the AutoMasker Stage window. Border display can be turned on or off in all view modes.

Using Interpolation

AutoMasker's interpolation linearly shapes the border of each frame between two specified keyframes. A keyframe contains the time at which the border changes and the shape of the border at that time. AutoMasker marks a keyframe as a diamond on the Time Ruler.

Interpolation in AutoMasker, as compared to interpolation in After Effects, provides the following added benefits:

• The interpolation mode is started automatically, once two keyframes are selected.

• Several paths can be simultaneously interpolated on the same layer.

• Anchor points can be added to keyframe borders as desired, without distorting the path.

> *Note: The following keyframe interpolation options in After Effects are not supported and do not affect interpolation in AutoMasker: Toggle/Hold Keyframe, Keyframe Interpolation, Keyframe Velocity, and Keyframe Assistance.*

Interpolating Multipaths

AutoMasker can interpolate several paths in each layer. The following applies when interpolating multipaths:

• If there is no correlation between the paths in the source and target keyframes, AutoMasker interpolates each path in the source frame with the path that has the nearest center in the target keyframe.

• Only the paths in the source keyframe that exist in the target keyframe appear in the interpolated frames in between the two.

Setting A Keyframe

In AutoMasker, the first border you mark is set as the first keyframe. If the first keyframe is not created in the first frame of a sequence, all previous frames will have the same border shape.

The following actions set a keyframe:

• Editing a border (sets a keyframe on the active frame)

• Using Find Border or Snap To Image

• Using Find Next/Previous, or Selective Find Next/Previous

• Checking the Keyframe box

Setting a keyframe when no border exists produces a full-screen Alpha and affects the neighboring frames. For faster results, place keyframes at motion extremes, then apply interpolation. If necessary, you can then make manual adjustments, or create new keyframes and interpolate again. Interpolation between keyframes can also be used to create shape animation.

Removing A Keyframe

To remove a keyframe, uncheck the Keyframe box when the desired keyframe is displayed. When a keyframe is removed, all the neighboring borders are automatically modified.

AutoMasker Tutorials

To use these tutorials, you must have AutoMasker installed in After Effects. In this section, you will learn how to:

- Start AutoMasker
- Select the layer to be masked

Basic Tutorial

To create an AutoMasked layer, take these steps:

1. Select your target layer (at frame 00) in the After Effects Time Layout window. You are now ready to activate AutoMasker.

2. From the Effects menu, choose AutoMedia|AutoMasker. The Effect Controls window and the AutoMasker Stage window will open.

3. In the AutoMasker Stage window, the source image of the layer at frame 00 is centered. The size of the window reflects the actual dimensions of the layer's source.

Now, we'll:

- Mark the segments that create the path
- Close the path
- Compute the marked path
- Edit the marked path
- Navigate and compute the path
- Interpolate frames
- Examine the mask
- Apply rendering attributes

Marking Path Segments

Marking the segments that designate the path of the masked object is the most important stage of your work. The accuracy of the path will determine the quality of the mask.

You'll mark Bézier segments by using the Pen tool, and freehand segments by using the Freehand Pen tool.

> Note: Use the Pen tool when the image outline is smooth and not very detailed. Use the Freehand Pen tool when the outline is detailed and distinct.

You can use these tools in any combination to accurately define the shape of the masked object per segment. Switching between the tools will let you mark segments that suit the curvature of the image. Before you start to mark the path, use the Zoom tool to magnify or reduce an area of the image. As you mark the path, AutoMasker scrolls the image to reveal the areas that are located beyond the edge of the window.

> *Note: Double-click on the tool to change the default color of segments (red for freehand segments, green for Bézier) and anchor points (pink for all). When you mark a picture, it is always recommended that you place your anchor points in accordance with the object you're masking. In Bézier segments, place the anchor points at the corners or at the peak of a distinct curvature. In freehand segments, place the points where the overall direction changes.*

Mark Bézier Segments

To mark Bézier segments:

1. From the toolbar, click on the Pen tool.

2. Position the cursor on the image, and the cursor appears.

3. Click on the bottom left side of the giraffe's neck. An anchor point appears on screen.

4. Click on the location for the next anchor point. Another anchor point appears. A straight Bézier segment connects the two.

5. Follow Steps 2 through 4 to create a straight line that connects this anchor point to the next.

6. To create a curved line, click on the desired location of the next anchor point and hold down the mouse button. Drag the mouse until the curve is shaped to your satisfaction. Bézier handles extend from this anchor point and follow your movements.

7. Release the mouse. A curved Bézier segment connects the two anchor points.

8. Follow Steps 6 and 7 to create a curved line that will connect this anchor point to the next.

Marking Freehand Segments

To mark the freehand segments, take the following steps:

1. From the toolbar, click on the Freehand Pen tool.

2. Position the cursor on the image. The cursor appears.

3. Draw as you would with a pencil on paper. Release the mouse when you wish to mark the next anchor point. The anchor points confine the segment and enable you to edit it.

Completing The Path

To complete the path, do the following:

1. Press G on the keyboard to switch to the Pen tool, and mark the initial Bézier segments.

2. Press Y to switch to the Freehand Pen tool, and mark the freehand segments.

3. Press G again to switch back to the Pen tool, and mark any additional Bézier segments.

Closing The Path

You should close the created path before you compute it; otherwise, it will be closed automatically by the computation function. To close the path, double-click on the location for the last anchor point. An anchor point appears there, and a Bézier segment connects this point to the first anchor point of the path. The path is now closed and ready to be computed.

> **A WORD ON PATHS**
>
> Paths are only shown in the After Effects Composition window when they are closed. After you have closed the path, you are now ready to view the matte.

Viewing The Matte

At this stage, you may want to evaluate the matte in its true context. Click on the View icon to view the matte from the AutoMasker Stage window. The After Effects Composition window is refreshed to show the masked object as it is masked in the AutoMasker Stage window. After you view the matte, you are now ready to compute the path.

Computing The Path

After the masked object is enclosed within a closed path, you can perform a computation that will make the selected segments of the path cling to the outlines of the masked object.

1. To select the path to be computed from the toolbar, click on the Pointer tool.

2. To select the entire path, hold down Option (Mac) or Alt (Windows) and click anywhere on the path. The lines of the selected segments become dashed, and their anchor points become solid.

3. To deselect any path, hold down Shift and click on the desired segments.

4. The lines of the deselected segments become solid, and their anchor points become unfilled.

Snapping The Path To The Image

To snap the path to the image, take these steps:

1. Click to open the Border Machine palette.

2. From the Border Machine palette, click on the Snap To Image icon. AutoMasker calculates the selected segments of the path according to the data of the current frame and adjusts them around the masked object.

> *Note: After calculation, the segments are deselected. Using Snap To Image is recommended when there is a drastic change between the current frame and the last computed frame.*

After you compute the path, you are ready to edit the path where needed.

Editing The Path

After you examine the results for the computation of the path for this frame, you can make corrections, as required.

Splitting A Segment

You can split a segment to adjust a Bézier segment to better fit the outline of the object or to redefine the boundaries of a freehand segment, as follows:

1. Position the cursor on the selected segment.

2. Click the cursor on the segment. An anchor point is added to the underlying segment, splitting it into two segments that are now selected.

Adjusting A Segment

If the marked segment does not accurately match the object being masked, it can be adjusted to the segment accordingly. To adjust a segment:

1. Click on any part of the segment and drag (inward or outward). The segment becomes selected. The anchor points that limit the segment you've just dragged remain stationary, and the segment adjusts.

2. Release the mouse button when you have adjusted the segment as required.

3. Before continuing to the next task, undo your changes. A segment can be dragged from any part of it. The place you click becomes the gravity point for the segment's new shape.

Redrawing A Freehand Segment

To redraw a freehand segment, take these steps:

1. From the toolbar, select the Freehand Pen tool.

2. Place the cursor so it touches the segment at the desired point.

3. Click and hold the mouse button to draw the curved part. Drawing beyond an anchor point starts to mark a new path.

4. Release the mouse button when the cursor touches the segment at the desired point. AutoMasker automatically removes the outer segment and adjusts the edited segment accordingly.

> **Note: You can use the eraser to erase parts of a freehand segment.**

The procedure for reshaping a Bézier segment in AutoMasker is similar to that in After Effects. After you have edited the path, you are ready to navigate to the next frame.

Navigating To The Next Frame

Once you are satisfied with the path in the current frame, you can proceed to the next frame. To step forward one frame, take these steps:

1. Advance to frame 01, and it appears with the path of frame 00.

2. Edit the path to match the image. To edit a single segment, you can select it, drag it toward the object, and click on the Border Machine palette to make it snap to the object.

3. Press the Q key to switch to the Pointer tool, and click anywhere on the image, but not on the path, to deselect it.

Using Find Next

To use Find Next, take the following steps:

1. Press Shift and select the desired segments.

2. From the Border Machine palette, click on and edit the border, if required.

3. From the Border Machine palette, advance to frame 02. It appears with the path of frame 01. The segments that were computed in frame 01 are momentarily selected and then computed; the path is then redisplayed, and the computed segments are adjusted to fit the boundaries of the image. You can now edit the border, if required.

4. From the Border Machine palette, advance to frame 03. It appears with the path of frame 02. All the segments of the path in frame 02 are momentarily selected and then computed; the path is redisplayed, and all the segments to the boundaries of the image are adjusted. Repeat this process for all the frames needed.

Interpolate Frames

AutoMasker interpolates frames that are located between keyframes. Interpolation requires that you:

- Start at a certain keyframe.

- Navigate to a nonconsecutive frame and modify its border. (This sets it to be a keyframe.)

- Navigate back to see an interpolated frame that lies between the two keyframes.

Interpolation between keyframes is not just a mapping tool, it can also be used for creating shape animation.

To Start At A Keyframe

Start at the current frame. Performing Find Next sets any frame to be a keyframe.

To Navigate To A Nonconsecutive Frame

To navigate to a nonconsecutive frame, take these steps:

1. Type in the frame number you want to navigate to. The frame is displayed. (At this stage, the frame is not a keyframe.)

2. Select the desired segments and edit the border from the Border Machine palette. Click on Done. The frame is now a keyframe.

To Navigate Backward To See An Interpolated Frame

To navigate backward to see an interpolated frame, follow these steps:

1. Drag backward until the required frame is displayed.

2. The border of this frame is an interpolation of the borders of the frames on either side of it.

3. Edit the path as required. The frame now becomes a keyframe. After you have interpolated frames, you are ready to examine the mask.

Examining The Mask

AutoMasker provides several view modes that enable you to examine the mask: Source, Alpha, Stencil, Invert, and Border. By default, Border is turned on, so the path is shown regardless of the activated mode.

Viewing In Stencil Mode

The Stencil view mode displays the image over a tinted background, at a specific level of opacity. To apply Stencil view mode:

1. From the View pop-up menu, select Stencil. The display in the AutoMasker stage window is refreshed. (The default color is red, with an opacity value of 50 percent.)

2. Edit the border to match the image. For information on how to change the color and opacity, see the AutoMasker User's Guide.

View In After Effects

Examine the matte in the After Effects Composition window. After you have examined the mask, you are ready to apply rendering attributes.

Applying Rendering Attributes

The created matte may be rendered using various attributes. The rendering attributes are set in the Effect Controls window (refer to Figure 36.1).

Setting The Offset Value

In some cases (for example, to include part of the background), you may want to expand the boundaries of the matte. To set the offset value:

1. Navigate to frame 00.

2. Set the Offset Value to 5.

3. View the matte in the After Effects Composition window.

4. Before continuing, activate Undo to reset the offset value.

Setting The Feather Value

In some cases (for example, if you want the masked object to merge into the background), you may want to create a soft edge for the matte. To set the Feather Value:

1. Set the Feather Value to 20.

2. View the matte in the After Effects Composition window. The feathering extends 10 pixels on the inner part of the edge and 10 pixels on the outer part of the edge. After you have applied rendering attributes, you are ready to create the final movie.

Creating The Final Movie

After you have masked the object, you can create a QuickTime movie. To create the final movie:

1. In After Effects, set the end of the work range to the desired frame.

2. Test render the movie with the following parameters:

   - Render Settings—Best Settings
   - Output Module—QuickTime
   - RGB—Millions Of Colors

3. Play the QuickTime movie back and examine the masked areas you created with AutoMasker. Save, or adjust and render as necessary.

Using Additional AutoMasker Attributes

You can fine-tune your work with other AutoMasker tools and options.

Setting A Computation Search Range

When you activate a computation, the border is computed within margins that are six pixels high and eight pixels wide (in both directions). In some cases, the size of these computation margins may need to be changed. For example, you may want to increase the range if the marked path is too far from the object, or decrease the range if the path is close to the object (to save computation time). To set the computation search range:

1. Navigate to the desired frame.

2. Select the segments to be computed.

3. Click to open the Border Machine palette. The Search Range palette is displayed with the Find tab open.

4. Enter 15 on the horizontal axis and 20 on the vertical axis.

5. Click on the Border Machine palette. The border now clings to the image. Placing the border close to the object and using a small search range provides the best and quickest results. After you have computed the search range, you are ready to evaluate the mask.

Using Onion Skin Mode

To efficiently eliminate jittering and motion blur, you can display the borders of neighboring keyframes in addition to the border of the current frame. This option lets you fine-tune the location of the current border in relation to the neighboring keyframes and to evaluate the degree of change.

To Turn The Onion Skin Mode On, from the View bar, click on the closed-eye icon or press the K key. The View bar will be displayed, as well as the borders of the current frame and the frames on either side of the selected frame. Onion Skin borders may not be edited.

To Turn The Onion Skin Mode Off

Click on the open-eye icon or press the K key. The borders of the preceding/succeeding keyframes are removed from the display. The Onion Skin mode is also useful while performing complicated marking tasks and not just when evaluating results. The Onion Skin palette enables you to set the number of preceding/succeeding keyframes and their color(s).

Tips From AutoMedia On Using AutoMasker Effectively

The following tips may make your use of AutoMasker all the more enjoyable and efficient.

When To Select Either The Freehand Tool Or The Pen Tool

Pen segments create a very smooth border, so you should use them in areas where you need smooth lines. Freehand segments create a border that exactly matches the outlines of the object. Use freehand segments for areas with complex or irregular shapes.

Find Border And Snap To Image

For a new segment, I recommend that you use Snap To Image. The segment is computed according to the data in the current frame. If a keyframe is several frames apart from the next/previous keyframe, use Snap To Image. Use Find Border when you are tracking segments that were computed in preceding frames. The segments are computed according to data from the current frame, as well as to data from the preceding frame. This computation method enables greater accuracy when tracking moving objects on complex backgrounds.

Converting A Segment

If the shape of the object changed so that the object now has finer details, convert the segments from Bézier to freehand. If there is less detail than before, convert freehand segments to Bézier.

Fixing A Computation-Move Error

If computation moved a selected anchor point to the wrong location, take these steps:

1. Use Undo to revert to the original condition.

2. Move the anchor point to its appropriate location.

3. Select one of the segments that extends from the anchor point and compute that segment.

4. Select the other segment that extends from the anchor point and compute it. Computing the segments, one at a time, does not affect the anchor point.

Placement Of The Anchor Points When Drawing A Path

It is recommended to place anchor points in locations that reflect shape change. In Bézier segments, place anchor points at the corners or at the peak of a distinct curvature. In freehand segments, place anchor points wherever the overall direction changes. Place as many anchor points as you need. Later, you may add/remove anchor points, as needed.

When Should Several Paths Be Drawn On One Object?

When the segments of an object intersect, it is recommended that you split the border into several paths, with each enclosing a part of the object with different shape behavior.

Transferring An AutoMasker Mask Between Layers

This is a simple procedure. All you need to do is duplicate the layer and replace the source.

For information on the purchase of AutoMasker or more information, email **support@automedi.com**.

QTVR Matte

QTVR Matte is a Mac-only application that lets you use any QTVR panorama movie as footage in After Effects. A QTVR panorama is normally viewed as an interactive file that can be rotated a full 360 degrees by simple mouse movements. QTVR movies are made with Apple's QTVR authoring software. Inquire at **www.apple.com** for information. The manipulations you perform with QTVR Matte's controls can create keyframes for an animation. The resulting keyframed animation can then be saved out as a standard movie file from After Effects (see Figure 36.3).

Figure 36.3
From left to right: three views of a QTVR movie with different tilts and rotations.

The following controls allow you to adjust the parameters of the QTVR Matte filter:

- *Pan*—This is a standard After Effects rotation controller. Using it, you can view the QTVR file from any horizontal angle. If you keyframe-animate the rotation values, the QTVR scene will rotate, just as if you were standing in the middle of the scene and spinning around.

- *Tilt*—This controller adjusts the vertical angle of view (from –90 to 90 degrees). Positive values move the camera up, and negative values make it point downward.

- *FOV* (Field of View)—You can use this controller as a zooming effect (from 0 to 180). The higher the value, the more of the view is displayed in the Composition window. At values of 30 and lower, the camera focuses on less of the image content, so it appears to be zooming in.

- *Correction*—You may select None, Some, or Full. (Full is the default.) This applies a correction to the distortions inherent in QTVR files.

- *Color Quality*—Select from Min, Norm, or Max. There is little reason not to select Max color quality all the time.

For more information about QTVR Matte, contact ElectricFish at **slithy@electricfish.com**.

AND CYCLONIST

CINELOOK, CINEMOTION,

37

This chapter examines three plug-in filters from DigiEffects that transform your footage to achieve the look of different media: CineLook, CineMotion, and Cyclonist. CineLook creates effects that resemble one of a selection of film stock looks, from 8mm and 16mm to more-customized effects. CineMotion is a collection of 10 diverse plug-ins that add a variety of effects to your footage. Cyclonist is a complete particle-painting system that allows you to create painterly effects that either replace or add particle strokes over the footage.

CineLook

The CineLook collection is made up of two separate plug-ins: CineLook and Film Damage. CineLook allows you to select from a list of industry-standard film formats and apply one to your footage. This is especially useful when you are creating an After Effects sequence that will be inserted into a larger sequence created in a film format (see Figure 37.1).

Some possible uses for the CineLook effect are:

- Use the Old Movie filter to give your footage the look of vintage Hollywood movies. This works great when you need to historically simulate the 1920s or 30s.

- Use the Day For Night preset to transform footage into a dark-blue duotone. This is particularly effective when you want to use footage as a background layer for bright text.

The following controls allow you to adjust the parameters of the CineLook filter:

- *Presets*—You'll start most of your CineLook explorations in this list of dozens of options. You can choose from dozens of Ektachrome, Fujifilm, and Agfa film formats, as well as a host of special effects. Preview each one so that you are familiar with what they do.

Figure 37.1
Three CineLook effects, from left to right: Funky, Old Movie, and Sunset.

- *Stockmatch*—These controls are for professional use only. If you have little or no experience with matching the exact components of industry-standard stock samples, stay with one of the preset options. If you do have the experience, the Stockmatch controls allow you to adjust for grain, smoothness, and defocus parameters to get a match a close as possible to the external footage you will be patching into.

- *Chromamatch*—These controls are also for professional use only, and you'll mostly likely stay with one of the preset options. (The Chromamatch controls allow a professional to adjust for RGB gamma and seven degrees of RGB and white channel mixes, as well as hue, brightness, and saturation modifications.)

- *Timematch*—These controls are also for professional use only. If you have little or no experience with matching the exact components of industry-standard stock samples, stay with one of the preset options. If you do have that experience, the Timematch controls allow you to adjust timing anomalies in the footage, as well as how much the overall footage effect will blend with the original (0 to 100).

Film Damage

The Film Damage effects are well titled: it is a collection of looks that you can apply to your pristine footage to damage or dirty it up in various ways (see Figure 37.2).

The following list shows some possible uses for the Film Damage effect:

- Use the Garbage Matte preset to dirty up the footage, and increase the number of scratches to 350 to emphasize the poor condition of the content.

- Use the Rust preset to give your footage an aged sepia-tone look.

The following controls allow you to adjust the parameters of the Film Damage filter:

- *Presets*—You'll start most of your Film Damage explorations in this list of dozens of options. Besides dozens of 8mm and 16mm damaged film formats, there is a list of special effects as well. Preview each one so that you are familiar with what they do.

- *Grain*—You can control the Grain Amount (0 to 1,000) and the Smoothness (0 to 1,000) to add specks of grain to your footage. Increasing the grain amount to 1,000 gives the footage a very stippled look; it tends to obliterate the content, too.

Figure 37.2
Three different Film Damage effects applied from left to right: Moldy, Junk On Negative, and Garbage Matte (with number of scratches set to 350).

- *Film Response*—These controls alter a number of different parameters. Iris Level (-5,000 to 5,000) adjusts the overall darkness and brightness of the footage. Pushing the Iris Level to 5,000 removes the footage content, so all you see are the damaging anomalies. Checking the Black And White box removes color information from the footage. When Black And White is checked, you can select which channel will be used as the source for the footage (red, green, blue, or luminance).

- *Flicker*—Want to really make the audience believe that the footage is damaged? Then add flickering to the movement. You can control the Amount (–5,000 to 5,000), Speed (0 to 5,000), and Variation (0 to 5,000). Using values larger than 500 in either the negative or positive direction creates so much flicker that the footage content can become indecipherable.

- *Vertical Scratches*—You can control the Number (0 to 30,000), Thickness (1 to 1,000), Speed (0 to 30,000), Vibration (0 to 30,000), Opacity (0 to 255), and Length (0 to 30,000) of Vertical Scratches applied to the footage, as well as the number of white scratches (0 to 30,000).

- *Micro Scratches*—Micro Scratches are more subtle than vertical scratches, and are better used to fine-tune the mix. You can control their number (0 to 30,000), size (0 to 10,000), and opacity (0 to 255), as well as the number of white Micro Scratches (0 to 30,000).

- *Hair*—You know how irritating it is to a movie audience to wait for the projectionist to remove a floating piece of hair from the lens. Now you can irritate your audience in the same way, by adding hair to the footage. You can control the number of black and/or white hairs (0 to 30,000), Size (0 to 10,000), and Opacity (0 to 255).

- *Trapped Hair*—Trapped Hair is even more annoying, because it stays put and doesn't move with the footage. You control the Size (0 to 10,000) and Opacity (0 to 255), as well as what part of the composition the trapped hair remains on.

- *Dust*—Dust is composed of specks of dirt, so it can be used as an image effect to pixelate the footage as well as an aspect of the footage age or condition. You control the Amount of black and/or white dust (0 to 30,000) and the Opacity (0 to 255).

- *Dirt*—Dirt comes in clumpy globs with semitransparent edges. You control the Amount of black and/or white dust (0 to 30,000) and the Opacity (0 to 255).

- *Duotone*—The footage that is damaged has a duotone look, usually sepia. To compose the duotone, you can select any colors you like (with the eyedropper or from the system palette).

- *Stains*—Stains are usually larger than dirt clumps, although they are commonly more transparent. You can control their hue to emulate coffee or more unique substances, and also their Number (0 to 30,000), Size (0 to 30,000), and Opacity (0 to 255).

- *Uneven Focus*—Uneven focus isn't so much a sign of damage or age, as it is of a bad camera operator. You control the Defocus Amount (0 to 1,000) and the Probability that it will occur (0 to 255).

- *Frame Jitter*—When the sprockets on a film projector get worn, the film skips whole or partial frames. This is known as frame jitter, and you can emulate it with this filter.

CineMotion

The CineMotion collection is composed of 10 different filters, each of which is used to alter one or more footage components to give you diverse media looks. The list includes Adaptive Noise, Banding Reducer, Film Motion, Grain Reducer, Interlace Aliasing Reducer, LetterBox, Selective HSB Noise, Selective HSB Posterize, Selective RGB Noise, and Selective RGB Posterize. You can think of all these filters as extended utilities for the DigiEffects CineLook options, which is why they are both in this chapter (see Figure 37.3).

Figure 37.3
Selective HSB Posterize presets from left to right: 2 Levels, 4 Levels, and 7 Bright Levels.

Adaptive Noise

 This filter creates noise that occurs only in smooth areas of the footage. You control the area size (0 to 100), and whether the noise is monochrome based on the red channel. You also control the Variance (0 to 255) and Noise Amount (0 to 255) for each of the RGBA channels.

Use Adaptive Noise to add some pixelated content to large single-color areas of the footage, or to match the footage to the film it is to be placed in.

Banding Reducer

 This effect smoothes out the color banding that results when certain effects are applied to footage. This irritating phenomenon occurs especially when you animate color glows around footage elements. Using this filter smoothes the banded boundaries.

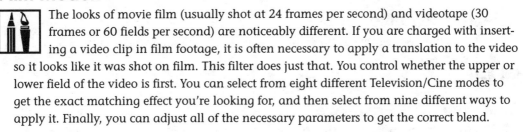

You control the Area Size (0 to 100), Variance Threshold (0 to 255), Replace Threshold (0 to 255), and the Blend With The Original (0 to 255).

Use this filter whenever you apply an effect that results in color-banding anomalies.

Film Motion

The looks of movie film (usually shot at 24 frames per second) and videotape (30 frames or 60 fields per second) are noticeably different. If you are charged with inserting a video clip in film footage, it is often necessary to apply a translation to the video so it looks like it was shot on film. This filter does just that. You control whether the upper or lower field of the video is first. You can select from eight different Television/Cine modes to get the exact matching effect you're looking for, and then select from nine different ways to apply it. Finally, you can adjust all of the necessary parameters to get the correct blend.

This is another one of those filters that is best left alone unless you have a solid amount of professional knowledge concerning film format matching.

Grain Reducer

Reducing the grain in footage blurs the image content. This filter gives you 10 different ways to reduce footage graininess.

This is another of those filters that is best left alone unless you have professional experience with matching film formats. You can, however, also use this filter as a blur effect.

Interlace Aliasing Reducer

This filter reduces the flicker often caused by interlaced video by applying a vertical blur to the footage. You control the distance (amount of the blur) in a range from 0 to 255, as well as how much the affected footage blends with the source footage (0 to 255).

You can also use this filter to create animated vertical blur effects on any footage.

LetterBox

To simulate wide-screen film formats on a video screen, the footage has to be "letterboxed"—that is, reduced vertically so that the entire horizontal content can be viewed. It's either that, or clipping the horizontal content. Using the LetterBox filter, you can create the following film-style aspect ratios: 16mm Aspect, 16mm Red, 35mm Panavision, and 35mm Wide. You can also adjust the vertical-inset dimension (0 to 4,000) to tweak the final ratio.

Selective HSB Noise

This filter allows you to add selective noise to any or all of the hue, saturation, brightness, or Alpha channels. This is done through any one of three modes. Adding noise to HSB channels allows you to modify each of the channels independently to create subtle alterations in footage color, while adding RGB or monochrome noise acts globally on the footage.

Selective HSB Posterize

Posterization reduces the apparent number of hues in an image. With this filter, you can apply posterization separately or in any combination to the hue, saturation, brightness, and Alpha channels. You can also use a list of presets as starting points, and then customize by altering the parameters for each channel.

Selective RGB Noise

This filter is the same as the HSB Noise filter, except that it works on the RGBA channels.

Selective RGB Posterize

This filter is the same as the HSB Posterize filter, except that it works on RGBA channels.

Cyclonist

Cyclonist is a DigiEffects filter factory that allows you to combine the attributes of a particle system with animated paint effects to create an infinite array of animated organics and other looks. It is by far the most complex DigiEffects plug-in and requires the most time to master (see Figure 37.4).

The following are some possible uses for the Cyclonist effect:

- Create animated backgrounds that resemble abstract paintings.
- Use a different source layer to control the way the particles animate.

The following controls allow you to adjust the parameters of the Cyclonist filter:

- *Presets*—Select from the presets list, or bring up the presets thumbnails to select a stroke type (see Figure 37.5).

Figure 37.4
Cyclonist effects, from left to right: Conch Shell preset with Constant Movement, Swirled Stroke with Random Movement, and the Clocks preset.

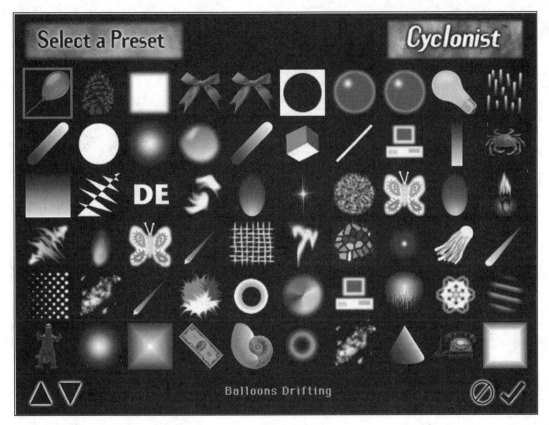

Figure 37.5
The presets thumbnail dialog box.

- *Stroke*—Select from the presets list, or bring up the stroke thumbnails to select a stroke type. You can also select any of your own images. It is automatically reduced to fit the Composition window and Cyclonist parameters (see Figure 37.6).

- *Coating*—The Coating parameters influence how the strokes interact with each other and how they composite in the composition. They can be placed as either constrained or moving. Moving creates random locations and pays attention to Perturb parameters. Constrained creates a stationary grid that moves in place. Movement By allows you to assign a layer in the stack to control the movement.

- *Chroma*—Chroma parameters control the color of each stroke for each particle. Perturb sliders control the degree of variation for Hue, Saturation, and Brightness. The source layer can be any layer in the stack or a color layer, and it controls the place the color is taken from. Separate translucency controls alter the opacity. Using Halftone Interaction mode, the stroke becomes black-and-white variations. Selecting any one of the 12 Modify modes alters the way the sampled values are adjusted for all of the other components. You should explore these modes to get an idea of how the footage responds.

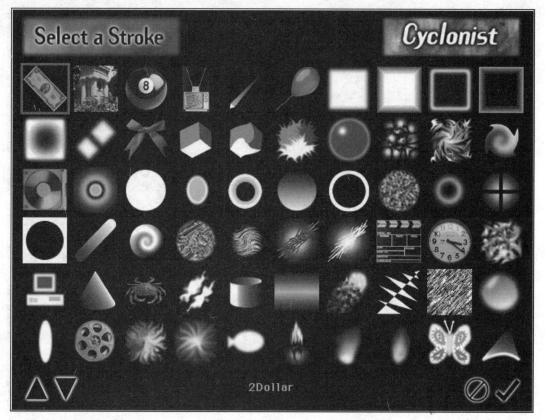

Figure 37.6
The stroke thumbnail dialog box.

- *Magnitude*—These parameters control the size of the stroke image for each particle. Minimum and Maximum control the size of the stroke in pixels. Choose any layer in the stack for source data, and use the Perturb sliders to add random variations.

- *Direction*—This controls the direction of the stroke for each particle. Again, Minimum and Maximum control the size of the stroke in pixels. Any layer in the stack can be sampled as the source, and the Perturb sliders add random variations.

- *Translucency*—This option allows you to alter the opacity of each stroke. The Perturb sliders add random variations.

- *Perturb*—The Perturb parameters are wave based and add random variance to the animation. Phase is randomly generated for each particle, so it looks like they all have independent movement. Higher amplitudes create larger variation, whereas higher frequencies create faster variations.

An Animated Cubist Painting

The following steps will walk you through creating a cubist abstract painting that you can later use as a background:

1. Select the CD Stroke from either the Stroke list or the thumbnail dialog.

2. Set Animated Stroke to None, and Animated Modification Layer to Solid.

3. Set the following Coating parameters: Stroke Interaction to Maximum Stroke, Ignore Alpha, and Moving Stroke Placement. Moving Number of Strokes set to 95. Set Movement to Hue and Source Layer to None. Leave all other settings at their defaults.

4. Under Chroma, set the following parameters: Source Layer to None, and Source Solid Color to Bright Red. Leave all other settings at their default.

5. Under Magnitude, set the following parameters: Magnitude by Luminosity, and Source Layer None. Minimum 85, Maximum 100, Perturb Frequency 222, and Perturb Amplitude 222.

6. Under Direction, set the following parameters: Direction by Random and Source Layer to None. Place the centroid at the top center of the footage, causing it to move upward during an animation. Set Minimum Rotation to –5 degrees, and Maximum Rotation to 6X+180 degrees. Leave all other settings at their default positions.

7. Under the Translucency option, use the following parameters: Translucency by Hue and Source Layer to None. Set both Minimum and Maximum to 255. Leave the other settings at their default positions.

8. Render and save to disk.

See the Cubist1 movie on the companion CD-ROM (see Figure 37.7).

Figure 37.7
Frames from the Cubist1 Movie, created with DigiEffects' Cyclonist.

DELERIUM

Delerium, from DigiEffects, is a collection of filters with effects you won't find in any other package. The most startling is TILT, a plug-in filter previously distributed by Cognicon. TILT allows Mac users of After Effects to incorporate QuickDraw 3D objects in their After Effects compositions.

This chapter covers the following DigiEffects Delerium filters: Fire, Gradients, Remap Color, Retinal Bloom, Snowstorm, Solarize, Specular Lighting, Supernova, Turbulent Noise, Visual Harmonizer, WarpFlow, and TILT. TILT is unique, so it has been removed from the alphabetical listing of the other filters to stand on its own at the end of this chapter.

Fire

The Fire filter adds flames to your selected layer and is a true particle effect (see Figure 38.1).

Some possible uses for the Fire filter are:

- Add flames to a color layer. Fade it out slowly to reveal a text block.

- Use the Fire effect on the inside of a masked text block to give the text a greater visual punch.

Figure 38.1
Examples of the Delerium Fire filter.

The following controls allow you to adjust the parameters of the Fire filter:

- *Presets*—Select from among the preset Fire parameters in the list.

- *Preroll Frames*—This value (ranging from 0 to 32,000) tells the effect how many frames have already passed before it begins on your footage. The default is 0, which means that the fire effect will be applied to your first frame.

- *Fire Generate*—This setting (ranging from 0 to 32,000) generates the strength of fire that is set.

- *Min/Max Size*—This value (ranging from 0 to 255) alters the size of the flames.

- *Min/Max Opacity*—This control alters the opacity of the flames, with 0 being transparent and 255 fully opaque.

- *Min/Max Lilt Amount*—This control (ranging from 0 to 1,000) sets the amount fo Lilt.

- *Min/Max Lilt Frequency*— These values (ranging from 0 to 1,000) determine the frequency of the Lilt over time.

- *Gravity*—Gravity acts to keep the flames from leaping too high. Keep this setting at 0 if you want the flames to leap the highest, and 1,000 to keep the flames from leaping at all.

- *Wind Horiz/Vert*—The settings for this control range from –100 to 100. Negative Horizontal Wind values push the flames left, and positive Horizontal Wind values push the flames right. Similarly, negative Vertical Wind values push the flames down, and positive Vertical Wind values push them up.

- *Gust Probability*—Set the probability (from 0 to 100) that gusts of wind will occur.

- *Gust Max Duration*—Set how long the gust will affect the flames with a value between 0 and 1,000.

- *Gust Max Speed*—Set the speed of the gust, again with a value between 0 and 1,000.

- *Fall on Layer*—Select the layer in the stack that will receive the fire effect.

- *Ground Layer*—The Ground layer sets the base layer for the flames.

- *Random Seed*—This control adds a random element to the fire's propagation, which changes the overall pattern of the fire. Settings range from 0 to 32,000.

- *Blend With Original*—At 0, the full effect of the gradient will be seen. As the values increase, the gradient becomes more transparent, with total transparency at the maximum value of 255.

Gradients

The Gradients filter allows you to create *ramps* (blended gradations from light to dark) across the footage or selected area. You can use gradients to alter the density of the footage at specific points by applying it to the Alpha channel of the footage. Doing this allows a layer under the source layer to show through where the gradient is dark and be blocked where it is light (see Figure 38.2).

Figure 38.2
Left to right: Square Gradient with Triangular Repeat Mode, Radial Gradient with Sawtooth Repeat and close centroid placement, and Cone One-way Gradient with Triangular Repeat.

Following are some possible uses for the Gradients filter:

- Create gradient Alpha layers as a way of adding transparent effects to source footage.
- Create gradient text blocks to emulate chrome and other metallic finishes.

The following controls allow you to adjust the parameters of the Gradients filter:

- *Presets*—Select from the preset gradients in the list.
- *Gradient Type*—Select from among the following types: Linear, Linear Mirrored, Square, Radial, Cone One-way, and Cone Matchup. You have more options here for creating gradients than with any other gradient filter plug-in.
- *Pixel Mode*—This control lets you determine the channel that the gradient will be rendered to. Select from among the following modes: RGB, Red Only, Green Only, Blue Only, or Alpha.
- *Color Mode*—The listed choices indicate the order of the gradient from light to dark. It includes RGB Start To End, RGB End To Start, HSB Clockwise, and HSB Counter-Clockwise.
- *Repeat Mode*—Select from the listed Repeat modes to create different gradient patterns. The selections are None, Triangular, and Sawtooth.
- *Blend With Original*—At 0, the full effect of the gradient will be seen. As the values increase, the gradient becomes more transparent, with total transparency at the maximum value of 255.
- *Start Point/End Point*—Place the centroids anywhere on the footage to determine the way that the gradient pattern is formed.
- *Start Color/End Color*—Use either the system palette of the eyedropper to select the initial color range.
- *Bias*—A value of 0 displays the default pattern, while pushing the value higher tends to thin the pattern out (if it repeats). At settings of 95 to 98 (the maximum is 100), repeated patterns start to develop moiré interference.

- *Multi-Gradient*—You can choose up to 15 additional gradient patterns to superimpose over the initial gradient. Each new gradient can have its own color, gradation mode, and mix setting. You can use any number of them—from just one to all 15—to produce colorful variants and a more complex, overall gradient. No guidance is offered, so you have to explore these options to get a feel for their infinite interactions and combination of effects.

Remap Color

Due to the inclusion of the Multi-Gradient option, the Remap Color filter creates some of the most startling posterized effects of any plug-in filter (see Figure 38.3). Following are some possible uses for the Remap Color filter:

- Create rich posterized footage by using all of the Multi-gradient options in the Remap Color mix.

- Keyframe animate the Bias values from 0 to 255 to alter the hues.

The following controls allow you to adjust the parameters of the Remap Color filter:

- *Presets*—Select from a list of preset values of the Remap Color filter.

- *Preview On*—View the Color Replace gradient without mixing in the source layer.

- *Pixel Mode*—To determine the channel that the gradient will be rendered to, select one of the following modes: RGB, Red Only, Green Only, Blue Only, or Alpha.

- *Color Mode*—The listed choices indicate the order of the gradient from light to dark: RGB Start To End, RGB End To Start, HSB Clockwise, and HSB Counter-Clockwise.

- *Start Color/End Color*—Use either the system palette or the eyedropper to select the initial color range.

- *Bias*—The minimum value of 0 leans toward the start color, while the maximum setting of 100 leans toward the end color.

- *Repeat Mode*—Select from the listed Repeat modes to create different gradient patterns. The selections are None, Triangular, and Sawtooth.

- *Multi-Gradient*—You can choose up to 15 additional gradient patterns to superimpose over the initial gradient. Each new gradient can have its own color, gradation mode, and mix

Figure 38.3
Left to right: Variations of the Remap Color effect, using the Multi-gradient options.

setting. You can use any number of them—from just one to all 15—to produce colorful variants and a more complex, overall gradient. No guidance is offered, so you have to explore these options to get a feel for their infinite interactions and combination of effects.

Retinal Bloom

The Retinal Bloom filter creates a widening, or *blooming*, of the lightest areas of your footage. The effect can be subtle or radical, depending on how much blooming is set and other footage specific factors (see Figure 38.4).

Following are some possible uses for the Retinal Bloom filter:

- Use Retinal Bloom when your footage has a backdrop of a bright sky. This will increase the effect the light has over the whole environment.

- Create a watercolor effect with a maximum value from 20 to 50 (depending on the footage).

The following controls allow you to adjust the parameters of the Retinal Bloom filter:

- *Preview Mode*—Check the Preview box to see a preview of the effect.

- *Effect Only*—Check this box to see only the affected areas of the footage.

- *Quality*—Select Low, Normal, or High. (Higher settings will increase rendering times.)

- *Bloom Shape*—Selections include Soft And Bright, Harsh Falloff, Dot, Rounded, Star, or Oval. These shapes affect how the bloomed area is written to the footage. Explore them to get a good feel of what each does.

- *Threshold Min/Max*—Altering the Threshold values (from 0 to 32,000) changes which parts of the footage receive the bloom.

- *Size Min/Max*—The larger the bloom, the less image content will remain intact. These settings also range from 0 to 32,000.

- *Angle Min/Max*—Select the angular components (from 0 to 360 degrees) of the bloomed areas.

- *Trans Min/Max*—This can be an interesting image effect, so explore the possibilities. Although the settings range from 0 to 32,000, values higher than 300 start to break the footage into pixelated elements.

Figure 38.4
Left to right: Variations of the Retinal Bloom effect applied at various settings.

- *Using A Single Color*—This control seems to have little effect. Checking this box and using any hue in the palette results in very little variation from leaving it unchecked.

- *Blend With Original*—At the minimum setting of 0, the full effect of the gradient will be seen. As the values increase, the gradient becomes more transparent, with total transparency at the maximum value of 255.

Snowstorm

The Snowstorm filter allows you to create wintry storms and blizzards on any layer (see Figure 38.5).

Following are some possible uses for the Snowstorm filter:

- Create a snowstorm over a wintry, pastoral scene.

- Use a snowstorm on a background layer behind an animated masked foreground to create an interesting animated backdrop.

The following controls allow you to adjust the parameters of the Snowstorm filter:

- *Presets*—Select from among preset parameters of the Snowstorm filter.

- *Preroll Frames*—This value tells the effect how many frames have already passed before the effect begins. The minimum setting (0) is the default, making your first frame the first frame of the Snowstorm effect. The maximum value is 32,000.

- *Snow Generate*—Set the value (from 0 to 32,000) to indicate the number of snowflakes.

- *Min/Max Size*—This control alters the size of the snowflakes. Its values can range from 0 to 255.

- *Min/Max Opacity*—This control alters the opacity of the snow, with the minimum value of 0 making the snow transparent and the maximum value of 255 making it fully opaque.

- *Min/Max Lilt Amount*—This control (ranging from 0 to 1,000) sets a range for the Lilt parameter.

- *Min/Max Lilt Frequency*—This control (ranging from 0 to 1,000) sets the number of times a Lilt is applied during the range of frames.

Figure 38.5
Left to right: Variations of the Snowstorm filter.

- *Gravity*—Gravity (ranging from 0 to 1,000) acts to keep the snow falling. A setting of 0 will make the snow fall at a more random rate.

- *Wind Horiz/Vert*—Negative Horizontal Wind (up to a value –100) pushes the snow left, and positive Horizontal Wind (up to 100) pushes the snow right. Negative Vertical Wind pushes the snow down, and positive Vertical Wind pushes the snow up. (These values also range from –100 to 100.)

- *Gust Probability*—Sets the probability (from 0 to 100) that a gust of wind will occur.

- *Gust Max Duration*—Sets how long the gust will affect the snow. The values range from 0 to 1,000.

- *Gust Max Speed*—Set the speed of the gust with values from 0 to 1,000.

- *Fall on Layer*—Select the layer in the stack that will receive the snow effect.

- *Ground Layer*—The Ground layer sets the base for the snowfall.

- *Random Seed*—This setting (from 0 to 32,000) will change the overall pattern of the snow.

- *Blend With Original*—At the minimum value of 0, you'll see the full effect of the snowstorm. As the values increase, the snowstorm becomes more transparent, with total transparency at the maximum value of 255.

Solarize

The Solarize filter removes all hue information from your layer, translating it to grayscale. (See Figure 38.6 for an example of this effect.)

Some possible uses for the Solarize filter are:

- Use inverted solarization to create a black-and-white negative of the footage.

- Use a Grain value of 255 to create a stippled effect.

The following controls allow you to adjust the parameters of the Solarize filter:

- *Invert*—Checking this box produces a negative image.

- *Contrast*—The higher the Contrast value, the fewer grayscales in the footage. The range of settings is from –127 to 127.

Figure 38.6
Left to right: The same image displaying alternate Solarize values.

- *Rotate*—This control rotates the grayscale values in the footage. Its values range from 0 to 255.

- *Solar Grain*—Grain adds pixelated noise to the footage. Its values also range from 0 to 255.

- *Blend With Original*—At the minimum setting of 0, the full effect of the Solarize effect can be seen. As the values increase, the solarization becomes more transparent, with total transparency at a maximum value of 255.

Specular Lighting

 The Specular Lighting filter adds a sun-like orb to your composition. You can control all of the parameters and animate them as well. A specular light is really the "hot spot" that appears on a surface when a light is shined on it, so this is also a perfect filter for any 3D object effects (see Figure 38.7).

Following are some possible uses for the Specular Lighting filter:

- Use this filter in combination with other lighting effects when you need to emulate a sun object.

- Use this filter on a TILT object to create a specular highlight on its surface. (For details on TILT, see the last entry in this chapter.)

The following controls allow you to adjust the parameters of the Specular Lighting filter:

- *Presets*—Select from a list of different Specular Lighting parameters.

- *Blend*—At the minimum setting of 0, the full effect of the Specular Lighting effect will be seen. As the values increase, the specular lighting becomes more transparent, with total transparency at the maximum value of 255. Keyframe animate this value to create glowing solar orbs.

- *ViewPoint*—Select the X, Y, and Z ViewPoints and Plane Normals to move the viewing camera around the composition. These values can range between –10,000 and 10,000.

- *Light Source*—Select Light Color, Light Type (Point or Directional), and Intensity (0 to 10,000). Note that intensities over 500 start to create white hot spots in the center of a

Figure 38.7
Left to right, variations of the Specular Lighting effect: Material Ambience at 60, Material Ambience at 100, and Spherical Bump Map at a Height of 255 with data taken from the same layer.

Point Light that obliterates the footage content. For Point Lights, use the XYZ Position controls to place the orb anywhere in the composition. For Directional Lights, use the XYZ Light Direction controls to determine the direction the light will "shine."

- *Material*—Here is a unique idea! These controls treat the footage as if it were made from a material that has its own light-reflectance properties, so that it reacts to the specular light. Use the controls to set the type of material makeup for the footage.

- *Bump Map*—Here's another perfect filter for a TILT object or any other 3D object effect. Bump Map adds a lumpy surface to an object, the texture of which is taken from any layer in the stack. The "height" of a bump map is taken from the lightness or darkness of a grayscale representation of the layer, with lighter areas being computed as "higher." You control all the parameters of the applied bump with these controls.

- *Environmental Map*—This mapping type is a flat texture taken from any layer in the stack. Using the Environmental Map control requires that bump mapping be also used because it really just compounds the Bump Map effect.

Supernova

The Supernova filter places a multirayed light (like an exploding star) on the selected layer (see Figure 38.8).

Some possible uses for the Supernova filter are:

- Use a supernova against a previously animated star backdrop.

- Use a pair of supernova layers to add animated glints to the eyes of a human or animal subject.

The following controls allow you to adjust the parameters of the Supernova filter:

- *Presets*—Select from a list of different Supernova parameter types. Use as is, or as a starting point to customized your own creations.

- *Center Point*—Place the centroid anywhere in the composition you want the supernova to be.

- *Nova Color*—Select the color from the system palette or with the eyedropper.

- *Radius*—Set the size of the Supernova's coverage in a range of settings from 0 to 10,000.

Figure 38.8
Left to right: Variations on the Supernova effect.

- *Spikes*—Set the number of rays emanating from the Supernova. The minimum value is 0, and the maximum is 10,000.

- *Random Hue*—Add a random hue to the Supernova. The range of values is again 0 to 10,000.

- *Blend With Original*—At 0 (the minimum value), the full Supernova effect will be seen. As the values increase, the supernova becomes more transparent, with total transparency at the maximum value of 255.

Turbulent Noise

The Turbulent Noise filter applies chaotic pixels to your footage (see Figure 38.9).

Following are some possible uses for the Turbulent Noise filter:

- Use Stretch XY values of 25 to create clouds.

- Use this filter with Turbulence Off to add abstract dropout areas to the Alpha layer.

The following controls allow you to adjust the parameters of the Turbulent Noise filter:

- *Presets*—Select from the list to create preset Turbulent Noise to the selected layer.

- *Use Turbulence*—Checking this option adds Turbulence parameters to the noise.

- *Contrast*—Heighten the contrast between the noise grayscales with values between 0 and 1,000.

- *Brightness*—Heighten the overall brightness of the noise with values between 0 and 1,000.

- *Detail*—Heighten the detailed areas of the noise at the areas where it normally blends. The settings can range between 0 and 10,000.

- *Stretch XY*—Increase the size of the noise blobs in either (or both) the X and Y directions. These settings also range between 0 and 10,000.

- *Offset XY*—Offset the noise in either (or both) the X and Y direction. You can choose from 0 to 360 degrees. Keyframe animate this setting to make the noise move like a fog bank.

- *Seed*—The Seed number (from 0 to 10,000) determines a pattern.

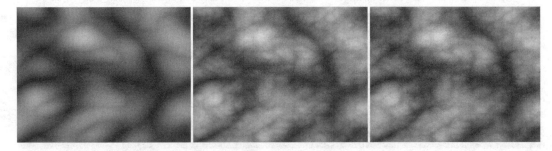

Figure 38.9
Left to right: Images display the Turbulent Noise effect with the same parameters except for Detail settings of 1, 20, and 75, respectively.

- *Animate Seed*—Checking this box animates the Seed number, thereby altering the pattern in an animation.

- *Make Tilable*—Checking this box makes the pattern a tiled one.

- *Blend With Original*—At the minimum value of 0, the full noise effect will be seen, but no source footage. As the values increase, the noise effect becomes more transparent, with total transparency at the maximum value of 255.

Visual Harmonizer

 The Visual Harmonizer filter is a wave-generation system, creating a variety of interweaving waveforms (see Figure 38.10).

Following are some possible uses for the Visual Harmonizer filter:

- Use the Visual Harmonizer in conjunction with an audio sample. As the amplitude of the audio sample changes, change the Amplitude setting (keyframe animate it) of the Visual Harmonizer. You wind up with a visual representation of your audio.

- Use this filter to create waveforms that appear on a screen on the deck of a starship.

The following controls allow you to adjust the parameters of the Visual Harmonizer filter:

Note: This filter is best used on a solid color layer.

- *Presets*—Select from the list to apply a preset Visual Harmonizer waveform to the selected layer.

- *Number of Frequencies*—Although this setting can range from 0 to 32,000, you should keep this value below 50 for most purposes or the waveforms will get too bunched up. Using more than 50 results in a more solid rendering.

- *Particle Shape*—Explore the six shapes listed here to see which one works best for your needs.

- *Start and End Points and Color*—Placing the Start and End Points creates a waveform that stretches between them. They can each be any hue you want.

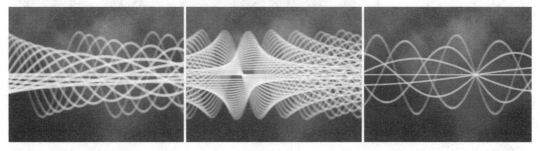

Figure 38.10
Left to right: Default values, Number of Frequencies raised to 50, and Number of Frequencies set to 7.

- *Start and End Size*—Again, although these values can range between 0 and 32,000, you should keep them below 10 as a default to prevent the waveform from blooming.

- *Spacing*—If you select to use spacing, you can set the Spacing Distance and the Spacing Phase. Although both of the settings can range between 0 and 32,000, good default values are from 1 to 5 for each.

- *Amplitude Start/End*—Set the Amplitude range with values between –10,000 and 10,000.

- *Frequency Start/End*—Set the Frequency range with values between –10,000 and 10,000.

- *Phase Start/End*—Set the Phase range with values between –10,000 and 10,000.

- *Blend With Original*—At the minimum value of 0, the waveform will be seen at full opacity. As the values increase, the waveform becomes more transparent, with total transparency at the maximum setting of 255.

See the Visharm1 animation on the companion CD-ROM.

WarpFlow

The WarpFlow filter is for users who are tired of the same old flat DVE effects. With this filter, you can curve and warp your flying logos and other footage (see Figure 38.11). Some possible uses for the WarpFlow filter are shown in the following list:

- Create a flying logo that twists and bends in smooth curves before it reaches its destination.

- Warp selected areas of an image to create bloating and other bulge effects.

The following controls allow you to adjust the parameters of the WarpFlow filter:

- *Presets*—Select from a list of preset warped surfaces and apply one to your footage.

- *XYZ Distance*—If you think of your footage as a 3D space, you'll understand how to manipulate the XYZ Distance controls. The X values represent left (negative) and right (positive) movements. The Y values represent up (negative) and down (positive) movements. The Z values represent movements in (negative) and out (positive) of the screen. You can also think of Z values as increasing (negative) or decreasing (positive) a zoom on the footage. These settings can range from –1,000 to 1,000.

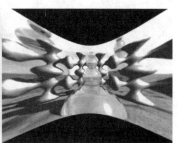

Figure 38.11
Left to right: Original footage, left and right upper corners warped to –27, and center points of the footage warped to –35.

- *XYZ Rotate*—Rotate each axis from 0 to 360 degrees.

- *Blend With Original*—At the minimum value of 0, the warped footage will be seen at full opacity. As the values increase, the warped footage becomes more transparent to the source footage, with total transparency of the warped footage at the maximum value of 255.

- *The Warp Matrix*—You can apply a warp to 16 possible areas of the footage, and each one affects the way the others address the footage. You can end up with some convoluted 3D planes, so it's best to alter the 16 values by small increments at first. (The values range from –1,000 to 1,000.) As you get the hang of it, the values can be more radically altered.

TILT

  The DigiEffects TILT filter (originally developed by Cognicon) might be the unique and most valuable filters you will ever run across in After Effects. It allows you to import a 3D object saved in the 3DMF format (QuickDraw 3D), and manipulate them inside the After Effects Composition window. This makes After Effects a 3D graphics and animation application. Unfortunately for Windows users, this filter works only on the Mac (see Figure 38.12).

Following are some possible uses for the TILT filter:

- Create your text block in a 3D application, and save it out as a 3DMF object file. Import it into After Effects for keyframe animation, using the TILT filter. (This allows you to animate in 3D much faster than most 3D applications.)

- Using TILT, import a 3D spaceship created in a 3D application and saved as a 3DMF object. Rotate the craft with a background of animated stars. This is a much faster and far easier than using a particle-generation system in a 3D application to do the same thing.

TILT is a collection of integrated options. The following controls allow you to adjust the parameters of each of the TILT options:

- *TILT Camera*—No matter what other TILT option you use, you have to have a camera or you won't see anything. So, it's a good idea to load the TILT Camera first. Simply select it from the Effects/Cognicon list. Don't tweak any of the settings right off, since you need an

Figure 38.12
These frames are from a TILT animation. All of the elements are 3DMF 3D objects that can be manipulated and lighted in 3D space.

object loaded first. The recommended loading order for the TILT options is Camera, Object, and Light. You can interface with the Camera controls either interactively or with control sliders. QuickDraw 3D objects have the advantage that they can be controlled through manipulation on a 3D interface, and TILT's camera can be controlled in this manner through the integrated 3D Manipulator interface (see Figure 38.13 for an example of the interactive controls).

You can also use the standard After Effects control sliders and rotation dials to manipulate the Camera—this includes XYZ Rotation (0 to 360 degrees) and Distance (0.1 to 1,000). Note that 0.01 is as close as you can zoom, and larger values cause the camera to zoom out. A value of 50 zooms out far enough to make the object disappear, so it is doubtful that you will need to use larger Distance values. You can also alter the FOV (field of view) of the camera, from 1 to 179. An XYZ "Look At" point can be set, so that—no matter how the Camera is altered—the same target remains in view.

- *TILT Simple Object*—TILT includes a number of sample 3DMF objects in the TILT folder. These can be used to augment imported 3DMF objects or to create an entire scene on their own. They include Box, Sphere, Cone, Cylinder, XZ Grid, Checker Board, Ngon, and Floor.

You can interface with the Simple Object controls either interactively or with control sliders. QuickDraw 3D objects have the advantage that they can be controlled through manipulation on a 3D interface, and TILT's Simple Objects can be controlled in this manner through the integrated 3D Manipulator interface (see Figure 38.14).

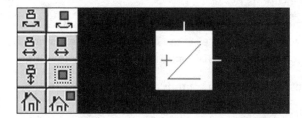

Figure 38.13
Using the interactive controls on the left of the TILT Camera Manipulator, you can rotate, move, and zoom the TILT Camera.

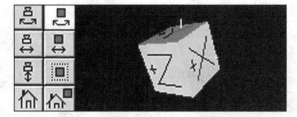

Figure 38.14
You can interact in real time with the TILT Simple Objects with the Manipulator interface.

You can also use the standard After Effects control sliders and rotation dials to manipulate the Simple Objects. This includes XYZ Rotation (0 to 360 degrees), XYZ Translation in space (–1,000 to 1,000), and Scale (0 to 1,000). Any layer in the stack can be used as a texture for the Simple Object. It can also take on any hue from the System palette or the eyedropper.

- *TILT File Object*—A File Object is a 3DMF object file that you have saved previously. You'll find a number of free sample 3DMF objects in the QuickDraw 3D/3DMF Models folder in the Apple Extras folder on your hard drive. It is also possible that you have set aside another folder on a hard drive for 3DMF models you have created yourself.

You can interface with the File Object controls either interactively or with control sliders. QuickDraw 3D objects have the advantage that they can be controlled through manipulation on a 3D interface, and TILT's Simple Objects can be controlled in this manner through the integrated 3D Manipulator interface (see Figure 38.15).

You can also use the standard After Effects control sliders and rotation dials to manipulate the File Objects. This includes XYZ Rotation (0 to 360 degrees), XYZ Translation in space (–1,000 to 1,000), and Scale (0 to 1,000).

- *TILT Far Light*—This is a distant light, equivalent to the sun. You can make it visible in the Composition window so you can aim it more effectively.

You can interface with the Far Light controls either interactively or with control sliders. TILT's Far Light effect can be controlled through the integrated 3D Manipulator interface (see Figure 38.16).

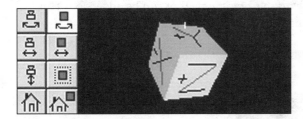

Figure 38.15
You can interact in real time with the TILT File Objects with the Manipulator interface. Animating an imported object with TILT is much faster than using a 3D application, although you don't have all the bells and whistles that a real 3D application offers.

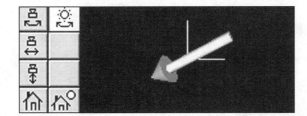

Figure 38.16
The TILT Manipulator interface for the Far Light effect.

You can also use the standard After Effects control sliders and rotation dials to manipulate the Point Light parameters, which include XY Rotation (0 to 360 degrees), Intensity (0 to 1), and Color.

- *Point Light*—A point light is a light that shines in all directions equally and can be compared to a light bulb. Point lights can be placed anywhere in TILT's 3D space.

You can interface with the Point Light controls either interactively or with control sliders. TILT's Point Light effect can be controlled through the integrated 3D Manipulator interface (see Figure 38.17).

You can also use the standard After Effects control sliders and rotation dials to manipulate the Point Light parameters, which include XYZ Position (–1,000 to 1,000); Attenuation (None, Inverse Distance, and Inverse Distance Squared); Intensity (0 to 1); and Color.

- *TILT Spot Light*—The TILT Spot Light can be positioned to cast light on any targeted object in TILT's 3D environment.

You can interface with the Spot Light controls either interactively or with control sliders. TILT's Spot Light can be controlled through the integrated 3D Manipulator interface (see Figure 38.18).

You can also use the standard After Effects control sliders and rotation dials to manipulate the Spot Light parameters. These parameters are XYZ Rotation (0 to 360 degrees); XYZ Position (–1,000 to 1,000); Attenuation (None, Inverse Distance, and Inverse Distance Squared); Falloff (Linear, Exponential, and Cosine); Hot Angle (0 to 90); Outer Angle (0 to 90); Intensity (0 to 1); and Color.

- *TILT VMesh Object*—This is the most variable object type that can be added to a TILT 3D scene. The object is constructed on the spot from an 8-bit grayscale bitmap.

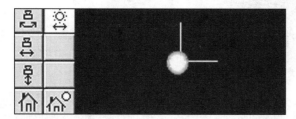

Figure 38.17
The TILT Manipulator interface for the Point Light effect.

Figure 38.18
The TILT Manipulator interface for the Spot Light effect.

Figure 38.19
The TILT Manipulator interface for the VMesh Object.

You can interface with the VMesh Object controls either interactively or with control sliders. TILT's VMesh Object can be controlled through the integrated 3D Manipulator interface (see Figure 38.19).

You can also use the standard After Effects control sliders and rotation dials to manipulate the VMesh Object parameters. These parameters are XYZ Rotation (0 to 360 degrees); XYZ Translation (–1,000 to 1,000); XYZ Scale (0 to 1,000); Height Field (choose the grayscale layer from the stack); Height From (select either R, G, B, Alpha, or Luminance Channel); Color; and Smoothing (if selected, smoothes aliased areas).

A TILT VMesh Project

To create a VMesh animation with TILT, follow these steps:

1. Open Photoshop, or another image-editing application that saves out 8-bit grayscale (256 gray toned) images (and TIFF or PICT format is best).

2. Work in RGB mode, and create a 320 × 200 grayscale graphic. Use a black background, and paint with solid white. Use your imagination.

3. Using the Blur tool, go over all of the edges of the white elements in the image, so that the edges blur into the black.

4. Transform the image into an 8-bit grayscale. Save it to disk.

5. Open After Effects, and make a new composition the same size as the graphic you just created.

6. Create a new color layer.

7. Target a TILT effect to the layer. Use the TILT Camera and Spot Light effect first.

8. Load the grayscale graphic into your layers list, and place it at the bottom. Turn Visibility off (because we want to use the layer, but don't want it to be seen in the layer stack as a graphic).

9. Make sure that the color layer is active. Open the TILT VMesh option. Under Height Field, find the graphic in the stack list. This allows VMesh to use the grayscale data as Height data for the Y axis of a 3D object.

10. Your graphic will transform into a 3D object.

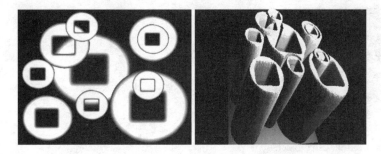

Figure 38.20
On the left is the original graphic, and on the right the graphic is transformed into a TILT VMesh 3D object.

11. Rotate and keyframe animate the object in TILT, and save the animation to disk (see Figure 38.20).

See the TILT_1 and the Teapots1 animations on the companion CD-ROM. Both animations display project ideas for the TILT plug-in.

COMMOTION

Puffin Design's Commotion is a Mac-only standalone application that is an essential add-on for After Effects. It offers users the tools for customizing footage either before or after it is processed in After Effects, which After Effects doesn't address. The set includes a full complement of painting tools for working directly on animated footage, onion-skinning attributes, spline editing, and more. (A working demo of Commotion is included on this book's CD-ROM.)

In this chapter, we have included Commotion tutorials so you can use the demo to create After Effects footage and get a feel for what Commotion does and how it works. The folks at Puffin Designs wrote this chapter and the tutorials.

Introduction

The following tutorials demonstrate how you can use Commotion for different types of projects. We included several clips that will serve as source and final footage for the projects you will work on. In this chapter, you learn how to accomplish the following tasks:

- Use Commotion's Playing Functions
- Paint and Onion Skin
- Use Super Cloning and AutoPaint to clean up a shot
- Create and apply Motion Trackers
- Paint and use rotosplines to create an articulate matte

Each tutorial makes use of a wide variety of Commotion commands, guiding you step by step through these processes to show you how to use Commotion's major features. This tutorial doesn't cover all the functions in Commotion, but instead gives you an idea of how the program works.

Note: Some of these tutorials ask you to load more than 30 frames. If you are using the demo version, you'll soon discover that you cannot load more than 30 frames. In this case, load as many frames as possible, starting with the first suggested frame of the tutorial.

Opening Footage, Using The Player Palette, And Painting

Commotion's creative tools are built on a playback engine that allows instant playback of your work. This means that you can paint, rotoscope, and motion track images without waiting for excessive rendering times. Your changes take effect immediately in Commotion, and they are always ready to be played back, reviewed, and edited.

What You Will Learn In This Lesson

You will be working with an image of an eagle, provided by Broadcast Services of Alaska. This clip is located in the Commotion demo part of this book's companion CD-ROM, in the folder Tutorials/1.Eagle. If you have the room, copy the contents of the Tutorials folder to your hard drive before beginning the exercise because doing so will speed up loading and saving files (the demo version doesn't allow saving). For this book, all the clips were compressed to save disk space. Commotion is designed to work with uncompressed media.

In this lesson you will be working with the following features:

- Opening clips
- The Player palette
- Viewer tool
- SuperClone tool
- AutoPaint functions

Opening A Clip

To open a clip, take these steps:

1. Launch Commotion and choose File|Open. The Open dialog box appears. Find the 1.Eagle.Movie file in the 1.Eagle folder on the CD-ROM. Click on OK.

2. The Load Frames dialog box appears (see Figure 39.1). This dialog box allows you to specify which frames of the clip are loaded into RAM. By default, Commotion will load as many frames of the selected clip as possible.

3. Click on OK to load the clip into RAM. When it has finished loading, it will appear in the Clip window on your desktop (see Figure 39.2).

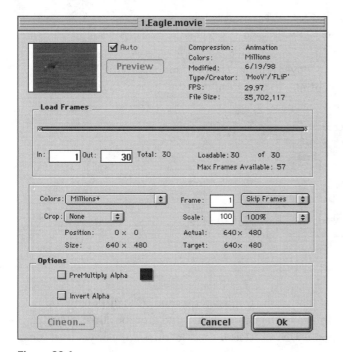

Figure 39.1
The Load Frames dialog box.

Figure 39.2
The footage appears in the Clip window.

Playing The Clip

To play a clip, take the following steps:

1. Click on the Play button in the Player palette. The clip will play to the end, loop back to the beginning, and continue to play until you stop it (see Figure 39.3).

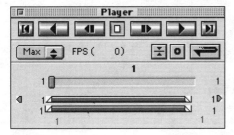

Figure 39.3
Play the clip by using the Play button (the right-facing arrow).

2. While the clip is playing back, look at the frames-per-second (FPS) display in the Player palette. This number indicates the actual frame rate that the clip is playing. You can use the frame rate pop-up list to select a specific frame rate, or you can choose Max to achieve the maximum frame rate.

3. To stop playback, click on the Stop button (the square icon in the center of the Player palette), or press the spacebar.

4. Click the Play Mode button, (the last icon in the second row of the Player palette). Commotion offers three different modes of play:

   - Once-Through (the right arrow): Plays the clip once through and stops.

   - Loop (right-pointing arrow with a loop at the top): Continually plays and loops the clip until you press stop.

   - Rock And Roll (arrow with both left and right points): Plays the clip through forward. When it reaches the end, it plays the clip backward. Play the clip using each of these settings.

   When you are done, set the Play mode back to Loop.

5. You can also scrub to any frame by using the Current Frame Slider in the Player palette.

Using The Viewer Tool

To use the Viewer tool, take these steps:

1. With the Clip window still open, select the View Window tool from the Tool palette (see Figure 39.4).

2. Pick an area you would like to view and make a selection around it by drag-clicking.

3. Press Play or use the spacebar to play the footage in the View Window.

4. With the footage playing, grab the window and drag it to a different location.

Figure 39.4
The View Window tool in the Tool palette.

5. Hold down the Shift key and make another selection. The View Window tool works in the same way as the other selection tools do. The Shift key adds area to a selection, and the Command key deletes area from a selection.

> Note: If you have made an existing selection with one of the other selection tools (such as marquee, lasso, or magic wand), Commotion keeps that selection in memory while you use the View Window tool to view the footage.

6. Click on Stop or press the spacebar to stop playback.

Painting On The Footage

Commotion is a full-featured paint program, providing real-time feedback of your 2D animation. With Commotion, you can easily create a brush and paint frame by frame on your clip.

1. Expand the Brush Control panel of the Tool Options palette. The size, feather, and spacing settings of the current brush are displayed here (see Figure 39.5).

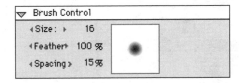

Figure 39.5.
The expanded Brush Control palette.

2. By clicking and dragging on the name of each setting, create a brush that is 16 pixels, with 100% Feather, and 15% Spacing. Notice how the preview window to the Feather Spacing right updates instantly as you change the brush settings.

3. Select the Paintbrush tool from the Tool palette or press the B key (see Figure 39.6).

Figure 39.6
The Paintbrush tool.

4. Click on the foreground color swatch in the Tool palette and choose a bright-red color.

5. Paint on several frames of the clip, using the Advance button in the Player palette to change frames.

Onion Skinning

Commotion offers an Onion Skin mode that allows you to see previous frames while you paint. This feature is vital to 2D animation.

1. Turn on Onion Skinning by selecting it from the Mode menu or by clicking on the Onion Skinning button in the lower left of the Clip window. The previous frame will appear semi-transparently over the current frame (hence, the term "onion skin").

2. Paint on several frames of the clip with Onion Skinning on.

3. At any time, you can get instant real-time feedback of your work by pressing the Play button.

> **Note: Turn off Onion Skinning before playing to improve playback speed.**

Shot Cleanup With SuperClone

You are now ready to use one of Commotion's most powerful tools, SuperClone. Unique to Commotion, the SuperClone tool is similar to Photoshop's Clone tool, with the added capability to clone from other frames in your clip, or from other clips altogether. In this shot, you will use the SuperClone tool to seamlessly remove the boat that crosses the top of the frame.

1. Double-click on the SuperClone tool, as shown in Figure 39.7. This will select the SuperClone tool and open the Clone Source palette (see Figure 39.8). This is where you choose the file and frames you want to paint with. You begin by painting on frame 5 with pixels from frame 18.

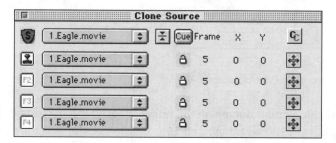

Figure 39.7
The SuperClone tool.

Figure 39.8
The Clone Source palette.

2. Go to frame 5. In the Clone Source palette, click on the frame number for the first clone source.

3. Enter frame 18 in the Clone Source dialog box, and select Absolute (see Figure 39.9).

> **Note: Make sure that you are on frame 5 when you set your clone source.**

4. Once set, the SuperClone tool will maintain the same time relationship between your current frame and your source frame. This way, when you advance to frame 6, the Clone Source will automatically become frame 19.

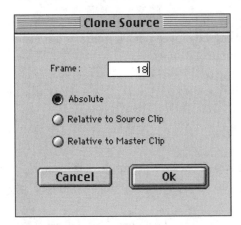

Figure 39.9
The Clone Source dialog box.

5. Create a new brush. Previously you used the Brush Control palette to do this. Commotion also allows you to create brushes in real time directly on the canvas! To make a real-time brush, hold down the Command and Option keys and click and drag above the eagle's wing to make a brush large enough to cover the area between the wing and the top of the screen. Don't let go of the keys or the mouse button.

6. When you add the Control key, you can interactively set the amount of feather for your brush. Press the Control key and drag the mouse inward, setting the size of the feathering to approximately 50 percent of the size of the brush.

Saving Time With AutoPaint

Commotion's AutoPaint feature can record and play back brush strokes over multiple frames. This powerful feature can save a lot of time. For example, in this shot, you'll only need to paint out the boat on one frame, and AutoPaint will do the rest.

1. Click on the Record button in the AutoPaint panel, located at the top of the Tool Options palette (the red circle) (see Figure 39.10).

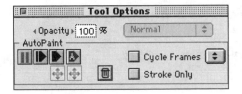

Figure 39.10
Click on the Record button.

2. Using the SuperClone tool, paint a single stroke (from right to left) across the top of the frame. Try to avoid the eagle's wingtip. You are now painting with pixels from frame 18.

3. Click on the Stop Recording button in the AutoPaint panel (see Figure 39.11). The stroke you made has now been recorded and can be played back a frame at a time, over a range of frames, or animated over a range of frames.

Figure 39.11
The Stop Record button.

4. To paint out the boat, you'll need to play the stroke back over a range of frames. This range is called the *selection range*, and it can be adjusted with the Selection Range slider in the Player palette.

5. Advance to frame 6 and press the minus key ("–") on the keyboard. This will set frame 6 as the "in" frame of the selection range.

6. Set the "out" frame by clicking and dragging the right point of the selection range slider to frame 18. You are now ready to automatically paint out the boat from the remaining frames.

7. Click on the Paint Over Range button in the AutoPaint panel and watch Commotion do the rest (see Figure 39.12)!

Figure 39.12
The Paint Over Range button.

> *Note: The EAGLE.STROKE file can be loaded from the 1.Eagle folder if you want to load it already made. Also, make sure that you check out the "AutoPaint Tips and Tricks" document at www.puffindesigns.com for more ideas about AutoPaint.*

Creating "Write-On" Effects

Commotion's AutoPaint features have a great deal of creative potential. Not only can they repeat your strokes over a range of frames, they can also animate them to create write-on effects.

1. Click on the Trash button in the AutoPaint panel (trashcan icon) to discard the previously recorded stroke.

2. Select the Paintbrush tool from the Tool palette, or press the B key.

3. Click on the Record button in the AutoPaint panel. With recording on, paint a word on the current frame.

4. Erase the strokes you just made by pressing Command+R and selecting Revert Current Frame.

5. Go to frame 1, and set the selection range so that it spans the entire clip. You are now ready to apply the write-on effect.

Figure 39.13
The Animate button in the AutoPaint panel.

6. Click on the Animate button in the AutoPaint panel (see Figure 39.13). The strokes you recorded will be animated over the entire clip. Play the clip back to see the results.

7. AutoPaint can also play back the recorded strokes using different brush settings. To try this, make a smaller brush and select a different color. With Stroke Only selected, click on the Animate button.

8. You can now see how easy it is to create complex brush strokes using AutoPaint. And, of course, any strokes you record can be loaded and saved from the pop-up menu in the AutoPaint panel.

9. Experiment with the Wiggle checkbox and Wiggle settings in the pull-down menu. Revert the clip and repeat step 6 with Wiggle checked.

Motion-Tracking Tutorial

Commotion's Motion Tracker is used to automatically "track" or follow a particular region or object within a moving image. The result is an editable motion path that can be used to stabilize images, automatically paint objects in or out of clips, change viewer perspective, and drastically accelerate the rotosplining process.

In This Section

For this tutorial, we will track several objects on a ferry boat (footage provided to us by Adventure Pictures). Open the file 2.boat.movie from the 2.boat folder. It isn't necessary to load the entire frame range of the clip, but load all 50 frames if you have enough RAM. This tutorial is written as though all 50 frames are loaded (see Figure 39.14).

Tracking Objects

To track track an object, take these steps:

1. Open the Motion Trackers palette. The palette can be reached by double-clicking on the Motion Tracker tool or by selecting Motion Tracker from the Windows menu (see Figures 39.15 and 39.16).

2. Create two new motion trackers by clicking twice on the New Motion Tracker button (lower right of the Motion Tracker palette).

3. Cue the clip to frame 1. When you set up a tracker, make sure you are at the beginning or end of a frame range that you want to track.

4. Move the Track Target and Track Region markers to select the area to track. The *Track Target* is the inner rectangle and represents the pixel pattern that the tracker will search for. The *Track Region* is the outer rectangle and represents the region to search on each frame.

Figure 39.14
The 2.Boat movie footage is loaded.

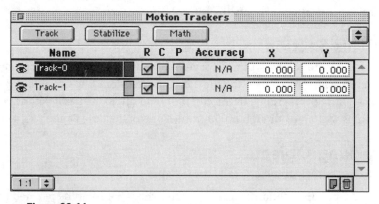

Figure 39.15
The Motion Tracker tool.

Figure 39.16
The Motion Trackers palette.

Note: The Track Region is a relative search area—if an object (black dot) is moving left to right across screen over a series of 100 frames—the track region needs to be only as big as the greatest movement from one frame to the next. It doesn't have to be as big as the entire frame. Picking the best track target and region is the trick to good motion tracking.

Here are some tips (for more, download the "Com-Motion Tracking" Tips and Tricks doc from the Puffin Design Web site):

- Track Targets should be high-contrast areas of the image that stay relatively constant in size and appearance (so that they can be recognized as they move). If you have problems tracking an object, try changing the size and position of your track target.

- When possible, try not to pick objects that are obscured halfway through a shot or that move offscreen. Commotion does have features to track objects like this, but it will require additional steps (see Motion Tracking in the Reference Section of the full product manual, or the aforementioned document).

- Track Regions should be just large enough to include the entire range of possible motion from frame to frame since the size of the track region greatly affects the performance of the motion tracking.

5. Position one tracker over the smokestack and place the other over the lifesaver on the right.

6. You can magnify a tracker and move it around to see precisely what you need to track. To do this, press 1 through 5 on the keyboard while the Tracker tool is selected, or select a magnification from the Tracker Zoom pop-up in the lower left of the Tracker palette (see Figure 39.17).

Figure 39.17
The Zoomed tracker areas.

7. When you are satisfied with the track target, shift-select both trackers in the Motion Trackers palette and then click on the Track button (see Figures 39.18 and 39.19).

Figure 39.18
The Track button.

Figure 39.19
The Motion Tracking Options dialog box.

8. A variety of options ensures that you are getting the best possible track. You can track pixels based on saturation or luminance, and you can select the degree of subpixel accuracy.

For this track, choose Luminance and make sure SubPixel Accuracy is set to 1/16th. Click on OK to begin tracking. Once the track is finished, an editable motion path and crosshairs are available to adjust the tracked data. To modify this path, you can simply click and drag any node or group of nodes. Because of Commotion's playback performance, you can easily evaluate your tracked data in real time. Once you are satisfied with your tracked data, then you can choose what to do with it.

Applying Tracker Data To Rotosplines

You can use tracked data in Commotion in a variety of ways. In this lesson, you'll be applying the tracked data to a rotospline. Rotosplines are one of Commotion's most powerful features, and are generally used to isolate objects to create animated Alpha mattes. You learn more about rotosplines in the following section, "Rotospline Tutorial."

1. If it isn't already open, press F7 to open the RotoSplines palette. Select Load All Paths from the pop-up menu in the upper left corner (see Figure 39.20).

Figure 39.20
RotoSplines palette.

2. Load the file LIFESAVER.PATH, which contains a rotospline for the lifesaver on the side of the boat. However, this spline was created for only the first frame of the clip. If you play the clip back, you will see that the spline doesn't line up with the

lifesaver because the boat is moving. Normally, you would have to manually adjust this spline frame by frame to accommodate the boat's motion. By applying the tracker data to this spline, Commotion can do this automatically.

3. Go to frame 1 and select the lifesaver spline in the RotoSplines palette. Click on the Motion Tracker button in the RotoSplines palette. In the Apply Tracker Data dialog box (see Figure 39.21), indicate whether you wish to apply the tracker data to the selected point(s) or to the entire spline (or multiple splines if more than one spline is selected). Choose Entire Spline and click on OK.

Figure 39.21
The Apply Tracker Data dialog box.

4. You can now select the track data that will be applied to this spline. Use the upper pop-up menu to select the tracker that you used to track the lifesaver. Make sure that the lower pop-up menu is set to None and click OK (see Figure 39.22).

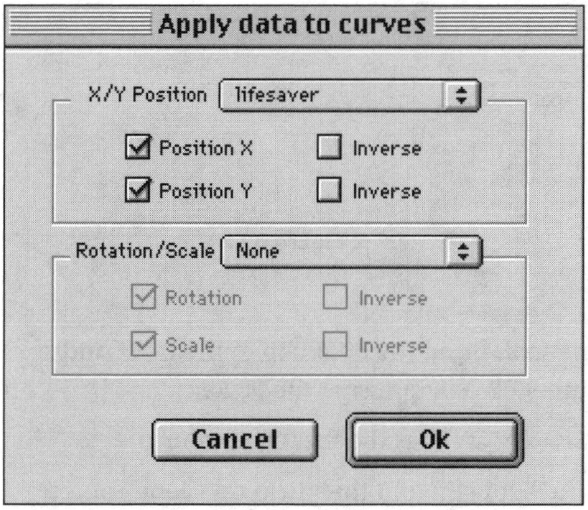

Figure 39.22
Apply Data To Curves dialog box.

5. Play the clip. Notice that the lifesaver rotospline is now correct throughout the shot. Before proceeding, hide the lifesaver spline by clicking the eyeball next to it in the RotoSplines palette.

Applying Tracker Data To Clone Sources

Motion tracking is fully integrated into many of Commotion's tools. In this section, you will apply an explosion coming from the smokestack by using the tracker data to control the position of a Clone source.

1. Open EXPLOSION.MOVIE. In the Load Frames dialog box, select frame 1 by entering 1 in both the In and Out fields. You need to load only the first frame, because the SuperClone tool can pull frames from disk as well as from RAM (see Figure 39.23).

2. Once EXPLOSION.MOVIE has loaded, collapse it by clicking the Collapse button (see Figure 39.24).

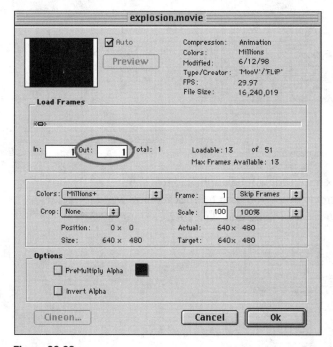

Figure 39.23
The Load Frames dialog box for the Explosion movie.

Figure 39.24
The Collapse button.

3. Next, you need to set up the SuperClone tool. Bring the boat clip to the front and open the Clone Source palette (see Figure 39.25) by pressing the F8 key.

4. Using the pop-up menu, select EXPLOSION.MOVIE as the first clone source.

5. Make sure that you are on frame 1 of the boat clip and then turn on Clone Source Overlay by pressing Option+'. This keyboard shortcut displays the current Clone Source semitransparently over the clip (see Figure 39.26).

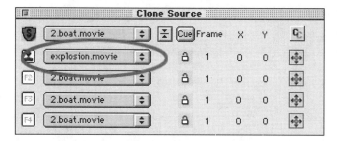

Figure 39.25
The Clone Source palette.

Figure 39.26
The Clone Source is displayed.

6. Hold down Shift while clicking and dragging in the Clip window to position the explosion so that it appears to be coming from the smokestack. After you have done this, use the Current Frame Slider in the Player palette to advance to frame 20. Notice that the explosion no longer lines up with the smokestack due to the motion of the boat. You will now compensate for this by applying the tracker data you previously created to the Clone Source.

7. Click on the Apply Tracker Data button (see Figure 39.27) to the right of the first Clone Source. Use the upper pop-up menu to select the tracker that you originally used to track the smokestack. Make sure that the lower pop-up menu is set to None and click on OK.

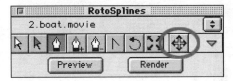

Figure 39.27
The Apply Tracker Data button.

8. Return to frame 20 by using the Current Frame Slider. Notice how the Clone Source is now correctly aligned with the smokestack, and no rendering took place. Before proceeding, return to frame 1.

9. Create a brush approximately 140 pixels in size, with a Feather value of 80%. Select Screen from the Transfer Mode pop-up list at the top of the Tool Options palette and turn on AutoPaint Recording (see Figure 39.28).

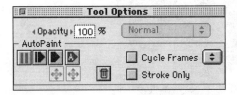

Figure 39.28
Turn on AutoPaint Recording.

10. Paint in the explosion around the smokestack. Remember, this stroke will need to be large enough to paint in all of the explosion as it grows larger, so make it big. (You can go to the last frame to see how big the explosion, and brush, will need to be.)

11. Click on the Apply Tracker Data button in the AutoPaint panel (see Figure 39.29). Commotion automatically applies the recorded stroke on each frame of the clip, following the tracker data as it goes. Now play back the clip and view your results.

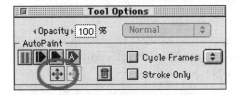

Figure 39.29
Click on the Apply Tracker Data button.

Rotospline Tutorial

Commotion is the best rotoscoping tool on the market on any platform. Rotosoping can be a time-consuming task by nature, but with Commotion the process becomes much easier. With an unlimited number of paths, Commotion provides the ultimate flexibility in shape creation. And all the spline paths can be played back over moving images, without rendering.

Rotoscoping is the art of isolating objects. The reason for the isolation can be for a composite, to apply an effect, or to create an animation. For this tutorial, you will use rotoscoping to create a composite. This is a *locked-down* shot in which the actor and the car were shot separately to ensure the actor's safety. You will use RotoSplines to create a matte so that the shot of the actor can be composited over the shot of the car.

In this section, you will be using several techniques to generate mattes and to touch up a plate:

- Rotosplines—A combination of multiple splines for different purposes.

- Painting to the Alpha channel directly to create an articulate matte.

- Using the Composite command to preview a composite while painting on an Alpha channel.

- Using the SuperClone brush to paint on the final composite to make the shot perfect.

Types Of Rotosplines

Commotion has two types of splines: Bézier and natural (natural splines are also called B-splines). We will be using natural splines for their ease of conforming to organic shapes quickly and efficiently. Natural splines work with "control points" rather than keypoints because the path direction is controlled by where the points are relative to each other. This may sound complicated, but the ease of natural splines will be self-evident after a little practice.

Using Natural Splines

To use the Natural Splines tool, take the following steps:

1. Open BG.CAR from folder 3.Roto on the companion CD-ROM. Load at least 15 frames beginning at frame 1 (see Figure 39.30).

2. On the Tool palette, double-click on the Pen tool to bring up the RotoSplines palette. When making a new spline, the New Spline button indicates either blue (Bézier) or orange (natural). To change the kind of spline you want to work with, pull down the RotoSpline Option menu and select Curve Options. You can set the kind of splines you want to work with here, or by Option+clicking to toggle between blue/orange on the New Spline button at the lower right corner of the RotoSplines palette (see Figures 39.31, 39.32, and 39.33).

3. Set the spline type to Natural (orange), then click the New Spline button to bring up an untitled spline. The orange border on the left of the spline name indicates the type of spline it is (orange for natural, blue for Bézier). This is useful when working with multiple splines of each type. The spline path will become the color shown in the Spline Color box next to the path name.

4. As a test, select the Roto Pen tool and begin drawing a spline around the edge of the car on any frame. You can lay down points as you want, but the fewer points you use, the smoother your matte will be. To close the shape, click on the first point that you laid down. (To make an unclosed path, press Esc.)

Figure 39.30
The BG.CAR movie is loaded.

Figure 39.31
The Pen tool.

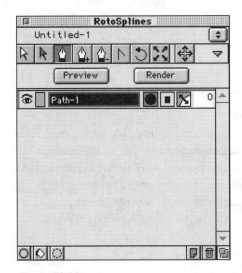

Figure 39.32
The RotoSplines palette.

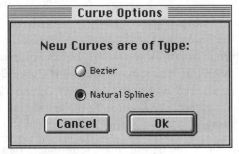

Figure 39.33
The Curve Options dialog box.

5. Select the Pointer tool to manipulate the natural spline. Pick a control point(s) and "push" or "stretch" the path in any direction to fit the shape. Experiment a little to get the feel for it (see Figure 39.34).

Figure 39.34
Experiment to get a feel for creating the spline.

> *Note: Natural splines can be plotted interchangeably with the traditional Bézier splines using the same keyboard shortcuts and interface controls with the exception of the Splitter tool, which works a little differently. Unlike Bézier splines, there are no tangent handles for fine-tuning the spline. Instead, natural splines can be laid down and manipulated with three settings of tension: "normal," "loose," and "tight," which will increase or decrease the curvature of the spline.*

To toggle through the tension settings, click the Splitter tool (see Figure 39.35) on the control point or group of control points that you want to adjust. As with Bézier splines, you can add and subtract points to natural splines, keyframe the splines to control the animation over time, and instantly play them back over your moving footage to evaluate your work in progress.

Figure 39.35
The Splitter tool.

Part 1: Create The Car Spline

To create the car spline, take these steps:

1. Using a natural spline, outline the car on frame 1.

2. Go to frame 50. If frame 50 isn't live, take the Live Frame selection slider in the Player palette and move the range forward so frame 50 is the last live frame.

3. With the Pointer tool, Option+click on any point on the car spline (or Command+A) to select all of the points in the spline. Then move the spline onto the car.

4. Because the car now takes up more of the frame, you have to scale the spline to fit around the car. Select the Scale tool (see Figure 39.36) from the RotoSplines palette, click once to establish an axis for scaling, then click-and-drag to scale the spline until it fits the outline of the car. (You can also use the keyboard arrow keys to nudge the scale.)

Figure 39.36
The Scale tool.

5. Use the Pointer tool to make finer adjustments to the control points so the spline fits precisely.

6. Play the frames you have worked on to review the spline movement. You may notice on frames 20 through 49 that the spline gets too big too quickly before the car moves into place. You can adjust this by going into the RotoSplines Keyframe Editor (Figure 39.37), which you access by clicking the arrow tab in the upper right corner of the RotoSplines palette.

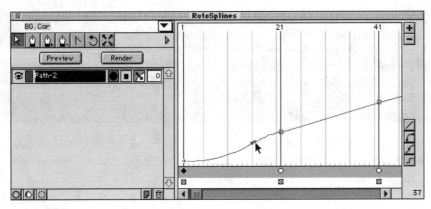

Figure 39.37
The RotoSplines Keyframe Editor.

7. In the Keyframe Editor, you can change the rate of interpolation for the splines. Select the first keyframe by clicking the selection box directly below keyframe 1 (see Figure 39.38). To change the keyframe interpolation type, choose the Easy Curve type (see Figure 39.39) from the Keyframe Type buttons on the right.

Figure 39.38
The Keyframe Editor selection box.

Figure 39.39
Easy Curve type.

8. While the clip is playing, adjust the spline interpolation and get immediate feedback to how that will affect the spline tracking. Adjust the tracking until you get the spline to roughly follow the outline of the car through frames 20 through 50, but don't worry if it isn't perfect.

9. Adjust the matte by adding new keyframes anywhere along the clip. Modify a shape, and a keyframe will automatically be added.

> **Note: Practice using the Keyframe Editor until you are comfortable with its capabilities. For the purposes of this demo, we provided a finished spline for you to use for the rest of the shot.**

Part 2: Painting A Matte

To paint a matte, take these steps:

1. Open the file FG.GUY and load as many frames as possible.

2. From the RotoSplines palette pull-down menu, pick Load Single Path and select SPLINE.CAR.PATH, which is included in the Car Chase folder in the Tutorial folder.

3. Play the clip and notice where the actor and the car spline cross paths at frames 9 through 27. Using the car path as a guide, you will create a matte of the actor in the Alpha channel (see Figure 39.40).

Figure 39.40
Notice where the paths cross.

4. To paint the matte, paint into the Alpha channel while viewing the Alpha overlaid with RGB. To set these modes, either click the Mode buttons (see Figure 39.41), or press Command+M (to overlay the matte) and Option+3 (to paint on Alpha).

Figure 39.41
The Mode buttons.

5. Select the Brush tool and black as your foreground color. Because the background is the same in both shots, rough strokes can be used to paint the actor's matte. The car spline will serve as a guide to where you need to be precise along the edges of the matte you are painting. (The overlaid Alpha is shown here as white—see Figure 39.42). You can also look at your matte while you paint it by pressing Command+4.

Figure 39.42
Painted Alpha layer.

6. You will need to paint accurate edges only from frames 9 through 27. For frames 1 through 8 and 28 through 50, paint a quick-and-dirty matte. Remember to paint the actor's shadow as well because you will want to composite it into the final shot (see Figure 39.43).

Figure 39.43
The painted matte.

Part 3: Check The Composite And Perfect The Matte Edges

The Alpha that you just painted should be checked. You'll use Commotion's Comp Against preview mode to view a preview of the FG.GUY clip composited against the BG.CAR clip.

1. Load 1 frame of the BG.CAR file.

2. With the FG.GUY clip active, Shift-click on the Preview button in the RotoSplines palette. Set the Preview Mode to Comp Against (see Figure 39.44), and select BG.CAR from the FilmClip pop-up list. Click on OK.

3. You will now see a preview of the current frame of FG.GUY as it will appear when composited against the BG.CAR clip (see Figure 39.45).

Figure 39.44
The Preview Mode dialog box.

Figure 39.45
The composited preview.

Part 4: Rotoscope Using Multiple Splines

Commotion's ability to create multiple splines is often more efficient, because using more than one shape offers a much more flexible solution than trying to create a single master shape. When you have multiple splines, think of them as a stack of layers, with one spline on each layer and the first spline being on the top layer. You can adjust the stack order in the RotoSplines palette.

1. With the FG.GUY clip, move your Live Frame range to include frames 50 through 90 (or as many as possible). Adjust the BG.CAR clip to have just one frame of it open, to make more RAM available.

2. To continue the matte you painted by hand up to frame 50, make a "garbage" matte of the actor using a Bézier spline. Create a rough outline of his entire body on frame 50, then move to frame 60 and make another shape. Check the interpolation from 50 to 60 to make sure that the shape never touches the actor's body. Once the actor intersects the car mask for the second time you will want to make precision mattes for every part of the actor's body that come in contact with the car matte (see Figure 39.46).

3. Start by making a rotospline for the actor's left thigh using a natural spline. (You can use a combination of natural and Bézier splines.) You'll want to maintain as much precision as possible when the actor's legs are overlapping the car (see Figure 39.47).

4. At this point you can either complete the rest of the rotosplines yourself, or load the file CAR CHASE SPLINES, which contains finished splines for this shot. Notice that the splines below the torso are very precise, while the upper body and head are less accurate (because the sky is the same in both shots).

Figure 39.46
Create the rough outlines first.

Figure 39.47
Maintain as much precision as possible in the overlapped areas.

5. Commotion can also add realistic motion blur that is based on the movement of your splines. Go to frame 70 and turn on Motion Blur for the paths of the runner's left shoe and thigh by clicking on the Motion Blur icon for each path (see Figure 39.48).

6. Shift-click on the Preview button to access the preview options. Select High-Con and click on the Motion Blur checkbox. Click on OK (see Figures 39.49 and 39.50).

7. Click the mouse or press Command+period to exit the Preview mode. Before proceeding, turn Motion Blur off on the runner's shoe and thigh.

Figure 39.48
Turn on Motion Blur for each path.

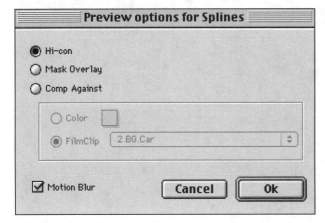

Figure 39.49
The Preview Options dialog.

Figure 39.50
A preview of the matte with a blur.

8. At this point, you must decide whether to render the Alpha channel as a separate clip to the Alpha of your current clip, or to perform the composite directly. In this example, you do the composite directly. To do this, click the Render button and check the Composite checkbox. Then select FilmClip and choose BG.CAR. This renders the foreground clip against the clip you chose, based on your splines as the matte.

Note: The first two options in the Render Options dialog box (see Figure 39.51), New Clip and To Disk, render the Alpha to a separate clip. New Clip automatically opens a new file; To Disk is saved directly to your hard drive.

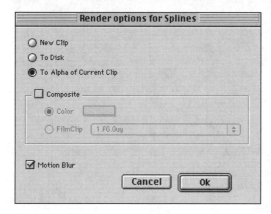

Figure 39.51
Render Options for Splines dialog box.

Part 5: Compositing The Clips

While it's likely that you perform your compositing in a dedicated compositing tool (such as Adobe After Effects), Commotion includes some basic compositing functions. If you want to render your matte as a separate clip and perform this composite in Commotion as a separate step, follow these steps:

1. Select Composite from the Calculate menu (see Figure 39.52).

2. With the FG.GUY clip active in the foreground, make the following selections in the Composite dialog box: select Normal from the Transfer Mode pop-up menu. In the Matte middle section, choose the clip you rendered as your matte (if a new clip, it will be open; if saved to disk, you need to load at least one frame). Check the checkbox. In Comp Against, choose BG.CAR from the Clip pop-up menu. At the bottom, choose Flatten, and click on OK. The FG.GUY clip will be composited with BG.CAR, based on the matte.

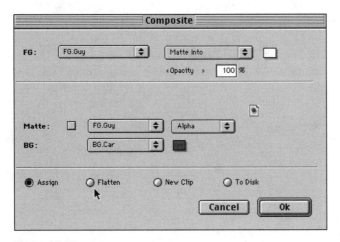

Figure 39.52
The Composite dialog box.

Conclusion

We hope that these tutorials have given you a taste of Commotion's power and the advantage of working in a real-time environment. Whatever your position in the production process, we are confident that Commotion will save you time and extend your creative range. Thanks for taking the time to learn more about Commotion. Please check out our Web site at **www.puffindesigns.com** for our latest tip and tricks documents, white papers, user testimonials, product demos, and much more.

Puffin Designs also sells products from Knoll Software, including the Knoll Lens Flare Pro for After Effects, an After Effects plug-in of particular interest to readers of this book. Downloadable demos are available at our Web site.

If you have questions about features that weren't covered in this demo or if you want to purchase Commotion, contact us at **www.puffindesigns.com**, by phone at 415-331-4560, or by email at **techsupport@puffindesigns.com**, **sales@puffindesigns.com**, or **info@ puffindesigns**.

INVIGORATOR

ZAXWERKS 3D

This chapter covers ZaxWerks 3D Invigorator, a plug-in that allows you to import an Illustrator vector shape, translate it into a 3D form, and animate it in 3D space.

If you think working in a 3D environment in After Effects is worth pursuing, you will definitely appreciate ZaxWerks' 3D Invigorator plug-in, a complete 3D art and animation system for After Effects. The 3D Invigorator for After Effects follows the Photoshop and Illustrator/FreeHand versions and uses the same basic interface. But, in After Effects, you can keyframe animate all your 3D manipulations.

How 3D Invigorator Works

ZaxWerks' 3D Invigorator works a bit differently in After Effects than it does in Photoshop or Illustrator/FreeHand. You develop Invigorator content in After Effects in the following manner:

1. Create a shape in Illustrator or FreeHand. This can be an open or closed shape, but if it's a text block, it has to be converted to paths.

2. Save the vector shape as an Illustrator file (with the extension .AI).

3. Open After Effects, and create a new composition. Create a new solid layer as a proxy to apply the 3D Invigorator effect to.

4. Select ZaxWerks 3D Invigorator from the Effects menu. The basic 3D Invigorator Effects interface will appear in the Effect Controls window (see Figure 40.1).

5. From this point, you have several choices. You can:

   • Click on Load, and select an AI file that was saved out from FreeHand, Illustrator, or any other application that exports AI files.

   • Click on Load, and then on the Fonts button to display a list of available fonts. The Size and Text Input boxes allow you to select a font, a size, and a text message. When all is okay, this text block will be written to the composition in 3D (see Figure 40.2).

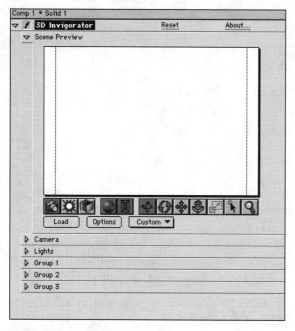

Figure 40.1
The 3D Invigorator controls as they appear in the Effect Controls window.

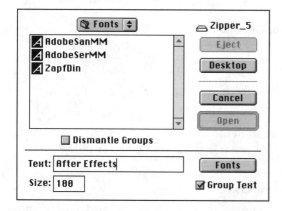

Figure 40.2
Click on Load and then the Fonts button to create a text block that can be further customized in 3D.

- Click on the Options Button in the Effects Controls window to display the full 3D Invigorator interface, giving you hundreds of ways to create and customize your imported AI files (see Figure 40.3).

As expected, keyframe animation controls are under the 3D Invigorator listing in the Effects list in the Time Layout window. You should take some time examining the 3D Invigorator interface.

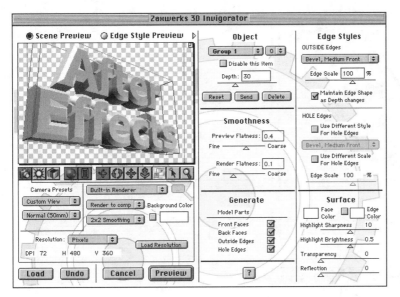

Figure 40.3
Click on the Options button to display the full 3D Invigorator interface.

Understanding The 3D Invigorator Interface

Let's look at each part of the 3D Invigorator interface to understand what it does and how to use it. It has eight major areas of interest: preview window, toolbar, rendering controls, object controls, smoothness options, generate options, edge styles controls, and surface controls.

Please note that the following details are meant to be only an overview of 3D Invigorator's tools and not a replacement for the extensive documentation found in the software's documentation and online help files.

Preview Window

The preview window displays either a representation of your finished 3D object or a wireframe view. The window is interactive, so you can maneuver your object by using tools in the toolbar below the window. The two buttons above the window select either the full 3D preview or an edge-on view of the 3D-shaped slice (see Figure 40.4).

Toolbar

The toolbar is below the preview window and consists of tools for viewing, lighting, and rendering options for your 3D objects (see Figure 40.5).

The key letters in Figure 40.5 represent the following options:

- *A*, *B*, and *C*—These are the three preset tabs for Camera, Lights, and Surface attributes. Selecting one of these presets brings its controls forward.

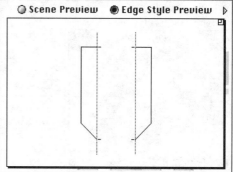

Figure 40.4
Click on one of the two buttons to select to see either the full 3D preview or an edge-on view of the 3D-shaped slice.

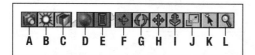

Figure 40.5
The toolbar and its icons.

- *D*—This is the Shader toggle. When off, the artwork in the preview window becomes a wireframe.

- *E*—This is the Bevel toggle. When off, the beveling attributes become invisible.

- *F*—This is the interactive 3D Rotation tool.

- *G*—This is the tool that rotates the object around the Z axis.

- *H*—This icon allows you to move the object around in its XY planes.

- *I*—This tool allows you to move the object in and out of the screen (its Z axis).

- *J*—This is the resizing tool.

- *K*—This is the Selection arrow, which allows you to select an object or objects in the scene.

- *L*—This is the Magnification tool, which allows you to zoom in or out of the scene.

Controls

The three preset tabs reveal their control options. Selecting the Camera preset tab allows you to access the camera controls. These controls allow you to alter the camera's focal settings and the view. You can also select whether to use the built-in renderer, or any other renderer you may have installed in the system. The art can be rendered to the composition, or to disk. Smoothing can be deactivated (a good idea when exploring your beveling options), or set to either 2×2 or 3×3. You can also set the background color here, as well as control the resolution of your image (see Figure 40.6).

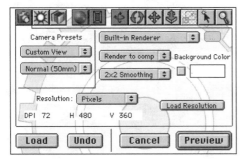

Figure 40.6
The camera preset controls.

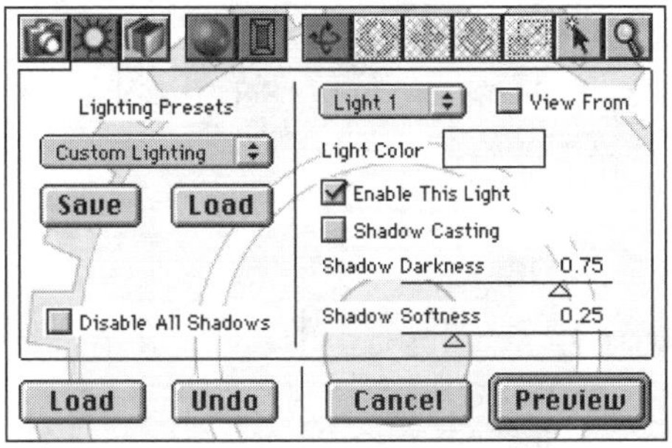

Figure 40.7
The light preset controls.

Selecting the Light preset tab provides access to the light controls, where you can load and save light presets, enable shadows, select from among six separate lights, assign color, and adjust shadow darkness and softnes (see Figure 40.7).

Selecting the Surface tab brings up its control panel. Remember that 3D Invigorator is a complete 3D application, so you can do all the things you might expect to do in 3D. As far as surfacing, you can apply a surface preset from a list of options that includes matte and luster finishes, metallics, and other options. You can also apply an image file as an environment map, further enhancing your surfacing capabilities.

> *Note: One way to use environment options is to select a frame from the background footage you are using as the environment map. This can make the 3D object look like it belongs in the environment you are placing it in, especially if it is surfaced with a metal or chrome look.*

The SpikeBuster control is also found here. Using SpikeBuster, you can tame any wayward spiking caused by point placement in your vector imports. The documents walk you through this attribute in detail (see Figure 40.8).

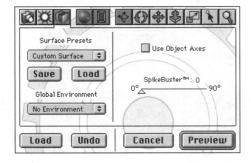

Figure 40.8
The surface preset controls.

Object Controls

These controls allow you to select the object(s) in the scene by name, and also to set their depth (see Figure 40.9).

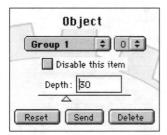

Figure 40.9
The Object controls.

Smoothness Options

The smoothness controls allow you to adjust smoothness for the preview screen and the final rendering in the composition (see Figure 40.10).

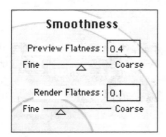

Figure 40.10
The Smoothness controls.

Generate Options

With these check boxes, you can toggle the visibility of front and back faces, and outside and hole edges (see Figure 40.11).

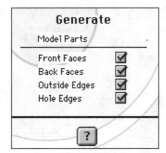

Figure 40.11
The Generate options controls.

Edge Styles Controls

The heart of 3D Invigorator is this control set. Edge styles refers to the shape of the extruded depth of the object. 3D Invigorator gives you control over the shape of the outside edges and the hole edges separately, thus greatly increasing the number of looks you can create. The outside and hole edges can also be scaled separately. The list of edge presets is extensive, with over 100 options (see Figure 40.12).

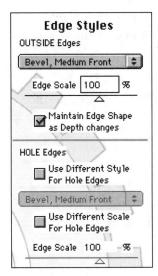

Figure 40.12
The Edge Styles controls.

Surface Controls

Four sliders allow you to control the surface properties: Highlight Sharpness, Highlight Brightness, Transparency, and Reflection. Reflection has to be set very high if you want an environment map to be seen. You can also set separate colors for the face and the edge (see Figure 40.13).

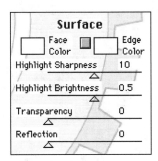

Figure 40.13
The Surface controls.

Creating An Invigorated 3D Logo Animation

Use the ZaxWerks' 3D Invigorator plug-in to create an animated 3D-logo animation. Just follow these steps:

1. Open Macromedia FreeHand, Adobe Illustrator, or any other vector-drawing application that can export Illustrator (AI) files. Create a drawing of your desired logo shape. (If this drawing includes text blocks, they must be changed to paths.) When finished, group all of the logo's parts as one, and export as an Illustrator (AI) file to disk.

2. Open After Effects, and create a new composition. Make the frame rate and size whatever you need.

3. Create a new color layer to act as a proxy for the 3D Invigorator content.

4. Select the 3D Invigorator plug-in from the ZaxWerks item in the Effects menu. The Effects Controls window will be displayed.

5. Click on Options to display the complete 3D Invigorator interface.

6. Click on Load and import the logo you created.

7. Use 3D Invigorator's preset controls to apply the depth, beveling, light placement, and surface properties you need. Select OK to return to the Effects Control window.

8. Use the keyframe animation controls in the Time Layout window to control the position and rotation of your 3D logo object over time.

PART V

UTILITIES

EVOLUTION AND IX ALIUS

ATOMIC POWER CORPORATION'S

Evolution, from Atomic Power Corp., is a next-generation set of professional plug-in animation systems for Adobe After Effects 3.1 and 4.

Evolution is targeted to digital video designers of motion graphics and special effects for film, broadcast, multimedia, Web, and games. Evolution consists of the following plug-ins: Multiplane, Shatter, Turbulator, Foam, Card Wipe, Card Dance, Vegas, Radio Wave, Radio Star, Radio Shape, WaveWorld, Caustics, and ColoRama. Note that these listings are not in alphabetical order. This is because many of these filters are meant to be used alongside others, so items are listed with this in mind. This has also been done at the request of the developer.

> *Note: At the developer's request, all detailed information concerning the control parameters and descriptions have been withheld. See the Evolution documentation for this information.*

Multiplane

  Multiplane enables true 3D-layer animation. A Multiplane composition is comprised of the source layers (with their visibility turned off) and a Multiplane "container" layer. Multiplane takes over AE's geometrics—position, scale, rotation, motion blur—and adds another control; depth. This allows users to precisely position up to 12 layers anywhere in 3D space. With adjustable lighting, layers can cast 3D shadows on each other. The Multiplane camera can be positioned to view the scene from any point in 3D space, and supports depth of focus for realistic compositing effects. The filter emulates a true multiplane camera: a popular animation technique used by Disney and others to create the illusion of depth within a scene comprised of 2D elements.

The following list describes some possible uses for the Multiplane effects:

- Use Multiplane whenever you need to create the illusion of 3D depth in a 2D animation.

- Use Multiplane to fly a text block over a solid backdrop, while it casts shadows.

The following controls allow you to adjust the Multiplane filter's parameters:

Mode, Motion Blur, Camera Position, Camera Depth, Camera Rotation, Depth Of Field Blur, Focus Depth, Depth Of Field, Camera Perspective, Enable Shadows, Shadow Saturation, Shadow Softness, Max Shadow Softness, Light Position, Light Depth, Ambient Lighting, Layer, Depth, Position, Rotation, Scaling, and Cast Shadows.

Detailed information regarding these controls is available from the Evolution documentation, after you purchase the plug-ins.

Shatter

With the powerful Shatter filter, a user can extrude a layer into 3D space, and then blow it up in an infinite number of entertaining ways! With two force points, complex "shockwave" explosions can easily be created. The user can blow up all of a layer or just blow holes in it. By animating a force point, the user can "paint with an explosive brush," carving a layer up bit by bit. Preset *shatter maps* include bricks, glass, puzzle pieces, and many others—plus the user has full control over creating custom shapes. The user can fine-tune the physics of the explosion, so it's easy to make the pieces behave as if they're made of Styrofoam—or made of stone. The shattered shapes are not merely flat polygons, but are actually extruded shapes, and the user can apply separate textures to the front, sides, and back of the extruded pieces. With full 3D camera and lighting controls, a Shatter effect can be easily composited into any scene.

You can also use a gradient to further control a Shatter explosion. A gradient allows the user to precisely control the order of an explosion via a third image, which means that if the user imports a picture of a client's logo, the user can use Shatter to blow a logo-shaped hole in a layer! Combined with the capability to generate custom shatter maps, Shatter offers the ultimate control in explosive effects. Shatter also contains Atomic Power's optional *corner pin camera*, a powerful, fast way to composite 3D effects into moving video via After Effects' motion tracker.

The following are some possible uses for the Shatter filter:

• Use this filter to blow a logo-shaped hole in a layer.

• Shatter footage to transition to new footage.

The following controls allow you to adjust the Shatter filter's parameters. Detailed information regarding these controls is available from the Evolution documentation when you purchase the plug-ins:

Render, Shape, Custom Shape Layer, Shape Repetitions, Shape Direction, Shape Origin, Extrusion Depth, Force 1 and Force 2 Parameters, Force Position, Force Depth, Force Radius, Force Strength, Rotation Speed, Tumble Axis, Randomness, Viscosity, Mass Variance, Gravity, Gravity Direction, Gravity Inclination, Color, Opacity, The Mode Settings, The Layer Settings, Camera X, Y, Z Rotation (Shatter-Camera only), Camera Position (Shatter-Camera only), Camera Depth (Shatter-Camera only), Focal Length, Camera Xform Order (Shatter-Camera only), Corner Pins, Corner Settings (Shatter—Corner Pin only), Auto Focal Length (Shatter—Corner Pin only), Focal Length, Light Intensity, Light Color, Light Position, Light Depth, Light Is, Ambient Light, Diffuse Reflection, Specular Reflection, Highlight Sharpness.

Turbulator

Turbulator is a powerful fractal-based displacement system, useful for generating convincing clouds, fire, and smoke. It works great with Atomic Power's Caustics—generating displacement maps for photo-realistic water—and also partners beautifully with Atomic Power's Caustics, generating incredible animated textures.

Within a single filter, Turbulator generates an animated fractal system, provides level controls for input and transparency, offers full displacement controls based on the animated fractal, and contains several effect points to precisely control the fractal system. For example, with Turbulator, the user can transform text into puffy clouds that slowly churn, dissipate, and drift off the screen. Fractal distortion points allow for the quick creation of tornadoes, galaxies, black holes, and so on.

The result of two years of development as an all-purpose special-effects generator for motion pictures, Turbulator is a special-effects power tool that offers ultimate flexibility and control (see Figure 41.1).

The following list shows some possible uses for the Turbulator filter:

- Transform text into puffy clouds that slowly churn, dissipate, and drift off the screen.
- Generate a cloud fly-through by increasing the level of detail in a Turbulator cloud.

The following controls allow you to adjust the Turbulator filter's parameters. Detailed information regarding these controls is available from the Evolution documentation after you purchase the plug-ins:

Presets, Type Of Noise, Detail, Alignment, Geometrics Center, Zoom, Aspect Ratio, X Origin, Y Origin, Time Origin, Horizontal Speed, Vertical Speed, Evolution Speed, Equalizer Input/Output Levels, Input Black, Input Gamma, Input White, Output Black, Output White, Displace, Horizontal, Vertical, Transparency/Fractal Influence, Transparency Input/Output Level.

Figure 41.1
Turbulator can create interesting image displacement effects. Left: Original footage. Center: Horizontal and vertical displacement of 6. Right: Horizontal and vertical displacement of 20.

Force Fields

There are four customizable Force Fields available for use in Turbulator: Attractor 1, 2, 3, and 4. Attractors are a class of distortions that don't work in pixel space, but rather in texture space. Attractor distortions don't blur or soften the displacement map, and as such, they preserve the details better than a classic distortion.

There are four types of Attractors:

1. Bubble is a repulsive punctual force field (it shoves pixels away).

2. Bubble 2.

3. Black Hole is an attractive punctual force field (it sucks pixels in).

4. Vortex creates a twirly distortion, like a spiral galaxy.

Attractor Parameter Controls

The Attractor parameter controls are: Center, Radius, Intensity, and Falloff.

Attenuation

Because you might not always want to displace an entire image or distribute the transparency of a Turbulator effect evenly across a layer, the Attenuation controls allow you to target the placement of the effect. They work just like the Ramp filter in After Effects. The controls include the following:

Type, Noise, Distort, Transparency, Start Intensity, Stop Intensity, Starting Point/Ending Point. Place the centroids to set and animate the starting and ending points of the attenuation gradient.

Foam

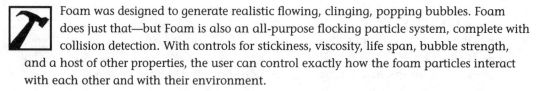 Foam was designed to generate realistic flowing, clinging, popping bubbles. Foam does just that—but Foam is also an all-purpose flocking particle system, complete with collision detection. With controls for stickiness, viscosity, life span, bubble strength, and a host of other properties, the user can control exactly how the foam particles interact with each other and with their environment.

The user can specify a separate layer to act as a *flow map*, controlling precisely where the foam goes—or doesn't go—on the screen. For example, the user can have particles flow around a logo, or fill it up with bubbles. Foam ships with 20 preset bubble-types but the user can define any layer (even an animated one!) as a custom *bubble map*. While perfect out of the box for beer spills, bubble baths, or toothpaste commercials, Foam's powerful controls make it a useful tool for other general-purpose flocking animations, such as swarming ants or crowd simulations (see Figure 41.2).

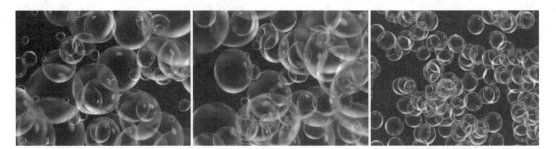

Figure 41.2
A selection of bubbles created with the Foam filter.

The following are some possible uses for the Foam filter:

- Use Foam to create bubbles escaping from an undersea diver or a fish.
- Use Foam to create an interesting bubbling backdrop for any footage.
- Create bubbles in a glass of champagne.

The following controls allow you to adjust the Foam filter's parameters. Detailed information regarding these controls is available from the Evolution documentation after you purchase the plug-ins:

View, Producer Point, Producer X/Y Size, Producer Orientation, Zoom Producer Point, Production Rate, Size, Size Variance, Lifespan, Bubble Growth Speed, Strength, Initial Speed, Initial Direction, Wind Speed, Wind Direction, Turbulence, Wobble Amount, Repulsion, Pop Velocity, Viscosity, Stickiness, Zoom, Universe Size, Blend Mode, Bubble Texture (this is used to either pick a one of the 17 preset bubble textures, or to tell Foam that you're going to use a bubble of your own creation), Bubble Texture Layer, Bubble Orientation, Environment Map (if you'd like an environment to be reflected in your bubbles, set the layer you wish to use here; it must be present in the comp, but its visibility can be turned off), Reflection Strength, Reflection Convergence, Flow Map, Flow Map Steepness, Flow Map Fits, Simulation Quality, and Random Seed.

Card Wipe (Camera And Corner Pin)

  You know how a large group of people at a college football game will hold cards above their heads, forming a picture, then flip them all over to make another picture? That's what this plug-in simulates. Like Shatter, Card Wipe is a full 3D effect, with lighting controls, full control over the number of rows and columns, built-in transition presets, jitter controls to add "human-ness" to the effect, and even the capability to use a gradient map to control the order of the card flips. Card Wipe also contains Atomic Power's optional *corner pin camera*, a powerful, fast way to composite 3D effects in perspective into moving video via After Effects' motion tracker.

The following are some possible uses for the Card Wipe filter:

- Create a message using a series of cards, and then animate the cards so they flip to reveal another message.

- Flip animated footage to reveal another animation on the other side.

The following controls allow you to adjust the Card Wipe filter's parameters. Detailed information regarding these controls is available from the Evolution documentation when you purchase the plug-ins:

Transition Completion, Transition Width, Back Layer, Rows, Columns, Card Scale, Flip Axis, Flip Direction, Flip Order, Gradient Layer, Timing Randomness, Random Seed, Camera System, Camera Position, Camera Position (Card Wipe—Camera only), Camera Depth (Card Wipe—Camera only), Focal Length, Camera Xform Order (Card Wipe—Camera only), Corner Pins, Corner Settings (Card Wipe—Corner Pin only), Auto Focal Length (Card Wipe—Corner Pin only), Focal Length, Light Intensity, Light Color, Light Position, Light Depth, Light Is, Ambient Light, Diffuse Reflection, Specular Reflection, Highlight Sharpness, X, Y, Z Jitter Amount, X, Y, Z Jitter Speed, X, Y, Z Rotation Jitter Amount, X, Y, Z Rot Jitter Speed.

Card Dance (Camera And Corner Pin)

  Card Dance uses the same 3D engine found in Card Wipe, but it allows the user to generate astonishing *card choreography* by controlling all geometric aspects of the cards via a second layer. With Card Dance the user can easily make a crowd "do the wave," or simulate one of those "extruded pin" sculptures, or have the letters of a logo floating lazily on the surface of a pond. A true designer's tool, Card Dance offers creative control never before seen in After Effects or any other package.

The following are some possible uses for the Card Dance filter:

- Make the letters of a logo look like they're floating lazily on the surface of a pond.

- Make the animated footage of a crowd into a wave pattern.

The following controls allow you to adjust the Card Dance filter's parameters. Detailed information regarding these controls is available from the Evolution documentation on purchase of the plug-ins:

Rows & Columns, Rows, Columns, Back Layer, Gradient Layer 1, Gradient Layer 2, Rotation Order, Transformation Order, Source Pop-ups, X, Y, Z Position Scale, X, Y, Z Position Offset, X, Y, Z Rotation Source, X, Y, Z Rotation Scale, X, Y, Z Rotation Offset, X, Y Scale Source, X, Y Scale, X, Y Scale Offset, Camera Position, Camera Depth, Focal Length, Camera Xform Order, Corner Settings, Auto Focal Length, Focal Length, Light Intensity, Light, Light Position, Light Depth, Light Is, Ambient Light, Diffuse Reflection, Specular Reflection, Highlight Sharpness.

Making A Card Dance With A Ramped Layer

Do the following:

1. Apply a black-to-white gradient to a layer using the Ramp filter.

2. Use that in Card Dance as a gradient layer to control the rotation of the cards (with a setting of 45).

Vegas

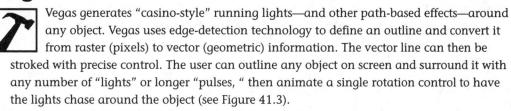

Vegas generates "casino-style" running lights—and other path-based effects—around any object. Vegas uses edge-detection technology to define an outline and convert it from raster (pixels) to vector (geometric) information. The vector line can then be stroked with precise control. The user can outline any object on screen and surround it with any number of "lights" or longer "pulses, " then animate a single rotation control to have the lights chase around the object (see Figure 41.3).

The following are some possible uses for the Vegas filter:

• Use this effect to outline a face with marquee-like lights.

• Use this filter to generate and animate fake "traffic" for an urban night scene.

The following controls allow you to adjust the Vegas filter's parameters. Detailed information regarding these controls is available from the Evolution documentation on purchase of the plug-ins:

Input Layer, Invert Input, If Layer Sizes Differ, Blend Mode, Value Channel, Value Threshold, Pre-Blur, Tolerance, Stroke Color, Stroke Width, Stroke Hardness, Length, Length Controls, Segments, Stroke Rotation, Random Stroke Origin, Random Seed, Start Opacity, Mid-point Opacity, Mid-point Position, End Opacity, Stroke Mode, and Contour.

Figure 41.3
A selection of Vegas effects applied to footage at alternate Valu4e Thresholds (left to right): 115, 16, and 38.

Radio Wave

  Radio Wave emits concentric polygons from an effect point. If the effect point sits still, the shapes will simply radiate outward, like the station ID for Comedy Central. Animate the effect point, however, and you'll realize that Radio Wave is a particle system, useful for generating pond ripples, or sound waves, or beautiful geometric patterns.

The user has control over the number of sides in the polygon; the width, color, and quality of the line; plus the speed, rotation, life span, and fade rate of the shapes. Turn on Reflection, and the emanating shapes will bounce off the sides of the layer, making Radio Wave suitable for generating realistic ripple displacement maps when combined with Atomic Power's Caustics filter (see Figure 41.4).

The following are some possible uses for the Radio Wave filter:

- Create a 1930s commercial that features a radio tower emitting these waves.

- Use this filter several times on the same layer to create interesting wave interference patterns.

The following controls allow you to adjust the Radio Wave filter's parameters. Detailed information regarding these controls is available from the Evolution documentation, on purchase of the plug-ins:

Producer Point, Parameters Are Set At, Wave Type, Shape Points, Curve Size, Curvyness, Shape Rotation, Wave Color, Wave Speed, Wave Frequency, Wave Start Width, Wave End Width, Wave Intensity, Lifespan, Fadeout Rate, Reflection.

Figure 41.4
Left to right, bell curve Radio Waves with varying wave speeds: 6, 10, and 20.

Radio Star

  Radio Star contains the same controls as Radio Wave, but is optimized to emit stars rather than polygons, with extra controls to adjust the number and length of points and the "roundness" of the star's corners (see Figure 41.5).

Figure 41.5
Left to right: Radio Star waves with maximum curve and curve sizes of: 0, .5, and 1.

The following are some possible uses for the Radio Star filter:

• Emit Radio Stars from a tower image in your footage.

• Use multiple Radio Star filters on the same layer to create intersecting star waves.

The following controls allow you to adjust the Radio Star filter's parameters. Detailed information regarding these controls is available from the Evolution documentation on purchase of the plug-ins:

Producer Point, Parameters Are Set At, Wave Type, Shape Points, Star Depth, Curve Size, Curvy-ness, Shape Rotation, Wave Color, Wave Speed, Wave Frequency, Wave Start Width, Wave End Width, Wave Intensity, Lifespan, Fadeout Rate, and Reflection.

Radio Shape

  Radio Shape contains the same controls as Radio Wave, but is optimized to emit custom shapes rather than polygons or stars. The user has full control over defining any shape, using the same edge-detection/rasterizing technology found in the Vegas filter. With these capabilities, waves shaped like logos, characters, or numbers can be easily added to a composition (see Figure 41.6).

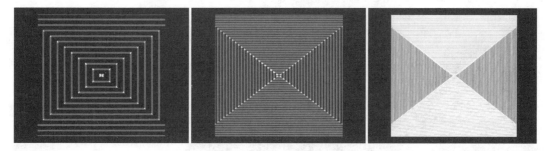

Figure 41.6
Left to right: Altering the Radio Shape Frequency: 2, 5, and 12.

The following are some possible uses for the Radio Shape filter:

• Use Radio Shape waves when you want to design the waves yourself.

• Use multiple Radio Shape filters on the same layer to create intersecting waves of your own design.

The following controls allow you to adjust the Radio Shape filter's parameters. Detailed information regarding these controls is available from the Evolution documentation on purchase of the plug-ins:

Producer Point, Parameters Are Set At, Wave Type, Gradient Layer, Gradient Center, Value Channel, Invert Input, Value Threshold, Pre-Blur, Tolerance, Contour, Curve Size, Curvyness, Shape Rotation, Wave Color, Wave Speed, Wave Frequency, Wave Start Width, Wave End Width, Wave Intensity, Lifespan (seconds), Fadeout Rate (seconds), and Reflection.

Wave World

 Wave World is a physics-based liquid wave generator. The user generates a top-down view of the virtual liquid and, by animating an effect point, drags a "digital finger" through it. The effect point can generate oscillating waves as it moves, or it can simply displace the water (like a boat wake). Waves emanate from the effect point, interacting with each other, and reflecting off their environment in a realistic fashion.

In other words, you can have a top-down view of a logo floating in water, and the waves in the water could appear to reflect off of the sides of the layer and the logo. This filter generates a grayscale displacement map only, which is interesting, but it's optimized to work in conjunction with Atomic Power's Caustics filter.

Additionally, the user can define a ground layer, which is essentially a grayscale height map. If the slope of the ground plane is steep enough to intersect with the water's surface, the resulting "shore" will also produce waves—you can use a logo, text, or other still to generate waves that emanate from complex shapes (see Figure 41.7).

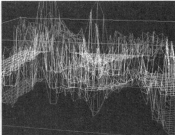

Figure 41.7
Wave World generates interesting maps for the Caustics filter. Left to right: Original footage, Wireframe Preview, and Height Map.

The following are some possible uses for the Wave World filter:

- Use Wave World to animate the waves generated by any moving object.

- Create a top-down view of a logo floating in water, and with Wave World, create waves in the water that appear to reflect off of the sides of the layer, and the logo.

The following controls allow you to adjust the Wave World filter's parameters. Detailed information regarding these controls is available from the Evolution documentation after you purchase the plug-ins:

View, Horizontal Rotation, Vertical Rotation, Vertical Scale, Brightness, Contrast, Gamma Adjustment, Render Dry Areas As, Transparency, Grid Width/Grid Height, Water Level, Wave Speed, Damping, Reflect Edges, Pre-Roll (seconds), Ground, Ground Steepness, Ground Height, Producer Type, Producer Point, Producer Height/Length, Producer Width, Producer Angle, Producer Amplitude, Producer Frequency, and Producer Phase.

Caustics

 The word *caustics* refers to the reflections of light you see at the bottom of a body of water, which are generated by the light refracting through the water surface. Atomic Power's Caustics generates just this effect, rendering ultra-realistic water surfaces when used in conjunction with Wave World, Turbulator, and/or Radio Wave. Caustics is also useful for generating general distortion effect, suitable for distressing type or other graphics (see Figure 41.8).

The following are some possible uses for the Caustics filter:

- Simulate the patterns generated on moving water at the bottom of a pool or lake.

- Simulate energy effects in science fantasy projects.

- Create Van Gogh-like paintings from any footage. Just use a Water Depth of 0.1.

The following controls allow you to adjust the Caustics filter's parameters. Detailed information regarding these controls is available from the Evolution documentation after you purchase the plug-ins:

Figure 41.8
Left to right: Original footage, same footage used as Water Surface with Water Depth of 0.1, and Water Depth of 1.

Bottom, Bottom Scaling, Bottom Repeat Mode, If Layer Sizes Differ, Water Surface, Wave Height, Water Depth, Refractive Index, Render Caustics, Surface Color, Surface Opacity, Smoothing, Light Intensity, Light Color, Light Position, Light Height, Light Is, Ambient Light, Diffuse Reflection, Specular Reflection, and Highlight Sharpness.

Colorama

  Colorama is the ultimate color management tool for AE. With Colorama the user can re-map the pixels of a layer to a custom palette composed of *any number* of colors. For example, the user could sample the luminance of a layer and re-map that source to a gold gradient, creating output video that looks like it's made of gold. Colorama can be used as a powerful levels-adjustment took, a powerful tinting tool, even a keying tool. The custom user interface allows the user to create a complex color palette on the fly or load a custom palette from Photoshop. The circular structure of Color Master's color palette allows for easy color-cycling effects, useful for pulsing lights or psychedelic effects (see Figure 41.9).

The following are some possible uses for the Colorama filter:

• Create backdrops that shimmer through cycled hues.

• Add multicolored cycling color to a text block.

The following controls allow you to adjust the Colorama filter's parameters. Detailed information regarding these controls is available from the Evolution documentation on purchase of the plug-ins:

Get Phase From, Add Phase, Add Phase From, Phase Shift, Use Preset Palette, Output Cycle, Interpolate Palette, Modify, Modify Alpha, Change Empty Pixels, Matching Color, Matching Tolerance, Matching Softness, Matching Mode, Mask Layer, Masking Mode, Composite Over Layer, and Blend With Original.

Figure 41.9
The images left to right display what alternate Phase values can create from a Negative Palette: 0, 180, and 270.

IX Alius

ImageXpress Alius plug-in is a multifeatured posterization environment that can be used to alter the look of your footage (see Figure 41.10).

Use IX Alius to do the following:

- Create animated stained glass footage by applying this filter to animated layers. Use the Radical Stained Glass setting.

- Use the Pastels and Outlines setting for a rotoscoped look.

Activating IX Alius brings up its interface, where all customization is applied. Blending the finished posterized footage with the original is all that can be keyframed.

The following controls allow you to customize IX Alius looks:

- *Reduce Image Detail*—It's a good idea to leave this checked as the default because too much detail can detract from the posterized effect.

- *Tonality*—This adjusts the lightness or darkness of the base footage, effecting the mid-tones of the posterization. The settings range from –0.5 to 0.5.

- *Saturation*—Values less than 0 tend to remove color, and a –100 creates a gray result. Higher saturated values add more color vibrancy. The settings range from –100 to 100.

- *Hue*—Adjust this slider to alter the color ranges.

- *Detail*—The setting ranges from 0 to 8. Lower values accentuate detail, while higher values smooth the detail out.

- *Number*—Determines how many tone stages are present in each channel of the base footage. The settings range from 5 to 15.

- *Base*—Select from three listed options: No Stages (uses original footage tonality), Detailed Stages (creates a harder-edged posterization), and Smooth Stages (creates a softer-edged posterization).

- *Intensity*—This effects both the strength and color of outlined areas of the footage. The settings range from 0 to 255. 0 maximizes the outlines, and 255 removes all of them.

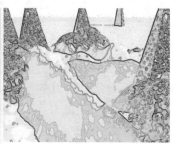

Figure 41.10
left to right: Original footage, Radical Stained Glass, and Pastels and Outlines.

- *Thickness*—This controls the thickness and weight (in settings of 1 to 9) of the outlines. Higher values increase both.

- *Color*—Select either Gray-Black or Chromatic to color the outlines.

- *Blend*—Select from among Darker, Lighter, Brighter, Base Image Only, or Outlines Only to alter the look of the footage.

- *Settings*—Use one of the presets in this list to apply a base look to the footage.

TOOLS

The Matte Wizard, Reality Check, and Style Tools plug-ins from Industrial Strength Effects Company cover a wide range of effects in four separate volumes.

The effects covered in the four volumes are: Image Tools (Alpha Clean, Color Matcher, Composite Blur, Denoiser, Faster Blur, Rack Focus, Wire and Rig Removal, and Zone HLS); Matte Wizard (Edge Blur, Edge Border, Edge Feather, Edge Feather Sharp, Light Wrap, Matte Cutter, Smooth Screen, and Spill Killer); Reality Check (Brimstone, Camera Blur, Clouds, Fire, Mirage, Real Shadows, Super Displacer, Tunnel, and Turbulent Distortion); and Style Tools (Alpha Ramp, Blender, Color Map, Framer, Grunge, Hall of Mirrors, Hall of Time, Outliner, Title Scroll, Turbulent Edges, Typewriter, and Video Feedback).

Image Tools: Alpha Clean

 ISFX Alpha Clean eliminates Alpha channel noise. It considers both the Alpha density and how separated a pixel is from other elements to determine which pixels will be transparent.

The following are some possible uses for the Alpha Clean filter:

- Use this filter to clean up any Alpha channel, especially scanned images.
- Use this filter to create image effects by smoothing out the Alpha channel beyond its standard contents.

The following controls allow you to adjust the Alpha Clean filter's parameters:

- *Size Threshold*—This controls the size of the area effected by a cleanup. The settings range from 0 to 100 percent. Increase this value to affect more of the area around the disconnected pixels.
- *Alpha Threshold*—The higher the value (with settings from 0 to 100 percent), the more pixels will be cleaned up.
- *Connection Threshold*—The higher this value (with settings ranging from 0 to 100 percent), the more pixels will be removed farther from major area elements.
- *Preview Alpha Only*—Checking this feature allows you to preview the Alpha channel only.

- *Blend With Original*—This sets the degree (in settings that range from 0 to 100 percent) of blend with the original footage.

Image Tools: Color Matcher

This filter allows users to match colors between and among layers in a composite.

The following are some possible uses for the Color Matcher filter:

- Use this filter when you have to match similar colors in two or more layers. A good example would be blue hues in multiple-layered sky footage.

- Use this filter when you want to create controlled solarizations by exploring the replacement of color ranges when the Source and Target layer are the same.

The following controls allow you to adjust the Color Matcher filter's parameters:

- *View*—The options are Changed Colors and Original Colors.

- *Strength*—This value determines the degree to which the Source Colors are moved toward the Target Colors. The settings range from 0 to 100 percent.

- *Sample Source/Sample Target*—By using these three color selection parameters (white, gray, and black), you can alter the hues in the image to match your requirements.

- *Target Layer*—Select any layer in the stack as the target for this effect.

- *Blend With Original*—This sets the degree of blend with the original footage. The settings range from 0 to 100 percent.

Image Tools: Composite Blur

ISFX Composite Blur is a very fast blur effect and is controlled by a third layer. Use it to create blurring between layers, using edge masks created by using the ISFX Edge Border filter for the control layer (see Figure 42.1).

The following are some possible uses for the Composite Blur filter:

- With None selected as the control layer, create a keyframe animation that moves from a Blur Amount of 100 to a final value of 1. This results in the footage coming into clear view from a hazy overlay.

- To mimic a hazy day, use the targeted layer as the control layer (preferably a nature scene), and set a Blur Amount of 100 and a Luminance control attribute. Keyframe the Control Gain from 9 to 1 to make the scene clear a little.

The following controls allow you to adjust the Composite Blur filter's parameters:

- *Blur Type*—Select between Better or Faster.

- *Blur Amount*—This value (which ranges from 0 to 100) determines the degree to which the target footage is blurred.

- *Alpha Channel*—When checked, the Alpha channel is blurred.

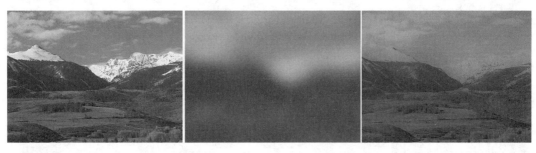

Figure 42.1
Left to right: Original footage, None as the control layer with a setting of 50, and the footage itself as the control layer with a setting of 100 and a Luminance control attribute.

- *Control Layer/Control Attribute*—Select any layer in the stack as the control layer. Explore different control attributes to see which creates an effect you like. Checking the Stretch Layer box stretches the layer to accommodate off-sizes.

- *Control Gain*—Boost the gain (in a range from 0 to 10) to apply more blur.

- *Control Polarity*—Checking this box inverts the application of the blur.

- *Blend With Original*—This sets the degree of blend with the original footage. The settings range from 0 to 100 percent.

Image Tools: Denoiser

Animated footage sometime contains jitter, often caused by unstabilized camera usage. This filter works to eliminate the jitter.

- Use this filter to correct frame jitter.

The following controls allow you to adjust the Denoiser filter's parameters:

- *Time Depth*—This value (in a range from 1 to 10) determines how many frames the filter will compare in order to remove the jitter. Note that excessive jitter in the footage may not be fixable by this filter.

- *Average Range*—Higher values allow the filter to attempt to remove more jitter. The settings range from 0 to 100 percent.

- *Blend With Original*—This sets the degree of blend with the original footage. The settings range from 0 to 100 percent.

Image Tools: Faster Blur

This is a basic blur filter that works very fast.

- Use this blur when you don't need bells or whistles.

The following controls allow you to adjust the Faster Blur filter's parameters:

- *Blur Type*—Select between Better or Faster.

- *Blur Amount*—This sets the strength (in a range from 0 to 100) of the blur. Checking the Blur Alpha box applies the blur to the Alpha channel.

- *Blend With Original*—This sets the degree of blend with the original footage. The settings range from 0 to 100 percent.

Image Tools: Rack Focus

This filter allows users to simulate a 3D environment by creating a depth-of-field effect. ISFX Rack Focus produces a high-quality variable blur controlled by another layer and provides control over the Focal Point, or the control value that produces no blur. If used with a depth map or Z-buffer, such as are produced by many 3D filters (the Boris AE perspective filters, for example), you can use Rack Focus to create a blurring of elements in the distance. By manipulating the Focal Point and Depth Of Field values, you can even add a 3D-like depth to 2D footage (see Figure 42.2).

- Use this filter to add 3D depth to your footage.

The following controls allow you to adjust the Rack Focus filter's parameters:

- *Max Blur*—This value sets the maximum amount (in a range from 0 to 200) of resulting blur.

- *Focal Point*—(0 to 100 percent) The control layer value that produces no blur. If set to 0 percent, then layer values of 0 produce no blur, and values of 255 produce the maximum blur. If set to 100 percent, then layer values of 0 produce the maximum blur, and values of 255 produce no blur.

- *Depth Of Field*—This controls the perceived depth (with settings that range from 0 to 10) of the low-blur area of the footage.

- *Control Layer/Control Attribute*—Select any layer in the stack as the control layer. Explore different control attributes to see which creates an effect you like. Selecting the Stretch Layer checkbox stretches the layer to accommodate off-sizes.

- *Control Polarity*—Checking this box inverts the application of the blur.

- *Blend With Original*—This sets the degree of blend with the original footage. The settings range from 0 to 100 percent.

Figure 42.2
From left to right: Original footage, Focal Point of 50 and a Brightness control attribute, and a Focal Point of 100 with the same control attribute.

Image Tools: Wire And Rig Removal

 This filter quickly eliminates wires and unwanted objects from a layer. ISFX Wire And Rig Removal replaces unwanted objects such as control wires and rigs with pixels stitched from either side of the unwanted elements. Time offset cloning is also available, allowing you to pull pixels from past or future frames to cover the unwanted elements.

The following are some possible uses for the Wire and Rig Removal filter:

- Use this filter to remove the control wires used in live special effects footage.
- Use this filter to remove anomalies from the footage that appear as discreet features, such as scratches.

The following controls allow you to adjust the Wire and Rig Removal filter's parameters:

- *View*—View the composition before or after the effect is applied to compare the results.
- *Replacement*—The options are Mask (cuts a hole in the Alpha, revealing the layer underneath), Clone (copies pixels from a space offset or time offset source), and Stitch (pulls pixels from the edges and duplicates them across the selection).
- *End 1/End 2*—Place the centroids at the start and end of the feature you want to remove.
- *Width*—This sets the pixel width of the replacement area. Settings range from 1 to 1,000.
- *Feather*—You can feather the edges of the replaced area to blend it more effectively. Settings range from 1 to 1,000.
- *Clone X/Y Offset*—(–10,000 to 10,000) Using either or both an X or Y offset allows you to take the replacement information from other areas of the footage. Settings range from –1,000 to 1,000.
- *Clone Frame Difference*—You can get the replacement information from previous or future frames by altering this value (in a range from –100 to 100).
- *Replacement Color*—Select a color that will act as the replacement color for the removed area.
- *Replacement Noise*—Sets the level of replacement noise for the area selected. The settings range from 0 to 100 percent.
- *Preview Alpha Only*—This checkbox allows you to preview only the Alpha channel.
- *Blend With Original*—This sets the degree of blend with the original footage. The settings range from 0 to 100 percent.

Image Tools: Zone HLS

ISFX Zone HLS controls the Hue, Saturation, and Lightness of a layer (see Figure 42.3).

The following are some possible uses for the Zone HLS filter:

- Use this filter to create a wide variety of image effects based on altering the HLS Channels.
- Use Zone HLS for tonal matching and correction to integrate layers in a composite.

Figure 42.3
Left: Original footage. Center: Shadows darkened to maximum. Right: Shadows darkened to maximum, and Highlights brightened to maximum.

The following controls allow you to adjust the Zone HLS filter's parameters:

- *Shadow Hue/Lightness/Saturation*—Set the parameters for the darker HLS components of your footage.

- *Midtone Hue/Lightness/Saturation*—Set the parameters for the midrange HLS components of your footage.

- *Highlight Hue/Lightness/Saturation*—Set the parameters for the brighter HLS components of your footage.

- *Blend With Original*—This sets the degree of blend with the original footage. The settings range from 0 to 100 percent.

Matte Wizard: Edge Blur/Edge Blur Pro

 This allows you to blur the edge of a layer. It works best when the layer is a masked cutout area (see Figure 42.4).

The following are some possible uses for the Edge Blur filter:

> **Note: Edge Blur and Edge Blur Pro are distinguished only by the extent of the Blur settings and that the Pro version includes adjustable Width parameters.**

- Use this filter to add a blur to the edges of a layer mask.

- Use this filter to create soft vignette blends to take the hard edge off of your layer content.

The following controls allow you to adjust the Edge Blur filter's parameters:

- *Blur Amount*—(0 to 200) and (0 to 1,000) for Pro version. This sets the overall strength of the blur.

- *Blur Width (Pro filter only)*—This value (with settings that range from 0 to 1,000) determines the pixel width of the blur.

- *Preview Alpha*—This checkbox allows you to view the Alpha channel only.

- *Blend With Original*—This sets the degree of blend with the original footage. The settings range from 0 to 100 percent.

Figure 42.4
Left: Original masked layer. Center: Blur Amount and Edge Width of 20. Right: Blur Amount of 50 and Edge Width of 75.

Matte Wizard: Edge Border/Edge Border Pro

This filter adds a smooth, white border around the layer's Alpha channel. Use it before you add an Edge Blur to create a better transition.

The following are some possible uses for the Edge Border filter:

• Use this filter prior to using the Edge Blur filter to create a smoother blurred transition.

• Use this filter to add a smooth border to any Alpha channel.

The following controls allow you to adjust the Edge Border filter's parameters:

• *Border Width*—(0 to 100) and (0 to 1,000) for the Pro version. This determines the pixel width of the added border.

• *Preview Alpha*—This checkbox allows you to view the Alpha channel only.

• *Blend With Original*—This sets the degree of blend with the original footage. The settings range from 0 to 100 percent.

> *Note: Edge Border and Edge Border Pro are distinguished only by the extent of the Border Width setting.*

Matte Wizard: Edge Feather/Edge Feather Pro

Here's another way to soften a hard edge of the Alpha channel.

The following are some possible uses for the Edge Feather filter:

• Use this filter as a substitute for Edge Blur.

• Use this filter to soften the edge of any Alpha channel.

> *Note: Edge Feather and Edge Feather Pro are distinguished by the fact that Edge Feather has only a Size setting, whereas Edge Feather Pro includes more customizing options.*

The following controls allow you to adjust the Edge Feather filter's parameters:

- *Feather Size (non-Pro version only)*—(0 to 1,000) This value determines the size in pixels of the feathered area.

- *Edge Pre-Blur (Pro version only)*—(0 to 100) This blurs the edge before it is feathered.

- *Edge Smoothing (Pro version only)*—(0 to 63) This controls the overall softness of the edge, with higher values making a softer edge.

- *Edge Threshold (Pro version only)*— This value determines where the edge begins, with higher values moving the edge inward. The settings range from 0 to 100 percent.

- *Feather Width (Pro version only)*—(0 to 200) Controls the width of the feathering in pixels.

- *Feather Slope (Pro version only)*—(1 to 8) This controls the abruptness of the transition, with lower values creating more gradual transitions.

- *Edge Post-Blur (Pro version only)*—(0 to 100) This value adds another blur to the edge, eliminating any stray jagged edges.

- *Preview Alpha*—This checkbox allows you to view the Alpha channel only.

- *Blend With Original*—This sets the degree of blend with the original footage. The settings range from 0 to 100 percent.

Matte Wizard: Edge Feather Sharp

 This filter is useful when you want to feather an Alpha channel edge without removing or softening the sharp angles.

The following are some possible uses for the Edge Feather Sharp filter:

- Use this filter to preserve the sharp edges of the Alpha channel while adding feathering.

- Use this filter in combination with the ISFX Edge Border filter to widen the edge before feathering.

The following controls allow you to adjust the Edge Feather Sharp filter's parameters:

- *Feather Width (Pro version only)*—(0 to 1,000) Controls the width of the feathering in pixels.

- *Feather Slope (Pro version only)*—(1 to 10) This controls the abruptness of the transition, with lower values creating more gradual transitions.

- *Alpha Blur*—(0 to 100) This value adds a uniform softness to the entire Alpha channel mask.

- *Preview Alpha*—This checkbox allows you to view the Alpha channel only.

- *Blend With Original*—This sets the degree of blend with the original footage. The settings range from 0 to 100 percent.

Matte Wizard: Light Wrap

This filter applies soft light from a selected background layer (see Figure 42.5).

The following are some possible uses for the Light Wrap filter:

- Use negative Brightness settings to add shadows to the selected layer.
- Use keyframe-animated Brightness settings to add pulsating glows to the selected layer.

The following controls allow you to adjust the Light Wrap filter's parameters:

- *Background Layer*—Select any layer in the stack to use as the background light source.
- *Background Blur*—(0 to 1,000) This value sets the amount of blur added to the light source, creating either sharper or softer lights.
- *Composite Mode*—Explore using different transfer modes to effect the composite.
- *Width*—(0 to 1,000) This value sets the width of the Light Wrap.
- *Brightness*—(–1 to 1) This sets the overall brightness of the Light Wrap. Negative settings create darker areas.
- *Blend With Original*—This sets the degree of blend with the original footage. The settings range from 0 to 100 percent.

Figure 42.5
Left: Source layer. Center: Target layer. Right: Blended composite, using the Light Wrap filter.

Matte Wizard: Matte Cutter

Using this filter, the next layer down in the stack is applied as a matte for your top layer (see Figure 42.6).

The following are some possible uses for the Matte Cutter filter:

- Use this filter to composite matte footage on another layer.
- Explore the inversion of the filter to create darker composites.

Figure 42.6
Left: Source of matte. Center: Target layer. Right: Composite using the Matte Cutter filter.

The following controls allow you to adjust the Matte Cutter filter's parameters:

- *Control Channel*—Select from among the options to apply the matte.

- *Invert Control*—This inverts the Control Channel option you have selected.

- *Blend With Original*—This sets the degree of blend with the original footage. The settings range from 0 to 100 percent.

Matte Wizard: Smooth Screen

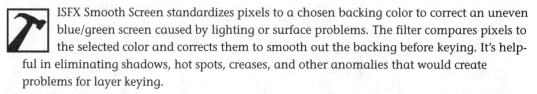

ISFX Smooth Screen standardizes pixels to a chosen backing color to correct an uneven blue/green screen caused by lighting or surface problems. The filter compares pixels to the selected color and corrects them to smooth out the backing before keying. It's helpful in eliminating shadows, hot spots, creases, and other anomalies that would create problems for layer keying.

The following are some possible uses for the Smooth Screen filter:

- Use this filter when the footage was shot against a blue or green screen for compositing, before you apply keying.

- Use this filter for more general background color correction.

The following controls allow you to adjust the Smooth Screen filter's parameters:

- *Screen Color*—Select the desired color with the eyedropper or from the system palette.

- *Hue Tolerance*—Selects the range of colors for pixel correction, from 0 (selects only the chosen hue) to all pixels for the maximum setting. The settings range from 0 to 100 percent.

- *Lightness Tolerance*—Selects the pixels to be corrected by variations in Lightness. Lower settings select less variations. The settings range from 0 to 100 percent.

- *Flattening*—Higher values apply more color correction. The settings range from 0 to 100 percent.

- *Blend With Original*—This sets the degree of blend with the original footage. The settings range from 0 to 100 percent.

Matte Wizard: Spill Killer/Spill Killer Pro

 ISFX Spill Killer mathematically analyzes and corrects for colored spill from screen backing. When a blue/green screen layer has reflected spill light on the foreground, Spill Killer corrects the contaminated pixels without harming the color.

Note: The Pro version of this filter allows you finer control over the parameters.

The following are some possible uses for the Spill Killer filter:

- Use this filter before applying a keying filter to footage shot against a blue or green screen.

- Use this filter to correct to correct for unwanted pixels in motion blurred areas.

The following controls allow you to adjust the Spill Killer filter's parameters:

- *Screen Color*—Select the dropout screen color: red, green, or blue.

- *Range*—The lower the setting, the more pixels are corrected. The settings range from 0 to 100 percent.

- *Tolerance*—The higher the setting, the more pixels are effected. The settings range from 0 to 100 percent.

- *Color Suppression*—This controls which pixels are effected, so exploring the best setting for your footage is recommended. The settings range from 0 to 100 percent.

- *Blend With Original*—This sets the degree of blend with the original footage. The settings range from 0 to 100 percent.

Reality Check: Brimstone

 This filter creates some of the most spectacular particle fire effects available for After Effects, and it's controlled by very intuitive commands. Creating volcanic fire or other types of pyrotechnics is easy and fun, and the rendering is fast compared to the complexity of the effects (see Figure 42.7).

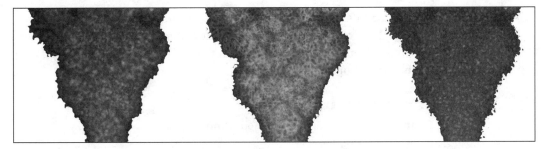

Figure 42.7
Three Brimstone types left to right: Clouds, Filaments, and Billows.

The following are some possible uses for the Brimstone filter:

- Use this filter to create billowing fire exiting a volcano.

- Create complex and organic-looking fire, water, smoke, mist, explosions, molecules, and many other particle effects.

The following controls allow you to adjust the Brimstone filter's parameters:

- *Quality*—Select Better, Faster, or Draft. Use Draft to create the particles, Fast to preview, and Better for the final rendering.

- *Composite Mode*—Explore different ways to composite the particles over the layer they are addressed to.

- *Preserve Transparency*—When this checkbox is activated, Brimstone acts as though the layer is a track matte. The Alpha is generated by multiplying the effect's Alpha with the layer's Alpha.

- *Slow Time 10X*—Checking this box slows down Brimstone's functions by a factor of 10, allowing you to create slow, graceful effects like water and fog.

- *Time Offset*—Usually, the effect starts at Frame 0, but using this control you can start the effect at any frame you want to.

- *Particle Controls*—The controls that fall under this heading are used to create the particles behaviors. Gravity, Spread, Lifetime, Velocity, Direction, Air Resistance, and Brownian Motion (internal wiggle). The documentation provides examples for various effects.

> **Note: A Gravity value of 0 is used to create explosions, or particles that flow from a central point.**

- *Color Controls*—The default color range is red and yellow, but you can set the color range to any hues you desire to create effects other than fire.

- *Cloud Controls*—The most important controls here are the Appearance options, allowing you to select Clouds, Filaments, or Billows Cloud types. After that, customize the ways that the particulate clouds interact with each other.

- *Flow Controls*—Setting the Influence Type allows you to select from among Gravity, Helix, Whirlwind, Spiral, and Slipstream. Gravity is the default, but more spectacular effects can be created by selecting one of the other options. From there you can determine the strength of the Influence settings.

Creating A Fiery Volcano

To use this filter to create a fiery volcano, do the following:

1. Select footage that displays either a dormant volcano or a snowless mountain, as seen from the front view, and place it in the Composition window.

2. Place another copy of the same footage on top of the original footage, at the same position. Create a mask and cut out just the volcano on the top layer. This allows

you to create the effect as though it were being generated from inside of the volcano. Make the top layer invisible, and select the bottom layer for the effect.

3. Select Brimstone from the ISVX Reality Check listing in the Effects menu.

4. Place the Producer centroid about a third of the way down from the top of the volcano.

5. Use the following parameter settings: Replace Composite Mode, Time Offset 40, Gravity –1. Beam Spread Angle 100, Velocity 3, Birthrate 60, Lifetime 40, Birth Radius 50, Birth Radius Variance 15%, Brownian Motion 25, Default Colors, Filaments Appearance, Detail 25, Rotation Enabled, Influence Type Gravity, and Influence .4. Leave all other settings at their defaults. Preview the results, and tweak where necessary. Render and record to disk.

Reality Check: Camera Blur/Camera Blur Pro

ISFX Camera Blur creates lens artifacts that make the blur look as though the footage were shot with a 35mm camera. Camera Blur Pro has the added feature of being able to create depth blurs using an 8-bit depth map. This enables you to create realistic depth of field and rack focus effects.

The following are some possible uses for the Camera Blur filter:

- Use this filter to create blurry, dream-like footage.

- Use this filter as a transition from hazy to clear.

The following controls allow you to adjust the Camera Blur filter's parameters:

- *Show*—You may select to display the blur effect, the reverse Sharp Zone, the Blur Control (depth map), or the Iris Artifact.

- *Maximum Blur*—This value (in a range of 0 to 200) sets the maximum level of blurring.

- *Blur Alpha*—Checking this box applies the blur to the Alpha channel as well as the RGB channels.

- *Blur Aspect*—The blur and lens artifacts can be stretched horizontally or vertically, in settings that range from –4 to 4.

- *Iris Blades*—This specifies the number of blades in the iris, from 3 to 12 and Round.

- *Iris Softness*—(0 to 100) Higher values create softer artifacts.

- *Iris Angle*—This value sets the angle, in a range of settings from 0 to 360 degrees of the iris blades.

- *Iris Edge Enhancements*—Explore these values (in settings that range from 0 to 100) to set the edge enhancement of the iris.

- *Gamma*—This value controls the artifact's relationship with bright pixels in the footage. Gamma settings range from 0 to 2. Lower settings create more artifacts.

- *Focal Point*—This value, which ranges from 0 to 255, controls the focal point based on the depth map. Explore various values for the focus needed.

- *Depth Of Field*—This value controls the parts of the footage that are blurred and those that remain in focus, based on the depth map. The settings range from 0 to 100 percent.

- *Near/Far Blur Gain*—Control the depth (in a settings range from 0 to 256) of the blur in front of and behind the Sharp Zone.

- *Control Layer*—Select the layer to be used as a depth map.

- *Conform Layer*—Checking this box resizes the depth map according to the selected layer's dimensions.

- *Control Attribute*—Select from any of the listed Channel Types to control the blur. Luminescence is the default.

- *Control Polarity/Invert*—In a standard depth map, black is closest and white is farthest away. Checking this box reverses this order.

- *Depth (Enable Obscuration)*—Leave this box checked as a default because it allows an algorithm to be applied that places the artifacts in their proper relationships.

- *Blend With Original*—This sets the degree of blend with the original footage. The settings range from 0 to 100 percent.

> *Note: Many 3D applications allow you to generate a depth map. One of these is MetaCreations Bryce 3D. Rendering the color footage and then the depth map footage is perfect when using this filter.*

Reality Check: Clouds

  This filter is perfect for generating and animating clouds, fog, and similar effects (see Figure 42.8).

> *Note: The best way to use this filter is to target it to a color layer with the Replace function enabled. Then use a Linear Color Key to drop out the darks.*

The following are some possible uses for the Clouds filter:

- Use this filter to generate a moving fog bank over your footage.

- Use this filter to emulate smoke resulting from the application of the ISFX Fire effect.

The following controls allow you to adjust the Cloud filter's parameters:

- *Color Map*—Customize the color map or select one from the list of options.

- *Transfer Mode*—Select an item from the list to decide how the clouds are to interact with the layer.

- *Appearance*—Select Clouds, Billows, or Filaments.

- *Detail*—This sets the amount of detail or sharpness, with lower values increasing the amount of detail. The settings range from 0 to 100 percent.

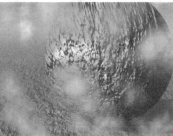

Figure 42.8
Left: Clouds. Center: Billows. Right: Filaments.

- *Scale*—This value controls the size of the cloud. The settings range from .001 to 1. Lower settings increase the size, and a value of 1 creates tiny particles. A value of .5 is a good starting point.

- *Bias*—Explore Bias settings (from 0 to 1) to alter the cloud shapes.

- *Gain*—The higher this value (which ranges from 0 to 1), the more different cloud shapes look from each other. The lower the value, the more similar the cloud shapes look.

- *Clipping*—Adjust Black and White Clipping levels (in settings that range from 0 to 1) to create different patterns based on the color range.

- *Aspect Ratio*—(0 to 100) A setting of 50 creates balanced clouds. Settings below 50 start to stretch the clouds horizontally, and at 0 they are horizontal streaks. Settings above 50 stretch the clouds vertically, and at 100 they become vertical streaks.

- *Rotation*—This value (which ranges from 0 to 360 degrees) rotates the cloud texture.

- *Position*—Place the centroid to generate the cloud center.

- *Mutation*—Select a Mutation Rate (0 to 100) and a Mutation Offset (0 to 10,000) to create more random movements for the clouds. Explore various values, and keyframe animate them.

- *Blend With Original*—This sets the degree of blend with the original footage. The settings range from 0 to 100 percent.

Reality Check: Fire

 Fire is one of the most requested filters, and the ISFX Fire filter is one of the most realistic (see Figure 42.9).

The following are some possible uses for the Fire filter:

- Use this filter to set a logo on fire as it moves.

- Create a fire coming from an image of a torch.

Note: Apply the Fire filter to a color layer with Replace or On selected. An Alpha map is automatically created in these cases, so the layers underneath show through.

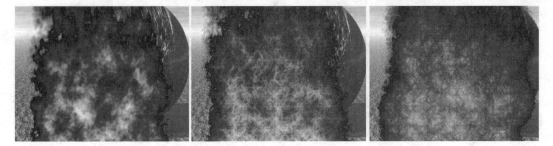

Figure 42.9
Left: Gasoline. Center: Plasma. Right: Kerosene.

The following controls allow you to adjust the Fire filter's parameters:

- *Color Map*—Customize the color map or select one from the list of options.
- *Texture*—Select Gasoline, Kerosene, or Plasma.
- *Paint Mode*—Select an item from the list to decide how the flames are to interact with the layer.
- *Smokiness*—Adds black smoke (with settings that range from 0 to 100) from the flames. The higher the value, the more smoke.
- *Detail*—(0 to 100) Adds increasing detail to the flames the higher the value is set.
- *Scale*—(.01 to 1) Alters the size of the flame texture.
- *Velocity*—Adjusts the speed of the fire for animation purposes. The settings range from 0 to 100.
- *Mutation*—Mutation includes Mutation Rate (0 to 100) and Mutation Offset (0 to 10,000). Exploring these values adds a random nature to the flames movements.
- *Direction*—(0 to 360 degrees) Change the direction the flame is headed.
- *Bias and Gain*—Altering the Bias (0 to 1) changes the position of the texture, and altering the Gain (0 to 1) alters the strength or amplitude.
- *Height/Height Cutoff Slope*—You can adjust and animate the Flame Height (0 to 100 percent); the Height Cutoff Slope value (0 to 100 percent) alters how abruptly the top of the flames will fade out (higher values create more gradual transitions).
- *Flame Width*—This value specifies how much of the width of the layer the fire will cover. The settings range from 0 to 100 percent.
- *Flame Edge*—This value is adjusted by: Scale (1 to 1,000), Amplitude (0 to 100 percent), and Slope (0 to 100 percent). All these adjust how the edges of the fire will be effected.
- *Flame Base*—As the values increase, the base of the fire is moved up relative to the layer. The settings range from 0 to 100 percent.
- *Acceleration*—This controls the "leap" of the flame, with higher values increasing it. The settings range from 0 to 100 percent.

- *Wind*—(–10 to 10) Negative values create a wind from the right, and positive values a wind from the left.

- *Wiggle*—Wiggle adds a left-right jitter to the flames. Some wiggle is always recommended. The settings range from 0 to 100 percent.

- *Fuel Supply Cutoff*—Checking this option allows you to keyframe animate spurts of flame.

- *Blend With Original*—This sets the degree of blend with the original footage. The settings range from 0 to 100 percent.

Create A Flame From A Rocket

Do the following to create a lame streaming from a rocket nozzle:

1. Create a composition with three layers. The layer in the background should contain stars, either moving or simply a still image. The middle layer should be a color layer. The top layer should have your masked rocketship.

2. Make the top layer invisible. You are going to apply the ISFX Fire filter to the color layer (the middle layer).

3. Resize the layer until it is the approximate size of the flame you want. Apply the ISFX Fire filter to the middle layer.

4. Adjust the Fire settings until you have the flame you want. Pay special attention to the Wiggle setting, giving it a value of 100. Select the Plasma fire type.

5. Make your top layer (the rocket) visible again. Move the fire layer under the rocket nozzle, and rotate as needed to make it look as though it's coming from the nozzle.

Preview, tweak as necessary, and render the movie to disk.

Reality Check: Mirage

  This allows you to create all manner of semitransparent shimmer effects.

The following are some possible uses for the Mirage filter:

- Use this filter to add a heat shimmer to the ISFX Fire effect.

- Add a heat shimmer to the exhaust of a rocket or jet.

The following controls allow you to adjust the Mirage filter's parameters:

- *View Mode*—Select to view the Normal Layer or the Distortion Field.

- *Gain*—This value (with settings that range from 0 to 100) determines the amount of distortion the Mirage creates.

- *Detail*—This value sets the amount of high-frequency distortion visible. The settings range from 0 to 100 percent.

- *Scale*—Generates the mirage waves, with higher values creating more waves. The settings range from 0 to 100 percent.

- *Aspect Ratio*—A value of 50 is the default. Values lower than 50 create vertical waves, and values higher than 50 create horizontal waves. The settings range from 0 to 100 percent.

- *Blur*—(0 to 1,000) Little or no blur creates distortions that look distant, whereas higher values create distortions that appear closer.

- *Velocity*—(0 to 100) Determines the speed of the animated distortion field.

- *Mutation*—Mutation includes Mutation Rate (0 to 100) and Mutation Offset (0 to 10,000). Exploring these values adds a random nature to the flame's movement.

- *Producer Point*—Move this centroid to the location you want the distortion to be the bottom of the distortion field.

- *Direction*—This sets the direction of the distortion field from 0 to 360 degrees.

- *Field*—These settings determine the parameters of the distortion field and how it reacts with the layer.

- *Bend*—(–10 to 10) Negative values bend the mirage to the left, and positive values to the Right.

- *Blend With Original*—This sets the degree of blend with the original footage. The settings range from 0 to 100 percent.

Reality Check: Real Shadows

 With this effect, you can add perspective shadows to any layer with an Alpha channel (see Figure 42.10).

The following are some possible uses for the Real Shadows filter:

- Give your text blocks 3D depth by adding shadows.

- Create shadows from a low-flying aircraft on a ground layer.

The following controls allow you to adjust the Real Shadows filter's parameters:

- *Color*—Make the shadow any color you want.

- *Opacity*—Set a transparency value for the shadow. The settings range from 0 to 100 percent.

Figure 42.10
Various Real Shadows. Left: Opacity 70, Softness 60, and Fadeout .8. Center: Opacity 25, Softness 0, and Fadeout 0. Right: Opacity 100, Softness 100, and Fadeout 1.

- *Softness*—Makes the shadow blurry, with higher values increasing the blur. The settings range from 0 to 100 percent.

- *Fadeout*—This causes the shadow to fade as it extends from the object. This control's settings range from 0 to 1.

- *Placement*—Use the centroids to place the shadow, or better yet, do it in real time by moving the interactive centroids in the Composition window.

- *Avoid Clipping*—It's good to leave this checked as a default because it allows the shadow to extend beyond the borders of the layer.

- *Hide Layer*—Checking this box displays the shadow only.

- *Blend With Original*—This sets the degree of blend with the original footage. The settings range from 0 to 100 percent.

Reality Check: Super Displacer

This filter creates high-quality distortion maps from a source layer (see Figure 42.11).

The following are some possible uses for the Super Displacer filter:

- Create distortions that warp your footage to generate steam and other effects.

- Add distortion to your animated logo at the start of an animation, and remove it at the end. This creates an interesting distortion transition.

The following controls allow you to adjust the Super Displacer filter's parameters:

- *Map Layer*—Select the layer to use as the displacement map.

- *Map Interpretation-Use Slope*—Choosing this option creates glass-like effects.

- *Map Behavior*—Stretch, Tile, and Center are the options that determine how different size layers will be treated.

- *Scale*—Scale (ranging from –100 to 100) determines the size of the displacement map. Commonly, values under 6 or over 6 are not advised.

- *Rotation*—(0 to 360 degrees) Rotate the displacement.

Figure 42.11
Left to right images display various Super Displacer Scale values: 1, 2, and 5.

- *Offset*—Place the centroid to alter the position of the layer.

- *Map Alpha Mode*—Use Alpha, Use Blue Channel, and Ignore Alpha are the options. Explore each one before your final rendering.

- *Blend With Original*—This sets the degree of blend with the original footage. The settings range from 0 to 100 percent.

Reality Check: Tunnel

  The Tunnel filter creates animated tunnels that draw you into their depths (see Figure 42.12).

The following are some possible uses for the Tunnel filter:

- Keyframe animate a tunnel and place an object layer over it. The object layer will seem as though it is traveling down the tunnel.

- Use the Tunnel filter to overlay tunnel layers over the eyes of a figure for a hypnotic effect.

The following controls allow you to adjust the Tunnel filter's parameters:

- *Color Map*—Use one of the presets or customize your own color map.

- *Transfer Mode*—Select one of the modes listed.

- *Appearance*—Select from Billows, Clouds, or Filaments to texture the tunnel.

- *Detail*—(0 to 100) Increase or decrease the level of detail.

- *Scale*—(.01 to 1) This value controls the size of the tunnel.

- *Bias and Gain*—Bias (0 to 1) and Gain (0 to 1) control the wave parameters that effect the tunnel shape.

- *Clipping*—(0 to 1) Adjusting the Black and White Clip values darkens or lightens the tunnel.

- *Fade*—The options are Fade Inner Radius (0 to 100), which controls the radius of the hole at the back of the tunnel, and Fade Width (0 to 100), which affects the way the hole blends into the rest of the tunnel. Larger values create a softer transition.

- *Zoom*—As the value increases (the settings range from 0 to 100), the tunnel appears deeper.

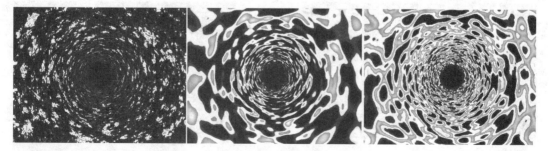

Figure 42.12
Left to right, the three tunnel types: Billows, Clouds, and Filaments.

- *Twist*—(–1 to 1) Twist smears the texture on the tunnel's sides either left (negative values) or right (positive values).

- *Rotation*—(0 to 360 degrees) This is an animation setting that rotates the tunnel as you zoom down it.

- *Velocity*—(–10 to 10) Negative velocity values make it seem as though you are exiting the tunnel, whereas positive values create the illusion that you are entering it.

- *Z Position*—Larger values (the settings range from 0 to 10,000) bring you closer to the tunnel's exit point, and finally through it.

- *Position*—Place the centroid where you want the center of the tunnel to be.

- *Blend With Original*—This sets the degree of blend with the original footage. The settings range from 0 to 100 percent.

Reality Check: Turbulent Distortion Pro

This filter allows you to distort images on either or both their horizontal and vertical axis with turbulent noise (see Figure 42.13).

The following are some possible uses for the Turbulent Distortion filter:

- Create the effect of a funhouse mirror by keyframe animating the degree of warp in the footage.

- Create an animated cubist painting with this filter.

The following controls allow you to adjust the Turbulent Distortion filter's parameters (note that these are repeated for both horizontal and vertical distortions):

- *Appearance*—Uniform Appearance resembles reflections in wavy water, whereas Turbulent Appearance resembles more fluid distortions. Mixing them for the horizontal and vertical components creates interesting varieties.

- *Detail*—(0 to 100) This sets the level of detail in the distorted footage. As detail increases, the edge between distorted and nondistorted aspects of the footage become harder.

- *Scale*—(.01 to 1) This value determines the size of the distortion field.

Figure 42.13
Left to right: Original footage, distortion using Uniform Appearance, and distortion using Turbulent Appearance.

- *Gain*—(0 to 100 percent) This setting controls the strength of the distortion field.

- *Aspect Ratio*—(0 to 100 percent) This controls the horizontal or vertical stretching of the footage.

- *Position*—Use the centroid to position the distortion center.

- *Mutation*—Mutation Rate and Mutation Offset control the speed and rate that the distortion changes over time.

- *View*—You can view either the distorted layer or the actual distortion field. Either can be rendered and animated.

- *Blend With Original*—This sets the degree of blend with the original footage. The settings range from 0 to 100 percent.

Style Tools: Alpha Ramp

This filter creates ramped alpha layers.

The following are some possible uses for the Alpha Ramp filter:

- Use this filter to control composite blending without creating an Alpha key.

- Use this filter to create, render, and save your own customized ramps for use as transitions.

The following controls allow you to adjust the Alpha Ramp filter's parameters:

- *View Mode*—The options are Normal (view the composite), Alpha (view the Alpha channel), and Ramp (view the ramp by itself).

- *Ramp Edge Point*—This is the placement for the top of a linear ramp or the center of a radial ramp.

- *Ramp Width*—(0 to 4,000) This is the width of the ramp in pixels.

- *Ramp Curvature*—A value of 0 creates a linear ramp, and 100 creates a radial ramp. Values in between mix the two. The settings range from 0 to 100 percent.

- *Ramp Angle*—You can adjust the angle (with settings that range from 0 to 360 degrees) of the ramp, which is more important for linear ramps.

- *Alpha Inversion*—The Alpha channel can be inverted. The settings range from 0 to 100 percent.

- *Blend With Original*—This sets the degree of blend with the original footage. The settings range from 0 to 100 percent.

Style Tools: Blender

ISFX Blender blends between previous effects and the unaffected layer, based on a Control Layer. Blender is a powerful tool that extends the precision and control of many other effects.

The following are some possible uses for the Blender filter:

- Control the exact areas of the footage that will be affected by filters.
- Use this filter to apply an effects mix to an unaffected layer.

The following controls allow you to adjust the Blender filter's parameters:

- *Control Layer*—This is the layer in the stack that controls the blending effect. A good choice is a ramp.
- *Control Channel*—Select which channel option will be used as the mask.
- *Invert Control*—Choosing this checkbox works like Invert Selection in Photoshop.
- *Stretch Layer*—Choosing this checkbox will make the control layer the same size as the target layer.
- *Blend With Original*—This sets the degree of blend with the original footage. The settings range from 0 to 100 percent.

Style Tools: Color Map

This allows users to animate two separate color maps for the layer.

The following are some possible uses for the Color Map filter:

- Use Color Map for spot matting using transparent bands, or psychedelic color transformations.
- Use Color Map to animate interesting color alterations by keyframe animating the Blend control.

The following controls allow you to adjust the Color Map filter's parameters:

- *Attribute To Map*—Select the channel of the layer to be mapped.
- *Preserve Alpha*—When this checkbox is selected, the Alpha is preserved.
- *Premultiply Colors*—Low areas of the Alpha are treated as darks when checked.
- *Color Map 1*—Edit the color for the selected channel. You may also select one of the presets.
- *Map 1 To Map 2*—This control blends Color Map 1 with Color Map 2. A value of 0 uses only Color Map 1, and 100 uses only Color Map 2. The settings range from 0 to 100 percent.
- *Color Map 2*—Edit the color for the selected channel, using the second color map. You may also select one of the presets.
- *Blend With Original*—This sets the degree of blend with the original footage. The settings range from 0 to 100 percent.

Style Tools: Framer

The Framer filter is used to create a rectangular frame around any part of the footage.

The following are some possible uses for the Framer filter:

- Keyframe animate the size of a framed area from 0 to 100.

- Create a rectangular mask by checking Use As Mask.

The following controls allow you to adjust the Framer filter's parameters:

- *Corners*—Place the top left and bottom right centroids to determine the dimensions of the frame.

- *Frame Width*—(0 to 500) Determine the pixel width of the frame.

- *Frame Color*—Use the system palette or eyedropper to determine the hue.

- *Act As Mask*—When this option is selected, the frame acts as a rectangular mask, and only the frame area content is displayed for that layer.

- *Blend With Original*—This sets the degree of blend with the original footage. The settings range from 0 to 100 percent.

Style Tools: Grunge

The Grunge filter adds torn edges to the Alpha layer or channel.

The following are some possible uses for the Grunge filter:

- Use this filter at maximum value and Acid Bath to create a corrosive effect.

- Create a torn page look on the edges of the Alpha.

The following controls allow you to adjust the grunge filter's parameters:

- *Grunge Styles*—Select Decay, Sand Blast, or Acid Bath as the Grunge look.

- *Grunge Amount*—This adjusts the quantity of grunge displayed. The settings range from 0 to 100 percent.

- *Grunge Smoothing*—Add Smoothing to the grunge edges. The settings range from 0 to 100 percent.

- *Blend With Original*—This sets the degree of blend with the original footage. The settings range from 0 to 100 percent.

> **Note: This filter works effectively after using ISFX Alpha Ramp on the layer.**

Style Tools: Hall Of Mirrors

ISFX Hall of Mirrors creates multiple reflections of the layer, with controls affecting the reflections (see Figure 42.14).

The following are some possible uses for the Hall of Mirrors filter:

- Simulating a hall with infinite mirror reflections.
- Create visual echoes and motion trails.

The following controls allow you to adjust the Hall of Mirrors filter's parameters:

- *Repetitions*—(0 to 100) This sets the number of times, in a range from 0 to 100, the layer will be replicated.
- *Scale*—Controls the scale of the layer. The settings range from .1 to 100.
- *Rotation*—(0 to 360 degrees) Sets a rotation amount for each successive mirrored layer.
- *Offset*—Place the centroid to determine the center of the effect.
- *Transfer Mode*—Explore a range of alternate transfer modes for different looks.
- *Fade*—This value (which ranges from 0 to 100) sets a fade as the mirrored layers recede.
- *Blend With Original*—This sets the degree of blend with the original footage. The settings range from 0 to 100 percent.

Figure 42.14
Left: Original footage. Center: 8 Repetitions and a Scale of .9. Right: 7 Repetitions, a Scale of .75, and a Rotation of 45 degrees.

Style Tools: Hall Of Time

 ISFX Hall of Time creates time-based reflections of the layer, generating an effect based on the sampling of previous frames to create complex time warping.

The following are some possible uses for the Hall of Time filter:

- Use this filter wherever you need to add a Time Echo to the Hall of Mirrors effect.
- Use this filter to create mirrored reflections when your animated footage contains jumps in content.

The following controls allow you to adjust the Hall of Time filter's parameters:

- *Repetitions*—This sets the number of times (in a range from 0 to 100) the layer will be replicated.

- *Echo Time (Seconds)*—This value (with settings that range from –30,000 to 30,000) allows you to sample previous (negative values) or future (positive values) frames for mirroring.

- *Scale*—(.1 to 100) Controls the scale of the layer.

- *Rotation*—Sets a rotation amount (0 to 360 degrees) for each successive mirrored layer.

- *Offset*—Place the centroid to determine the center of the effect.

- *Transfer Mode*—Explore a range of alternate transfer modes for different looks.

- *Fade*—(0 to 100) This value sets a fade as the mirrored layers recede.

- *Blend With Original*—This sets the degree of blend with the original footage. The settings range from 0 to 100 percent.

Style Tools: Outliner

 ISFX Outliner generates a smooth outline around a layer's Alpha.

The following are some possible uses for the Outliner filter:

- Use this filter when you want to create precise halos, glows, and frames around a complex Alpha mask.

- Use this filter in combination with the other ISFX Alpha filters.

The following controls allow you to adjust the Outliner filter's parameters:

- *Edge Smoothing*—(0 to 32) Smoothed edges composite more effectively.

- *Outline Distance*—(–10,000 to 10,000) A value of 0 creates the outline on the Alpha edge. Higher values move it farther away. Negative values move it inside of the edge.

- *Outline Width*—(0 to 1,000) This value determines the width of the outline in pixels.

- *Outline Color*—Select any color you need from the system palette or with the eyedropper.

- *Outline Blur*—(0 to 100) Use this value to add a blur to the Alpha.

- *Combination Mode*—Explore various combination modes to preview their look, then settle on the one that is best for your composition.

- *Avoid Clipping*—Checking this option allows the outline to render beyond the confines of the layer.

- *Blend With Original*—This sets the degree of blend with the original footage. The settings range from 0 to 100 percent.

Style Tools: Title Scroll

 ISFX Title Scroll creates scrolling titles from a standard text file.

The following are some possible uses for the Title Scroll filter:

- Use this filter when you are need of adding titles or credits to your AE production.

- Use this filter to add text that can then be affected by other filters as it scrolls.

The following controls allow you to adjust the Title Scroll filter's parameters:

- *Start Offset*—Place the centroid to determine where the text will be positioned.

- *Scroll Rate*—(0 to 100) A setting of 0 creates no scrolling. As values increase, scrolling increases speed.

- *Text Color*—Select any text color you need from the system palette or with the eyedropper.

- *Character Size*—(0 to 1,000) This value enlarges the text in accordance with the setting.

- *Aspect Ratio*—A 50-percent setting is the default. Smaller values make the text taller than wide, and larger values make the text wider than tall. The settings range from 0 to 100 percent.

- *Text Blur*—(0 to 100) This can be used as an effect or to remove jaggies.

- *Leading*—(0 to 100) This value effects the spaces between the letters.

- *Corners*—Place the centroids to determine the scroll width.

- *Shadows*—You can determine the shadow distance, angle, and color, as well as its blur and opacity.

- *Fade Distance*—This value (ranging from 0 to 100) sets the way the scrolled text fades before it reaches maximum distance from the top border.

- *Composite Mode*—Options include Replace, Behind, and In Front for different layered scrolls.

- *Field Rendering*—When selected, field rendering is enabled. This can result in smoother scrolls; it is a vital option for broadcast media.

- *Blend With Original*—This sets the degree of blend with the original footage. The settings range from 0 to 100 percent.

Style Tools: Turbulent Edges

The Turbulent Edges filter allows you to add turbulence to the edge of Alpha masks.

The following are some possible uses for the Turbulent Edges filter:

- Use this filter to add a stylistic look to layer edges.

- Use this filter to add a more organic edge to environmental effects.

The following controls allow you to adjust the Turbulent Edges filter's parameters:

- *Mutation Rate*—This is an animation control that sets the rate of change for the Turbulence. The settings range from 0 to 100 percent.

- *Scale*—(0 to 100) This sets the area magnitude of the turbulence.

- *Sharpness*—Values above 0 create sharper turbulent edges. The settings range from 0 to 100 percent.

- *Gain*—(0 to 500) This sets the strength of the turbulence.

- *Blend With Original*—This sets the degree of blend with the original footage. The settings range from 0 to 100 percent.

Style Tools: Typewriter

T This is a character generator for After Effects.

The following are some possible uses for the Typewriter filter:

- Use this filter to create animated text that looks as though it is being typed to the screen.
- Use this filter to zoom text into or out of the composition by keyframe animating the font size.

The following controls allow you to adjust the Typewriter filter's parameters:

- *Font* Size—(0 to 1,000) This value determines the overall size of the text in Points.
- *Width Scale*—(0 to 25) Alter the width with this control.
- *Position*—Place the centroid to position the text centered on its baseline.
- *Color*—Select any text color you need from the system palette or with the eyedropper.
- *Raster Effect*—The options are Off, Easier, and More Control (customizes the effect). This control creates raster lines through the text.
- *Completion*—Keyframe animate this setting, from 0 to 100 percent, to have the text "typed" to the screen.
- *Leading Scale/Tracking Scale*—The Leading Scale (–100 to 100) controls the vertical space between lines of text. The Tracking Scale (–100 to 100) sets the space between letters.
- *Kerning*—With kerning activated, allows the text to be kerned according to its built-in kerning table. This allows specific pairs of letters to be spaced more attractively.
- *Typing Effect*—Options are Normal and Random. Normal types the letters on left to right, whereas Random brings them on in no particular order. Random is interesting for titles.
- *Transfer Mode*—Select one of the transfer modes for different ways the text interacts with the layer.
- *Cursor Mode*—When selected, this places a cursor with the text. Select a cursor type from the list.
- *Blinking*—(0 to 30) This setting controls the speed of blinking for text and cursor.
- *Space-Time Scale*—(1 to 1,000) This value controls the amount of time spaces and returns occupy. Use a high value to make the typing look more natural.
- *Typing Rate Variance*—Adding some variance to the typing rate makes it look less mechanical. The settings range from 0 to 100.
- *Raster Controls*—If raster lines are activated, you can customize their appearance with these controls.
- *Grunge Amount*—(0 to 100) Adds a degraded look to the text for that worn-out effect.
- *Dot Scatter*—Breaks the text into pixels (with settings that range from 0 to 1,000), with more breakup at higher settings.

- *Fade Mode*—You can control the parameters of a fade by using these controls.

- *Fade Completion*—Control the completion amount of the fade. The settings range from 0 to 100 percent.

- *Blend With Original*—This sets the degree of blend with the original footage. The settings range from 0 to 100 percent.

Style Tools: Video Feedback

The Video Feedback filter creates multiple iterations of the selected layer (see Figure 42.15).

The following are some possible uses for the Video Feedback filter:

- To generate unique chaotic patterns.

- To create the infinite looped effect achieved when you point a video camera at its own monitor.

The following controls allow you to adjust the Video Feedback filter's parameters:

- *Scale*—(.1 to 100) This sets the scale difference between each iteration.

- *Rotation*—Set this value to determine the rotational spin, in a range from 0 to 360 degrees, of the iterated layers.

- *Offset*—Use this centroid to place the iterated components.

- *Transfer Mode*—Select one of the transfer modes for different ways the iterated layers interact with each other.

- *Fade*—(0 to 100) This sets the fade rate between each iteration.

- *Blend With Original*—This sets the degree of blend with the original footage. The settings range from 0 to 100 percent.

Figure 42.15
Left to right: variations of the Video Feedback effect.

THE FOUNDRY

The following AE external filters are from The Foundry. They include T_Kaleid, T_LensBlur, and T_Sparkle.

T_Kaleid

This filter creates kaleidoscopic animations based on position, size, and spin parameters (see Figure 43.1).

The following are some possible uses for the T_Kaleid effects:

* Create flowing kaleidoscopic animations as a background for your text.

* Map a kaleidoscopic movie on one of the After Effects 3D objects to accompany a logo animation.

The following controls allow you to adjust the T_Kaleid filter's parameters:

* *Prism Size*—(0 to 2,000) This value sets the size of the kaleidoscopic elements.

* *Prism Spin*—(0 to 360 degrees) Keyframe animate the spin to create hypnotic kaleidoscopic movies.

* *Prism Center*—Place the centroid wherever you want the kaleidoscopic effect to be centered.

Note: See the Kaleid1 movie in the CH_43 folder in the Anims directory on the companion CD-ROM.

Figure 43.1
Left to right: Original footage, Prism Size 128 with a Prism Spin of 45 degrees, and Prism Size 170 with a Prism Spin of 180 degrees.

T_LensBlur

With the T_Lens Blur filter, you can apply a blur and an associated bloom at the same time (see Figure 43.2).

The following are some possible uses for the LensBlur effects:

- Use the Bloom feature to create a watercolor look to the footage.
- Keyframe animate the Size parameter from 500 to 0 to start with a hazy color that becomes a clear image at the end of the animation.

The following controls allow you to adjust the LensBlur filter's parameters:

- *Aperture*—You can select from the following options: Circular, Pentagonal, Hexagonal, Septagonal, and Octagonal. Each influences the bloom in a different way.
- *Size*—(0 to 1,000) A value of 0 shows the original footage. As the value increases, more blur is applied. Even at a Blur of 0, you can still apply blooms.
- *Spin*—(0 to 360 degrees) Rotate the Blur and Bloom effect.
- *Gain %*—(0 to 30,000) The default is 100. Decreasing it below 100 turns the footage darker, and at 0, the footage becomes transparent to the layer beneath. Increasing the Gain above 100 increases the strength of the Bloom value.
- *Bloom Threshold %*—(0 to 100) Set the Threshold to determine what areas of the footage receive a bloom. Setting it at 0 causes all of the footage to bloom, while a value of 100 dampens the bloom throughout.
- *Bloom Amplify %*—(0 to 30,000) use this control to amplify the bloom further.

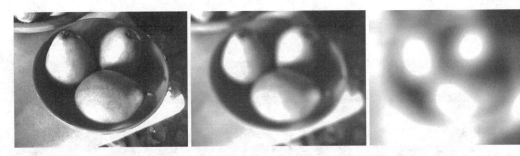

Figure 43.2
Left: Original footage. Center: Blur 10 and Bloom 10. Right: Blur 50 and Bloom 40.

T_Sparkle

T_Sparkle creates the same effects as a star filter does with a camera (see Figure 43.3).

The following are some possible uses for the T_Sparkle effects:

- Create a starfield with sparkling stars.
- Add sparkles to any footage content, especially metals and liquids.

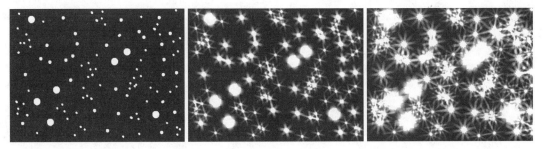

Figure 43.3
Left: Original footage. Center: Sparkle Size 20, Number of Lines 6, Spin 45, Threshold 0, and Amplify 120.
Right: Sparkle Size 35, Number of Lines 10, Spin 45, Threshold 0, and Amplify 145.

The following controls allow you to adjust the Sparkle filter's parameters:

- *Sparkle Size (Pixels)*—(0 to 1,000) This is the size of the radius of the sparkle.

- *Number Of Lines*—(1 to 1,000) Set this value to determine the number of arms for each sparkle.

- *Spin*—(0 to 360 degrees) This angle represents the rotation of the sparkle. Keyframe animate this setting to create revolving sparkles.

- *Threshold %*—(0 to 100) At 0, every bright pixel will be effected. At 100, the effect is dampened.

- *Amplify %*—(0 to 30,000) Usually, a setting of 125 or less is quite enough amplification. Above that, all brights in the footage start to bloom and become ovals.

Create A Basic Animated Starfield

To create a basic animated starfield, do the following.

1. In Photoshop or another bitmap-editing application, create an image the same size as the movie you want to create in After Effects.

2. Make the background solid black.

3. Paint variable sized white dots on the image to represent stars.

4. Save the image to disk. Start After Effects and import it as footage for a new composition sized the same as the image.

5. Open the Foundry Sparkle filter in the Effects menu.

6. Set the parameters as follows: Sparkle Size 20, Number of Lines 6, Spin 0, Threshold 0, and Amplify 120.

7. Keyframe animate the Spin value from 0 for the first frame to 360 degrees at the last frame.

8. Render to disk as an animation.

You have just created an animated Starfield, with the stars spinning around their Z axis. You can use this as a background layer, or add other effects as you like.

PART VI

SPECIAL
PROJECTS

PROJECTS

This chapter focuses on three projects. You can follow along and see how we developed the compositions, and afterward, develop compositions of your own, using the same elements.

All the elements used in these compositions are found on the book's companion CD-ROM. Look in the Projects folder. There, you will see three folders: Docum, Tour, and Sci-Fi. Docum is a project based on an opening for a documentary on Egypt. In it, you will find a layered file called Egypt.PSD (it is a Photoshop layered composition). After importing into After Effects as Photoshop layered footage, you can apply different effects and movements to each layer. The Tour folder contains another Photoshop layered image in which you can use the elements to create a composition for a travel company that offers a visual display of images of California. The Sci-Fi folder contains text blocks and three QuickTime movie files for developing an opening for a TV science fiction show. In this chapter, we present examples on how each of these compositions might be put together. Walk through the tutorials just to see how we went about it. After that, experiment with the same elements on your own to create your own unique After Effects compositions.

> **Note: Important warning! Although the Project files are included for these projects in their respective folders on the companion CD-ROM, you can use them only if you have the indicated third-party filters installed!**

The Docum Project

The documentary film has become a widely used form in the past 10 years. Whether based on studies of the natural world, history, geography, technology, or any of a multitude of other topics, documentary projects dominate many cable channels. In this example, you will create an opening sequence for a documentary called "Egypt: a history." In the Docum folder is the Egypt.PSD footage, which contains all the needed elements. Remember, an infinite number of "right" ways exist to go about creating this Composition, and the solution presented here is only one of many (see Figure 44.1).

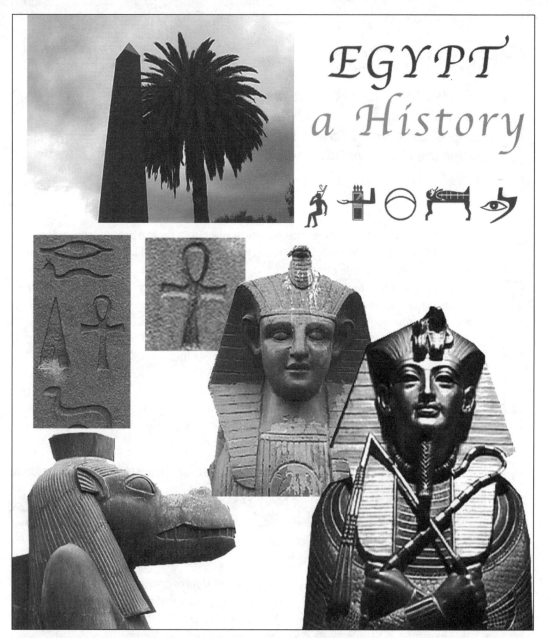

Figure 44.1
The layered elements in the Docum folder consist of these images and text blocks.

Note: You will use several external AE filters for this project that have to be purchased separately. If you do not own these filters, use internal AE filters or other plug-ins you might have to create alternate composition examples.

Note: All the footage displayed in Figure 44.1 and contained in the Docum folder on the companion CD-ROM are copyright free. The author took them on a visit to the Egyptian Museum in San Jose, California. You may use this footage in any way you wish.

Creating The Docum Project

With all your AE Projects, the idea is to surprise the viewer. Why else would you spend so much time and money collecting all of the fancy plug-ins detailed in this book? It would be easy enough to just bring all of the elements in this composition on screen one after the other, which would be guaranteed to bore your audience to tears, causing many to switch channels and skip the documentary that followed...perhaps causing you to lose employment. However, if you have diligently worked through the tutorials in this book and purchased the plug-in collections that interested you (and have also availed yourself of the hundreds of animated examples of various effects on the companion CD-ROM), then you are already aware of thousands of ways to develop a composition with more than simple sliding footage elements.

In this project, you will create some interesting visual prior to the title coming on screen. The basic elements consist of a background layer, and a collection of alternate image layers to be layered above the background in a moving stream. Then, the title is brought on. There are three separate title blocks: "Egypt", "a History", and a row of hieroglyphs.

To create a composition based on the Docum elements, do the following:

1. Open a new composition in After Effects. Make it 360 frames long at 30 fps (equaling 12 seconds), and size the composition to 480x360 pixels.

2. Import the Egypt.PSD footage in the Projects/Docum folder on this book's companion CD-ROM as a Photoshop Comp.

3. Reduce your composition view to 1/2, which will allow you to see the empty border area of the composition. In the Project List, open the Egypt.PSD folder so you can see the contents. Load the Backdrop layer first, so it can act as the background for all your other footage. Now load the other named layers to the Composition window in exactly the following order and place each layers contents outside of the composition window in the empty border area. This allows all the other content to be animated from off screen in the first frames: Ankh, Hiero, Hippo, Sphinx, Tut, Text 1, Text 2, and Text H. You won't be able to see the content of the footage outside of the Composition window, but just the border indicators (see Figure 44.2).

4. Now you're going to do something that may seem strange at first, but I'll explain it in a moment. Load the backdrop footage again, so that it is now the topmost layer. Make sure that it lines up exactly with the same footage used as the background layer.

5. Double-click on the layer you just added, which will bring up the editing window. Use the Pen tool to carefully outline just the obelisk, and quit the editor. Do you

Figure 44.2
Your reduced Composition window should look like this, with all of the content layers added on the outside.

know what you have just accomplished? If you place any of the other objects in the composition, you will see that they pass in front of the palm tree, but behind the obelisk. You have just added a dimensional layer to your composition, making anything that is done from this point on more interesting.

6. Click on the Ankh graphic layer to activate it. Keyframe animate it so that starting at time 2:00, it moves from off screen at the upper left of the Composition window to off screen at the lower right at time 6:00. It will pass behind the obelisk. This is a simple position animation. During this same time, keyframe animate its rotation geometrics from 0 degrees to 360 degrees.

7. Now select the Hier_1 layer. It should be keyframe animated to move from just outside of the rightmost border of the composition to outside of the left border. This will also pass it behind the obelisk, and in front of the ankh. Keyframe animate this movement from second 1:00 to second 4:00.

8. You're not through with the Hier_1 layer yet. It's time to add some effects to it as it moves. You need to have purchased AlienSkin's EyeCandy AE plug-ins to do this part of the tutorial. You are going to add a pulsating glow to the moving Hier_1 layer. With the Hier_1 layer selected, go to the EyeCandy effects and activate the Glow filter.

9. Set Opacity to 40%, and use a bright yellow hue. Keyframe animate the width value so that it starts at 30 at time 1:00, and moves back and forth a few times to 50 before it reaches time 4:00. Don't make the pulse too regular. The result is a pulsating glow.

10. Select the Tut layer, and using the Layer menu, bring it to the front. This places the Tut layer in front of everything, even the obelisk. Place the Tut layer outside of the Composition window, below and to the left of the obelisk. Keyframe animate it starting at time 6:00 and ending at time 10:15 so that it rises and sits next to the obelisk (see Figure 44.3).

11. At time 00:00, place the Sphinx layer on the right side of the composition. This next step requires that you installed the DigiEffects Berserk plug-ins. Go to the DigiEffects Berserk effects, and select Ripploid. Keyframe animate the Strength to –3,000 at time 00:00. This causes the Sphinx layer to disappear completely. Set the Number of Waves to 20, and leave it there. At time 6:00, set the Strength to –2,999. At time 6:00, set the Strength to –500, which causes the rippled layer to start to become visible. At time 9:00, set the Strength to –200, and at time 10:00 to –50. Finally, keyframe the Strength to 0 at time 11:00, making the layer completely visible.

12. Reduce the size of the Hippo layer until it's about half the height of the composition. Move it outside of the composition at the top, about halfway between the obelisk and the right border of the composition.

Figure 44.3
The Tut layer rises and remains in place next to the obelisk from time 10:15 to the end.

13. We are going to move this layer from the top outside of the composition downward, until it disappears at the bottom. Start the keyframed move at time 4:00, and make sure that it is completed and keyframed out of sight at the bottom at frame 6:00.

14. This step requires that you own the DigiEffects Delerium plug-ins and have them installed. Go to the Delerium list in the Effects menu and select Solarize. Set the Contrast to 50, Solar Grain to 10, and Blend to 0. Keyframe animate the Rotate values from 0 at time 4:00, to 255 at time 5:00, and back to 0 at time 6:00. This creates a moving sheen across the surface of the layer.

15. Now it's time to animate the Text_H layer, which is a series of hieroglyphs in a row. Click on the layer in the Time Layout window, and resize it proportionally so that it's half as tall as the Composition window. Place it at the bottom of the Composition window so that it is resting on the bottom of the frame, with its left edge lined up with the left edge of the frame. You will see that much of its content is invisible and hangs outside of the Composition window to the right.

16. In the Time Layout window, move the Text_H layer's frames so that instead of starting at time 00:00, they start at time 2:00. This causes this layer to suddenly pop up at time 2:00 (see Figure 44.4).

17. Click on the Scale Geometrics to keyframe these settings at time 2:00. Now go to time 6:00, and reset the Scale to 0%, effectively reducing the size to make the layer invisible. It will shrink during the time between 2:00 and 6:00.

18. Now for the titling text. There are two separate layers, Text 1 ("Egypt") and Text 2 ("a History"). Select Text 2. Go to the Layer menu and select Bring To Front. This text needs to be in front of everything else. Now go to the last frame, and position this text at the bottom right of the Composition window. This is where it will wind up.

19. The text is a light blue-green and doesn't show up clearly against the images. You could change its color, but part of the text is against a light backdrop and part against dark. No color change would make much difference. One solution is to place a glow around it to pop it out. Select the Glow filter from the EyeCandy AE plug-ins (obviously, you have to have them installed). Set the Width to 10 and Opacity to 90, with a dark blue hue. This pops the text out nicely.

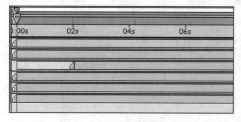

Figure 44.4
Move the Text_H layer's frames so that they start at time 2:00.

20. This is how the text will look on the last frame, but not where it will be at the beginning. In the Time Layout window, move the frame block for this layer so that it starts at time 11:00. This pops the text on at that time, making it invisible before that.

21. You're almost finished. One item left, the word "Egypt". You'll want to make sure that it's in its final placement before the words "a History" come on screen, or the composition will not read correctly. Click on the Text 1 layer to activate it. Bring it to the front layer.

22. This text is in red, and it suffers from the same clarity problems as Text 2. Treat it the same way that Text 2 was treated, with the EyeCandy AE Glow filter. The only difference is that you should make the color of the glow bright yellow.

23. Use the last frame for placement. Set it centered just over the Text 2 block. Now it's time to plan how to get it there. Certainly you don't want to just pop it on because you have more creative options. Besides, Text 2 pops on, so you should try a different approach.

24. For the effect that will bring this text on, you need to have the FE Twister filter installed from the FE Complete plug-in collection. Slide this layer's frame bar so that it starts at time 8:00. Go to the Transitions Effects list, and select FE Twister.

25. Set the Axis control to –90 degrees. Keyframe the Completion value to 100 at time 8:00, and to 0 at time 10:00. Make sure that Shading is not selected. Preview the results of your alterations, and change anything that doesn't look the way you want. When satisfied, render the animation to disk.

Congratulations! You can explore countless ways to develop alternate projects with this same footage. If you want to see the final rendering of this example, view the Egypt.mov animation in the CH_44 folder in the Anims folder on the companion CD-ROM. Figure 44.5 shows selected frames from this project.

Figure 44.5
Selected frames from the Egypt project animation.

The Tour Project

Travel agencies have grown accustomed to using multimedia presentations, whether in their waiting rooms or on the Web, to display various tour packages and promotions. In this example, you'll put together a 12-second piece of footage that might serve as an opening to a larger narrative. You will find all of the elements for this Project in the Tour folder, which is

Figure 44.6
These are the layer elements in the Photoshop Bueno.psd file. They include a stack of images of California and some text.

in the Projects folder on this book's CD-ROM. The file you want is called Bueno.psd (see Figure 44.6).

> **Note: All the footage displayed in Figure 44.6 and contained in the Tour folder on the CD-ROM are copyright free. They were taken by the author on a visit to California. You may use this footage in any way you wish.**

Creating The Tour Project

In large part, this project centers on the creation of a slide show of images, followed by the text blocks. A simple way to do this would be to start each image at a later point in the time line, making the text blocks the last items in the time line. Yes, this would be easy...and boring to watch. Your task then is to find more interesting ways to bring the images and the text on screen. Do the following:

1. Open After Effects. Set a new composition to 480×360 pixels, with a total time of 12 seconds. Import the Tour.psd file as a Photoshop Comp.

2. Open the Bueno.psd file, and load in the layer elements in exactly the following order: DarkSea, L2 Sea, L3 Sea, L SanF, and on top, L5 Brdg. This stack represents the order of the slide show images.

3. The top layer, an image of the Golden Gate Bridge, is rather poor because it was taken on a hazy day. That's OK because we will add some image effects to it so that it's more interesting, while we mask its poor quality at the same time.

> **Note: One secret of selecting which effects to use for any footage is that, if treated with care, lower-quality footage can still serve as a component of your composition.**

4. To apply this effect, you need the Evolution plug-ins from Atomic Power and have them installed. Go to the Effects menu, and select the Evolution plug-ins, activating the Colorama option.

5. Leave everything at its default. All you will keyframe animate is the Phase Shift values. Keyframe a Phase Shift of 0 degrees at time 00:00, and a Phase Shift of –180 degrees at time 4:00.

6. Now apply a channel blend effect to this same layer. Select Blend from the Channel Effects list. Make sure that Crossfade is selected in the Mode list, and that None is selected in the Blend With Layer list. All you want to do is to fade out the Bridge layer to reveal the next layer down. Keyframe the Blend With Original value as follows: 100% at time 00:00, 99.9% at time 2:00, and 0% at time 4:00. Preview your work so far to see what all of this does.

7. Now you will develop a transition effect for the next layer down, the San Francisco cityscape. First, create a new solid layer, and make it bright red. Send it to the back of the stack, and turn its visibility off.

8. You need to have the Boris AE 2 plug-ins installed to create this next effect. Activate the Page Turn filter from the Boris AE 2/Perspective options. Set the following parameters: Direction 285 degrees, Flap Radius 36, Flap Opacity 100, Light 70, Shadow 100, and Trails 0. Select the solid color layer you just created as the Alternate Back layer.

9. Keyframe animate the Offset values as follows: 0 at time 00:00, 0.1 at 4:00, and 100 at 5:15. Preview the effects so far and tweak as necessary.

10. The next layer down is L3 Sea. You will apply the same Page Turn filter to it, but with a different Direction setting and different Offset keyframe values. Apply the Page Turn effect to this layer, set the Direction to 60 degrees, and set the Solid layer as the Alternate Back Layer. Use the previous values for all other settings, except for the Offsets. Keyframe this layer's Page Turn Offset values as follows: 0 at time 5:15, 0.1 at time 6:10, and 100 at time 7:00. This completes the Page Turn at time 7:00, allowing you to see the next layer below: L2 Sea.

11. The same Boris AE 2 Page Turn filter is applied to this layer. Apply the Page Turn effect to this layer, set the Direction to 290 degrees, and set the Solid layer as the Alternate Back layer. Use the previous values for all other settings, except for the Offsets. Keyframe this layer's Page Turn Offset values as follows: 0 at time 7:00, 0.1 at time 8:10, and 100 at time 9:15. This completes the Page Turn at time 9:15, allowing you to see the next layer below: DarkSea. This layer remains as it is for the entire animation, providing a nice dark backdrop for the text components.

12. Force layer Cal 1 to pop on at time 10:00, layer Cal 2 at time 10:05, and layer Cal 3 at time 10:10. Arrange them top to bottom as shown in Figure 44.7.

13. Set the time slider to 10:15, and place the Bueno layer in the composition. This text reads "Bueno Tours". Place it on the right side of the composition, about a third of the way up from the bottom.

14. For this effect, you need to have the FE Complete plug-ins installed. With the Bueno layer still selected, activate the FE Scatterize filter from the Effects/Stylize menu. Leave all the parameters at their defaults. Keyframe the Amount value at time 10:15 to 15, and at time 11:05 to 0. This allows the Bueno Tours text to start as scattered particles, and to resolve to clarity at time 11:05.

15. Only adding the phone number remains to be done. Each numeral of the phone number is on a separate layer, so by simply telling each numeral when to appear, and lining it up, the phone number will appear as if it were being typed to the screen. The total phone number is "555-2000". You want to place it so that it's centered under the Bueno text. Place the layers in this order: 5A, 5B, 5C, Dash, 2, 0A, 0B, and 0C. Each should appear on screen two frames apart, starting at time 11:05. Do it.

You can explore countless ways to develop alternate projects with this same footage. If you want to see the final rendering of this example, view the Tour1.mov animation in the CH_44 folder in the Anims folder on the companion CD-ROM. Figure 44.8 shows some frames from the completed Tour project.

Figure 44.7
Arrange the Cal 1, 2, and 3 layers top to bottom as shown here.

Figure 44.8
Selected frames from the Tour project animation.

The Sci-Fi Project

Here's an opening for a Sci-Fi movie series, a "gather-around-the-tube-on-Saturday-night" special. It has graphic and movie elements. The Sci-Fi folder in the Projects folder on the companion CD-ROM contains the following project elements: a SciFi.psd Photoshop file with the text blocks, Alien1.mov, Veepah1.mov, and Veepah2.mov (see Figure 44.9).

> **Note: All the footage displayed in Figure 44.9 and contained in the Sci-Fi folder on the companion CD-ROM are copyright free. The author created them especially for this project. Use the footage in any projects you like.**

1. Open After Effects, and create a new composition that is 15 seconds long at 30 fps. Size it to 480×360 pixels. Create a new solid layer. Make it dark blue (an HSV of 240, 90, 50 works well). You need to have the DigiEffects Berserk plug-ins installed for the next step.

2. Select the StarField filter from the DigiEffects Berserk options. Set the parameters as follows: Star Shape = Star, Number of Stars 75, Speed 50, Twist –100, Streak 0, Birth Fade Up 20, Min/Max Sizes = 20/310, with all other settings at their defaults. This creates a starfield that looks as though you are traveling through it.

3. For this step, you need the Knoll Lens Flare Pro plug-in. Activate the Knoll Lens Flare filter from the Effects menu. Use any Lens Flare type you like. Keyframe animate the Angle so that it rotates twice from the first to the last frame. Keyframe animate the Scale value so that it pulsates several times during the animation, from a value of 1

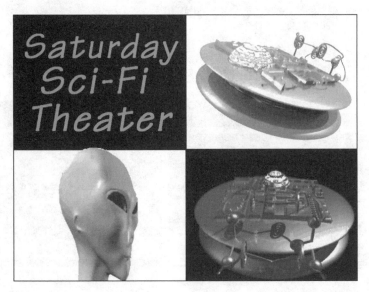

Figure 44.9
The contents of the Sci-Fi folder on the companion CD-ROM include a selection of text layers and movie files.

Figure 44.10
The Knoll Lens Flare and StarField are targeted to the background color layer.

to 1.5. Keyframe animate the Brightness value so that it pulsates several times during the animation, from a value of 40 to 60 (see Figure 44.10).

4. Import the Veepah2.mov footage to the composition. Note that it's only 12 seconds long, so either you have to stretch its time, or it must be manipulated within the total composition so that its length doesn't matter. The latter option is what you will work with in this case.

5. Notice that this movie footage shows a moving craft against a blue background. It is necessary to drop out its background so the craft can be seen against the starfield we created on the color layer. You can use the standard AE Color Key to accomplish this quite well. Activate the AE Color Key from the Keying Effects list. Use the eyedropper to select the ship's blue background as the dropout color. Set its parameters as follows: Color Tolerance 11, Edge Thin 3, and Edge Feather 1.6. You want to remove any blue halo from around the ship, so you may have to adjust these values a bit.

6. Move the ship straight down at time 00:00, so that it is out of the composition frame. Now, keyframe animate its position. Leave it in place for time 00:00, and keyframe the position to one that show it completely in the frame at time 8:15.

7. Keyframe animate the ships Scale to 100% at time 00:00, 90% at time 06:00, and 0% at time 8:15. The result should be a ship that enters the composition at the bottom, and that appears to be flying into the Knoll Lens Flare, completely disappearing at frame 8:15 (see Figure 44.11).

Figure 44.11
The ship enters the frame from the bottom, and flies straight for the lens flare, where it vanishes.

8. Add the Veepah1.mov to the Composition. It has a white background that must also be dropped out. Use the same Color Key filter to accomplish this. Apply the following parameters: Color Tolerance 39, Edge Thin 1, and Edge Feather 3.6. You have to play with the settings until the white halo is removed.

9. Reduce the Scale of the Veepah2.mov ship to 35 percent, and place it outside of the composition at the upper right. Keyframe animate the position of the Veepah2.mov ship so that it flies from outside the frame at the upper right to outside the left border around the center of the composition. It must be no longer visible, having flown out of the frame at the left, by time 12:00 because it is only a 12-second movie (see Figure 44.12).

10. Import the Alien.mov, and place it in the composition. This is an alien head created by the Zygote Modeling Group and rendered in MetaCreations Poser. Place the head so that it sits on the bottom left of the composition. It is a 12-second animated movie. Stretch it to 15 seconds by selecting the Time-Stretch option from the Layer menu and changing 12:00 to 15:00. Now the rotating alien head movie is the same length as our composition.

11. Notice that the alien has a white background that must be dropped out. Use the AE Color Key, with the following parameter settings: Color Tolerance 27, Edge Thin 0, and Edge Feather 3. You have to play with the settings until the white halo is removed.

Figure 44.12
The Veepah2 craft enters the composition at the upper right and exits center left.

12. Now you'll add some strange flames emanating from the alien's head. To do this, you'll need AlienSkin's EyeCandy AE filters installed. Open the EyeCandy Fire filter. Set the parameters as follows: Flame Width 10, Height 140, Movement 30, Inside Masking 100, Edge Softness 5. Make Color User Defined, and select a light blue-green for the Inner Color and a medium violet for the Outer Color. Set the Flow Speed at 340.

13. It's time to pop on the title text. At time 12:06, pop on "Saturday", at 12:15 pop on "Sci-Fi", and at 12:20 pop on "Theater". Place an EyeCandy AE Glow around each text block, with a Width of 7 and an Opacity of 70. Make the glow around "Saturday" yellow, and the other glows light green. Place the text as shown in Figure 44.13.

Figure 44.13
The titling is added.

14. One last item. On the Starfield layer, increase the Brightness of the Flare to 90 and the Scale to 2 when the "Sci-Fi" text pops up at time 12:20.

You can explore countless ways to develop alternate projects with this same footage. If you want to see the final rendering of this example, view the SciFix.mov animation in the CH_44 folder in the Anims folder on the companion CD-ROM. Figure 44.14 shows some frames from this project.

Figure 44.14
Selected frames from the SciFi project animation.

APPENDIX A: ICE

This book would be noticeably incomplete without a mention of ICE. ICE is a leader in desktop special-effects solutions used in digital post-production, compositing, visual effects, broadcast, and animation.

ICE's hardware and software accelerate effects creation within the leading 2D finishing applications, including After Effects, Avid, Media 100, Commotion, CineLook, Ultimatte, BorisFX/BorisAE, and ICEblast. The BlueICE board is a single PCI hardware card that fits in a PCI slot of standard Macintosh or Windows NT system. BlueICE is the first ever desktop-based system to support film and HDTV-image resolution rendering.

FE Complete

Final Effects Complete is a premium set of 60 motion-graphics effects plug-ins for Adobe After Effects that create professional special effects for film, video, and other digital video production.

ICE has taken over the development and distribution of Final Effects Complete from MetaCreations (see Chapters 25 to 31 in this book). Final Effects Complete offers the capability to generate rain, snow, fire, smoke, bubbles, liquid mercury distortions, explosions, 3D particles, liquid displacement and lighting effects, a multitude of stylistic transitions, and other video effects.

Features And Benefits

The following list describes FE Complete's features and capabilities:

- Advanced particle systems for creating complex smoke, fire, rain, confetti, gas particles and explosions.

- Extremely fast rendering allows the user to experiment and control the tools.

- Quality effects that are essential tools—not just tricks.

- Multiprocessing support for superior performance.

ICE'd Motion Tracker For Commotion

This software, an add-on module for owners of Puffin Designs' Commotion, is a visual effects, playback, paint, and rotoscoping tool that brings high-end workstation performance to motion tracking on the desktop (refer to Chapter 39). Commotion is a key tool for professionals who create TV commercials, video, film, or HDTV projects.

Features And Benefits

ICE'd Motion Tracker offers the following advantages over other tools:

- Up to 50 times faster than the built-in software tracker at the highest resolution.

- Work at the highest resolution with no speed penalty.

- Able to track two targets as fast as one target.

- Functionally equivalent to the Commotion software tracker, so there is nothing new to learn.

- Tracking data can be exported to After Effects, Flame, A/W Composer, or Stratasphere for further finishing.

- Resolution independent (like all ICE products).

ICEblast

ICEblast, ICE's new standalone special-effects editing application, is a true complement to the ICEfx family of products. ICEblast provides you with a powerful way to create effects for Adobe After Effects.

ICEblast's streamlined workflow allows you to apply effects to a video clip, adjust settings, quickly render, and preview the results with real-time software playback. You can take control of effects parameters with the Keyframe Editor and unique Curve Editor, and ICEblast also supports Alpha channels, which is essential for text and logo treatments.

Software-Based Playback Engine

ICEblast's playback engine offers the following features:

- Real-time uncompressed playback of media at full speed

- Native QuickTime and OMFI Media Files support for push-button integration

- Resolution independent up to 4000×4000

- Supports 32-bit images (8 bits RGB + Alpha)

- Supports frame or field-based media (24/25/30 fps, NTSC and PAL)

Unique Special Effects Capabilities

ICEblast's special effects give you the following features:

- Effects window for applying one or more superfast ICEfx effects

- Dynamic sliders for quickly adjusting parameter values

- Effect menu for easily applying After Effects-compatible plug-ins to a clip
- Full alpha channel for text or logo treatment
- Composite toggle for viewing video background while applying effects
- Effect settings for saving and reapplying customized effects

Project Window

One powerful tool ICE supplies is the project window, an excellent utility for managing your work. The following list describes the features of this tool:

- Effect list displaying applied effects and their parameters
- Parameter list toggles for customizing views
- Timeline with time marker for viewing entire clip's duration
- Effect range specifies section of time over which effect occurs
- Resolution and quality controls
- Preview control for fast rendering and real-time previewing

Keyframe Editor With Intuitive Controls

- Keyframe controls for animating effects over time
- Keyframe handles for quick manipulation (select, move, cut, copy, and paste keyframes)
- Keyframe interpolations (hold, linear, or Bézier)

System Requirements

Macintosh:

- PowerPC-based Macintosh
- 64MB of RAM (128MB is recommended)
- Apple Mac OS 8 or greater
- CD-ROM, Apple QuickTime 3
- Color display

ICEfx For After Effects

ICEfx lets you work your effects magic at full resolution. ICEfx for After Effects renders your ideas from 2 to 20 times faster, giving you unheard of freedom and creative flexibility. Added power lets you view the impact of your work at eye-popping high resolution.

ICEfx gives you the following features:

- 2 to 20 times faster than comparable special effects packages
- Resolution independent
- Create projects in film, HDTV, D1 resolutions with the same system

Specifications

- Adobe After Effects
- Mac OS and Windows NT
- Integrates directly into the After Effects interface
- ICEfx Softfx for After Effects also available (unaccelerated and doesn't require the ICE hardware)

ICEfx For AE Effects

ICEfx for After Effects includes the following effects: 3D Relief, Blur, Brightness/Contrast, Bulge, Chroma/Luma Blur, Color Balance, Emboss, EZ LazyWaves, EZ Ripple, Fractal, Gamma/Ped/Gain, Glow, Invert, Lens Star, LightBlast, LightWhirl, Median, Motion, Noise, Power Ramp, Replace Color, Sharpen, Simple Shadow, Soften, Spherize, Spin, Tint, Twirl, Video Fragment, Water Waves, and Zoom.

From DigiEffects For ICEfx

DigiEffects supplies the following tools: AgedFilm, Chaotic Noise, Chaotic Rainbow, Fog Alpha, FogBank, Starfield, and Videolook.

From Ultimatte For ICEfx

Ultimatte for ICEfx includes the following effects: Grain Killer, Screen Correction, and Ultimatte.

ICE'd Edges

ICE'd Edges is an optional set of nine filters for ICEfx for After Effects. Use these unique ICE compositing-type effects to highlight the edges or border of a layer, with full animation control at the speed of ICE.

To run ICE'd, your system needs to be set up as follows:

- Adobe After Effects
- MAC OS and Windows NT
- ICE'd version requires ICE hardware
- ICE'd SoftEdges also available (unaccelerated and does not require ICE hardware)

ICE'd Edges includes the following nine effects: ICE'd Spot Blur, ICE'd Spot Feather, ICE'd Spot Frame, ICE'd Spot Tatter, ICE'd Gradient Blur, ICE'd Wiggle Edges, ICE'd Sparkle Edges, ICE'd Burn Edges, and ICE'd Super Shadow.

ICE'd CineLook

ICE'd CineLook is an accelerated version of DigiEffects acclaimed "film look" software, ported to run on the ICEfx desktop effects system. ICE'd CineLook renders 5 to 10 times faster, so you can try 5 to 10 preset film stocks in the same time it used to take to see just one.

ICE'd CineLook gives you the following features:

- 5 to 10 times faster than original DigiEffects CineLook
- 50 of the most common film presets

Specifications

- Adobe After Effects
- Mac OS (Windows NT in late '98)
- ICE'd version requires ICE hardware
- Available as an upgrade to DigiEffects CineLook

ICE

460 Totten Pond Road
Waltham, MA 02451
USA
Telephone: 781-768-2300
Fax: 781-768-2301
Email: **sales@iced.com**
Web site: **www.iced.com**

APPENDIX B:

ARTBEATS' REELS

ArtBeats' Reels is the most comprehensive and high-quality set of nature footage available, well worth exploration and investment.

ArtBeats is a company dedicated to developing the highest quality CD-ROM volumes of backgrounds and textures. At various places in this book, ArtBeats' Reels footage was used as a layer to develop the animations on this book's companion CD-ROM. Using ArtBeats' Reels allows you to include authentic scenes of nature in your projects, just perfect for animated backdrops and Alpha channel effects.

The Reels collections feature both high-resolution single-frame sequences of various lengths and low-resolution preview movies. The content covers the range of natural and environmental footage, including multiple footage of clouds in motion, water in motion, animated textures, fire, and explosions. Most of the footage comes with separate Alpha content, so compositing the effect in an After Effects composition is simple.

Web address: **www.artbeats.com**

TOTAL AE

If After Effects is a new creative realm that you are just beginning to explore, you would do well to check out the videotape series, Total AE, from Total Training, Inc. and Maff/x Inc.

The series consists of nine tutorial- and demo-packed videotapes that feature acclaimed AE master Brian Maffitt doing the narration and examples. The tapes walk you through every corner and edge of After Effects, so that by the time you've worked through them, you'll be ready for any project challenge. The AE 4 series was in production during the writing of this book, and it should be out by the time you read this. Based on the AE 3 series of tapes, here are the categories represented: The Interface and Animation Basics; Keyframes and Compositions; Velocity Controls and File Prep; Masking and Advanced Animation; Effects; Keyframe Assistants; and Motion Math.

206.728.0892
206.728-.0893 Fax
www.totalae.com

Appendix D:

VENDOR CONTACTS

Many developers have contributed to the contents of this book. Look for many more plug-in effects from developers in the future. In the following list, you'll find the contact information for the developers represented. You may contact them to purchase their wares or to remain updated on what they are planning for the future.

Adobe Systems Inc.
345 Park Avenue
San Jose, CA 95110
Phone: 408.536.3019
Fax: 408.537.4040
www.adobe.com

Artel Software
(Boris AE)
Phone: 617.451.9900 ext. 102
Fax: 617.451.9916
janicef@artelsoft.com

Atomic Power Company
(Evolution)
Phone: 805.884.0714
tom@AtomicPower.com

AutoMedia Ltd.
(AutoMasker)
Jacob Pedhatzur-Wiedhopf
Vice President, Sales & Marketing
Phone: (+972) 3-9220444 ext. 246
Fax: (+972) 3-9220355
Jacob_pw@automedi.com

DigiEffects
Dan Prochazka/Director of Marketing
Phone: 415.826.0921
danp@digieffects.com

ElectricFish
(QTVR Matte)
slithy@electricfish.com

(The) Foundry
20 Rupert Street
London. W1V 7FN
Phone:+44 (0)171 434 0449
Fax:+44 (0)171 434 1550
www.thefoundry.co.uk

Hollywood FX Incorporated/Synergy International, Inc.
300 East 4500 South Suite 100
Salt Lake City, UT 84107
Phone: 801.281.0237
Fax: 801.281.0238
www.hollywoodfx.com

ICE
(Final FX Complete)
Phone: 888.ICE THIS
Phone: 781.768.2300

ImageXpress, Inc.
(Alius)
3545 Cruse Rd., Ste. 103
Lawrenceville, GA 30044
Phone: 770.564.9924
Fax: 770.564.1632
www.ixsoftware.com

Intergraph Corporation
(VizFX)
Huntsville, AL 35894
kdjost@ingr.com

ISFX
sb@isfx.com
www.isfx.com/

MetaCreations
(Painter)
Phone: 805.566.6464
www.metacreations.com

Pixelan Software
(Spice Rack)
4107 Harrison Street
Bellingham, WA 98226
pixelan@earthlink.net

Puffin Designs
(Commotion)
mike@puffindesigns.com

RayFlect
Phone: +33 1 42 60 61 82
Fax: +33 1 42 60 61 83
alexandre_c@rayflect.com

Total Training, Inc.
Total AE
Tom Sullivan, VP Sales & Marketing
Phone: 805.884.0714
tom@totaltraining.com
www.totaltraining.com

ZaxWerks
zax@zaxwerks.com

BORIS AE 3

By the time you read this, a demo version of Boris AE 3 will be available for download at ***www.BorisFX.com***.

Boris AE 3 adds more than 10 new filters and improves functionality to all of the existing Boris AE 2 filters listed in this book. Boris AE 3 is available for After Effects 3.1 and 4 on Macintosh and Windows platforms. The new filters are detailed in the following sections.

3D Text

This plug-in introduces a true 3D title creator to AE users. Without having to go to another application, AE users now can generate true 3D text, including the following:

- Full XYZ rotation, position, scaling, tracking, and pivot point control.

- Extrusion depth, bevel size, and style (Straight, Convex, and Concave).

- The capability to take any layer in your composition and texture map it onto the Front, Back, Bevel, and Extrusion.

- Three different light sources, with ambient and diffuse lighting.

- Camera position in true XYZ space.

- Wireframe, Flat, or Phong shading.

- Versatile Flat 3D-text generator with full XYZ rotation, lighting, and camera controls. Ideal to create title scrolls, rolls, and lower thirds. Although the text is "flat," the user still has full control over the XYZ rotation and true 3D lighting and camera. This feature includes character stroking and font manipulation.

3D Frame Shatter Filter

This filter has fully customizable particle shapes, dispersion maps, and advanced motion control. Break up any layer in a multitude of objects with full control over the behavior of particles. By using alternate layers, a number of custom-defined shapes can be randomly selected and applied as particles over the course of an effect. This creates some very realistic and unique-looking effects not available anywhere else on the AE platform.

Advanced Edge Lighting Filters

Add depth and style to your text and images. These filters make any text, Illustrator files, or bitmaps come to life with full control over the light direction, highlight and shadow intensity, color, and pre- and post-blur. This filter is perfect to make your type or images look like plastic, metal embossing, or glowing.

New Clouds And NoiseMap Filters

These filters generate realistic cloud formations and organic noise. The Clouds filter is ideal as a background plate because it is auto-animated. A unique cloud shape feature allows you to take any layer's Alpha channel and use it as the shape of the cloud. This makes it incredibly easy to have random cloud formations become a logo! The versatile NoiseMap is a great companion to the Boris AE Displacement map filters or to use as a texture map on the new 3D text.

Matte Choker And Composite Choker

These filters add choking to the standard version of AE and are perfect companions to the powerful array of keys available in Boris AE. Composite Choker is a unique two-stage simple choking filter with compositing modes between each choke stage. This allows you to quickly create text or image outlines.

> *Note: In addition, Boris AE 3 has an improved user interface to take advantage of all of AE 4's new features. All Boris AE filters now support the control grouping functionality introduced in AE4. This enables extended plug-ins to be a lot more manageable and take less space in the filter window.*

INDEX

COLOPHON

From start to finish, The Coriolis Group designed *After Effects 4 In Depth* with the creative professional in mind.

The cover was produced on a Power Macintosh using QuarkXPress 3.3 for layout compositing. Text imported from Microsoft Word was restyled using the Futura and Trajan font families from the Adobe font library. It was printed on a Heidelberg 1250 press using four-color process, metallic silver ink, and spot UV coating, on 12-point Silverado matte cover stock.

Select images from the color studio were combined with new figures to form the color montage art strip, unique for each Creative Professionals book. Adobe Photoshop 5 was used in conjunction with filters from Alien Skin Eye Candy 3.0 and other software to create the individual special effects.

The Color Studio was assembled using Adobe Pagemaker 6.5 on a G3 Macintosh system. Images in TIFF format were color corrected and sized in Adobe Photoshop 5. The Studio was printed using four-color process on 90 pound Silverado gloss paper.

The interior layout was built in Adobe Pagemaker 6.5 on a Power Macintosh. Adobe fonts used include Stone Informal for body, Avenir Black for heads, and Copperplate 31ab for chapter titles. Adobe Photoshop 4 was used to process grayscale images. Text files originated in Microsoft Word.

Imagesetting and manufacturing were completed by Courier, Stoughton, Mass.

WHAT'S ON THE CD-ROM

The *After Effects* companion CD-ROM contains elements specifically selected to enhance the usefulness of this book, including:

- *After Effects 4*—Trial version (Mac OS 7.5, and Windows 95/98 and later). AE 4 is the standard for post-production effects.

- *Media Cleaner Pro*—Trial version (Mac only). See what makes Media Cleaner Pro the most powerful solution for crunching your QuickTime files into more compact file sizes that take less disk space and stream online much faster. If you are a QuickTime moviemaker, you'll find Media Cleaner Pro a necessary component of your moviemaking toolbox.

- *Commotion 1.6*—Trial version (Mac only). Commotion adds painting and editing parameters to After Effects that are necessary for professional editing and compositing. Commotion is both a standalone application and a necessary partner for After Effects (see Chapter 39).

- *RAYflect plug-in demos* (Photoshop plug-ins):

  - Four Seasons—The powerful and photorealistic sky and atmosphere generator extension for Photoshop.

  - PhotoTracer—Allows every level of user to easily and quickly add 3D graphics to their creations.

- *Animations/Projects*—These animations illuminate the filters, plug-ins, and features covered in this book. Chapter 44's folder (named Projects) includes materials to produce three complete projects.

System Requirements

Software:

Windows
- Windows 95, 98, NT 4 or higher

Macintosh
- System 7.5 or higher (OS 8+ recommended)

Both Platforms
- A full copy of Adobe After Effects 4 is needed to complete the projects included in this book.
- You need a full copy of QuickTime to view the tutorial animations detailed in the chapters included on this book's CD-ROM.
- Additionally, many chapters in this book are devoted to plug-in effects found only in applications that you must purchase separately.

Hardware:

Windows
- Windows 95 (minimum requirement)

Macintosh
- A PowerPC processor

Both Platforms
- A Pentium processor is strongly recommended.
- 32MB of RAM is required on either platform (128MB of RAM is highly recommended for professional work; more if you plan to load more than three effects packages to the program).
- A color monitor (16 million colors) is recommended.